From Winchester
to
Cedar Creek:

The Shenandoah Campaign of 1864

by
Jeffry D. Wert

South Mountain Press, Inc., Publishers
Carlisle, Pennsylvania
1987

Photographs: pp. 1, 13, 116, 146, 156, 195, 220, 238, 251, 252, 253, 254, 324, 325
Maps: pp. 2, 14, 46, 70, 100, 115, 196, 219

Published and Distributed by South Mountain Press, Inc.
Please address all inquiries to the publisher:

South Mountain Press, Inc.
37 West High Street, P.O. Box 306
Carlisle, PA 17013-0306
Telephone: (717) 245-9251

Maps drawn by Mark Pfoutz

Contents

Dedication

To Gloria, Jason and Natalie, with love.

Preface

In the evening darkness of October 19, 1864, Confederate Lieutenant General Jubal A. Early stood atop Fisher's Hill, south of Strasburg, Virginia. Around him were the broken elements of a routed army. It had been slightly over four months ago when Early and his command, under orders from Robert E. Lee, raced to the Shenandoah Valley. For much of that time, Early had achieved his commander's objectives but, during the previous thirty days, the Confederates suffered three decisive battlefield defeats. Early's string of losses was unmatched by any other commander of an army in the Civil War. In numerous ways, Jubal Early stood alone that night on the crest of a hill.

That same night, a short distance to the north, across Cedar Creek, a different scene was transpiring. Early's opponent, Major General Philip H. Sheridan, was celebrating the day's achievement with a coterie of officers around a glowing bonfire. The Northerners, indeed, had reasons to rejoice for, within a span of approximately ten weeks, they had crippled the best corps in the Army of Northern Virginia and had brought flame and destruction to the granary of the Confederacy. A symbol of Southern victory, the Shenandoah Valley, no longer stood unconquered. For Sheridan, the accomplishments brought contemporary and historic renown. Many stood beside him in the blackness of an autumn night.

The Shenandoah Valley Campaign of August–October 1864 shattered the stalemate in Virginia during the Civil War's fourth year, marking the beginning of the end of the Confederacy in the Old Dominion. Fought during the final months of the most crucial presidential election campaign in American history, the struggle for the Valley of Virginia, combined with the strategically more important successes of William T. Sherman in Georgia, retrieved Abraham Lincoln's faltering reelection campaign, broke Southern morale and gave resolve to the Northern populace. Atlanta, Third Winchester, Fisher's Hill and Cedar Creek forged a tide of Union success that could not be stayed by a beleagured Confederacy.

The final campaign for the Shenandoah Valley, however, has been neglected by Civil War historians. A number of reasons might be offered for this lack of study. Some historians regard the operations in the region of minor importance once Early failed to capture Washington, D.C., in July. This view ignores the grave concern expressed by Lincoln's administration, Ulysses S. Grant's linking of his operations at Petersburg with those in the Shenandoah and Robert E. Lee's decision to detach one-fourth of his infantry in an effort at refashioning the strategy used in the spring of 1862 by Thomas J. "Stonewall" Jackson.

Secondly, the campaign has been overshadowed by Sherman's capture of Atlanta and subsequent "March to the Sea" and the ten-month duel at Petersburg between Grant and Lee. The struggle between Sheridan and Early, to be sure, does not possess the historic significance of the campaigns in Georgia, the Carolinas and at Petersburg. Sheridan's victory, however, wrecked Lee's bold gamble, eliminating the Confederate's last hope of unloosening Grant's deathgrip on Petersburg. The campaign's outcome insured Southern defeat in Virginia.

Finally, the number of troops involved and the casualties inflicted in sheer numbers do not rival other major engagements of the war. But, the fighting in the Valley of Virginia in 1864 was some of the bloodiest of the war in relation to numbers engaged and casualties inflicted. Early's percentage of losses at Third Winchester, for example, approached Lee's losses at Gettysburg. The opposing armies hammered each other with the skill and valor of veterans.

This book, consequently, is the first study of the campaign in the Shenandoah in a quarter of a century. It is also the first account which relies heavily upon the unpublished and published writings of the participants. My purpose was to write a detailed account, utilizing manuscript sources and the published regimental histories, diaries, letters, memoirs and reminiscences of the men in the ranks, officer and enlisted alike, in both armies.

A second purpose was to present a balanced reexamination of the operations. Both the victors and the vanquished share the pages. The military and political factors, the roles of Grant and Lee, the generalship of Sheridan and Early, the qualities of the opposing armies have all been restudied. Not all the questions, the controversies, the conflicting versions have been answered or settled but, in my judgment, the accounts of the operations from early August to mid-September, of Third Winchester, of Fisher's Hill, of "The Burning," and of Cedar Creek are the most detailed yet presented.

This campaign, in the end, led toward resolution. It had been a Confederate gamble against lengthening odds from the outset; it resulted in a decisive defeat because of those odds. Reputations were made; reputations were lost. Young men on both sides fought for their beliefs and fell in battle because of them. What was won and what was lost in the Shenandoah Valley in the late summer and early autumn of 1864 comprise this book.

Jeffry D. Wert
Centre Hall, PA.
December 1986

Acknowledgements

This book has been several years in the making and, along the way, the author has incurred innumerable debts to individuals, whose assistance, advice, criticism and friendship have made this a better book. I gratefully thank each one, while stating that errors of omission and commission are solely the author's responsibility.

Historians could not possibly complete their research without the assistance of librarians and archivists. I have in the course of my work found the following uniformly helpful, capable and kind in their responses to my requests for manuscripts from their libraries' collections: Ellen G. Gartell, Duke University, Durham, North Carolina; David E. Estes, Emory University, Atlanta, Georgia; Harriet McLoone, The Huntington Library, San Marino, California; Paul Heffron, The Library of Congress, Washington, D.C.; Thomas A. Smith, Rutherford B. Hayes Presidential Center, Fremont, Ohio; Marie T. Capps, United States Military Academy, West Point, New York; Nancy Bartlett, the University of Michigan, Ann Arbor; Gregory A. Johnson, University of Virginia, Charlottesville; Waverly K. Winfree, Virginia Historical Society, Richmond; Judith M. Arnold, Virginia Military Institute, Lexington; Paul I. Chestnut, Virginia State Library, Richmond; Richard W. Oram, Washington and Lee University, Lexington, Virginia; Peter Gottlieb, West Virginia University, Morgantown; George Miles, Yale University, New Haven, Connecticut; and the staffs of Chicago Historical Society; the Historical Society of Pennsylvania, Philadelphia; the Pennsylvania State University, University Park; the University of North Carolina, Chapel Hill.

Gretchen Hanks, interlibrary loan librarian, Centre County Library, Bellefonte, Pennsylvania, earned my special gratitude as she secured many rare regimental histories and soldiers' memoirs for me over the course of three years. Without her patient efforts, many of these valuable works would not have been available.

Dr. Richard J. Sommers, noted Civil War author and archivist at the United States Military History Institute, Carlisle Barracks, Pennsylvania, was most helpful as I pursued my research among the Institute's vast collections of manuscripts. Dr. Sommers and his assistants, David Keough and Valerie Metzler, guided my research with expertise and generosity.

Others deserve recognition and thanks for their advice, knowledge and/or friendship:

The United States Military History Institute for its award of an Advanced Research Grant for my book, which permitted me to spend a period of time utilizing their archival holdings and library.

William C. Davis, President, Products Division, Historical Times, Inc. and one of the foremost Civil War scholars, for his advice and counsel.

John E. Stanchak, editor of *Civil War Times Illustrated*, for his friendship and for his numerous efforts in my behalf.

The late Patricia L. Faust, editor *Historical Times Illustrated Encyclopedia of the Civil War* and former editor of *American History Illustrated* and *Virginia Cavalcade*, for her belief in my work.

Ben Ritter and James Tubbesing of Winchester, Virginia, for walking with me over the remains of the battlefield of Third Winchester and for reading my chapters on that engagement and correcting my errors.

Allan Tischler of Star Tannery, Virginia, for his sharing of his knowledge of the Cedar Creek battlefield.

Nick Picerno of Springfield, Vermont, for his friendship and for the photographs included in the book from his collection on the Shenandoah Valley Campaign.

Father Peter J. Meaney, O.S.B., of the Delbarton School, Morristown, New Jersey, and the author of *Engagement at Cool Spring, July 18, 1864*, for reading part of my manuscript and offering advice based upon his knowledge of operations in the region and for his friendship of many years.

John Kallmann, my publisher, for his modifications in the manuscript and for this chance.

Finally, my wife, Gloria, for the love, support and patience she has given me throughout our years together. She also typed every word of the manuscript, tolerated my changes, sustained me during the periods of doubt and forgave me when the research and writing overshadowed other things. Also, our children, Jason and Natalie, for their understanding when their father spent long hours at a desk. This book could not have been possible without them and, for these reasons, it is dedicated to them with my love.

Jacket Photograph: Left to Right: Brig. Gen. W. Merritt, Brig. Gen. David McMurtrie Gregg, Maj. Gen. Philip H. Sheridan, Brig. Gen. Henry Eugene Davies, Brig. Gen. James Harrison Wilson, Brig. Gen. Alfred T. A. Torbert. USAMHI.

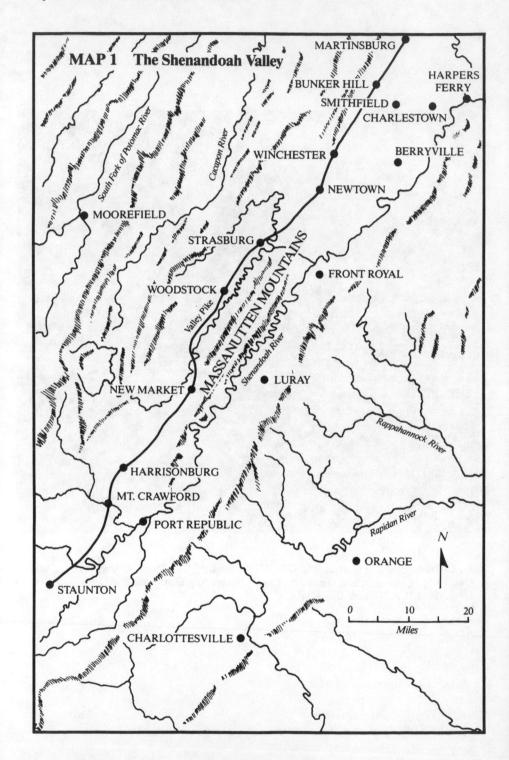

MAP 1   The Shenandoah Valley

1

Virginia Stalemate, Summer 1864

Lieutenant General Ulysses S. Grant, General-in-Chief of the armed forces of the United States, arrived at Monocacy Junction, Maryland, on the evening of August 5, 1864. Accompanied by two aides, the Union's ranking officer had traveled from his headquarters at City Point, outside of Petersburg, Virginia, to the railroad stop three miles from Frederick for a conference with one of his key subordinates. Critics of the general could have argued that with recent developments in western Maryland and northern Virginia the trip was overdue. Grant, to be sure, had only lately and, only after mounting pressure from Washington, D.C., come to appreciate the importance of and the Union administration's sensitivity to the unexpected Confederate successes during the previous month. But, in Grant's defense, this region west of the Federal capital was only one area of operations for which he had responsibility and, wherever he might have looked, final victory still seemed like a dim dream.

In this, the Civil War's fourth summer, stalemate, more than resolution, characterized the military situation. The embattled Confederate States of America, though crippled by significant reverses in 1863 at Gettysburg, Pennsylvania, Vicksburg, Mississippi, and at Chattanooga, Tennessee, endured. The direst warnings of 1861 had not foreseen the conflict's length and staggering costs in money and blood. The war, by 1864, had become a testing of national wills, both in the North and in the South. Or, as President Abraham Lincoln told an audience in Gettysburg on November 19, 1863, it was "for us to be dedicated to the great task remaining before us . . . that we here highly resolve that these dead shall not have died in vain."

For all Americans, Northerner and Southerner alike, the tragic war must have seemed like a passage through hell. The maiming and the killing had visited hundreds of thousands of homes in nearly every village and city in the country. The issues and arguments of the 1850's had lost to grieving parents, wives and children some of their importance next to the posted casualty lists. One question stood paramount: could the mounting human toll be justified by the goals of union and the abolition of slavery.

No one, perhaps, better understood that question and its future implications than Lincoln. His 1860 election had precipitated the secession of Southern slave states, and his executive actions during March–April 1861 had led to an outbreak of fighting. No other chief executive in the nation's history had been subjected to such virulent criticism as had Lincoln. The president, however, withstood the condemnations by newspapers and politicians, convinced of the justness of the Northern cause. But, would the citizens of the loyal states stand by Lincoln and his uncompromising policy of victory in the forthcoming autumn presidential election. The president's reelection and the Northern people's determination to see the war through to a conclusion were inextricably linked and, as Lincoln in the summer of 1864 also looked upon the military impasse, he was less than sanguine over his and the nation's future.

The politics of 1864, therefore, were governed, to a significant degree, by the outcomes upon battlefields. Lincoln and the Republican party needed military victories, a pattern of successes which gave Northerners a reassurance that "these dead shall not have died in vain." For three years Lincoln and his advisors had sought a general who could bring with him the final victory. Finally, early in 1864, the president believed he had found that man in Grant. Lincoln asked Congress to revive the rank of lieutenant general, following this with a request to the Senate for Grant's confirmation in the new rank. The general arrived in Washington on March 8, met the president, received his new commission and assumed command of the Armies of the United States.

Grant was not quite 42 years old, an Illinoisan like Lincoln, when he took direction of the Union war effort. Described by Assistant Secretary of War Charles A. Dana as "an uncommon fellow—the most modest, the most disinterested and the most honest man I ever knew," Grant had fashioned an unrivaled string of victories in the western theater.[1] His capture of Vicksburg, the city and Confederate fortress on the Mississippi River, and his defeat of Confederate forces besieging Chattanooga were the most brilliant of his achievements, which dated back to the winter of 1862. As Lincoln had told someone earlier, Grant could not be spared for he fought.

The new lieutenant general—only George Washington had held the rank previously—was an uncompromising hard man of war. He understood the arithmetics of killing and maiming, knowing that in an unrelenting struggle of attrition the North's resources and economy and larger manpower pool gave him a clear edge over his Confederate opponents. He, consequently, fashioned a grand offensive for the spring of 1864, a concerted hammering by Federal forces against Southern armies, and the cities, railroads, farmlands and factories which sustained them.

Grant focused his plan upon two vital bastions of the Confederacy —
Richmond, its capital, and Atlanta, Georgia, its railroad hub. He ordered
Major General William T. Sherman, with three armies at Chattanooga, to
march upon Atlanta in the Southern heartland. As for Richmond and Virginia, the commanding general developed a three-prong thrust. While Major
General George G. Meade's Army of the Potomac, under Grant's personal
direction, advanced directly against its old nemesis, General Robert E. Lee's
Army of Northern Virginia, Major General Benjamin F. Butler and the Army
of the James was ordered south of its namesake river toward the railroad
center of Petersburg, twenty miles south of Richmond. The third operation —
one upon which Grant placed little importance — was in the Shenandoah
Valley, where Major General Franz Sigel, with a small army, was assigned the
task of penetrating southward into the upper valley, severing Lee's rail links
with the fertile region. The Union had never launched such a coordinated
operation.

The offensive began during the first week of May. Sherman found the
going slow in northern Georgia as Confederate General Joseph Johnston and
his Army of Tennessee withdrew from one defensive position to another. The
campaign became one of maneuver and countermaneuver with little significant combat. Butler, whose military skill was in inverse proportion to his
political acumen, landed at Bermuda Hundred, a neck of land between Richmond and Petersburg. A small Southern force stalled Butler's advance and
finally bottled up the numerically superior Federal army on Bermuda Hundred. In the Shenandoah Valley, Sigel's command collided with a makeshift
Confederate army under Major General John C. Breckinridge at New Market
on May 15 and suffered a defeat, forcing the Yankees into retreat.

The Army of the Potomac, meanwhile, crossed the Rappahannock and
Rapidan rivers into the battle-scarred region between Fredericksburg and
Richmond. Lee, his army outnumbered nearly two-to-one, raced his veterans
eastward from their winter camps around Culpeper and struck the Federals
on May 5 in a demonic landscape of brush and scrub trees known locally as
The Wilderness. The unexpected Confederate assaults initiated the so-called
Overland Campaign. For the next forty days, with infrequent respite, the old
foes butchered each other: at the Wilderness, May 5–6; at Spotsylvania, May
8–20; along the North Anna River, May 23–25; and at Cold Harbor, June 1–11.
Throughout the campaign, Grant, endeavoring to place Meade's army between the Confederates and their capital, sidled leftward or southward. But
Lee, utilizing interior lines, intercepted the Federal thrusts, forcing them to
attack his troops, who had rapidly become experts in the construction of
fieldworks. Grant's most grievous mistake was the ordering of a frontal assault
on June 3 against Lee's virtually impregnable line at Cold Harbor. The Southerners erased the Union assault lines in approximately thirty minutes, inflicting several thousand casualties.

By the second week of June, therefore, Grant's grand offensive noticeably had not accomplished much: Sherman, crawling southward, seemingly had been swallowed up in Georgia; Butler sat quietly; Sigel was long gone; and Grant, on the Virginia Peninsula, was no closer to Richmond than George B. McClellan had been two years earlier. It had the look of another fruitless summer without final victory, but with staggering human costs. Northerners were stunned by the slaughter—Grant's casualties exceeded the entire strength of Lee's army, averaging nearly 2,000 per day. How could the results justify the butchery when the end appeared no closer than it had with McClellan in June 1862?

Grant was no McClellan, however. Though Lee could claim tactical victories on each battlefield, the Union General-in-Chief had not turned back. As he stated earlier in a dispatch, he proposed "to fight it out on this line if it takes all summer."[2] On June 12, the Army of the Potomac abandoned its trenches on the Peninsula's sweltering bottomlands, stole a march on Lee's troops, crossed a hastily erected 2,000-foot-long pontoon bridge over the James River and, by the 15th, was advancing on a weakly garrisoned Petersburg. Grant had executed another brilliant maneuver, which fell short of seizing the vulnerable railroad center because of cautious, inept generalship by some subordinates, erroneous orders and command paralysis. By June 18 the bulk of Lee's army manned the Petersburg works. The siege that both Grant and Lee—for different reasons—had hoped to avoid had begun. Lee's command remained intact, but Grant had locked it in place, restricting its offensive prowess. It was a stalemate, a gnawing away which might lead to resolution if the national wills in either the North or South could be sustained. Time might be the ally of either Grant or Lee.

At headquarters, Army of Northern Virginia, in Petersburg, a protracted siege, however, could mean a slow death. Lee, unable to assail the numerically superior Yankees, worried about his ranks being bled white in the trenches. The 57-year-old Virginian was in his third year at the helm of the army. Ironically, despite his previous accomplishments, his masterful defensive campaign against Grant perhaps was Lee at his best. Yet, he did not prevent the siege, and the depletion in the army's ranks could not be readily staunched. Confronted with this situation and with Union threats in other parts of the Old Dominion, Lee risked a gamble, a refashioning of the strategy used successfully in the spring of 1862 by himself, as the military advisor to President Jefferson Davis, and Thomas J. "Stonewall" Jackson.

When the two armies lay opposite each other at Cold Harbor, Lee learned that Grant had sent Major General Philip H. Sheridan with two cavalry divisions westward on a raid against the Virginia Central Railroad, the vital lifeline which supplied Lee's men with the harvests of the Shenandoah Valley. The Confederate commander dispatched his horsemen in pursuit. The mounted commands clashed on June 11 at Trevilian Station with the

Southerners blunting Sheridan's thrust. Temporarily, at least, the indispensible track had been secured. Additionally, during the same week, reports reached Lee that another Union army had returned to the Valley of Virginia. Commanded by Major General David Hunter, this 20,000-man force had already passed Staunton and occupied Lexington, wrecking railroads, burning warehouses and supply depots. Lee had no force in the region to match Hunter's troops, who posed a major threat to Lynchburg, where the Orange and Alexandria, the Virginia and Tennessee and the Southside railroads intersected. Lynchburg and the railroads could not fall to the Federals.

On June 10, General Braxton Bragg, Davis's current military advisor, wrote the president that "it seems to me very important that this force of the enemy should be expelled from the Valley. If it could be crushed, Washington would be open to the few we might then employ." Davis referred it to Lee, offering no comment or advice. Lee replied the next day: "I acknowledge the advantage of expelling the enemy from the Valley. The only difficulty with me is the means. It would [take] one corps of this army." If Davis and Bragg deemed it prudent "to hazard the defense of Richmond," Lee added, he would send a corps.[3]

The Confederate general, between the time he wrote to Davis on the 11th and the next morning, decided to assail Hunter. Lee later wrote that he resolved to send a force "that would be adequate to accomplish that purpose effectively, and, if possible strike a decisive blow." Lee not only wanted Hunter's threat eliminated; he planned a raid upon the Union capital which might compel Grant to weaken Meade's army by sending detachments northward, thereby presenting Lee with an opportunity for a resumption of offensive operations at Petersburg.[4]

Lee consequently summoned Lieutenant General Jubal A. Early, commander of the Second Corps, to army headquarters on June 12—the day Grant started for the James River. The pair conferred privately. Lee outlined his plan, directing the corps commander to leave early on the 13th, take all three of his infantry divisions and two battalions of artillery, and attack Hunter. If successful, added Lee, Early should march northward, down the Shenandoah Valley, cross into Maryland, seizing military stores and supplies, and threaten Washington and Baltimore. For Lee, it was a bold scheme, a willingness to restrict his own mobility by giving up a fourth of his undermanned infantry force if the outcome might match the accomplishments of two years earlier. Once begun, however, the audacious operation accelerated in importance, affecting the strategic balance in Virginia for the summer and autumn of 1864. It was Lee's major attempt at breaking the stalemate.

Early's Second Corps departed at the designated time on June 13, racing westward by forced marches and by rail, and reached Lynchburg four days later. Hunter, confronting these veteran troops, lost his nerve and scampered into the Allegheny Mountains. With the Shenandoah Valley cleared of Yankees, Early headed northward. By the first week of July, his command, augmented by some cavalry and an infantry division under John C. Breckinridge, were spilling into western Maryland. On the 9th the raiders arrived at Frederick, where a hastily gathered Union force, under Major General Lew A. Wallace, barred the roads to Baltimore and Washington. The Confederates defeated the Federals in the so-called Battle of Monocacy and continued toward the enemy's capital. Slowed by oppressive heat, dust and a drought, the Rebels approached Washington's miles of forts and earthworks on the afternoon of July 11. Early tested the defenses later in the day and the next, but found them unassailable to his few numbers. Insuring the capital's safety was the arrival of two divisions of the Union VI Corps, belatedly dispatched by Grant from Petersburg.[5]

A few minutes past midnight on July 13 the final contingent of Early's troops abandoned their lines west of the capital. A feeble, disjointed Union pursuit ensued, but the graycoated raiders eluded the Federals, except for two brief clashes, and were safely back in the Shenandoah Valley a week later. When the major component of the Federal force returned to the capital, Early struck a 9,500-man detachment, under Brevet Major General George Crook, on July 24, in the Second Battle of Kernstown, routing the Yankees and clearing the northern end of the Valley of Federals.[6]

Early, keeping the initiative, sent two brigades of cavalry into southern Pennsylvania. An unforgiving type, the general ordered the horsemen to Chambersburg because of Hunter's incendiarism in the upper Valley. "It was time," Early wrote, "to open the eyes of the people of the North to this enormity, by an example in the way of retaliation." The Southerners, led by Brigadier General John McCausland, entered the Pennsylvania community on July 30. McCausland demanded a tribute of $100,000 in gold or $500,000 in cash but, when town officials refused, the grayjacketed troopers began looting and burning. The conflagration engulfed eleven squares and over 400 buildings, including 274 private dwellings. The Commonwealth of Pennsylvania later paid the victims $1,628,431 for the damages.[7]

The burning of Chambersburg concluded the operations associated with Early's raid and its immediate aftermath. In slightly over a month the Confederate general had carried the war to the doorstep of the Union capital, embarrassed Lincoln's administration and forced Grant into a slight detachment of troops from Petersburg. The populace of the North was astonished by the July developments. "The thing seemed so much out of keeping with the position of affairs elsewhere," editorialized the New York *Times*. It was "the old story over again," the newspaper argued. "The back door, by way of the Shenandoah Valley, has been left invitingly open."[8]

The newspaper's editorial possessed considerable truth. Union authorities, in fact, had lost nearly all control over the unfolding events in the

Shenandoah Valley and western Maryland, resulting in an appearance of helplessness in confronting the bold Southern movement. The cause of much of this was structural. The Union command system, like an outmoded engine wheezing under the strain, faltered. Four departments—West Virginia, Middle, Susquehanna and Washington—encompassed the area penetrated or endangered by the Southern raiders. Fears and rumors multiplied as each layer in the command bureaucracy flooded the War Department with their individual concerns.[9]

The man responsible for overseeing this organization was the Federal Chief of Staff, Major General Henry Wager Halleck. Nearly sixty, West Pointer, author of a translation on tactics, Halleck had achieved modest success in the west in 1862 when Lincoln plucked him from that theater to coordinate the burgeoning Union departments. Unfortunately by the summer of 1864, the Chief of Staff had become inured to the ways of bureaucracy. He vacillated under pressure and continually avoided responsibility.[10]

"Old Brains," as Halleck was dubiously termed, acted primarily as the communications link between Lincoln and Grant and between the General-in-Chief and his seventeen department commanders. It was through Halleck's eyes that most situations unfolded for Grant. As the Confederate operation in the region developed, Halleck funneled the news to Grant, shrugging off any responsibility for the deteriorating Union operation.[11]

Compounding the defective command organization was the lieutenant general's attitude toward the area of operations. Grant viewed the Shenandoah Valley as a subsidiary theater and took little initial interest in Early's advance northward. Perhaps Grant refused to believe that his Confederate counterpart had committed such a large portion of his infantry to such a dubious operation. The Illinoisan only slowly came to appreciate the embarrassing storm descending upon the Northern administration and its political implications for Lincoln and the Republican Party. When he finally reacted to Halleck's alarm, he sent the VI Corps and rerouted the XIX Corps, which was enroute from Louisiana to Petersburg. The reinforcements reached the capital by the slimmest of margins and subsequently participated in the lethargic pursuit of the raiders.[12]

Grant's irresolution during the initial phases of the Confederate raid changed to a grim determination by the final week of July. Two factors contributed to this. First of all, he concluded that the four departments embracing the capital, Maryland, Pennsylvania and the Shenandoah Valley had to be merged into one. Lincoln, Secretary of War Edwin Stanton, assistant secretary Charles Dana and Halleck in a series of messages suggested such a restructuring of the command system. When the pursuit failed so miserably and Crook was routed at Kernstown, Grant had little choice but to order the change and appoint a commander. A merger, as Grant told Halleck, was "absolutely necessary."[13]

Secondly, Grant's appreciation of the impact of events in the Shenandoah Valley on other areas in Virginia, especially his own operations at Petersburg, had increased considerably since May when he expected little benefit from Franz Sigel's advance up the Shenandoah. The fertile granary of the Confederacy and the metal lifelines which connected it to Lee's besieged army at Petersburg now became Grant's objective. If a Union force of greater strength and with abler leadership could extend Hunter's June expedition, Grant would retain the VI and XIX Corps in the region. The destruction of the Virginia & Tennessee, the Southside, the Virginia Central and the Orange & Alexandria railroads would deny Lee's troops their sustaining rations. The Union General-in-Chief finally linked operations in the Shenandoah Valley to those at Petersburg. "It seemed to be the policy of General Halleck and Secretary Stanton," he subsequently wrote in his memoirs, "to keep any force sent there, in pursuit of the invading army, moving right and left so as to keep between the enemy and our capital; and, generally speaking, they pursued this policy until all knowledge of the whereabouts of the enemy was lost. . . . I determined to put a stop to this."[14]

During the final days of July and the initial week of August, The General-in-Chief acted. On July 25, the day after Crook's defeat at Kernstown, Grant wrote a letter to Lincoln which he had his Chief of Staff John Rawlins carry personally to the president. In it, Grant reiterated his belief that the four departments should be merged under one commander. "All I ask," Grant stated to Lincoln, "is that one general officer, in whom I and yourself have confidence, should command the whole." Earlier, Grant had suggested Major General William B. Franklin, a former McClellan supporter, for the post, but he was rejected. Now the lieutenant general chose George Meade, commander of the Army of the Potomac. With Meade in control, Grant argued, "I would have every confidence that all the troops within the military division would be used to the very best advantage from a personal examination of the ground, and [he] would adopt means of getting the earliest information of any advance of the enemy, would prepare to meet it." Perhaps anticipating Lincoln's reaction to his surprising choice, Grant concluded that "many reasons might be assigned for the changes here suggested, some of which I would not care to commit to paper, but would not hesitate to give verbally." If Lincoln needed such information, Rawlins could supply it.[15]

Rawlins conferred with Lincoln at the White House on the morning of July 26. The president responded to Grant's words with a request, submitted through Stanton, that the commander-in-chief and his top officer meet personally at Fortress Monroe. Any time after Thursday, the 28th, would suit, Lincoln said. Grant replied to the summons that night, expressing his willingness to confer directly with Lincoln, but it would have to be after the 29th because "I am commencing movements to-night from which I hope favorable results," added Grant.[16]

The movements Grant referred to eventually concluded on July 30 with the explosion of a Federal mine under a portion of Lee's works at Petersburg. The ensuing Union assault into the breach resulted in the bloody fiasco of the so-called Battle of the Crater. This was also the same day McCausland burned Chambersburg. Later that day Grant wired Lincoln, telling the latter he would meet him the next day at Fortress Monroe.[17]

Details of this July 31 meeting between the president and the lieutenant general are sketchy for neither ever said much about it. What the two talked about and resolved, however, is reasonably certain. The agenda probably encompassed what Lincoln jotted on the back of Grant's July 30 telegram: "Meade & Franklin / McClellan / Md. & Penna." Both men understood and were committed to the unification of the four departments and a force of sufficient strength to operate successfully in the region. Grant had funneled the remainder of the XIX Corps and one of the three cavalry divisions of the Army of the Potomac to Washington. What this private session had to resolve was who would command it.[18]

Lincoln initiated the meeting by asking Grant whether Meade was interested in the appointment. The lieutenant general had broached the idea days earlier to Meade, who responded by saying he was "ready to obey any order that might be given me." The army commander actually preferred the appointment to independent command for it would return to him control over troops, something he no longer possessed with Grant accompanying the army. Lincoln, however, rejected Meade, arguing that for months he had been opposing efforts calling for Meade's dismissal. The president had no desire to appear to be bowing now to that pressure.[19]

The inclusion of former Major General George B. McClellan's name on the list referred to a proposition making the rounds in Washington and New York. Various moderate Republican leaders, hoping to prevent McClellan's nomination as the 1864 Democratic presidential candidate, wanted the popular officer returned to rank and given the independent command. It was reported that Francis B. Blair, Sr., father of Lincoln's Postmaster General, met with McClellan, urging the latter to apply for an assignment. But McClellan refused to commit himself and never did apply. More importantly, however, Lincoln probably thought little of it, but he surely wanted to discuss it with Grant.[20]

This McClellan proposal served, at least, to remind Grant of the political pressures confronting Lincoln during this election year. The administration could not stand for a repetition of Early's raid, nor for the continual cavalry incursions north of the Potomac River which culminated in events similar to Chambersburg's, whose ashes were still warm as the two conferred. The president was also under increasing pressure from John W. Garrett, the president of the Baltimore & Ohio Railroad. Garrett was a brilliant administrator and a trusted advisor of Lincoln and Stanton. He, as much as any single man, except for perhaps Lew Wallace, managed to secure the capital in mid-July by having his trains ready to funnel troops to Washington. Fortunately for Garrett, Grant shared his belief that the operation of the railroad was indispensable. For Union authorities the situation along the upper Potomac, both politically and militarily, was presently intolerable.[21]

Lincoln and Grant departed from Fortress Monroe the same day, with the question of who would command unsettled — the president had left it with his General-in-Chief. Grant did not wait; the next morning, August 1, he told Meade that his choice was the army's cavalry commander, Philip H. Sheridan. At 11:30 a.m. he telegraphed Halleck:

> I am sending General Sheridan for temporary duty whilst the enemy is being expelled from the border. Unless General Hunter is in the field in person, I want Sheridan put in command of all the troops in the field, with instructions to put himself south of the enemy and follow him to the death. Wherever the enemy goes let our troops go also. Once started up the Valley they ought to be followed until we get possession of the Virginia Central Railroad. If General Hunter is in the field give Sheridan direct command of the Sixth Corps and cavalry division.

On the 2nd, Grant, in Special Orders No. 68, formally ordered Sheridan and his staff to Washington.[22]

In Washington opposition to Sheridan's appointment arose within a day. Lincoln, Stanton and Halleck voiced misgivings about the 33-year-old cavalry commander, believing that he was too young for the post. Once more, telegrams raced back and forth between Washington and City Point. Finally, on August 4, Grant decided upon a personal visit to David Hunter's headquarters at Frederick, Maryland, and so informed Lincoln. The time had come for a wresting of the strategic initiative in the Shenandoah Valley from the Confederates, so Grant traveled to Monocacy Station.[23]

The lieutenant general, upon his arrival, found the VI Corps, a portion of the XIX Corps, Hunter's Army of West Virginia and part of the cavalry covering the fields around the railroad stop and Frederick. Hunter met Grant, and the superior officer wasted little time in getting to the heart of the matter. Where were the Rebels, Grant asked the department commander. Hunter admitted he didn't know; the conflicting orders from Halleck and Stanton had caused him to lose "all trace of the enemy."[24]

If Hunter couldn't find Early, Grant could. He ordered a general advance of the entire force at Frederick to Halltown, Virginia, four miles southwest of Harpers Ferry. When Early learned of this movement, the Union commander surmised, he would have to respond, probably by concentrating near Martinsburg, Virginia. Grant then wrote out the instructions for Hunter, who was directed to give Sheridan field command while he established his headquarters somewhere. To this, Hunter said that since Halleck so distrusted his fitness for command, he thought that he should be relieved. Grant said, "very well then," and telegraphed Washington for Sheridan. Hunter, Grant wrote in his memoirs, "did not want, in any way, to embarrass the cause; thus showing a patriotism that was none too common in the army."[25]

Sheridan came by train to Monocacy Junction the next day, August 6. The pair conferred briefly; Grant handed Sheridan the written instructions prepared the night before. Within two hours, Grant boarded a train for Washington and Sheridan another for Harpers Ferry. Weeks of uncertainty in Washington and City Point ended at a stop on a railroad with probably a handshake and a salute. This was indeed a strange war, the outcome of which in Virginia now rested with two men who came from the West, from the heartland of the nation.[26]

As the late summer days shortened into autumn, the campaign for the Shenandoah Valley began. Its genesis lay in the gambling strategy of Robert E. Lee. The Confederate general had refashioned an earlier, successful operation and, with its achievements in July, brought a response from Ulysses S. Grant. The stakes, both political and military, became high for both antagonists. If the summer stalemate in Virginia were to be broken, it would be beyond the Blue Ridge Mountains in the Shenandoah Valley.

Lieut. Gen. U. S. Grant at Cold Harbor. USAMHI.

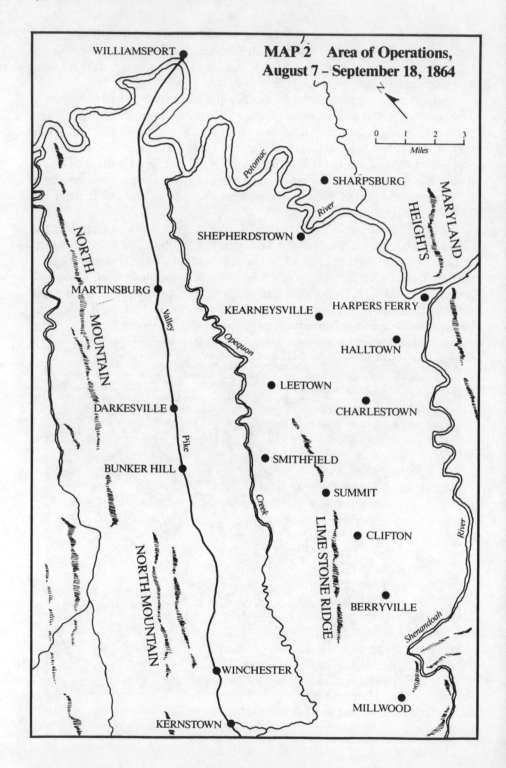

MAP 2   Area of Operations,
August 7 – September 18, 1864

WILLIAMSPORT

SHARPSBURG

SHEPHERDSTOWN

MARTINSBURG

KEARNEYSVILLE

HARPERS FERRY

HALLTOWN

LEETOWN

DARKESVILLE

CHARLESTOWN

SMITHFIELD

BUNKER HILL

SUMMIT

CLIFTON

BERRYVILLE

WINCHESTER

MILLWOOD

KERNSTOWN

NORTH MOUNTAIN

NORTH MOUNTAIN

MARYLAND HEIGHTS

LIME STONE RIDGE

Potomac

River

Valley

Pike

Opequon

Creek

River

Shenandoah

0   1   2   3
Miles

2

Armies On The Land

The railroad freight cars groaned under the weight of the soldiers who crowded within and blanketed the roofs. Beside the tracks, columns of blue-coated Yankees, stretching out of sight, tramped in the heat and dust. Many had been at Harpers Ferry, Virginia less than a week ago, and now they were heading back. This day, August 6, 1864, ended a week most preferred to forget.

It had been seven days ago, July 31, a Sabbath as hot as Hades, when these soldiers had marched out of Harpers Ferry. The Confederate raid on Chambersburg the day before had brought orders for a return to Frederick, a place many left only three days earlier. The Sunday movement "was the hardest march we ever made," recalled a tough Vermonter of the VI Corps. "The heat was intense; the day was the very hottest of all the season; the clouds of dust were actually blinding; the pace almost a gallop." Hundreds collapsed from sunstroke, with a number dying. The ceaseless campaigning for nearly a month had already taken its toll, and this march intensified it. "The men was about as near plaid [sic] out as ever saw them," Second Lieutenant Charles R. Perkins, 2nd Rhode Island Battalion, wrote his sister on the 30th. The exhausted Yankees stumbled into Frederick, nearly 25 miles from the ferry, at sunrise the next morning.[1]

The infantry and cavalry camps covered the fields encircling Frederick and along the banks of the Monocacy River until Ulysses Grant issued his orders for an advance on the evening of August 5. By the time Philip Sheridan met Grant at the depot, nearly all the regiments had been on the road for hours or had spent a fearful ride on a "rickety train." Men of the XIX Corps, who rode back to Harpers Ferry in the freight cars, asserted later that they had been safer on a transport in a gale off Cape Hatteras, North Carolina, than on this railroad hurtling westward at 45 miles per hour. Many of them thrust their bayonets into the roofs to steady themselves. But for those clinging to the tops, this practice only increased anxieties. Before midnight on the 6th, most of the command was encamped just south of Harpers Ferry, near Halltown.[2]

The next day, August 7, Grant formally reorganized the Middle Department and the Departments of Washington, D.C., Susquehanna and West Virginia into the Middle Military Division. Sheridan's appointment was also officially announced. For the men in the ranks, they would be designated in time as the Army of the Shenandoah. Union authorities, for the first time in the war, created a command structure and fielded an army of sufficient strength to oppose Confederate forces in the Shenandoah. Even the officers and privates understood the reasons behind the change. "It seems to be necessary," Major William Knowlton, 29th Maine, wrote his wife on the 3rd, "for quite a large force to be kept somewhere about here for it has always been the case as soone [sic] as we all left this section the rebs have come up here and got the start of us."[3]

The Army of the Shenandoah was thus formed to prevent the Rebels from getting "the start of us." It was an amalgam, a hybrid army merged together because of the recent Confederate operations in Maryland and the Valley. The army contained the second largest corps in the Army of the Potomac, a corps from the Department of the Gulf, which had been rerouted on its way to Petersburg, the Army of West Virginia which had bled before in the Shenandoah and, within a week, two veteran cavalry divisions from the Army of the Potomac. For the most part the soldiers in the ranks were battle-tested veterans, with many capable and, a few brilliant, combat officers. Forces beyond their control brought them together at the confluence of the Potomac and Shenandoah Rivers and under the command of an officer of unknown quality to all, except for the horse soldiers and a handful of former comrades.

Private James F. Fitts, 114th New York, a member of the XIX Corps, probably typified most of the soldiers' view of the appointment of Sheridan. "I think," recalled Fitts, "that the prevalent feeling among the corps was one of surprise and disappointment." It had not been any different four months earlier, in April, when Grant brought Sheridan east to lead the cavalry corps. To the seasoned troopers, who had finally been able to fight Major General J. E. B. Stuart's knights of Virginia on even terms, the selection of an infantry officer from the West was, as Trooper Charles E. MacConnell wrote, "anything but welcome news." But, under Sheridan, the Union horsemen inflicted crippling losses on the Rebel cavalry, and even killed the irreplaceable Stuart. The Union troopers soon learned what the Army of the Shenandoah was about to find out — Sheridan was, as one of Meade's staff officers perceptively saw, the "superior to any officer there."[4]

The rise of Philip Henry Sheridan during the war can best be described as meteoric. The son of Irish immigrants, born March 6, 1831, probably in

Albany, New York, Sheridan grew up in Somerset, Ohio, before entering West Point, where he was graduated in the bottom third of his class in 1853. Eight years of duty on the frontier followed until the outbreak of the war. He initially served as chief quartermaster and commissary of the Army of Southwest Missouri. On May 25, 1862, he was appointed colonel of the 2nd Michigan Cavalry, but soon was promoted, on September 13, to date from July 1, to brigadier general. He commanded an infantry division at Perryville, Kentucky and at Stone's River, Tennessee with skill and aggressiveness. Promoted to major general on March 16, 1863, Sheridan lost over a third of his division at Chickamauga, Georgia, in September. Then on November 25, his men, without orders and under the admiring eye of Grant, scaled Missionary Ridge, outside of Chattanooga, Tennessee, and wrenched it from its Confederate defenders. Grant remembered Sheridan's headlong combativeness and, when the Illinoisan came east in March 1864, Sheridan followed within a month to command the cavalry.[5]

What struck people, when they first met Sheridan, was his size. A cavalry officer, in the spring of 1864, figured Sheridan stood about five feet, three inches and weighed between 115 and 120 pounds. Colonel Charles S. Wainwright asserted that Sheridan "certainly would not impress one by his looks any more than Grant does. He is short, thickset and common Irish-looking. Met in the Bowery, one would certainly set him down as a 'b'hoy'; and his dress is in perfect keeping with that character." Sheridan was broad-shouldered, with a robust chest, but he possessed inordinately short legs. Orton S. Clark, 116th New York, when he saw Sheridan in August, described him simply as "the little man who rode so large a horse." To his men, he was "Little Phil."[6]

Another feature of Sheridan's appearance which elicited comments was his peculiarly shaped head. It looked somewhat like a slightly flattened minie ball. It "was not a common head," remarked Dr. A. D. Rockwell, 6th Ohio Cavalry. The Ohio surgeon, with the profoundness of a learned medical man, attributed "this singular shape" to "certain irregularities called by phrenologists bumps of combativeness." These "bumps," Rockwell added, "greatly inconvenienced him as well as his enemies." The soldiers even speculated that Sheridan had difficulty wearing a hat, which explained why in battle he generally held it in his hand. Few generals of the war had a head which drew so much attention.[7]

But this diminutive commander possessed fire, a combativeness which Grant admired. "Little Phil" was preeminently a man of action; to those who saw him, he appeared restless, with what an infantryman described as "nervous animation." Captain Henry DuPont, Crook's artillery commander, who saw Sheridan closely in the forthcoming campaign, described the army commander as "naturally eager and impulsive." Intense, energetic, Sheridan was also self-confident. He didn't doubt his abilities nor his capacities; he faced his duty squarely and expected no less from others.[8]

Few things aroused the fury of "Little Phil" more than this latter point. Major Benjamin W. Crowninshield, a member of his staff, described his commander as "always affable," unless someone displeased him. Sheridan "had no favorites but the men who best carried out his orders," said Crowninshield. Colonel J. Warren Keifer, a VI Corps brigade commander, found Sheridan, in quiet moments at headquarters or on the march, to be "rollicking and free and easy." But Sheridan could be merciless to an officer whom he perceived to have failed. Keifer believed that there was a petulance to this "nervous, restless" man.[9]

If Sheridan demanded much from those under him, he possessed the ability to inspire them. Few officers in either army had the charisma of "Little Phil." One of his biographers stated that he "had an undeniable talent for bravura—calculated bravura in the frontier style." This was particularly true of Sheridan when he rode along a line of troops engaged in battle. He became "ablaze with enthusiasm" during combat, according to Crowninshield. Though he relished combat, inspired men to go beyond their limitation, Sheridan "never lost his head," said Keifer.[10] No previous Union general, commanding an army in the Shenandoah Valley, possessed the intrinsic qualities of Sheridan. Confident, aggressive, brave, inspirational, "Little Phil" believed that an army existed to fight, to bring war to his opponent. He was unquestionably the type of leader Grant wanted in the strategic area.

The doubts of Lincoln, Stanton and Halleck were justified, however. Could Sheridan handle an entire army with the same skill he directed an infantry division or a cavalry corps? Could he direct a campaign in unfamiliar terrain, fashioning a strategy of victory? Could his aggressiveness, his penchant for a headlong attack be enough against a wily foe, who led perhaps the finest body of defenders in any army, both Union and Confederate? The answers rested with him and also with the officers and soldiers of the Army of the Shenandoah.

The bedrock of the new Army of the Shenandoah, both in size and grit, was the VI Corps of the Army of the Potomac. Three infantry divisions, divided into eight brigades which contained thirty-eight regiments and three battalions from eleven Northern states, comprised the unit. Though the heavy casualties sustained in May and June brought in many raw recruits and conscripts, the corps maintained its reputation for steadfastness and reliability. Little in their record had been spectacular—public renown had gone to other corps—but these veterans had seen enough of the elephant to be sturdy fighters.[11]

Their present commander, Major General Horatio G. Wright, was a man much like his command. Though Wright had faltered under the burdens of independent command during the pursuit of Early, he had the qualities an army commander would want in a ranking subordinate and corps commander. Cautious by nature, not particularly ambitious, the Connecticut native was an exceedingly careful, painstaking officer. One of his brigade commanders described Wright as the "unassuming, sturdy solid kind—never pryrotechnic" and "especially fitted to command infantry." Lieutenant Colonel Theodore Lyman of Meade's staff called him "the stout-hearted General," "a sterling soldier." If he had a fault, Lyman believed, it was simply "poor luck."

At divisional command, Wright had three very capable West Point-trained, old Regular Army professionals. Brigadier General David A. Russell led the First Division. A friend and former superior of Sheridan, Russell was one of the most trusted and well liked officers in the corps. Brigadier General George Washington Getty, who joined the corps just before the Wilderness, commanded the Second Division. He then directed it with the ease and skill of a man long in such a post. A Vermont soldier argued "that the army did not contain a better Division General" than Getty, while a veteran New Yorker confided in his journal that "General Getty is a splendid specimen of a soldier and always handles his div in gallant style." The Third Division belonged to Brigadier General James B. Ricketts, who had, said Lew Wallace, "fought magnificently" at Monocacy. A quiet, generous man, Ricketts possessed "great personal courage." This redoubtable fighter particularly enjoyed having his wife, Fanny, with him in the field.[13]

Of the eight brigade commanders, only two were professionals and only three had acquired their brigadier's star. Brigadier General Frank Wheaton was the senior brigade officer and a deserving successor if any division commander fell in battle. Brigadier General Daniel D. Bidwell, a former police justice or magistrate in Buffalo, New York, had commanded his four regiments and two battalions with skill and gallantry for over a year. The third brigadier was Emory Upton, a 24-year-old West Pointer. War consumed this thin, wiry, freckle-faced officer, it was his "ardent love." He coveted military fame, studied assiduously the principles of warfare and wanted nothing less than a chance to acquire greatness. He had already become a marked man, the corps' rising star. Of the four colonels and one lieutenant colonel, who led the remaining brigades, Colonels Oliver Edwards, J. Warren Keifer and James M. Warner headed the list, each highly regarded and battle wise.[14]

The corps was composed overwhelmingly of men from New York, New Jersey, Pennsylvania and New England. The command's most renowned unit was probably the Vermont Brigade in Getty's division. A rugged outfit, they fought with the tenacity and sturdiness of their beloved Green Mountains. A member attributed their record to "steadiness in critical positions, perserverance against all odds, and inability to admit defeat." But his words could have described most of the corps, men, like the Vermonters, of "steady, perser-vering, confident pluck."[15]

The two divisions of the XIX Corps, or officially the "Detachment, XIX Corps," when compared to the VI, was "far behind it in discipline and effi-ciency," according to the artillerist, Henry DuPont. Six weeks ago, in June, these troops had been in Louisiana recuperating from Major General Nathan-iel Banks's ill-fated Red River Campaign when Grant ordered them trans-ferred to Virginia. The General-in-Chief intended them for Petersburg, but Early's Washington raid caused Grant to redirect them to the capital and, now, they found themselves in the Shenandoah Valley. For most of the men in the ranks, the trip brought them much closer to home. Of the command's 35 regiments, 15 came from New York and 12 hailed from all the New England states, except Rhode Island.[16]

Major General William Hemsley Emory, a 52-year-old academy graduate and career soldier, commanded the corps. He had fought with distinction as a division commander under Banks but, for reasons not altogether clear, he wanted out of the Department of the Gulf, requesting in June a leave of absence for ninety days, which was declined. A coarse, profane, rather eccen-tric man, Emory had ability and enjoyed great popularity with his troops, who affectionately called him "Old Brick Top" because of his sandy hair. Major Crowninshield, Sheridan's aide, subsequently described him as "a fine speci-men of the old United States army officer. Though Sheridan's senior by many years, he showed none of the jealousy so common during the war among West Point officers."[17]

Emory, unlike Wright, was burdened with officers at division and brigade level of questionable caliber. The most prominent was Brigadier General William Dwight, commander of the First Division. Dismissed from the mili-tary academy in 1853 for "deficiency in studies," Dwight had only recently been appointed to the post. During the Red River Campaign he acted as Banks's chief of staff, with the principal duty of shipping captured cotton north to Massachusetts mills. Dwight lacked combat experience at this level and, perhaps, personal courage. The commander of the Second Division, Brigadier General Cuvier Grover, had still not rejoined the corps. When he arrived, Grover came with a proven combat record, having directed his bri-gades for over a year. Of the seven brigade commanders, four—Brigadier Generals James W. McMillan and Henry W. Birge and Colonels Edward L. Molineux and Jacob Sharpe—had definite promise. But, as the ensuing cam-paign would reveal, this corps had to prove its mettle to Sheridan.[18]

Little Phil's third infantry command was the Army of West Virginia, veterans of the Valley, who after Second Kernstown, wanted another go at Early's Confederates. At the head of this unit, Sheridan not only had, per-haps, his best subordinate, but his West Point roommate and close friend—Major General George Crook. He had been clearly whipped by Early at

Kernstown, but Crook possessed his officers' and men's unquestioned confidence and a keen tactical mind. A VI Corps officer described him as "an ideal soldier."[19] Sheridan, more importantly, trusted Crook and would seek his advice and opinions. For the Union cause, this reunion portended much; for the two friends, it portended something else.

Of Crook's subordinates at division and brigade command, none had been trained to the profession; the war had been their tutor. The division commanders, Colonels Joseph Thoburn and Isaac H. Duval, "were most capable and energetic officers," according to DuPont. Thoburn, a physician before the war, was the better of the two. An officer in his brigade described him as "a rock" on a battlefield. Duval, a wanderer in the West before 1861, was relatively new to the responsibilities, but he had shown much promise at Kernstown. Of the five brigade commanders, Colonels Rutherford B. Hayes and George D. Wells were the most outstanding, both highly respected by their men and highly regarded by their superiors. Except for a regiment from Massachusetts and a battalion from New York, Crook's command was entirely composed of troops from West Virginia and Ohio.[20]

A dozen batteries of field artillery were attached to the infantry corps. Wright's command had half the batteries, six four-gun batteries of Napoleons and 3-inch rifles under Colonel Charles H. Tompkins, an experienced, able officer. The XIX Corps had three batteries of light artillery, containing a dozen Napoleons. Captain Albert W. Bradbury commanded one battery, while Captain Elijah D. Taft directed the corps's Reserve Artillery of two batteries. Crook's two divisions were supported by a battery of six 3-inch rifled cannon, a battery of six 10-pounder Parrott guns and a battery of four Napoleons. Captain Henry DuPont, a West Pointer, class of 1861, commanded Crook's artillery. The captain, a Delaware DuPont, was an outstanding artillery officer of great personal courage. Sheridan maintained this organization, keeping the batteries with the infantry corps and not appointing a chief of artillery.[21]

The third component of the Federal army, three divisions of cavalry, joined the Union infantry and artillery units within a week after Sheridan assumed command. The Union general soon afterwards organized the mounted units into an unofficial corps, directed by Brigadier General Alfred Thomas Archimedes Torbert. A 31-year-old West Pointer, Torbert had led infantry for three years until appointed commander of the First Division of cavalry in April 1864. As the senior officer in the cavalry, Torbert was entitled to the position as chief of the cavalry. Sheridan knew Torbert well and apparently did not hesitate to give him the post. But others questioned the selection. Captain George B. Sanford, one of Torbert's aides, described his boss as "a handsome, dashing fellow, at this time, a beautiful horseman, and as brave as a lion; but his abilities were hardly equal to such large commands."[22]

Torbert's three divisions contained, argumentatively, some of the finest, if not best, regiments and brigades in Sheridan's army, who were led by young, brash, but excellent, officers. The two divisions dispatched by Grant from Petersburg were a strike force the Confederates could not match in the Valley. Three years of combat against Stuart's mounted legions had forged these troopers into a body of tough, no nonsense fighters. Two solid officers commanded the divisions—Brigadiers Generals Wesley Merritt and James Harrison Wilson. Their brigade commanders were officers of distinguished merit and promise. Torbert's other division, two brigades under William Averell, did not equal Merritt's and Wilson's troopers but, when Averell's men combined with the other two divisions, Torbert's command was indeed a formidable weapon.[23]

Of the 29 cavalry regiments, two detachments and one battalion in the Union army, fifteen regiments were completely armed with Spencer repeaters and three partially armed with the excellent firearm. With the Spencers, the horsemen possessed a firepower even some Confederate infantry units could not match. Eight batteries of horse artillery supported the mounted units. Altogether, the cavalry corps was a powerful command, as tough as tempered steel.[24]

Union authorities, finally, had brought to the Shenandoah Valley a command—in strength, leadership and combat prowess—worthy of the strategic value of the region. The Army of the Shenandoah exceeded, in numbers alone, any previous Union force in the Valley. Sheridan would begin the forthcoming campaign with nearly 35,000 infantry and artillery effectives and 8,000 cavalry. If the separate Military District of Harpers Ferry, commanded by Brigadier General John D. Stevenson, numbering nearly 5,000, were included, Sheridan had, at hand, approximately 48,000 troops. His Middle Military Division also embraced the nearly 29,000 troops in the Department of Washington, the 2,700 soldiers in the Department of the Susquehanna and the approximately 5,900 Federals in the Middle Department.[25]

On August 7, then, the bluecoated infantry and artillery, lying in the camps surrounding Halltown, waited for the orders to advance, while from the east and the west the mounted horsemen were coming. To the southwest, however, their opponents also waited, confident that the Shenandoah belonged to them.

The Confederates lay in camps near Bunker Hill, Virginia. It had been two months, less five days, since Jubal Early received the orders from Lee returning him to the Valley. He and his veterans had achieved all that had been asked of them. He could only have had immense satisfaction with the past sixty days of operations. The trust and confidence Lee reposed in "his bad old man," Early had returned in full. But his successes over the past two months had brought not relief, nor security, but a Federal army with a mission and a commander with evident capability. The general, officially commander of the Valley District, and his Army of the Valley confronted a task greater than that which they undertook when they left Cold Harbor. The credits and debits of both Early and his veterans would count for much when the Yankees came south.

The 47-year-old Early, whom the men called "Old Jube" or "Old Jubilee," enjoyed the respect and liking of the soldiers in the ranks. He might have been "a bundle of inconsistencies and contradictions," but it was his very eccentricity that endeared him to the men. "A queer fish" was Early, said one of them, but the troops had "a great fondness for him," though they showed it in a peculiar way. "Whenever he came along the line," remarked a graycoat, "there was a laugh and then a cheer, both of which things were very disagreeable to him, and looking as preternaturally solemn as a country coroner going to his first inquest. After he had passed, some wag would shout after him one or another of the old army gags of those days. He would wheel his horse to see who had insulted him, but nobody knew, and he had no means of finding out."[26]

The irascible general and the troops in the ranks were men of kindred spirit. Early shared their affinity for whiskey and apple brandy, and he could cuss with the best of them. His honesty, his abhorrence of pretentiousness, his cynicism, his sauciness appealed to the independent-minded soldiers. They particularly enjoyed recalling the time Stonewall Jackson, following a day's hard march, sent a note to Early inquiring why he had seen so many stragglers in the rear of the subordinate's division that day. Old Jube sent Jackson his compliments and explained that the corps commander had seen so many stragglers trailing Early's column "probably because he rode in rear of my division." The privates knew only Early and Stuart dared to send such a note to that stern Presbyterian warrior.[27]

"That grand old fellow," as a gunner called Early, could also be found with his veterans along a battle line. "He was always ready for a fight, and was never happier than when in a battle," claimed one of them. Captain Samuel Buck, 13th Virginia, concurring, stated that "I have seen him at times and places that tried men's souls, and he was always in the thickest of the battle."[28]

Such bravery, such belligerence especially suited a brigade or division, perhaps even a corps, commander. In an army commander, particularly one facing superior numbers, it could be a dangerous trait, however. Major General John B. Gordon, no admirer of Early, spoke of this in his memoirs after the war. Old Jube, asserted Gordon, was "an able strategist and one of the coolest and most imperturable of men under fire and in extremity," but he lacked "the courage of one's convictions." Early fought boldly, but blindly, unable to perceive the weak and the strong points of an adversary. "He strikes in the dark," concluded the division commander, "madly, wildly, and often impotently."[29] Gordon's criticisms reflected the bitterness between the two men, but the able Georgian's censure had some validity. Though Early showed wise restraint at Washington a month earlier, he clearly preferred aggressive offensive warfare. He had been schooled in strategy by Jackson and Lee, two generals who confronted the long odds by audacity and two men Early admired above all others.

Early had other flaws of character and leadership which could adversely affect his ability to direct an army. None were, perhaps, more serious than his reluctance, even indisposition, to act upon the suggestions and advice of his ranking subordinates. This probably indicated more than a man imbued with self-confidence or one who cared little for or knew not of the art of ingratiation. He could not have asked, in the war's final year, for finer combat generals than John Breckinridge, Robert Rodes, John Gordon and Stephen Dodson Ramseur. But there was a quirk in Old Jube's make-up which seemingly brought forth his worst attributes for officers he must have viewed as rivals. Though Early had given Breckinridge command of an unofficial corps of two divisions, no relationship developed between the two generals comparable to that of Sheridan and Crook. Breckinridge, by his stature and experience, was worthy of such confidence and trust, but Early did not fully utilize the Kentuckian's talents. Old Jube's treatment of Gordon perhaps best indicated the commander's response to a rival. Gordon, based on his battlefield record, seemed destined for higher command, but Early clearly resented the brilliant Georgian. Instead of praise, the lieutenant general gave the division commander silence; jealousy warped the superior officer's conduct. Jubal Early commanded the Army of the Valley, and no one would likely be given the chance to forget it.[30]

A career infantry officer, the lieutenant general possessed a prejudice against the mounted arm. It may have resulted from a foot soldier's natural dislike for those he viewed as glory seekers or Early's lack of understanding of the role of cavalry in military operations. During the winter of 1863–1864, Old Jube, while commanding the Valley District, developed this prejudice when he saw the ill-disciplined units he directed. His biased view increased during the raid on Washington as he thought the cavalry performed without any particular merit.[31]

Early's dim assessment of his five cavalry brigades had some justification. By the summer of 1864 certain critical factors had begun to debilitate the effectiveness of Confederate mounted units, and those in the Valley were particularly affected. Lack of discipline, inadequate or ineffective arms and a crippling shortage of mounts and equipment characterized many of the regiments serving under him. Bradley Johnson described William E. "Grumble" Jones's brigade, which the Marylander inherited in June, as about 800 "half-armed and badly disciplined mountaineers from Southwest Virginia, who would fight like veterans when they pleased, but had no idea of permitting their own sweet wills to be controlled by any orders, no matter from whom emanating."[32]

Shortages of good weapons, horses and equipment compounded morale problems. Most of the horsemen carried Enfield rifles, a cumbersome, nearly useless weapon in mounted combat. "I would rather command a regiment," groused one officer about the Enfields, "armed with good oaken clubs." Improperly armed, the cavalrymen also wrestled with insufficient mounts, forage and horseshoes. The problem of good horseflesh became acute for Confederates in 1863 and 1864. The troopers owned their own mounts and, as the toll of dead and disabled horses increased, they found it more difficult to replace their mounts. A cavalryman without a horse was called a "camp dog," and the regiments had too many "camp dogs" by the summer of 1864.[33]

Finding forage for those animals still in service aggravated the situation. During the winter of 1863–1864, the lack of feed became serious and grievously affected the fighting capabilities of the units. "I have pulled grass in December for my horse until my fingers bled," recalled one. The summer's grass lessened this, but many of the horses had been badly weakened during the cold months and the constant movement only added to the number of unserviceable mounts. The scarcity of horseshoes additionally contributed to hampering the quality of the regiments. A typical scene in a Southern horse regiment was later described by one of the brigade commanders in the Valley. "I have seen my men many a time," wrote Colonel Thomas T. Munford, who joined Early in mid-August, "have the hoof of a dead horse strapped to their saddles, which they had cut off at the ankle with their pocket-knives, and would carry them until they could find a smith to take it off with his nippers, and thus supply their sore-footed steeds."[34]

Worsening Early's judgment of his mounted units was his dim assessment of the cavalry commanders. He came to have an abiding distrust of John McCausland. The army commander also thought very little of John Imboden's abilities and was not particularly certain of William Jackson's and John Vaughn's. Bradley Johnson, however, seemingly maintained Early's trust. Old Jube thus confronted the Federals with a mounted command hampered by morale, discipline and equipment problems, led by officers Early had little faith in. Except for the strength of his army, the Southern general faced no graver disparity between him and Sheridan than in cavalry.[35]

Such then was the officer and the man, with all his flaws and attributes, who directed the Army of the Valley. Early was an enigma, a bundle of inconsistencies—magnanimous and charitable to his few friends and intimates, critical and deprecating to his numerous enemies. But he had earned his position, for he had unquestioned talent. A professional soldier, West Point, class of 1837, veteran of the Mexican War and a former attorney, Early had distinguished himself on a number of battlefields. He had fought with bravery, skill and aggressiveness. Since Lee had assigned him to command of the Second Corps on May 27, Old Jube had clearly fulfilled Lee's desires and orders. He didn't look like much of a warrior, for rheumatism had bent his frame and his dark eyes and full gray beard made him look like "a very malignant and very hairy spider." But Early could be a formidable opponent and, if he needed anything in this August, it was more troops.[36]

The Confederate Army of the Valley, in numbers of effectives, paled before the Federals flooding into Harpers Ferry. Early counted only between 13,000 and 14,000 troops in all three branches. His five cavalry brigades in August amounted to barely over 4,000 troopers. The three battalions of artillery, divided into nine batteries, mustered 40 cannon and 800 artillerymen. The army's main component, the four infantry divisions, totalled less than 9,000 muskets. As Sheridan prepared to move against his opponent, the Federal army enjoyed a superiority of at least three-to-one.[37]

Though significantly outnumbered, the Confederates bivouacked around Bunker Hill were still a deadly antagonist. The gray-clad infantry, in officers and men, had few equals as fighters. Early had in Breckinridge, Rodes, Gordon, Ramseur and Gabriel Wharton some of the finest combat commanders in Virginia. At brigade level Cullen Battle, Bryan Grimes, Philip Cook, William Cox, Robert Johnston and William Terry were top caliber. As for the men in the ranks, none were better. A Yankee officer, seeing them earlier in the spring of 1864, said of them that "a more sinewy, tawny, formidable-looking set of men could not be. . . . Their great characteristic is their stoical manliness."[38] And supporting these veteran infantrymen were three excellent battalions of artillery under the capable direction of Colonel Thomas H. Carter and the three battalion commanders—Lieutenant Colonels Carter M. Braxton, William Nelson and J. Floyd King.

As the second week of August began, these Southerners "in all their rags and squalor," looking "like wolf-hounds," waited for the Yankees.[39] The wait would not be long as the Army of the Shenandoah came south within days, into a region of breathtaking beauty, which had served as a warpath for centuries.

The Shenandoah Valley appeared in 1864 much as it had two years earlier when Confederate Brigadier General Richard Taylor saw it for the first time. As Taylor crossed the Blue Ridge Mountains, he looked upon a scene he never quite forgot. "The great Valley of Virginia was before us in all its beauty," the brigadier later wrote. "Fields of wheat spread far and wide, interspersed with woodlands, bright in their robes of tender green. Wherever appropriate sites existed, quaint old mills, with turning wheels, were busily grinding the previous year's harvest; and grove and eminence showed comfortable homesteads. The soft vernal influence shed a languid grace over the scene."[40]

In days before men wrote such things down, Indians lived and fought in the fertile region they called the "Daughter of the Stars." In the eighteenth century, Europeans, pushing their grip inevitably westward, entered the Valley. These first were the fierce Scotch-Irish, and they wrenched the Shenandoah from the Indians, put down roots and stayed.[41]

With the peace following the American Revolution, sturdy, hardworking Germans, from the Cumberland Valley of Pennsylvania and Maryland, poured into the Shenandoah. They were farmers and craftsmen and they made the Valley flourish. In such towns as Staufferstadt (Strasburg) and Muellerstadt (Woodstock), the Germans prospered with flour and lumber mills, iron forges and woolen, shoe and pottery factories. The fertile area acted as a conduit of trade between the North and South. Buyers from all over the country came to purchase the prime horses and mules which grazed heartily on the lush pastures. Farming was the backbone of the Valley, and it was no wonder that on one of its farms Cyrus McCormick tested his new reaper. By 1860 towns like Winchester, Staunton and Lexington, with their red brick and gray limestone houses, testified to the natural and man-made richness of the Valley.[42]

The Civil War brought bloodshed once more to this natural warpath. Angling from the southwest to the northeast, the Shenandoah pointed, like a giant's lance, at the Union's heart, Washington, D.C. A Union officer called it "a sort of a back alley, parallel to the main street wherein the heavy fighting must go on." For three years its butternut defenders and terrain defied a succession of Union operations, while the Valley's farmers fed their warriors from the brimming barns and mills of the granary of the Confederacy. "There seemed to be for our arms," another Yankee officer admitted, "something akin to fatality in the Shenandoah Valley."[43]

The Valley itself contributed significantly to Union frustration and defeat in the region. Any Federal army confronted the difficult task of subduing a huge corridor which stretched for 165 miles southward from Harpers Ferry to Lexington. On the west the ranges of the Allegheny Mountains stood as formidable sentries guarding that flank. On the east the Blue Ridge Mountains, which "looked as though a race of titans had been at war, and had thrown up these long ridges as breastworks for opposing forces," separated the back alley from the main street. But any Rebel units, lying east of the Blue Ridge and operating on interior lines, could readily enter the Valley through a string of gaps in the Blue Ridge—Snicker's, Ashby's, Chester, Swift Run, Brown's and Rockfish. As a Union army moved southward up the Valley, a Confederate force could march through one of these defiles and advance on the Federals' flank and supply lines.[44]

Confederate defender, conversely, withdrawing before such a Union movement, benefitted from better defensive positions and a closer connection with the railroads which ran through the upper Valley. Generally thirty miles in width, the Shenandoah, about twenty miles above Winchester, narrowed and became two, severed by the Massanutten Mountains, "the glory of the Valley," said Richard Taylor. The Massanutten, which in an Indian language meant simply "big mountain," equalled the Blue Ridge in height, but with sharper peaks and steeper sides. The "big mountain" towered over the Valley floor, like a brooding, sleeping dinosaur, for forty-five miles from Strasburg to Harrisonburg, dividing the Luray Valley from the main valley. Only the New Market Gap notched its backbone, permitting a road from Luray to connect that town to the defile's namesake in the Valley and the site of John Breckinridge's victory in May. At the Massanutten's northern end, Fisher's Hill rose up from the floor, like a mistake committed during the creation. Fisher's Hill nestled for four miles between Massanutten on the east and Little North Mountain, an intrusion of the Alleghenies, on the west. The high ridge, manned by Southerners, was an intractable barrier for a Union army.[45]

When a Confederate army chose to retreat up the Shenandoah, it moved nearer to the railroads which connected the region to the rest of the Old Dominion. Reinforcements from Richmond or Petersburg or southwestern Virginia could be hurried to the Valley on the rails. The chief line, the Virginia Central Railroad, permitted Lee to dispatch troops from his command at Petersburg to Gordonsville or Charlottesville, where the units could march through a gap of the Blue Ridge to reinforce Jubal Early. Three other railroads intersected at Lynchburg, with the Southside being a direct line to Petersburg. These railroads gave Lee and Early critical links in their advantage of interior lines.[46]

This green and golden deathtrap of Union armies then stood unconquered when Grant handed Sheridan his orders on August 6. The General-in-Chief had finally determined to change the past, with a weapon created for the task and with instructions that meant a new, grim-visaged war.

3

"Mimic War"

The orders Philip Sheridan received from Ulysses Grant on August 6 outlined a sharp, vigorous and swiftly concluded campaign. It should also be hard, punishing, as the lieutenant general stated:

> In pushing up the Shenandoah Valley, as it is expected you will have to go, first or last, it is desirable that nothing should be left to invite the enemy to return. Take all provisions, forage, and stock wanted for the use of your command; such as cannot be consumed, destroy. It is not desirable that the buildings should be destroyed; they should rather be protected; but the people should be informed that so long as an army can subsist among them recurrences of these raids must be expected, and we are determined to stop them at all hazards. Bear in mind the object is to drive the enemy south, and to do this you want to keep him always in sight. Be guided in your course by the course he takes.[1]

Sheridan undertook his superior's instructions immediately after his arrival at Harpers Ferry on the night of August 6. He formed a staff, organized the Army of the Shenandoah and hastened preparations for an advance. Sheridan knew conclusively on the evening of the 7th that Early was encamped at Bunker Hill, 12 miles west of Halltown. The Federals would be moving south, up the Shenandoah and, on the 9th, Sheridan issued orders for the march. His purpose and the tactical and strategic considerations for the campaign, he summarized in his official report, written in February 1866. "On entering the Valley," Sheridan stated, "it was not my object by flank movements to make the enemy change his base, nor to move as far up as the James River, and thus give him the opportunity of making me change my base, thereby converting it into a race-course as heretofore, but to destroy, to the best of my ability, that which was truly the Confederacy—its armies. . . . Every officer and man was made to understand, that when a victory was gained, it was not more than their duty, nor less than their country expected from her gallant sons."[2]

On August 9, the Union army commander, in detailed instructions, ordered a general forward movement commencing between four and five o'clock on the morning of the 10th. The Federals' objective for the day was Berryville, fourteen miles south of Halltown and a dozen miles east of Winchester. With the Confederates at Bunker Hill, Sheridan, by moving to Berryville, placed his command beyond Early's right and rear with a direct path to Winchester. To protect his supply line to the upper Valley and to prevent being caught between the Northerners and the Potomac River, Early would have to pull back, probably beyond Winchester. In one day's march, Sheridan could rid the lower Valley, north of Winchester, of the Southerners.[3]

Sheridan's proposed flank movement was a sound utilization of the terrain — ground which figured in the campaign for the next six weeks. Halltown lay at the northeast corner a quadrangle of the lower Valley which extended west from Halltown to Martinsburg, then south to Winchester, east to Berryville and then back north to its starting point outside Harpers Ferry. Opequon Creek, a stream rising approximately ten miles southeast of Winchester and scouring northward through the limestone region for nearly forty miles to the Potomac, sliced this area into two. The Opequon, with numerous fords, served as a natural barrier between the opposing armies. Ten miles east of the Opequon, the Shenandoah River rolled towards its meeting with the Potomac at Harpers Ferry. Halltown and Berryville lay between the Opequon and the Shenandoah, while Martinsburg and Winchester, connected by the macadamized Valley Pike, were west of the Opequon. The creek bended to within less than four miles of Winchester. Numerous country roads and so-called Pikes crisscrossed the area, connecting the many small towns to each other. The key points to be guarded by either army lay where these roads crossed the Opequon.[4]

Sheridan's orders of August 9 for an advance had not been altogether unexpected by the officers and men of the Union army. With Sheridan's arrival, Chaplain William C. Walker, 18th Connecticut, claimed, "it was the universal conviction that it meant hard marching and harder fighting." Colonel Rutherford B. Hayes informed his wife in a letter on August 8 that "we are likely to be engaged in some of the great operations of the autumn." A Yankee infantryman put it more graphically to his wife than Hayes, when he wrote her on the 7th, saying that "I wish we could Ketch them Some Some place and Kill every Son of a Bitch the[y] are nothing But Regular Raiders and Thiefs."[5]

The Army of the Shenandoah marched southward at the designated hours on the 10th. While cavalry rimmed the western flank along Opequon Creek, the infantry tramped via Charlestown to Berryville, arriving about 5:00 p.m. To the west Jubal Early's Army of the Valley abandoned their position at Bunker Hill and, as Sheridan expected, withdrew toward Winchester. Some Confederate infantry skirmished with Union cavalry, but that was the extent of the day's fighting. By nightfall Early's infantry and artillery blanketed the ground around Winchester with his cavalry guarding the rear north of the village.[6]

The Union advance and the Confederate retrograde movements continued throughout the 11th and 12th. Both days were blistering hot; the sun baked the Valley floor, and the "sufferings of our men exceeded previous experience," claimed a Yankee. Early, with Sheridan threatening his right flank and rear, pulled back to Fisher's Hill, a steep bluff which shadowed the village of Strasburg. As on the 10th, combat flared periodically between Federal cavalrymen and Confederate infantrymen. The clashes heated occasionally with the foot soldiers keeping the horsemen at a distance. By nightfall of August 12 the two armies lay only four miles apart, with the Yankees bivouacked along Cedar Creek south of Middletown, and the Rebels bedded down on Fisher's Hill. Videttes dotted the ground between the foes within gunshot range of each other. In three days of maneuvering Sheridan had driven Early out of the lower Valley.[7]

Before Sheridan slept for the night, he prepared a message for Henry Halleck in Washington. The Union commander had been updating the Chief of Staff daily, and again he summarized the day's march. "The enemy," Sheridan wrote, "have made some show of resistance in front of Strasburg. I am yet unable to determine its character, and could not get my command sufficiently in hand to attack him this evening." Little Phil added that he would have to wait at Cedar Creek until his supply train came up, though he expected the wagons the next day. His present concerns were the absence of part of William Emory's Second Division, XIX Corps, and the cavalry divisions of William Averell and James Wilson. He also had received conflicting reports that the First Corps, Lieutenant General James Longstreet's command, had reached the Valley. If these Confederates had entered the Shenandoah, particularly if they had come in by Front Royal beyond the Union left flank, Sheridan's army was in a perilous position with its extended supply line. "I would like to hear from Lieutenant-General Grant in reference to the truth of this report." "I am exceedingly anxious," he concluded, "to hear whether Longstreet has left to come here or not."[8]

On the morning of August 13, Sheridan, consequently, acted with caution, ordering only a reconnaissance in force toward Strasburg with the VI Corps and a few regiments from George Crook's command. The Yankee foot soldiers forded Cedar Creek and advanced to Hupp's Hill, north of Strasburg. "We were told that we might stop all day and perhaps not more than an hour," as First Sergeant Henry Keiser, 96th Pennsylvania, jotted it in his diary. The Federals stayed all day, peering up at Fisher's Hill, where the bristling Confederate works could be clearly seen. Some sporadic skirmishing characterized the combat.[9]

The bulk of the Union army remained north of Cedar Creek that day and throughout August 14. Increasingly anxious about the reports locating the Confederate First Corps at or approaching Front Royal, Sheridan hesitated to renew the probing between the two battle lines. He wisely ordered Thomas Devin's cavalry brigade to Cedarville on the road to Front Royal. Later during the day Colonel Norton P. Chipman, from the Adjutant General's office in Washington, reported to Union headquarters. Chipman, with a cavalry escort, had been on the road since early on the 13th, carrying a vital message from Grant. Addressed to Halleck, the General-in-Chief's August 12 telegram stated:

> Inform Sheridan that it is now certain two divisions of infantry have gone to Early, and some cavalry and twenty pieces of artillery. The movement commenced last Saturday night [August 6]. He must be cautious and act now on the defensive until movements here force them to this [detachment] to send this way. Early's force, with this increase, cannot exceed 40,000 men, but this is too much for Sheridan to attack. Send Sheridan the remaining brigade of the Nineteenth Corps. I have ordered to Washington all the 100-days' men. Their time will soon be out, but, for the present, they will do to serve in the defenses.[10]

When Sheridan received the message, he "at once looked over the map of the Valley for a defensive line—that is, where a smaller number of troops could hold a greater number—and could see but one such. I refer to that at Halltown," as he later stated. He decided to retreat to Halltown, while implementing Grant's earlier directive to destroy crops in the Valley. Sheridan started the preparations on the 15th. The skirmishers across Cedar Creek were pulled back before noon. He also dispatched two cavalry brigades to Front Royal to delay the oncoming Confederates reported by Grant. Finally, at 7:45 p.m., Sheridan ordered Emory's XIX Corps to move at 11:00 p.m. to Winchester.[11]

Before the XIX Corps started north, it began to rain heavily for the first time in many days. "It was a dismal night," remarked a New Hampshire veteran, "with the rain falling heavily. The camp-fires were ordered to be replenished and to be left burning brightly. They cast strange shadows of an army stealing away from its position in front of a vigilant foe." Emory's troops marched all night through the intermittently heavy showers. D. H. Hanaburgh, 128th New York, remembered the miserable night and withdrawal as "peculiar for its torture. Every one seemed stupid with a sleep that could not be thrown off." The corps reached the southern outskirts of Winchester at 6:00 a.m., on the 16th, and formed a line, stacked arms and bivouacked. "The men dropped like stones." said one of them.[12]

Back at Cedar Creek, the members of the VI Corps and Crook's command spent an uneventful 16th. Sheridan, before moving his headquarters to Winchester, issued orders to Crook and Horatio Wright to start moving north at 8:00 p.m. With these final instructions issued, Sheridan and his staff headed for Winchester. While passing through Newtown, the Union party heard cannonading from the direction of Front Royal. When he reached his destination, Sheridan learned from couriers sent by Wesley Merritt that Grant's warning had been confirmed—the Yankee cavalry were engaged with Southern horsemen and infantry. Sheridan had not acted too soon.[13]

This presence of a significant Confederate force at Front Royal resulted from Grant's decision during the first week of August to augment the strength of the Army of the Shenandoah and Lee's moves to counter this buildup. The shifting and countershifting of troops by Grant and Lee reflected how closely the operations at Petersburg and in the Shenandoah were now and would be intertwined. For the Confederate chieftain, the stakes were higher, however. Lee's gamble of June 12 gave him the initiative in the region for nearly two months. Grant, under pressure from Washington, finally responded, and Sheridan then unlocked Early's grasp on the lower Valley. Lee, hoping for a signal victory by Early, knew that he and his army could not sustain a major defeat in the Valley which might threaten the destruction of the Virginia Central Railroad. The Virginian had already committed a fourth of his army to the region, and he determined to raise the ante. The Shenandoah attracted Lee, like a magnet; it held for him the possibility of relieving Grant's death grip at Petersburg. Lee expected much from Jubal Early—a burden that cannot be overlooked when evaluating Old Jube's generalship in the campaign.

On August 4, Lee learned through his intelligence sources that additional Union troops were moving down the James River. The Southern commander wrote Jefferson Davis that day, stating that "I fear that this force is intended to operate against General Early, and when added to that already opposed to him, may be more than he can manage. Their object may be to drive him out of the Valley and complete the devastation they commenced [Hunter's] when they were ejected from it." Lee added that he could not attack Grant's formidable works, so he could detach, perhaps, two infantry divisions to Early. "If it is their intention," wrote Lee, "to endeavor to overwhelm Early I think it better to detach these troops than to hazard his destruction and that of our railroads, etc., north of Richmond, and therefore submit the question to the better judgment of Your Excellency."[14]

Lee followed this message by personally traveling to Richmond, where on Saturday, August 6, he conferred with Davis and Lieutenant General Richard H. Anderson, commander of the First Corps, who had replaced Longstreet when "Old Peter" fell seriously wounded at the Wilderness in May. The Confederate president and the two generals decided to send Major General Joseph B. Kershaw's infantry division, Major Wilfred E. Cutshaw's artillery battalion and Major General Fitzhugh Lee's cavalry division to Culpeper just east of the Blue Ridge, where Anderson's command could menace the Union army's flank and rear if, or when, it advanced up the Valley.[15]

The Confederate movement began that same day as the van of Kershaw's 3,500-man division entrained at Chester's Station on the Richmond and Petersburg Railroad. Anderson and his staff followed on the 7th and by the evening of the 8th, Anderson had Kershaw's entire command with him at Mitchell's Station, a stop on the Orange & Alexandria south of Culpeper. This expeditious movement was possible by the utilization of three rail lines, with the Virginia Central the major link. The cavalry and artillery moved overland, arriving at Mitchell's on the 11th.[16]

Sunday, August 14, found Anderson's command arriving at Front Royal at the northern end of the Luray Valley. These Southerners had been on the march since the 12th, when Anderson received Lee's instructions to move north of Culpeper. For three days they marched at sunrise, passing through Virginia's Piedmont toward the Shenandoah. Most of them had not been in the region for a year and were amazed at the scarring of the land. "The whole of Culpeper county," Captain William F. Pendleton, 50th Georgia, lamented, "was stripped of the beautiful forest which had been there the year before." By nightfall of the 14th they were encamped at Front Royal, where the North and South Forks of the Shenandoah met.[17]

Anderson's decision to enter Luray Valley was based upon Lee's communication of the 12th which stated that Early had fallen back to Newtown and that the Federals were apparently trying to reach Old Jube's rear perhaps by way of Front Royal. Lee suggested that Anderson move closer to the Shenandoah, "be governed by circumstances," and "keep in communication with Early." The First Corps commander then wisely closed the Luray avenue to Sheridan by occupying its northern end. Once he reached Front Royal, however, Anderson hesitated to act. Ignorant of the present situation beyond the Massanutten, he remained encamped on the 15th. Late in the day, Major Mann Page of Early's staff rode over from Fisher's Hill. Page surely brought Anderson current intelligence but, if Old Jube broached any specific plan, it remains unknown.[18]

The arrival of Anderson's command at Front Royal forced Sheridan, as noted previously, into a two-step withdrawal from Cedar Creek during the nights of the 15th and 16th. Wright's and Crook's troops reached Winchester about 7:00 a.m., on the 17th. During the afternoon the reunited infantry corps marched to Berryville. South and west of the foot soldiers, Wesley Merritt's cavalry division implemented Sheridan's orders to burn all haystacks, corn cribs and barns laden with grain and to seize all livestock. Columns of smoke, running in an arc from the Valley Pike eastward toward Berryville, marked the progression northward of the devastation.[19]

When Jubal Early, from atop Fisher's Hill, saw at daylight of the 17th the vacated Federal lines at Cedar Creek, he ordered an immediate pursuit and signalled Anderson to move toward Winchester. The cavalry preceded the infantry, exchanging shots with Union horsemen engaged in burning. Late in the afternoon the van of Early's column collided with Sheridan's rear guard south of Winchester. The Southerners routed the Yankees in a brief, nasty firefight before encamping around the village for the night. Anderson, meanwhile, approached Winchester from the southeast.[20]

Rain, torrents of rain, swept into the Valley during the night of August 17–18, continuing intermittently through the 20th. The dry creeks and parched ground soaked it up. For armies on the move, however, the weather slowed the pace. Sheridan resumed his withdrawal, marching northward slowly and incrementally from Berryville to Halltown, where his troops filed into their old lines on Monday, the 22nd. Early's legions trailed the retreating Federals and occupied Charlestown on that same Monday. The only significant combat occurred on the 21st when Early attacked a portion of Sheridan's lines west of Charlestown with Robert Rodes's infantry division. The fighting lasted for several hours, costing the Federals 250 men and Rodes 160.[21]

Tuesday, August 23, for the first time since the 10th, no component of either army undertook any major movement. Slight skirmishing reminded the foes of their closeness. Sheridan attempted a reconnaissance with Crook's infantry, but it amounted to little. The Confederates did little more than watch for, as Captain John DeForest, 12th Connecticut, wrote to his wife, "if Early attacks us here we shall whip him dreadfully unless he is very numerous." The graycoats, however, received a grateful welcome from the local populace — "They are loyal to the backbone," a brigadier, Bryan Grimes, said in a letter to home — and they opened their cupboards to the veterans.[22]

In the Union ranks, morale remained high, though two weeks of campaigning had brought them back to where they had started. One wag began calling the army "Harper's Weekly," because of the frequency of their departure and return, and the name stuck. But, if Sheridan's obvious caution before the Confederates did not diminish his men's fighting will, it clearly baffled them. The Connecticut officer, DeForest, stated that "of course the general understands it all, and perhaps Omniscience does, but nobody else." A Vermonter, writing many years later, remembered this time: "The army knew no better than the country at large what it was doing so vigorously, and we have never even yet been able to entirely comprehend our mysterious moneouvers [sic]."[23]

Sheridan's conduct of operations was governed by a number of factors. His defensive strategy at Charlestown on the 21st and his retreat to Halltown during the night were explicable because of disturbing reports from Washington and from scouts and spies in the Valley. On the morning of August 21, Major General Christopher C. Augur, commander of the Department of Washington, wired Sheridan that 2,500 Confederates were reported at Warrenton and 10,000 more at Culpeper. Two days later, his scouts, who had remained in Winchester, reported that the divisions of George Pickett and Charles Field had entered the Valley. Sheridan doubted this intelligence because Grant's messages from City Point still placed those units at Petersburg. But as he told Halleck in a telegram on the night of the 24th: "These various reports are embarrassing." The army commander had little choice but to fortify his lines at Halltown and remain on the defensive until the validity of this crucial information had been verified or proved incorrect.[24]

If the wily Lee, by utilizing the railroads, had again managed to remove secretly two entire infantry divisions and shuttle them to Early, the Army of the Shenandoah was outnumbered. William Averell, whose cavalry division was stationed north of the Potomac, sent Sheridan a detailed listing of Early's and Anderson's combined strengths. Obtaining his information from a deserter, Averell ascribed to the Confederates 22,800 infantry, 8,000 cavalry and 42 cannon. If the troops of Pickett and Field were added (they may or may not have been the 10,000 reported by Augur east of the Blue Ridge), Sheridan confronted a vastly strengthened opponent.[25]

These were the cold figures Sheridan wrestled with, numbers given to him in reports he could not ignore. There was more to it, however — an underlying, unspoken factor which affected Union strategy in the Shenandoah. Sheridan alluded to it in his words to Grant on August 22, when the subordinate explained his withdrawal to Halltown because of his "bad" position at Charlestown and "much being dependent on this army." This "much," he referred to, was both military and political; it was not so much satisfying headquarters at City Point as it was calming fears in the corridors of political power in Washington. The 12th Connecticut's Captain DeForest, with perception, attributed Sheridan's wariness "perhaps because of instructions from high political authority." "With so many elections at hand, including the presidential," the officer told his wife, "it would not do to have this army beaten and the North invaded."[26]

The concern shared by Union officials was genuine. The grand Federal offensive, begun simultaneously in Virginia and in Georgia in May, had so far brought no decisive victory. Military stalemate remained the course of things; and, in Chicago, within a week, the Democrats were to gather, probably adopt a platform calling for peace and nominate George B. McClellan for president. On August 23, as Sheridan learned of approaching Southern reinforcements, President Lincoln met with his cabinet, asking each member to sign an unread memorandum. The conflict and Lincoln's political fate had come down to these words: "This morning, as for some days past, it seems exceedingly probable that this Administration will not be re-elected. Then it will be my duty to so co-operate with the President elect, as to save the Union between the election and the inauguration; as he will have secured his election on such ground that he can not possibly save it afterwards."[27]

What the administration could not withstand was another battle lost, particularly so close at hand as in the Shenandoah Valley. This political reality evidently had been impressed upon Sheridan by Secretary of War Edwin Stanton, most likely when the officer passed through the capital to assume command of his new army. Whether Grant was informed of these restraints on his subordinate is not altogether clear. The lieutenant general's orders for Sheridan outlined a vigorous prosecution, not a timid defensive without risks. Grant, in his memoirs, wrote of this: "I had reason to believe that the administration was a little afraid to have a decisive battle fought at this time, for fear it might go against us and have a bad effect on the November elections." If this were Grant's belief, he still pressed for a punishing campaign in the region. The General-in-Chief would counsel Sheridan to be cautious, but the commander also directed his subordinate to watch closely the Confederates and, if Early returned troops to Lee, Grant expected Sheridan to "push with all vigor. Give the enemy no rest."[28]

Sheridan addressed the political factor directly in his memoirs. Since Grant had counseled restraint, Little Phil stated: "I deemed it necessary to be very cautious; and the fact that the Presidential election was impending made me doubly so, the authorities at Washington having impressed upon me that the defeat of my army might be followed by the overthrow of the party in power, which event, it was believed, would at least retard the progress of the war, it, indeed, it did not lead to the complete abandonment of all coercive measures."[29]

This assertion naturally benefitted from hindsight and as a possible defense against charges that he had been too cautious with his numerical superiority. But Sheridan's conduct during these August days support his statement. His initial movement to Strasburg was an unquestioned implementation of Grant's instructions but, once Anderson reached Front Royal, he ordered a withdrawal to Halltown, ignoring a possible opportunity of overwhelming that Confederate before Early could combine with the First Corps troops. The Union general's decision had justification, even if it did appear baffling, maybe even contradictory. A decidedly safe course, it also served to draw Early again northward into the lower Valley, where the Southerner would have difficulty sustaining his troops. It would additionally give the Federals another chance to sever Early's communications or engage the Rebels on more favorable terrain.

If Sheridan's withdrawal from Cedar Creek to Halltown demonstrated his caution and bewildered many of his troops, it had planted in Jubal Early's mind the dangerous idea that his opponent "possessed an excessive caution which amounted to timidity." The mission of the Rebels had really not changed in its essentials since Early returned to the Shenandoah in mid-July. "The object of my presence there [in the lower Valley]," he later wrote, "was to keep up a threatening attitude towards Maryland and Pennsylvania, and prevent the use of the Baltimore & Ohio Railroad, and the Chesapeake and Ohio

Canal, as well as to keep as large a force as possible from Grant's army to defend the Federal Capital." To accomplish these goals, to remain close to the Potomac, however, endangered Early's lines of communication up the Valley and required his men to harvest and to grind their subsistence in an area already suffering from the Federals' destruction. It was a strategy of daring, even rashness, predicated upon Early's growing belief that Sheridan "was without enterprise."[30]

"My only resource," Old Jube argued in his memoirs, "was to use my forces so as to display them at different points with great rapidity, and thereby keep up the impression that they were much larger than they really were." Another Confederate officer described Early's tactics as to "scatter to subsist, and concentrate for battle." John Gordon, however, thought of it differently, for when he wrote subsequently of what Early had in store for the army, he remembered it as a time of "marching and countermarching toward every point of the compass in the Shenandoah Valley, with scarcely a day of rest, skirmishing, fighting, rushing hither and thither to meet and drive back cavalry raids." This then would be Early's pattern—a "reckless game under his [Sheridan's] nose," said Major Henry Kyd Douglas—evidently decided upon when the Confederates stared at the Yankees before Halltown. The Southern commander knew he lacked Sheridan's numbers; he understood the perils; and, in keeping with his character, he always maintained that his strategy and his view of his opponent were the correct ones.[31]

On August 25 and 26, while Anderson's command held the works at Charlestown, Early took his troops up the Potomac River to make the impression that another invasion of Maryland and Pennsylvania was imminent. The movement made no sense, unless Early hoped that Sheridan might shuttle part of the Federal army across the river. If so, then it possessed only a modicum of wisdom, for it still left Anderson in danger of being annihilated if the Northerners attacked the nearly empty lines at Charlestown. But Sheridan, who was still wrestling with the intelligence reports of Confederate reinforcements, let the tactical opportunity of the campaign slip by. Finally, on the 27th, Early abandoned the ruse of an invasion and reconcentrated around Bunker Hill. Sheridan followed the next day, reoccupying Charlestown and pushing his cavalry south and west along Opequon Creek, which ignited skirmishes between the opposing horsemen. By the end of the month, the armies were in roughly the same locations they had been on August 10. This state of affairs moved one Union officer to describe the campaign as "mimic war."[32]

The pattern of August, the "mimic war," however, stretched into the initial fortnight of September. On the 3rd, Sheridan's army abandoned Charlestown, marching to Berryville. Throughout the next day the Yankees constructed fieldworks which extended from Berryville to Summit Point, a

distance of eight miles. Behind these entrenchments the Federals were virtually unassailable by the Confederates. Early probed Sheridan's new lines on
the 4th and 5th, before retiring to the vicinity of Winchester. Rain storms
blew in on the 6th, lasting for several days. Movement basically halted; from
the 6th until the 18th the two armies remained stationary, divided by the
Opequon.[33]

In letters, diaries and subsequent memoirs the common soldiers in both
armies wrote of this welcomed interlude. For the Yankees, it was campaigning
at its best. "The Shenandoah Valley," stated a Massachusetts veteran, "is the
richest country we ever campaigned in." An Iowan informed his family that
"we are living on the best that the country can afford." Two or three hogs daily
appeared in the Iowans' camp. Livestock, honey, apples and peaches, washed
down by cold spring water, were the main items on the Northerners' menus.
The area between Summit Point and Berryville had not been scoured of its
contents until this time, so much remained in the larders, springhouses, barns
and orchards of the residents. But the Federals, said a Pennsylvanian, "are
sweeping it clean of its contents."[34]

The Confederates, in contrast, were neither as well-fed nor as well-
clothed as their opponents. Foraging also supplemented their meager rations,
but they were reluctant to clean out the cupboards and granaries of fellow
countrymen. Every day details from regiments threshed wheat—"it shows to
what straits we have been reduced," Captain Robert Park confided in his diary.
They stoically accepted the conditions; morale hadn't suffered. Park added
that his fellow Alabamians remained "patient and uncomplaining," "cheerful
and hopeful." The brigadier, Bryan Grimes, informed his wife that his North
Carolinians "go into action with spirit." Lieutenant Colonel Alexander
"Sandie" Pendleton, Early's chief of staff, summarized well the lull: "The
Yankees are seemingly content to be left alone, & we are glad to rest."[35]

A major topic of conversation around the campfires of both armies was
the events in Georgia. On September 2 William T. Sherman informed the War
Department that "Atlanta is ours, and fairly won." As the news of the fall of
the rail center spread across the North, its citizens erupted in jubilation. The
months of stalemate suddenly had been shattered; it looked as though the
North was indeed winning the war. Sherman, an officer who studiously
avoided politics, delivered to Lincoln the turning point in the president's reelection campaign. Atlanta's capture, coming only two days after the Democrats formally nominated George B. McClellan and adopted a peace platform,
altered the fortunes of Lincoln and his party. The belief started to emerge
that the appalling sacrifices were not in vain. It was an idea which perhaps
needed more victories to sustain it, but the sense of it had clearly arrived. The
winds, military and political, had decisively shifted, with direct bearing on
operations in the Shenandoah Valley.

The fortnight of inactivity in the Valley resulted from a determined policy of Sheridan. In his report filed on the campaign, the Union commander explained his strategy:

The difference of strength between the two opposing forces at this time was but little. As I had learned beyond doubt from my scouts that Kershaw's division, which consisted of four brigades, was to be ordered back to Richmond, I had for two weeks patiently awaited its withdrawal before attacking, believing the condition of affairs throughout the country required great prudence on my part, that a defeat of the forces of my command could be ill afforded, and knowing that no interests in the Valley, save those of the Baltimore and Ohio Railroad, were suffering by the delay. In this view I was coinciding with the lieutenant-general commanding.[36]

The accurate intelligence regarding Confederate plans for Anderson's command was evidently supplied by a body of scouts and operatives formed between September 4 and 7. The Union general had been quite dissatisfied with the intelligence system in place when he assumed command. The "need of an efficient body of scouts" moved Sheridan to organize a battalion of scouts under the direction of Major H. K. Young of his staff. The battalion numbered between 58 and 60 members, whose primary duty was to operate within Confederate lines every day and night. The scouts disguised themselves in Rebel uniforms when necessary and received payment for their information in relation to its value. Young commanded the battalion, while Sergeant Joseph E. McCabe of the 17th Pennsylvania Cavalry had daily charge of the scouts. Their penetration of the Confederate camps was illustrated by the information they secured about Anderson. Sheridan retained the services of Young's battalion for the remainder of the campaign.[37]

Sheridan's policy of wait and see had the approval of Grant at City Point. The lieutenant general, on the 8th and again on the 9th, cautioned his subordinate against undertaking an offensive "with the advantage against you." Grant accepted Sheridan's estimate of near parity between the two armies and the difficulties and risks of a Union attack under the circumstances. The General-in-Chief's patience, though unstated to Sheridan, however, was thinning. With Sherman's victory at Atlanta, Grant was moving toward some decisive action to break the standoff in the region. He still deferred to Sheridan's policy, telling the latter on the 9th that he "would prefer just the course you seem to be pursuing—that is, pressing closely upon the enemy, and when he moves, follow him up, being ready at all times to pounce upon him if he detaches any considerable force."[38]

Two days later, September 11, Sheridan again summarized the situation confronting his army and the attendant problems. With the Confederates occupying the west bank of the Opequon and guarding the fords, "it is exceedingly difficult to attack him [Early] in this position," Little Phil telegraphed Grant. "The Opequon Creek is a very formidable barrier; there are various crossings, but all difficult; the banks are formidable. I have thought it best to remain on the defensive until he detaches, unless the chances are in my favor. The troops here are in fine spirits. . . . There is no interest suffering here except the Baltimore and Ohio Railroad, and I will not divide my forces to protect it."[39]

Until the reported detachment of Anderson's troops occurred, Sheridan proposed to keep on the defensive. But, within three days of his telegram to Grant, a decision was reached at Confederate headquarters regarding this command. Either on the 13th, or most likely on the 14th, Early and Anderson agreed to return the First Corps troops to Petersburg. With Sheridan remaining steadfastly on the defensive, the two probably concluded that Lee had more need of Kershaw and the artillery battalion than Early. There was more to it, however. Anderson had evidently tired of the anomalous command situation and probably of his dealings with the crotchety Old Jube. He intended to return to Petersburg, with or without his troops. He might have offered to Early that the Valley commander retain the First Corps veterans; if he did so, Early turned him down. Brigadier General James Conner, one of Kershaw's brigade commanders, subsequently addressed this in a letter to South Carolina. "Had Early been less selfish and more harmonizing," Connor argued in early October, "our Division need never have left Winchester. If he had told Anderson that he needed it Anderson would have left it, but they did not harmonize." The brigadier also claimed that Early's subordinate officers wanted Kershaw retained.[40]

Anderson moved swiftly. At sunrise, Thursday, September 15, the First Corps command departed Winchester, marching south up the Pike. The passing troops watched local farmers sowing their winter wheat. Nightfall found them on the North Fork of the Shenandoah River opposite Buckton. For the next three successive days, the command moved at sunrise, through Front Royal, up the Luray Valley and out of the Shenandoah at Thornton's Gap. They bivouacked on the 18th two miles east of Woodville in the Virginia Piedmont.[41]

Anderson's leaving on Thursday, the 15th, coincided, ironically, with a Union scheme to obtain current intelligence about the Rebels. Sheridan recently had learned from Crook that a loyal Quaker woman, a teacher of a small private school in Winchester, might supply the Federals with information. Young's scouts, additionally, discovered a black man, living near Millwood, who had entry through Confederate lines to sell vegetables three times a week in Winchester. Late at night on the 14th then, the scouts brought the black, one Tom Laws, to Sheridan's headquarters. The Union general interviewed the civilian, and "I was soon convinced of the negro's fidelity." Laws told Sheridan he knew the teacher well and would deliver a message.[42]

The next morning Sheridan asked Crook for the lady's name. It was Rebecca Wright. Little Phil then wrote a message:

> I learn from Major-General Crook that you are a loyal lady and still love the old flag. Can you inform me of the position of Early's forces, the number of divisions in his army, and the strength of any or all of them, and his probable or reported intentions? Have any more troops arrived from Richmond, or are any more coming, or reported to be coming?
>
> I am, very respectfully, your most obedient servant,
>
> P. H. Sheridan, Major-General Commanding. You can trust the bearer.[43]

Laws, with his vegetables and the message wrapped in tin foil and placed in his mouth, entered Winchester on the 16th. The black farmer visited Miss Wright's house, handed her the dangerous document and said he would wait for a reply. Sheridan claimed in his memoirs that Miss Wright, who was 26 years old, reacted nervously when she read the note and consulted her mother, Rachel, before answering. In a stroke of good fortune for the Federals, the previous evening a convalescing Rebel officer told the young Quaker teacher that Anderson's troops had left that morning for Richmond.[44] Rebecca Wright decided to take the risk. She wrote:

> I have no communication whatever with the rebels, but will tell you what I know. The division of General Kershaw, and Cutshaw's artillery, twelve guns and men, General Anderson commanding, have been sent away, and no more are expected, as they cannot be spared from Richmond. I do not know how the troops are situated, but the force is much smaller than represented. I will take pleasure hereafter in learning all I can of their strength and position, and the bearer may call again.
>
> Very respectfully yours,[45]

Laws returned to Sheridan's headquarters later that day with the message. The vital intelligence was surely more than Sheridan anticipated—he had been waiting nearly two weeks for this information. "This was my opportunity," as he later stated. He immediately began preparations for a movement by the army toward Newtown, beyond Early's flank and against his communications. While busily engaged, Sheridan received another message, delivered by a courier: Grant was at Charlestown and wanted to meet Sheridan that same day.[46]

The General-in-Chief had concluded that he had to take matters in the Valley personally in hand. He made the decision to go to Sheridan on the 14th, perhaps because of Halleck's message of that date relating the concerns of businessmen in Baltimore and Washington, regarding the continued interruption of the Baltimore & Ohio. The civilians feared, Halleck stated, a crippling shortage of coal during the approaching winter. Grant responded with dispatch, wiring the Chief of Staff that he would be leaving on the morrow for the Valley but would not pass through Washington.[47]

For the lieutenant general, the time had come for Sheridan to drive the Confederates out of the fertile region and destroy the crops. "I knew it was impossible for me," Grant wrote in his memoirs, "to get orders through Washington to Sheridan to make a move, because they would be stopped there and such orders as Halleck's caution (and that of the Secretary of War) would suggest would be given instead, and would, no doubt, be contradictory to mine."[48]

Sheridan rode from his headquarters at Clifton to Charlestown immediately after the courier delivered Grant's note. The two soldiers from the West met alone under a large oak tree. Bending over a map, Little Phil did most of the talking, Grant most of the listening. The subordinate told his superior, dressed in a nondescript uniform coat and chewing on a cigar, that he could "whip them." Grant, who kept the plans he had drawn up in his pocket, only asked if Sheridan could advance by Tuesday, four days hence. "O yes," Sheridan replied, "could be off before daylight on Monday." That was enough for Grant, and he simply said, "Go in." It was the briefest order the Illinoisan issued during the war.[49]

Nearby, a group of soldiers from the Vermont Brigade had been watching this momentous conference. One of the Vermonters had never seen Grant and asked his sergeant who was with Sheridan. "That's Grant," exclaimed the sergeant. "I hate to see that old cuss around. When that old cuss is around there's sure to be a big fight on hand."[50]

The two then parted; Sheridan back to Clifton, Grant to Harpers Ferry. The lieutenant general was satisfied—he could do no more; he had left the outcome to an officer he had personally chosen and trusted. For the moment then the war could wait; Grant decided to visit Julia and the children in Burlington, New Jersey. He so informed Halleck the next day in Baltimore while he changed trains. He was going ostensibly "to make arrangements for sending my children to school." This hard man of war needed to see his wife periodically, to talk to her and to enjoy the children. He planned to return to City Point, and the war, on Monday, the day of Sheridan's advance.[51]

While Grant journeyed by train to visit his family, Sheridan spent the 17th preparing plans, which had been interrupted by the meeting with Grant, for the advance on Newtown. With Early's army positioned around Stephenson's Depot and Winchester, he intended to outflank his opponent and to sever the Confederate's line of communications up the Valley. Early, his strength reduced by Anderson's departure, would have no choice but to give battle at a disadvantage. Sheridan's proposed movement basically duplicated his initial advance southward during the second week of August. He issued no detailed instructions to his subordinate commanders this day, evidently deciding to wait until the eighteenth.[52]

Sunday, September 18, dawned cloudy, with a threat of rain in the air; brief showers did pass through but this Sabbath was generally fair and fine. In the Federal camps, drills and inspections were interspersed with church services. The demanding, young professional, Emory Upton, even held a formal review of his brigade. A supply train from Harpers Ferry arrived, and quartermasters dispersed rations and ammunition to the units. After the midday meal, orders came down through the chain of command to send all baggage to the rear and to be ready to march at three o'clock. The "dog tents" were collapsed; knapsacks were filled; rifles and ammunition boxes received a final inspection. In the midst of the feverish activity, the Ohio colonel, Rutherford Hayes, took time to pen a note to his wife: "As usual the order to move comes on Sunday. We go [in] what direction or why I don't know." But, then, before the designated hour, countermanding orders were announced—the army would move at 2:00 a.m. on the 19th. Grumbling soldiers repitched their tents, cooked dinner and waited for the evening church services.[53]

This sudden change resulted from fresh intelligence Sheridan received from William Averell. In a message, dated noon, the cavalry officer reported that a Confederate cavalry brigade and the infantry divisions of Rodes and Gordon were enroute to Martinsburg. The news fired Sheridan—Early had committed a serious blunder by so rashly dividing his infantry. Instead of trying to outflank the Rebels, Little Phil decided to crush Ramseur's and Wharton's divisions before the Southerners could regroup. "The disjointed state of the enemy giving me an opportunity to take him in detail, unless the Martinsburg column should be returned by forced marches," Sheridan later explained the alteration in orders. The Union general had new orders cut— the target would not be Newtown, but historic Winchester, scene of two previous Civil War battles.[54]

Early's dispatch of half his infantry force and a cavalry brigade to Martinsburg—"his wild goose chase," as one Rebel derisively called it—imperiled his entire army. He began the march on the afternoon of the 17th after he received a report that work crews were repairing the railroad. The duty of thwarting these details belonged rightly to cavalry, not infantry. Historians have criticized Old Jube for his ignorance of the proper utilization of the mounted arm and his outspoken lack of confidence in his cavalry units. But, in his defense, Early had reasons for his mistrust. Time after time, during the previous weeks, the superiorly armed and mounted Union horsemen bested his. The deterioration in the effectiveness of Confederate cavalry, their resultant combat record and Early's judgment of that failure might more accurately explain his use of his cavalry than an old infantry officer's lack of understanding. The fault-finding commander simply turned to his infantry.[55]

Up to this point, Old Jube had conducted the campaign with consummate skill. Outnumbered, he resorted to audacity, keeping the Yankees at bay, searching for opportunities to punish them, preventing their use of an important railroad, while maintaining his army in the lower Valley, where it could feed itself and protect the granary to the south. When he erred, as on August 25–26, it was on the side of boldness, even rashness. "My only resource," as he stated after the war, "was to use my forces so as to display them at different points with great rapidity, and thereby keep up the impression that they were much larger than they really were." His mistake, his fatal error, was the belief that Sheridan "possessed an excessive caution which amounted to timidity." It probably underlaid his willingness to lose Kershaw and why he split the army for a "wild goose chase."[56]

With William Jackson's troopers in the lead, Rodes and Gordon started from Bunker Hill at daybreak on this Sunday, arriving about nine o'clock. The railroad crews were nowhere to be found. The cavalrymen destroyed a bridge over Back Creek, while ordnance officers purchased coal for forges with Federal money. Early, who had accompanied the column, learned at the telegraph office of Grant's visit with Sheridan. Old Jube knew for the Union commander to come to the Valley from City Point, something had to be astir. The men in the ranks, too, heard the news, and a Georgia private, like the Vermont sergeant, realized that with Grant came death. "This made us, private soldiers, feel very bad," Private G. W. Nichols admitted, "for we knew if it were true, we would soon have trouble."[57]

Early hastily ordered a return march. Back up the Valley Pike the Southerners raced. By evening Rodes's division encamped at Stephenson's Depot, Gordon's at Bunker Hill, with instructions to march at daylight for Stephenson's. Early had partially reconcentrated his army; his northernmost infantry command, Gordon's, lay approximately fourteen miles from his southernmost, Ramseur's, whose three brigades bivouacked east of Winchester across the road to Berryville.[58]

Intermittent rains resumed with the fall of night. For those on picket duty or without tents, the showers brought discomfort. For many of the 40,000 Yankees and 12,500 Rebels, it was to be their final night before the unending blackness.[59]

One of these thousands of soldiers, Private I. Norval Baker, 18th Virginia Cavalry, had spent the Sabbath quietly on picket duty along the Opequon. Baker knew nothing of the preparations ongoing east of the creek or of the countermarch of his comrades to the west. What this Virginia private recalled of the day was the sounds. "The enemy are having lots of music in their camp," Baker scribbled in his diary. "I never heard so many bands playing at one time."[60] What he thought it meant, Baker never put on paper. Perhaps, the coming fury needed a herald.

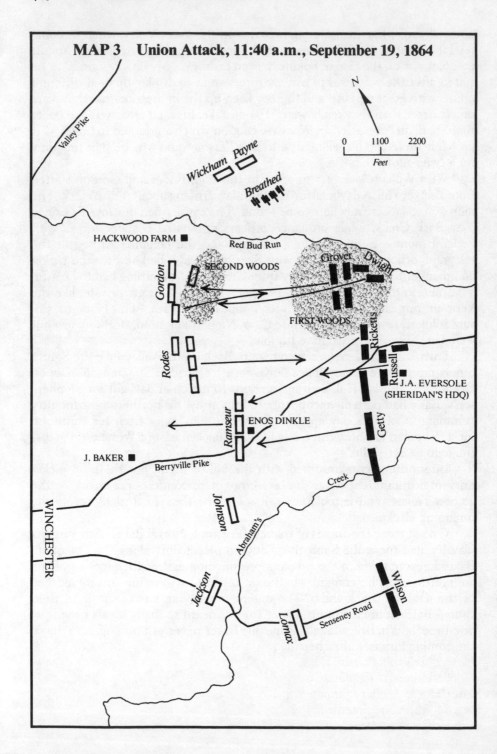

MAP 3   Union Attack, 11:40 a.m., September 19, 1864

N

0   1100   2200
Feet

Valley Pike

Wickham   Payne

Breathed

HACKWOOD FARM   Red Bud Run

Gordon   SECOND WOODS   Grover   Dwight

FIRST WOODS   Rickets

Rodes   Russell   J.A. EVERSOLE
(SHERIDAN'S HDQ)

Ramseur   ENOS DINKLE   Getty

J. BAKER   Berryville Pike   Creek

WINCHESTER   Johnson   Abraham's

Jackson   Wilson

Lomax   Senseney Road

4

A Stand-Up Fight

The "general call" sounded before 1:00 a.m. on September 19. The Army of the Shenandoah stirred from its bivouac, with the soldiers stretching their limbs, striking tents and boiling coffee. An hour later, in accordance with Sheridan's orders, James H. Wilson's 3,300 troopers mounted and cantered westward on the Berryville Pike toward the Opequon Creek. Wesley Merritt's cavalrymen, under the personal direction of A. T. A. Torbert, followed shortly, angling northwestward toward the Opequon's lower fords. Between two and three o'clock Sheridan's three corps of infantry swung into ranks and shuffled along each side of the pike while the wagon train and artillery units rumbled upon the road.[1]

This march into the Virginia night differed from the wearisome advances of the previous month—and the veterans knew it. Since "that old cuss" Grant's visit the army abounded in rumors and speculations. Gone were the regimental wagons, the superfluous baggage, the infirm and wounded. Gone, too, were the days when they "backed and filled," the fatiguing hours of countering Early's maneuverings.[2]

Wilson's troopers, in the vanguard, outdistanced the infantrymen and arrived opposite Spout Spring or the Berryville crossing of the Opequon probably before 4:30 a.m. Across the ford Daniel Wood's mill and stone house, formerly used as a fort and tavern, sat at the entrance to the Berryville Canyon through which the road passed. Wilson's instructions specified that his division clear the canyon and seize a foothold on the open ground beyond the narrow ravine. Brigadier General John B. McIntosh, accordingly, deployed his leading regiments, the 2nd and 5th New York Cavalry, for the attack. The 18th Pennsylvania Cavalry formed in their rear as support and to add mettle to any breakthrough. Captain Charles H. Pierce's Batteries B and L, 2nd United States Horse Artillery prepared to follow the charging troopers. McIntosh's remaining three regiments and Brigadier General George H. Chapman's brigade waited in the rear.[3]

Captain Walter C. Hull's 2nd New York Cavalry, mounted and dismounted, plunged into the two-mile-long canyon. The front of the assault column, narrowed by the wooded slopes of the gorge, struck the Confederate picket at the western entrance. The startled graycoats, the 23rd North Carolina under Colonel Charles C. Blackmall, immediately broke to the rear before the Spencer-firing Northerners. Blackmall, mounted on his horse, tried to rally his men before being struck in the ankle with a bullet. The Federals seized the wounded officer, who refused amputation and lingered in agony until his death on November 6. The North Carolinians, however, regrouped and withdrew slowly "making stand after stand" against Hull's troopers, whose attack was now augmented by Major Abram H. Krom's 5th. In the shadowy light the Federals debouched out of the ravine forming a blue ribbon across the pike.[4]

The North Carolinians fell back upon their brigade, which was formed behind "a slight elevation of rails" several hundred yards from the canyon.[5] The brigade commander, Brigadier General Robert D. Johnston, dispatched a courier to inform his superior, Dodson Ramseur, of the attack and deployed his command of five North Carolina regiments. The Tarheels, numbering probably less than 600 effectives, stabbed at the Union cavalrymen spilling out of the gorge.

Though the few Confederate accounts offer conflicting versions, Ramseur apparently responded quickly to Johnston's report and to the increasing musketry which sounded like the rapid tearing of canvas. The 27-year-old Ramseur had earned a reputation for battlefield prowess excelled by few officers in that proud command. But now as "a glaring and blood-red sun" tinted the eastern horizon, the intensely ambitious officer had already committed a major tactical blunder. His deployment of Johnston several hundred yards from the canyon, the establishment of a lone regiment at the western mouth and his neglect to post an advance vidette at Spout Spring permitted Wilson's troopers to surprise the pickets and acquire a foothold on the open terrain. If Johnston's brigade had barricaded the gorge's embouchure, no enemy force, charging along a front the width of the road, could have penetrated the brigade's line. Sheridan's dangerous enterprise could have died aborning, instead Ramseur's isolated division faced annihilation and Early's army a piecemeal destruction.[6]

Ramseur dispatched Brigadier General John Pegram's five Virginia regiments forward to bolster Johnston's left front and flank. Pegram abandoned his position in the large tract of woods which extended to Red Bud Run north of the Berryville Pike and probably began to align his brigade on Johnston's left rear. The Tarheels, behind their modest works, meanwhile, skirmished with Wilson's dismounted troopers. It was now nearly six o'clock, the morning's light crept across the land making an increasing swath like a gang of farmers preparing a field for harvest.[7]

With the sun at their backs, the New Yorkers finally came. Johnston's men blunted the charge with a volley. Behind Johnston, a battery belonging to Lieutenant Colonel William Nelson's battalion, supported the butternut infantry, punctuating the musketry with shell fire. The New Yorkers stumbled back toward the gorge, where McIntosh had deployed the 18th Pennsylvania Cavalry and Pierce's two unlimbered batteries. The bloodied 2nd and 5th New York Cavalry regrouped while the Pennsylvanians swirled forward in a mounted charge.[8]

The Southern fire twice staggered the cavalrymen, wounding and capturing the Pennsylvanians' commander, Lieutenant Colonel William P. Brinton. The brigade commander, McIntosh, fell with a grievous wound in his left leg which was amputated below the knee that night. "We killed a greate [sic] many of them," a North Carolinian claimed. The Pennsylvanians regrouped and, supported by the New Yorkers and Pierce's guns, plunged again toward the Confederate ranks. Union shell bursts and a withering fire from Spencers cracked the gray front with Pegram's partially deployed brigade breaking initially. Johnston's veterans followed. "This was awful [sic] time on our side to give back then," a Tarheel exclaimed, "but we wer [sic] forced to do it in a open field to go throug [sic] then when they wounded a good maney [sic] of our boyes the balls came as thick as hail at us it is a mistery [sic] to me how we got out." According to Ramseur, his men "did some tall running."[9]

Ramseur, a boyish-looking man who concealed his youth under a flowing beard, ordered one regiment, the 57th North Carolina from Brigadier General Archibald C. Godwin's brigade, forward to stabilize the line. He then galloped into the midst of his broken brigades, grabbed a musket and rode among his soldiers, knocking down any man who refused to stop. Ramseur's conduct and the efforts of his aides and brigade officers stemmed the retreat in some woods bordering the pike only 500 feet behind their lines. The mingled commands repulsed the pursuing Yankees, who withdrew to the ground near the canyon.[10]

The action was ebbing when Sheridan, accompanied by his staff, rode on to the field. The Union commander paused to tell a wounded McIntosh that "you have done nobly." He then halted upon a "conspicuous elevation," probably on J. A. Eversole's farm, near the mouth of the ravine, where he established his headquarters. It was certainly before seven o'clock when the short, broadchested commander scanned the terrain. Little Phil carefully examined the ground and selected the positions for his infantry, who then were marching into the canyon. But his timetable had already been wrecked.[11]

Back at Spout Spring, Sheridan's plan for a prompt advance lay ruined, entangled in wagons and cannon. While Wilson engaged Ramseur, Horatio G. Wright funneled his VI Corps infantry into the canyon. The advance element of the corps, Brigadier General Daniel D. Bidwell's brigade of George W. Getty's Second Division, entered the gorge about the same time Sheridan established his headquarters. James B. Ricketts's Third Division, trailing Getty's three brigades, splashed across the Opequon about seven o'clock. Behind them on the pike rumbled Wright's artillery and wagons and his First Division under David A. Russell. Two miles from the ford, William H. Emory's two XIX Corps divisions rested in the fields, watching the wagons and Russell pass.[12]

As prescribed by Sheridan's orders, Emory was to report to Wright upon the XIX Corps's arrival at the crossing. Emory obeyed, met Wright at Spout Spring and learned that his units must wait until the VI Corps passed. But as wagon followed slow-moving wagon, "Old Brick Top" Emory became "swearing mad." Staff officer after staff officer rode to Wright asking that the wagons clear the road and the ford for Emory's men. Finally the infuriated and exasperated Emory personally galloped to Spout Spring, where the stubborn Wright maintained his authority and insistence. Emory sent Captain Robert F. Wilkinson back to the columns and ordered his infantry to advance, bypassing the wagons. It was nearly 9:00 a.m., the final units of Russell's division, which had been entangled in Wright's "stupendous oversight," were entering the canyon. One hour had passed since Bidwell's brigade reported to Sheridan.[13]

Cuvier Grover's First Division, XIX Corps, forded the Opequon shortly after nine. The sound of distant artillery fire—Nelson's guns welcoming the VI Corps—like "the dull rustling of air which is hardly more than a vibration," wrote Vermonter George N. Carpenter, could be heard. Wagons, cannon, caissons and ambulances crowded the road in a "stupid, mischievous clutter." Grover's men abandoned the pike for the hillsides, struggling over rocks and across rain-carved gutters. "On every knoll and under every thicket," remembered John DeForest, "gravely watching us pass, sat the hundreds of men who belonged to any army but never fight: the cooks, the officers' servants, the hospital gangs, the quartermasters' people, the 'present sick' and the habitual skulkers."[14]

Wilson's troopers in "jammed squadrons" added to the congestion while surgeons operated on their comrades. "The shaded grass for some distance flanking the pike was covered with wounded men, the results of the cavalry fight of the early morning. A field hospital had been established and the surgeon's knife was in full play," Francis H. Buffum, 14th New Hampshire, recalled. The infantrymen paled at the sight, with one of them asking the inevitable question:

"Are there many Johnnies ahead?"

"Oh, yes, plenty of them," replied a trooper, "and they are gritty this morning. They mean to fight to-day."

"Have you had much of a fight," the infantryman rebutted.

"Yea, we've had a close twist, but we couldn't budge 'em, and we had to wait for you fellows to come up."[15]

Stumbling, cursing, inquiring, Emory's jumbled columns emerged from the gorge soon after 10:00 a.m. Glancing to their left, they saw Sheridan, an angry little man mounted on a large horse. "Though short in stature, he did not appear so on horseback," as one of them described Little Phil. "His stirrups were high up, the shortness being of leg and not of trunk. He wore a peculiar style of hat not like that of any other officer." His frustration at the delay, soured to rage by the time Emory appeared, caused Sheridan to berate the corps commander, who had been victimized by Wright's obstinacy, and the "stupid clutter" in the gorge. But for Sheridan, his opportunity—the tactical opportunity of the day—had passed.[16]

This chance of destroying Early in detail was lost, the Union commander later stated, by the "unavoidable delays by which I was prevented from getting the Sixth and Nineteenth corps through the narrow defile and into position early enough to destroy Ramseur while still isolated. So much delay had not been anticipated," he concluded. These "unavoidable delays," however, resulted from Sheridan's serious misjudgment to funnel over 20,000 soldiers through a confining gorge. More importantly, Sheridan, with several courses available, chose the worst. His cavalry and intelligence network had furnished him with the locations of Early's divisions; he knew on the 18th that, according to a Confederate brigadier, "Early had his troops stretched out and separated like a string of glass beads with a knot between each one." His movement thus required speed upon several avenues of advance but marching two corps through the canyon with alacrity was "plainly impracticable, if not impossible."[17]

Sheridan possessed three routes of advance upon Ramseur's position, the key to his plans. His decision sending Wilson crashing through the ravine, seizing the open ground, was sound. But the commitment of only two VI Corps divisions as support for the cavalrymen would have given him overwhelming numerical superiority against Ramseur's front. Wright's third division, by entering a country road 500 yards beyond Daniel Wood's and marching two miles, could have overlapped the Confederate right making Ramseur's position untenable. This neglected road Ramseur perceived as a threat and, even while Union infantry replaced cavalry along his front, he maintained part of Godwin's brigade on the road. Emory's corps, moreover, swinging south and then west upon the Senseney Road in two hours of marching, or by nine o'clock, could have been one mile from Winchester and the Valley Pike, Early's artery of communications and supplies.[18]

In his memoirs Sheridan maintained the correctness of his decision. "I have always thought," he wrote, "that by adhering to the original plan we might have captured the bulk of Early's army." His plan, however, was exceedingly faulty and proved to be nearly disastrous, except for his vast numerical superiority. Little Phil ordered the impossible, expected its accomplishment and fumed at its miscarriage.[19]

His Southern counterpart, conversely, responded swiftly to the Union attack. Old Jube—"he looked more like an animated scarecrow than the commanding general of any army," asserted a graycoat—received Ramseur's message of Wilson's attack about daylight at Stephenson's Depot, five miles north of Winchester where he had his headquarters the night of September 18–19 and where Robert E. Rodes's division was bivouacked.[21]

Early stirred Rodes's men for an advance and then departed for Ramseur's line. He rode knowing that this Union movement periled his army, whose month-long campaign of threatening Maryland, of audacious marches, of infantry acting as cavalry could now result in a disastrous defeat.

"The relative positions which we occupied," Early later explained, "rendered my communications to the rear very much exposed, but I could not avoid it without giving up the lower Valley." Convinced that Sheridan "was not an energetic" commander, Early separated his "glass beads" with a rashness that courted destruction, but which was understandable given Lee's orders and Early's interpretation of them.[21] If Wilson's attack portended a major Union advance against his communications, the Confederate commander needed time—the commodity Sheridan's advance through the canyon insured. When the stoop-shouldered general joined Ramseur, he properly assessed Sheridan's movement and ordered a reconcentration of his army.

Rodes's four brigades (commanded by brigadiers Bryan Grimes, William R. Cox, Philip Cook and Cullen A. Battle) were already prepared to march when Early's orders arrived. Rodes, a tall, stalking Virginian, led his division southward. These veterans moved briskly, "the health and spirits of the men were good, and they were always pleased to be in motion," noted a North Carolina colonel.[22]

Between nine and ten o'clock, as Wright's Federals filed out of the gorge, Grimes's brigade passed Winchester on the east and deployed. As the columns arrived, Rodes aligned three brigades in open fields and a patch of woods 300 to 400 yards north and west of Ramseur's left. Cook anchored the division's left; Cox, behind a stone wall, held the center, and Grimes manned the right. Battle's Alabamians acted as a reserve extending behind and beyond Cook's left. On the division's left rear and right front, guns of Lieutenant Colonel Carter M. Braxton's artillery battalion unlimbered. The unit's sharpshooters, Colonel H. A. Brown commanding, stepped forward, ringing the front. The Rebels then lay down and rested, unbothered by the artillery duel between Ramseur and Wright.[23]

While Rodes completed his line, the vanguard of Early's second division, under Major General John B. Gordon, approached the field. Gordon had been at Bunker Hill, an additional seven miles north of Rodes, with orders to move at daylight for Stephenson's Depot. Wearied by the march to Martinsburg on the previous day and the little sleep they managed to steal, Gordon's men were nevertheless enroute when the boom of distant cannon was heard. "Considering this shot in our front to be a part of the daily attack, we paid little attention to it," remarked Private John Worsham. Passing Rodes's abandoned camps at the depot, Gordon met Early's chief of staff, Sandie Pendleton, who ordered the division commander to Winchester. (A previous message from Early had never reached Gordon.)[24]

Gordon closed his ranks and hastened the step. The treble of distant musketry and the scurrying about of aides and couriers, like a hive of swarming bees, convinced the veterans that this was not another daily skirmish. "We decided that it was a general attack by Sheridan," Worsham wrote, "but we knew we could whip Sheridan easily, notwithstanding the large odds we believed he had against us." Gordon soon abandoned the Valley Pike, posting the brigade of Brigadier General Clement A. Evans, under Colonel Edmund M. Atkinson, 26th Georgia, on the left flank to avoid an ambush, and marched across the fields. Before 10 o'clock Gordon arrived, his troops and Rodes's adding slightly over 5,000 muskets to Early's line.[25]

Gordon's lines extended over the "old Hackwood farm," a local landmark built in 1777 by Revolutionary General John Smith and owned in 1864 by Lewis P. Hartman. Brigadier General William Terry's Virginians covered the division's right front. On Terry's left, Brigadier General Zebulon York's Louisianans held Gordon's center. Atkinson's Georgians lengthened the line through the trees to the country lane which crossed the Hackwood farm. North of the lane, seven cannon of Braxton's battalion protected Gordon's left and covered the ground to Red Bud Run. Early's reconcentration had been completed well over an hour before the Union assault.[26]

Old Jube consolidated his line by pulling back Ramseur when Rodes and Gordon arrived. Ramseur's men, for five hours, engaged the Federals, limiting the cavalry penetration, skirmishing with bluecoated infantry and enduring constant shell fire while maintaining an isolated position. "I can say," Ramseur boasted to his brother-in-law, "that I made Early's old Divn do splendid fighting at Winchester. I held my position unaided from early dawn until 10 o'clock." "Never did that division or any other do better work," concluded a proud staff officer. "It was a hopeless fight, but a hot one."[27]

Ramseur's redrawn lines overlapped the Berryville Pike around a conspicuous barn and farmhouse owned by Enos Dinkle, Sr. The Confederate front stretched along the largely wooded plateau between Abraham's Creek and Red Bud Run. Brigadier General Bradley Johnson's cavalry brigade, which had protected Ramseur's right throughout the morning, guarded the approaches along Abraham's Creek. South of Johnson, across the Senseney Road Brigadier Generals Lunsford Lomax's and William L. "Mudwall" Jackson's troopers faced Wilson's horsemen who had withdrawn after the Union infantry arrived. On Early's northern flank, across Red Bud Run, six cannon of Major James Breathed's Battalion of Stuart's Horse Artillery were posted. From their position, protected on the left by timber, the horse gunners could sweep the fronts of Rodes and Gordon with an oblique fire. Supporting the horse artillery were Brigadier Generals Williams C. Wickham's and William H. Payne's brigades of horsemen, under the direction of Fitz Lee.[28]

The Southerners, with their line completed, watched across the intervening ground the Northern columns maneuver into position. Eleven hundred yards of undulating terrain, consisting of fields of pasture and ripened corn, belts of timber overgrown with underbrush and ravines with steep sides, separated the two foes. For the Yankees the ascent would be gradual until it neared the plateau where the Rebels waited. Only Ramseur's brigades and their sharpshooters and skirmishers, sniping at the Federals, were visible from the Union lines, appearing as "white specks on the cornfield, and clustered in groups around barns and houses," stated a Yankee. Rodes and Gordon remained concealed by the trees. These intrepid fighters had manned stronger positions, but few of the lounging veterans probably doubted the outcome for no body of Yankees had ever driven them from a field they defended.[29]

From Eversole's hill, Sheridan, with increasing impatience and irritation, likewise watched the crawling Union deployment. When Getty's leading brigade, Bidwell's, arrived about eight o'clock, he directed it southward to form his left. As each successive unit debouched from the gorge, aides specified its location. Rebel gunners greeted the Federal soldiers with shellfire.[30]

Getty's line extended from Abraham's Creek to the Berryville Pike. Bidwell formed his line in a cornfield with his left across the creek, where it eventually connected with Wilson's troopers. Brigadier General Frank Wheaton's brigade of Pennsylvania and New York regiments aligned itself on Bidwell's right. Colonel James M. Warner's Vermont Brigade, forming on Wheaton's right, completed the division front to the pike. Wheaton's and Warner's troops, protected by a skirt of pine woods, suffered little from the Confederate artillery fire, while Bidwell's soldiers lay under the cornstalks, enduring the fire and suffering casualties. The division, because of the length of the front, formed in one line.[31]

Across the pike Ricketts's two brigades lengthened the front. Formed under the crest of a hill, Colonel William Emerson's command deployed next to the pike and Colonel J. Warren Keifer's brigades manned the division's right front. By nine o'clock Ricketts had completed his formation.[32]

Wright's final division, under Russell, filed into position as support for Getty and Ricketts. The New Jersey Brigade, commanded by Lieutenant Colonel Edward L. Campbell, deployed behind Getty while Colonel Oliver Edwards aligned his four regiments and two battalions also on the left of the road as support for Ricketts. Russell ordered his final brigade, Brigadier General Emory Upton commanding, to remain on the pike in column to move by either flank. Shortly after ten o'clock the VI Corps infantry had been deployed.[33]

While Russell's men shuffled into position, Getty and Ricketts sent their skirmishers forward against Ramseur's "white specks." The Union probing quickly added the fitful crackling sound of musketry to the deep bellowing of the Confederate cannon fire. "See how cheerfully they go in," a Rebel soldier said as he saw his comrades engage the Yankees. "How rapidly they load, fire and reload. They stand six and twelve feet apart, calling to each other, laughing, shouting, and cheering, but advancing." The sharpshooters stalked forward, like dancers performing a ritual ceremony, taking aim, squeezing the trigger, downing an enemy. The skirmishers performed their roles throughout the morning.[34]

Supporting the blue-clad sharpshooters was the VI Corps artillery now rolling into position. Colonel Charles H. Tompkins, commanding the corps artillery, sent Captain James McKnight's Battery M, 5th United States Artillery to the extreme left of the line behind Getty. First Lieutenant Jacob H. Lamb's Battery C, 1st Rhode Island Light Artillery unlimbered to the right of McKnight's Regulars in a cornfield. Captain Greenleaf T. Stevens placed one section of his Battery E, 5th Maine Artillery on the left of the pike and three remaining pieces across the road. Finally, the 1st New York Independent Battery, under First Lieutenant William H. Johnson, wheeled into line behind Ricketts's right. Tompkins's remaining two batteries—Battery A, 1st Massachusetts Artillery, Captain William H. McCartney, and Battery G, 1st Rhode Island Light Artillery, Captain George W. Adams—acted as mobile reserves, their guns attached to the caissons and teams.[35]

The Union gunners soon added counterfire to Nelson's artillerists', who had enjoyed unfettered control. Federal salvo after salvo slammed into the ground around Dinkle's barn, where Ramseur's veterans hugged the earth. "Their artillery seemed to be without limit," a Confederate remarked of the Union gunners, "so constant and fierce was their fire." Smoke enveloped the two lines.[36]

While the opposing gunners rammed their charges into the heated muzzles, Emory, the recipient of Sheridan's furious impatience, and his XIX Corps began filing into line. Grover's leading division angled to the right beyond Ricketts and entered a large expanse of timber (hereafter designated as the First Woods). Grover aligned his four brigades into two lines. Colonel Jacob Sharpe deployed his five regiments along the division's left front; Brigadier General Henry W. Birge's brigade held the right front. In Sharpe's rear, Colonel Edward L. Molineux placed his six regiments. To Molineux's right and Birge's rear, Colonel David Shunk's four regiments formed. Grover relieved some of Ricketts's skirmishers with his own men and detached the 9th Connecticut from Birge as a flanking regiment along Red Bud Run. Sheltered by the trees and not under enemy artillery fire, Grover's men relaxed, bantered with each other and cooked dinner.[37]

William Dwight's two brigades (his third brigade was detached on duty at Harper's Ferry) trailed Grover's men into the woods. Emory met Dwight and ordered the division commander to form his brigades en echelon, in column of regiments, to guard Grover's right flank and rear. Colonel George L. Beal's five regiments followed Emory's directions and formed behind Shunk. Brigadier General James W. McMillan positioned his brigade in a similar formation to Beal's left and rear. Dwight then sent a strong line of skirmishers along the marshy Red Bud Run, where the division commander personally examined the terrain before returning to his command and receiving orders for the attack.[38]

Up and down the Union line the instructions Dwight heard were repeated from command to command—Sheridan's error-plagued attack would commence with the firing of a signal gun, units to charge, guiding on the Berryville Pike. The intensity of the artillery duel slackened; the men in both armies ceased their talking, looked inward, speculating on their chances. "Awaiting orders!" as a Northerner described this moment. "That is the time that tries the courage of the bravest. Once in the heat and hurry and inspiration of the battle, the average soldier forgets fear in the excitement of the hour; but to stand at a safe distance, though within easy sight and hearing of the conflict, ready, expectant, every nerve strung, awaiting the word of command to march into a hailstorm of death, that is the crucial test. It is at such a time that all the mental struggle involved in a soldier's death is undergone, leaving nothing but the mere physical pang of sudden dying to complete the sacrifice."[39]

Francis Buffum, 14th New Hampshire, resting in the woods with his XIX Corps comrades, remembered the waiting. "There was little premonition of the impending carnage," he wrote, "for nothing more than desultory firing was heard along out front, and that was the preliminary death-play of the skirmishers." Buffum also recalled that "it was one of the most beautiful of early-autumn days: the air was cool and mellow, the sun shed a tempered warmth and the whole face of nature smiled in the harvest-time."[40]

At precisely 11:40 a.m. a Union signal gun boomed—the harvest of hell commenced.

Grover's two front brigades, Sharpe's and Birge's, burst out of the First Woods into a large open field measuring 600 yards across to a second belt of trees (hereafter designated as the Second Woods). Immediately Confederate musketry from the distant treeline and Breathed's six cannon across Red Bud Run opened fire. The two Union brigades moved across the barren terrain, its advance "slow, deliberate, and in perfect order." But Breathed's horse gunners' oblique fire "made lanes in this mass of the enemy," wrote an admiring gray cavalry officer. To one of the Yankees enduring the artillery bursts, the shell-fire seemed like a "heavy shower." "They had the best of range on us," the Northern told friends back home, "and I tell you that the ground fairly worked under our feet and there is one great mistery [sic] that is how we ever so many of us got off alive." The Confederate horse cannon "walked death in our ranks."[41]

The blue-bloused soldiers endured the grape and canister and lanced across the field. One of them, however, apparently unable to withstand the carnage, lay on the ground and a comrade shot him through the calf of the leg. The pair exchanged places and repeated the procedure.[42]

Emory and Sheridan had intended the line to lie down in the field but, as the two brigades neared the middle of the expanse, a drunken staff officer galloped to the front of Birge's brigade and shouted: "Charge bayonets! Forward! double-quick!" The soldiers immediately swirled forward toward the Second Woods. Rebel musketry rippled from along the treeline, but the volleys were high. "The terrible whistle and ping of Minie bullets just above their heads initiated the men into the society of death," Buffum wrote of his novice comrades in the 14th New Hampshire.[43]

Birge's line rapidly outdistanced Sharpe's four regiments. The five regiments swarmed into the woods driving back the enemy skirmishers. To the rear of the Second Woods, Atkinson's Georgians were deployed in a ravine. The fleeing Rebels were quickly greeted by: "What's the matter? What's the matter?" "You'll soon see," shouted a sharpshooter. Colonel John H. Lowe, 31st Georgia, then saw the oncoming Federals and ordered a charge. The Georgians marched out the ravine, halted, and "a sheet of fire flashed out from one end of the brigade to the other."[44]

Birge's men momentarily staggered and then replied. "The roar of battle," said Lieutenant Carroll B. Wright of Birge's staff, "as the two lines fairly met, sounding in a thunderous burst of volleys, pealed up from that woods; and smoke and flame streamed out in a long line, as though the whole forest had been suddenly ignited. The conflict was as fierce as the fiercest battle fought by Grant, from the Rapidan to Petersburg." The Georgians responded in kind; clusters of men in both lines slumped to the ground in agony and death. Shells, from Breathed's guns, screaming through the trees and lopping off branches, intensified the fury and casualties.[45]

Sharpe's four regiments, units from New York and Massachusetts, finally plunged into the woods on Birge's left. The combat mounted; waves of minie balls thudded into trees and shattered the bodies of young men. "I hope I may never be compelled to pass through another scene like the one of the 19th," Captain Peter Eltinge, 156th New York, informed his father a week later: "To see the men lie wounded and dying all around you and thus still falling is indeed terrible." Every regimental commander in Sharpe's brigade, except one, fell. The "most desperate fighting of the day" occurred here, according to Buffum, who waved his regiment's flag and shouted: "Boys, if I fall, don't forget that I did my duty." The two Union brigades, clubbing and stabbing the Georgians in a hand-to-hand melee, cracked the Confederate line and sent it reeling to the rear. For the first time in their history, the Georgians had broken.[46]

Grover quickly ordered a halt but his men, "so much excited by the sight of the enemy in full retreat," pursued the fleeing butternuts. Before the sweeping, badly mingled Union commands seven Confederate cannon, hub-to-hub north of the Hackwood lane, appeared. Braxton's pieces exploded, belching forth sheets of canister. The Union front lurched to a halt, like a spent fighter incapable of delivering another punch. "So many of our men fell," a New Yorker recalled, "that the line swayed and weakened." The artillerists, with "splendid service," according to Old Jube, slammed round after round into the Federal masses. Grover's assault had crested; already clusters of men, like eddies from a river, were trickling rearward.[47]

Emerging from some woods and from behind a rock ledge south of Braxton's guns, was Gordon's additional two brigades and the hurriedly regrouped Georgians. Though Early's natural disagreeableness and a festering jealousy poisoned his relationship with Gordon, the army commander could not have wished for a better fighter than this Georgian at this critical moment. Son of a Baptist preacher, a lawyer, newspaper reporter and manager of a coal mine before the war, Gordon had no previous military training when elected captain of the "Raccoon Roughs," a company in the 6th Alabama. Rising to command of the regiment, Gordon served in the brigade of Rodes. At Sharpsburg, Maryland, he was hit five times, and a bullet hole in his hat, as he lay unconscious on the ground, prevented his drowning in his own blood. Rewarded with a brigadiership and brigade, then divisional command, the Georgian had compiled a superlative record by the summer of 1864. His combat prowess had a freshness, an originality, a daring to it. He was the coming warrior, a marked leader in the Army of Northern Virginia.[48]

Six feet tall, straight as a sword blade and just as wide, Gordon was "a man of striking appearance and commanding presence." He possessed black hair, high cheekbones and eyes which could seemingly examine a man's soul. Artillerist Robert Stiles described him as "a superb, magnetic leader," "the most glorious and inspiring thing I ever looked upon." To another soldier, the ramrod Georgian was "the most prettiest thing you ever did see on a field of fight. It'ud put fight into a whipped chicken just to look at him."[49]

His presence, his carriage, his galvanizing voice made him an inspirational officer equalled by few, a general worth an additional brigade himself. Gordon's veterans loved him, for he was always with them, whether in camp, on a skirmish line or in the midst of combat. He had a remarkable memory and usually knew many soldiers by their names. "Gordon always had something pleasant to say to his men," Worsham recalled, "and I will bear my testimony that he was the most gallant man I ever saw on a battlefield. He had a way of putting to the men that was irresistible, and he showed them at all times that he shrank from nothing in battle." Once, during a battle, Gordon delivered a stirring speech before sending his men forward. One of his veterans said he wished he never heard Gordon speak again. "Why?" asked a comrade. "Because he makes me feel like I could storm hell."[50]

What, if any, words the Georgian had for his men just south of the Hackwood farm on this day went unrecorded, but his veterans hit the mass of Federals like a hammer. Overlapping the Yankees' flanks, the screaming gray-coats ravaged the enemy ranks. Sharpe fell wounded with a bullet in the groin, along with many in his command. Back into and through the Second Woods, the Northerners streamed. The 14th New Hampshire was "so nearly annihilated" by Gordon's counterattack. A New Hampshireman, Private Henry C. Mace, stopped during the flight and curiously picked up a tin cup. Mace kept it for nineteen years when, during an excursion through the Valley of Union veterans, returned the cup to its rightful owner, Private Frank S. Berry, 26th Massachusetts of Birge's brigade, who had scratched his name on the bottom with a nail and had lost it in the charge through the First Woods.[51]

The shattered ranks of Sharpe and Birge plunged through the woods, disrupting the lines of Grover's remaining two brigades under Molineux and Shunk. When Birge and Sharpe advanced, Grover ordered Molineux into the gap between the two brigades as Sharpe conformed to the left to keep on the VI Corps's right. Now Molineux's command, six regiments from five different states, encountered the fury of Gordon's assault. Once more in the Second Woods, the two opponents crashed in raging combat.[52]

The Southerners delivered a withering fire into Molineux's ranks. The 22nd Iowa on the left and the 11th Indiana on the right suffered heavily from the overlapping Rebel lines. One Hoosier, Sergeant Charles H. Seston, bravely waved the 11th's flag in the frenzied combat, winning a Medal of Honor but losing his life. In the brigade's center the 159th New York and 13th Connecticut held firm, but along the flanks the Union ranks were melting under the fire and flowing rearward. Molineux ordered a retreat; for the 159th and 13th it was too late. The Southerners swarmed around their flanks and captured most of the regiments' men. Gordon's men had wrecked a third brigade.[53]

Grover's last brigade, under Shunk, soon joined the other three. Aligned on Molineux's right rear, the four regiments of Iowans and Indianans likewise suffered "under one of the most withering fires of shot, shell and canister I have ever witnessed," reported Lieutenant Colonel Bartholomew W. Wilson, 28th Iowa. The Confederates closed to within a scant sixty yards. "I tell you that that was as close as I wanted to get to them," Nathan Dye, 24th Iowa, stated in a letter to friends. At this point-blank range, Shunk's veterans endured for but a short time, until the butternuts overlapped the 8th Indiana on the right, "showering the iron hail along and almost parallel with our ranks and mowing down our men by the score." One half of Shunk's officers fell in these woods. One of the wounded, First Lieutenant D. S. Dean, 28th Iowa, ordered his son to stay in the ranks "until the rebels were whipped."[54]

Caught between musketry from three sides, however, the Union line collapsed. Orders were shouted to retreat; "we was all ready to get out of that," admitted Dye. When the Yankees turned and ran, the Southerners "raised one of the awflest yells that ever met my ears," added the Iowan. The Northerners sprinted toward the First Woods under a blizzard of bullets. Suddenly another Federal would fall to the ground and would "screech out and cry for help and that is what will send horror to the bravest heart." One of the fleeing Yankees, the son of Lieutenant Dean, carried his wounded father in their race against death or capture.[55]

A Union officer described the scene as the mangled remnants of Grover's division cascaded toward the First Woods. "A small number of men belonging to the Nineteenth Corps on our extreme right began to emerge from the woods, their dark blouses looking like black spots on the sunburnt vegetation; many others soon followed and in a few minutes the four brigades of the Second Division of that corps, which constituted its first line of battle, broke to the rear and came pouring out of the woods."[56]

Breathed's horse artillery renewed its fire upon the exposed Northerners. "Our battery," said an officer, "if possible, excelled itself, and a more murderous fire I never witnessed than was plunged into this heterogeneous mass as they rushed back. We could see the track of the shot and shell as they would scatter the men, but the lanes closed up for another to follow." No Union counterfire responded to Breathed's bursts because Captain Albert W. Bradbury's Battery A, 1st Maine Light Artillery, positioned in the open field, was silenced by the swarming Federals. Captain William T. Rigby, 24th Iowa, rallied some men and saved Bradbury's cannon. "We had made a clean sweep—not a Yankee could be seen in our front," boasted a Virginian.[57]

Along the edge of the First Woods rode "Old Brick Top," his complexion even redder. Mounted on his "familiar yellow horse," Emory tried to restore order. He reached for a regiment's colors, saying: "Here, give me those colors; I will lead you myself!" The color sergeant refused the offer. Emory's efforts were in vain for Grover's was a defeated, decimated command. Every regimental commander lay either killed or wounded; casualties totalled nearly 1,500. But Grover's men had joined a circle of veterans whose membership one bought in blood—they had met Old Jack's foot cavalry in a stand-up fight, and lost. Dwight's division was about to join the brotherhood.[58]

The corps commander found Dwight already engaged in advancing his two brigades. The two generals exchanged words, Emory directing Dwight to deploy along the treeline. Before leaving, Emory said: "Have this whole nonsense stopped at once." The division officer quickly directed Beal's brigade forward and sent an aide to advance McMillan. Dwight then rode forward to aid in halting, as he reported, "the flying panic" of Grover's division.[59]

The 114th New York of Beal's brigade cleared the woods as the final stragglers from Grover's division crossed the scorched field. These New Yorkers had been lying and sitting on the grass, reading letters, munching on crackers. Several officers were sharing a lunch spread on top of a large rock when the bugle sounded the advance. The regiment hurriedly formed into a battle line. Their peaceful relaxation ended before the New Yorkers came out of the trees. Breathed's gunners, with Grover's troops no longer in front, directed their fire toward the First Woods. The first Rebel shell killed Colonel Samuel R. Per Lee's horse; the second the major's horse, the third, exploding above the ranks, caused some casualties. One fragment struck a corporal, "literally demolishing him."[60]

With their officers shouting to guide right, fix bayonets, keep steady, "don't flinch from those devils in front," the New Yorkers plunged into that basin of hell between the two woodlands. Gordon's troops immediately directed their fire toward the Union regiment. "The result was perfectly horrible, revolting, heart rending," wrote Harris Beecher. The New Yorkers froze under the musketry. Per Lee, on a borrowed horse, rode along his ranks, cheered his men and ordered an advance before falling with a piece of shell in his side. The 114th, delivering a volley, bolted about 500 feet across the ground and dropped in the grass. The Yankees loaded on their backs and fired lying down.[61]

The Confederate musketry sang like a scythe through the field, levelling the 114th's ranks. Orton S. Clark, 116th New York, witnessing the regiment's plight, admitted that "it was subjected to the most awful fire that ever a regiment received." Per Lee rejoined his battered command only to fall again with a musket ball in the neck. "The veterans of Stonewall Jackson fired amazingly low," Beecher remembered, "so that the grass and earth in front of the regiment was cut and torn up by a perfect sheet of lead." For twenty minutes the 114th New York clung to its grass line before being ordered back into the woods.[62]

Resting briefly, the 114th, joined by the 116th and 153rd New York, recharged across the lethal terrain. A "murderous volley" from the Rebels, who had withdrawn into the Second Woods, greeted the renewed assault. With their heads bowed low, the New Yorkers leaned into the storm. Smoke entirely enveloped Gordon's front, where the flaming discharges blazed from among the trees. Two color bearers and the entire guard of the 114th were shot. Lieutenant Edward E. Breed seized the flag and fell mortally wounded. Reaching a fence 200 yards from the Confederates, the New Yorkers halted and began a "violent file-firing." Their ammunition expended, the three regiments retreated across the field into the First Woods.[63]

The members of the 114th New York halted, looked about and saw a decimated unit. Entering the battle with less than 350 effectives, the 114th suffered 188 casualties or 60 per cent of the command. Dwight subsequently thanked the men for his "high appreciation of the noble conduct displayed and signal services rendered by the regiment. . . . The loss sustained but too clearly attests the position held and the devotion shown by the regiment."[64]

While the 114th was proving its mettle, two of McMillan's regiments surged into the field. The 12th Connecticut and the 8th Vermont, personally directed by Emory, emerged from the woods as Gordon's men "raised jeering yells" as Beal's New Yorkers finally retreated. The two regiments deployed upon an open knoll near the treeline. Bradbury brought up two brass howitzers and replied to the enemy artillery. Emory ordered an attack. Lieutenant Colonel Frank H. Peck, commanding the 12th Connecticut, shouted: "Officers, rectify the alignment." A Confederate shell burst above Peck's head and the officer tumbled from his horse. Earlier that day Peck told an aide that "we of Dwight's division will have no fighting today. The first line alone will take care of the enemy." Bradbury's two cannon were also hit, and an artilleryman "staggered to one side with a ghastly face."[65]

The two regiments clung to the exposed knoll, a place Emory described as a "slaughterhouse." Captain Sidney E. Clark, who replaced Peck, finally waved the 12th forward. The regiment wheeled to the right and double-quicked across the meadow toward a ripple of ground 200 yards from the Confederates. "We were a loose swarm," recalled an officer, "the strongest in front and the feeble in the rear." Enroute one veteran skulker dove into the hollow of an unrooted tree. A lieutenant spanked him with a side of his sword and the skulker bolted up only to be killed instantly by a minie ball. Suffering few casualties, the soldiers fell panting to the ground.[66]

On their left, the 8th Vermont, minus three companies, arrived. The 8th belonged to its colonel, Stephen Thomas. Fifty-three years old, a staunch Democrat, former assemblyman, state senator, candidate for lieutenant governor and judge, Thomas had recruited, armed and equipped his regiment. He was the first Vermont colonel appointed directly from civil life without previous military experience. When Clark waved the 12th forward, Thomas shouted: "Attention, old Vermont!" before leading them across the field.[67]

The Vermonters sprawled on the ground, their only protection from the merciless rifle fire was thin clumps of grass. "What a change comes over men" at this moment, Private Herbert E. Hill averred. Grimly, silently, the soldiers from the Green Mountain state loaded the rifles on their backs and stood to pull the triggers. It was dangerous work to expose themselves as such, and the numbers hit began to mount. Private Walter Pierce died first, instantly, when a bullet smashed into his face. Nearby a tall Vermonter had his forehead cleaved open; another member of the regiment had his chin shot away, leaving his tongue dangling over his throat. Both men crawled toward the rear to die. "There is absolute equality for the time being," stated Hill of combat's perverse democracy. "All are on the same plane, so to speak, the rich and the poor, the high and low, the learned and unlearned. The minie ball and the screeching shell make no distinction, but plough their cruel furrows until exhausted, or pass on like invisible fiends."[68]

The Confederate bullets seemingly never abated, buzzing over the prone Vermonters like "angry hornets." Private Charles Blood died, then Corporal

James Black. Sergeant Francis E. Warren, rising to look at the Rebels, was killed on the spot when a bullet entered his eye socket and came out near his ear. Beside Private Hill, Edmund Fisher, over fifty years old, collapsed on the ground, shot in the right hip. "I'm killed! I'm killed!" Fisher screamed. "My home! my home!" Hill quickly examined the wound and, using his fingers, popped the bullet from the hip bone. A grateful Fisher then started hobbling to the rear; he went only a few feet when another round ripped into his back, killing him.[69]

But the 8th Vermont steadfastly and courageously clung to their position. For the next two hours they and their comrades in the 12th Connecticut engaged Gordon's division. The Northerners shot at puffs of smoke among the trees. The Vermonters' Springfield rifles fouled from the constant use, but plenty were available from the dead and wounded. Three times Sergeants Henry Downs and Lewis Lamb crawled back to the First Woods to bring up ammunition. In the midst of this fury, unscathed, Thomas sat on his horse, refusing to dismount, and encouraged all that could hear him. He could not have been more proud of his valiant regiment, whose bloody ranks bore testimony to the fearful combat.[70]

Along side the Vermonters, in the ranks of the 12th Connecticut, the scene differed little. "Some of our men got shot in five places," asserted a Yankee. One member of the 12th was killed by a minie ball which penetrated his blanket roll and stuffed knapsack into his chest. Once the dry grass in front of the regiment burst into flame, and Corporal Augustine Gray dashed forward and smothered it. Captain Clark twice ordered his men to spare their ammunition.[71]

As the action became routine, the Northerners joked, laughed and smoked. Several of them stood up, fired and shouted:

"Here's one for Corporal Gray!" Others followed with different refrains:

"Here's one for Sheridan!"

"Here's one for Lincoln!"

"Here's one for McClelland [sic] who'll pay us off in gold!"

"Here's one for Jeff Davis!"[72]

The musketry between the two foes eventually slackened into a fitful, isolated firefight. The advance of the 8th Vermont and 12th Connecticut into the grassy whirlpool concluded Emory's attack, which had been wrecked by 1:00 p.m. While Thomas's and Clark's men died, Old Brick Top fashioned a jagged line in the First Woods. Dwight's brigades mingled with those of Grover. Gordon, whose men still hammered at the two exposed Union regiments, meanwhile chose, probably wisely, against an assault on Emory's battered ranks. His losses had been fairly heavy; Zebulon York, commanding the Louisianans, was lost with a shattered arm which required subsequent amputation, while William Terry escaped unharmed after his horse was killed under him. Gordon's victorious soldiers needed a respite. Besides, the action south of him had already reached a climax.[73]

The bloody debacle on the Union right flank had occurred beyond Sheridan's view. Little Phil received the discouraging reports probably with little surprise, but he cursed them anyway. Emory's troops were not his best fighters and he knew it. Sheridan, however, witnessed his toughest veterans, Wright's VI Corps, assault Early's center. The results staggered the Union commander, nearly destroying his army. Blame for it rested with him.[74]

Getty and Ricketts also advanced with the signal gun at 11:40 a.m. Getty's left brigade under Bidwell abandoned its shell-swept cornfield and guided right. Nelson's Confederate gunners quickly responded. Bidwell conformed his line on his right regiment, the 122nd New York. Lengthening the 122nd's left was the 43rd New York, 49th New York and the 7th Maine. The brigadier dispatched the 61st Pennsylvania across Abraham's Creek to protect his left, while the 77th New York served as support. The Union line then charged up a hill and drove back Godwin's forward pickets. Confederate artillery fire, described as "very severe," slowed the attack.[75]

To Bidwell's right, Wheaton's five regiments pushed back Pegram's skirmishers. Wheaton's brigade, charging through woods, rapidly lost cohesion but dislodged the Rebels. His advance soon halted when Confederates beyond his right enfiladed the lines. In the center, the 102nd Pennsylvania, still moving ahead, captured 10 officers and 171 men. Sweeping forward "with the greatest gallantry and enthusiasm," the brigade forced a battery to withdraw. Wheaton halted his command, while both he and Bidwell prepared for the attack on Ramseur's main line. Bidwell, meanwhile, ordered McKnight's Battery M, 5th United Artillery forward for artillery support.[76]

Warner's Vermonters, on Wheaton's right, found the going much more difficult. The brigade initially outdistanced Wheaton's men until it reached a ravine, on whose opposite crest gray sharpshooters lay. The Vermonters fell to the ground as the Confederates opened fire. At this location, the pike veered to the left and, under orders to guide on the road, the Vermonters, "almost by common consent," plunged into the ravine. The marshy hollow, with steep slopes covered with six-foot-high evergreens, afforded some protection. But a body of Southerners, probably some of Pegram's men, swung beyond the Union right flank and enfiladed the brigade. "The slaughter was for a few moments murderous," wrote Aldace Walker. Unable to retreat, the Vermonters "floundered on, our coherence entirely lost, entered the clusters of evergreens." The confused mass huddled under the crest, opened fire for the first time all day and waited for Ricketts's attack to close.[77]

The two brigades of the Third Division encountered difficulties from the outset. Assigned the critical task of guiding the Union assault and maintaining an unbroken front with Getty on the left and the XIX Corps on the right, Ricketts's veterans stumbled before the rugged ground and the crashing Confederate artillery fire, "a perfect storm of shot and shell." Emerson, on the left, adjoining the Berryville Pike, only reached his skirmish line before the shell bursts halted the advance. Major Edwin Dillingham, commander of the 10th Vermont, already lay mortally wounded from a piece of shell. Emerson re-formed his line behind his skirmishers, the 151st New York, and ordered the attack. A second regimental commander, Major Peter Vredenburgh, Jr., 14th New Jersey, died instantly from a shell fragment in the chest. The enemy fire "made sad havoc in our ranks," remarked an officer, but the brigade, formed in two lines, veered left and into the ravine east of Warner's Vermonters.[78]

Keifer's brigade on Emerson's right proceeded into the broken ground of Ash Hollow. Protected by the scarred terrain, Keifer's men groped forward steadily. Keifer conformed his advance to Emerson's leftward sidle but lost contact with Grover's swarming lines on his right. A dangerous gap slowly appeared in the Union front. Sheridan's orders specifying that the attack follow the pike were a serious error. Six hundred yards beyond the main Union line the road veered sharply to the south, angling towards Dinkle's farm. At this point Warner, initially, then Emerson and finally Keifer adjusted their advance in conformity with the orders. If Ricketts discovered the danger he failed to rectify it. Pounded by cannon fire, raked with musketry, the two VI Corps divisions marched toward disaster. From his headquarters, Sheridan, the man responsible for the tactical blunder, could view his mistake.[79]

When Keifer's first line came abreast of Emerson's brigade, the division charged up the hill which rose about 90 feet above the Yankees. Warner, then Wheaton, then Bidwell pressed forward. Ramseur's Virginians and North Carolinians replied with a blazing volley, but the Union assault, finally coordinated, drove toward the farm. Rebel Colonel William Nelson ordered his two batteries to the rear. Emerson's brigade ruptured the Confederate center at the Dinkle farm with the fighting swirling around the farmhouse. Clusters of butternuts fought from behind Dinkle's barn before being dislodged by Emerson's and Keifer's soldiers. Ramseur's division streamed toward Winchester. From an oak grove rimming the home of Josiah Baker, 1,000 yards west of Dinkle's barn, Major Thomas J. Kirkpatrick's Amherst Battery opened fire on the Yankees with their new cannon forged at the Tredegar Iron Works. Eight cannon from Braxton's battalion, positioned in front of the woods concealing Rodes, added to Kirkpatrick's salvos.[80]

Across the open plateau Keifer saw the brigades of Sharpe and Birge driving Atkinson's wrecked command. The Union colonel directed the 67th and 138th Pennsylvania and the 110th Ohio toward Braxton's eight guns. The Pennsylvanians and Ohioans double-quicked across the plain into the muzzles of the cannon. They got to within 200 yards of the artillery pieces before dropping to the ground and opening fire. The gunners began falling before the combined musketry of the three regiments. Within minutes the cannon fell silent, abandoned by the crew members who had not been hit. Approximately at this time Gordon unleashed his counterattack and, from the woods in front of the Pennsylvanians and Ohioans, Confederate gunfire erupted.[81]

The time neared 12:30 p.m. Acrid smoke blanketed the field, obscuring the action and choking the maimed lying in hollows and among leveled corn-stalks. Along the Union front the two VI Corps divisions rimmed Dinkle's farm, with individual regiments clinging to ground while off to their right the treble of Gordon's musketry, creeping eastward, indicated the collapse of Grover's attack. A gaping hole, extending for several hundred yards, loomed along Sheridan's front. In the Confederate center, screened by a belt of woods, Rodes's division adjusted its ranks, weathered the storm of shrapnel from Tompkins's five VI Corps batteries and prepared to charge. The morning's action moved toward its climax.

Rodes's four brigades had suffered minor casualties from the shellfire as the VI Corps's attack dislodged Ramseur. During the early stages of the Union assault Rodes and Gordon, two close friends, conferred. When Grover's charge crumbled Gordon's left, the Georgian returned to his lines and sent his division forward. Rodes rode along his command's rear shouting orders. His left brigade under Cook briefly became disrupted when Gordon charged, while Cox and Grimes snipped at the oncoming Union infantry.[82]

The unabating Union artillery fire crashed into the woodland as Rodes shifted Cullen Battle's brigade from behind Cox's ranks to a position from which the brigadier could launch a counterattack into the massive hole yawn-ing across the Union front. Battle's men were Alabamians all, men Rodes knew well for they had been his. Rodes had trained them, drilled them, disciplined them; he had watched them charge through the swamps near Seven Pines, cling tenaciously to a barren hill on South Mountain and die bravely in the Bloody Lane at Sharpsburg. As Battle waved his graycoats forward, the division commander, while trying to calm his skittish black stal-lion, shouted: "Charge them, boys! Charge them!" Another shell exploded above the mounted general. Rodes leaned forward, and then fell back off his horse. He had been killed instantly, his skull shattered. Early's army suffered an irreparable loss, and the charging Alabamians lost their mentor.[83]

Jubal Early was also at hand, and as Captain Robert Park, 12th Alabama, passed him, "I lifted my hat to the old hero as we ran forward (through the trees), and noticed how proudly he watched our impetuous advance." The Alabamians came out of the woods like a whirlwind. The two opposing lines—Battle's and Keifer's—stiffened at the contact. "The brave Alabamians," said a Southerner, "rushed at the enemy like tigers, and for a time the two lines were so near each other that the paper of their cartridges flew into our faces." Keifer's three isolated regiments buckled under the furious assault and finally were swept rearward "like grasshoppers." Battle pressed the advantage, disintegrating Ricketts's entire line. Keifer's other regiments and Emerson's brigade scrambled off the plateau in an amorphous mass. With his right turned, Getty also abandoned the ridge but his division maintained a sem-blance of order.[84]

Private G. W. Nichols, lying on the ground between the lines, witnessed the Alabamians' charge. The Yankees were "all mixed up and running for dear life," he stated. The Confederates reached the ground north of Dinkle's and fired. "I have never seen such a deadly volley fired as those noble Alabamians fired at the retreating enemy," exclaimed the veteran Nichols. "It was so terrible that it really looked sickening. It seemed that the first volley cut down half of their line."[85]

The discharges burned the ground, raking Ricketts's broken command. Lieutenant Colonel A. W. Ebright, commanding 126th Ohio, died at once; nearby Lieutenant Rufus Ricksecker, leading a company in his first battle, was killed. In the 9th New York Heavy Artillery, Private Myron Fish died with a bullet in his head. Moments later Fish's father, a lieutenant, tumbled to the ground severely wounded. To escape the lethal cauldron, a number of Yankees dove into a ditch, where they stayed until the Confederates were repulsed. One undaunted color bearer, however, stopped, faced the oncoming Rebels and emptied his pistol while walking backwards. On the Confederate left the 156th New York of the XIX Corps, which had eluded Gordon's assault, stumbled into the midst of Battle's charge, lost over 100 men in a few minutes and quickly retreated into some woods.[86]

Sheridan and Wright witnessed the Confederate counterstroke, the disintegration of their line and the resultant rout. The Union army faced defeat, if not destruction, and Little Phil reacted swiftly. He ordered Russell's remaining division into the breach; as Wright reported, "the fate of the day depended on the employment of this force."[87]

In the Union center the 1st New York Independent Battery and Battery E, 5th Maine Artillery stood fast, firing over the heads of the blue-clad fugitives, slowing the Confederate rush and buying time for Russell to advance. Already two of Russell's brigades were double-quicking toward the guns. West Pointer, Regular Army, David A. Russell had his command in motion before Sheridan's orders, through Wright, reached him. Earlier in the day as his division filed into their reserve position, Russell asked Sheridan, who served under the division commander in the pre-war army: "Phil, why do you put me in the rear?" "Because I know," Sheridan replied, "what I shall have there in a commanding officer if the line should break at or near that point."[88]

Lieutenant Colonel Edward L. Campbell deployed his three New Jersey regiments—4th, 10th, 15th—astride the Berryville pike behind Johnson's New York gunners. To his right, behind the Maine battery, Colonel Oliver Edwards positioned his brigade of four regiments and two battalions. While personally superintending the maneuver, Russell was hit in the left breast by a minie ball but refused to abandon the field. The two brigades then pitched into the ravine, which slowed Ricketts's advance, and scrambled up the opposite bank onto a slight rise. The 37th Massachusetts on the right flank flushed out a body of Rebels, dislodging them with their Spencer repeaters. Before them, across a cornfield and a skirt of woods were the Confederates—Rodes's entire division.[89]

While the Alabamians ripped into the Union line in their riveting attack, the other three Confederate brigades advanced. Battle's men, winded by their charge and slowed by the Union gunners, paused and regrouped, permitting the entire division to deploy. Grimes swung his North Carolinians beyond Battle's right; Cox and his Tarheels extended the Alabamians' left and Cook's Georgians completed the front. The unit then swirled forward against the two Union brigades. For the next thirty minutes a fearful, stand-up battle raged between the two opponents.[90]

Up and down the two fronts the musketry crackled, the stabbing flames creating an unending blaze. Like automatons, the veterans loaded and fired, repeating the procedure until the rifle barrels sizzled from the heat. The 37th Massachusetts found that their Spencers were a great weapon in a "tight place" like this. But even with their repeaters, the Bay Staters suffered their "largest percentage loss" of any battle they were in during the war. An officer in the 119th Pennsylvania reported that the Rebel fire was "doing great execution to our line."[91]

In the early minutes of the combat, the two Union brigades suffered their most serious and lamented loss—David A. Russell. Like Rodes, Russell died instantly from an exploding shell which pierced his heart. Captain Charles R. Paul, a staff officer in the New Jersey brigade called Russell's death "an irreparable loss; he was unusually loved," noted Paul. Wright wrote of his subordinate that he was "an officer whose merits were not measured by his rank, whose zeal never outran his discretion, whose abilities were never unequal to the occasion." Years later his friend, Sheridan, writing in his memoirs, recalled his own anguish at the news of Russell's death. "In the early days of my army life," Sheridan stated, "he was my captain and friend, and I was deeply indebted to him, not only for sound advice and good example, but for the inestimable service he had just performed, and sealed with his life, so it may be inferred how keenly I felt his loss."[92]

Along the jagged Union front, amid the dead and wounded, the survivors clung to the rise. The Confederate division, commanded now by Grimes, nevertheless drove forward. They had few equals as fighters—"they aimed better than our men," a Yankee officer admitted, "they covered themselves (in case of need) more carefully and effectively; they could move in a swarm, without much care for alignment and touch of elbows. In short, they fought more like redskins, or like hunters, than we." Still Campbell's and Edward's beleaguered men blunted the thrust. Finally, beyond the Union right, advancing obliquely across their front, Russell's third brigade, under Brigadier General Emory A. Upton, charged.[93]

When Russell ordered the advance of his division, he sent Upton's brigade (reduced to three regiments because the 95th and 96th Pennsylvania were guarding the wagons at Spout Spring) into the woods where Emory's shattered command was regrouping. Probably no other man on the battlefield this day wanted to be there more than this thin, wiry, freckled-face, 25-year-old brigadier. Upton, a New Yorker, an 1861 graduate of West Point, had been dreaming of military fame and glory since his childhood. Even as a young boy he refused to sleep with a pillow because the practice might make him round-shouldered and thus detract from a proper military posture. His goal had been to attain a general's star by the age of 45, and it came to be understood in the Army of the Potomac that no enterprise was too risky for Upton if it might lead to promotion and renown.[94]

Upton was more than just a headlong, ambitious fighter; he was a serious student of warfare, a scholarly warrior. An officer in his former command, the 121st New York, stated that his superior had "the appearance of a man who was deeply impressed with the seriousness of warfare and has mastered its science." Another New Yorker believed that "of all the men that I have ever met, no one was more thoroughly in earnest than Colonel Upton." His friend, James Wilson, the cavalry officer, claimed that the fearless New Yorker was "incontestably the best tactician of either army."[95]

Upton's shining moment had come earlier at Spotsylvania on May 10. He conceived of a tactical scheme to puncture the Confederate salient, dubbed the "Mule Shoe," lobbied for the plan's implementation and, receiving approval, led the spearhead. Massing a dozen regiments on a narrow front, Upton ruptured a section of the Rebel works and overwhelmed its defenders. He might have made a permanent lodgment, but support troops failed him and gray reinforcements retook the entrenchments from his outnumbered units. The assault so impressed Grant that the General-in-Chief used the same formation, but on a larger scale, two days later and crushed the apex of the "Mule Shoe." The lieutenant general also recommended Upton for a brigadier's star.[96]

It was such an officer which now led his command into the trees at the edge of Ash Hollow. The 121st New York, nicknamed "Upton's Regulars," formed his left, the 65th New York the center, and the 2nd Connecticut Heavy Artillery on the right. The line extended beyond the left of Grimes's division at an oblique angle. The brigadier ordered bayonets fixed and not to fire until he gave the command. "Upton's military instincts showed him what ought to be done," Henry DuPont stated, "and he took responsibility of doing it."[97]

Upton waited until the advancing Confederates closed to within 200 yards and then shouted: "Ready, aim, fire." A slicing volley cut into Cook's stunned Georgians. He then yelled: "Forward, charge." The three Union regiments stormed from their concealment. A Yankee, witnessing the attack, wrote that "the charge of this brigade was the finest spectacle in the infantry battle of the day. Gen. Upton himself rode at the advance of his lines, and drawing his sword sat his horse like a centaur, calling his men to follow." The Confederates, their left crumbled, scurried to the rear. Part of the 14th North Carolina, including its colonel, were captured in the swift Federal charge. Campbell and Edwards added their brigades to the attack. The Confederates retreated back to their original position, regrouped and, once more, stopped the Federals. The Union division disengaged and, with Gordon's and Emory's fighting flickering to an end, the action subsided. Both armies—temporarily—had had enough.[98]

Wright, in his report, termed Upton's counterattack "the turning point in the conflict." In over ninety minutes of searing combat Old Jube's matchless foot soldiers wrecked one wing of the Union army and fought the other to a standstill. Early's officers displayed daring, skill and energy in exploiting advantages and directing the counterstroke, for the Union army tottered momentarily on the verge of disaster. Sheridan's last reserve on the field saved the army. Little Phil possessed one more division—Old Jube's was enroute to Richmond.[99]

Back at his headquarters on Eversole's knoll, Sheridan had earlier turned to his West Point roommate and close friend, George Crook, and told him to advance his two divisions. From the north, several miles away, he heard muffled sounds of battle filtering back. The army's cavalry was moving on Winchester. The cessation of agony was only an interlude.

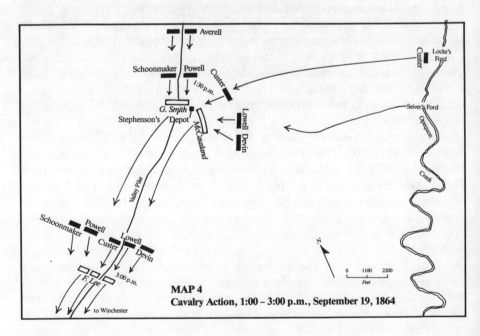

MAP 4
Cavalry Action, 1:00 – 3:00 p.m., September 19, 1864

5

"Whirling Through Winchester"

Alfred Torbert's instructions for his cavalry for September 19, stated the situation bluntly: "the move means fight." While James Wilson's division preceded the infantry into Berryville Canyon, Wesley Merritt's three brigades were directed to two lower fords of the Opequon and "if opposed only by the enemy's cavalry, you will cross the creek at daylight and follow them up." Torbert told Merritt that Early would have to concentrate his infantry against Sheridan's, permitting the division commander and William Averell, who was ordered to advance south up the Valley Pike, to "pitch into their rear." The cavalry commander ended his directions by stating that "the greatest promptness will be exercised in the above."[1]

Wesley Merritt was one of those young, dashing, highly-capable officers, barely out of West Point, who had come, through combat experience, to lead Union horsemen in the war's final year. Merritt—thirty years old, New Yorker by birth, Illinoisan by residence, academy graduate, class of 1860—had served as an aide to Philip Cooke in 1862, commanded the Reserve Brigade in 1863 and had been a brigadier for slightly over a year. When Sheridan appointed Torbert to command of the army's cavalry, the division post fell to the clean-shaven, boyish-looking Merritt. A staff officer of Torbert described him as "tall, slender, and intellectual-looking. He had a constitution of iron, and underneath a rather passive demeanor concealed a fiery ambition." One of the division's regimental commanders thought Merritt to be charming, gentlemanly and modest, with an absolute coolness in battle. Merritt had handled the division with skill for the previous six weeks, and neither Torbert nor Sheridan expected him not to fulfill his instructions on this day of battle.[2]

Merritt's troopers, like Wilson's, were the first to stir on the 19th, many of them rising at midnight and cooking breakfast. Saddled up by 1:30 a.m., the division marched soon after Wilson's men clattered toward Spout Spring.

Colonel Charles Lowell's brigade, the division's wagons and horse artillery, then Colonel Thomas Devin's brigade moved on the Summit Point road, while Brigadier General George Custer's brigade cantered across country. At Summit Point the horsemen turned west toward the Opequon. Halting at Seiver's Ford, Merritt sent Custer, who one cavalry officer described as "Merritt's life-long rival," downstream to cross at Locke's Ford. The Virginia night still shielded the Yankees as Merritt completed his preparations.[3]

Across the Opequon, guarding the crossings, were the cavalrymen of Brigadier General John McCausland's brigade. The paucity of Confederate accounts of the action on this sector of the field make it difficult to locate precisely McCausland's five regiments. The 14th Virginia Cavalry, Colonel James Cochran commanding, picketed Seiver's Ford; the 22nd Virginia Cavalry, under Colonel Henry S. Bowen, barred Custer's path at Locke's. The whereabouts of the brigade's other three regiments, Virginia units all, cannot be pinpointed. McCausland evidently had the task of holding the crossings from north of Spout Spring to near Smithfield, where his line then ran in an arc westward until it connected with Colonel George Smith's mounted brigade, formerly John Imboden's, which stretched across the Valley Pike, opposite Averell's division. McCausland's 16th Virginia Cavalry, under Colonel Milton J. Ferguson, evidently connected with Smith's right near the Pike. Dispersed across the farmlands and woodlots, McCausland's troopers, numbering perhaps 800, could only hope to delay the Federal division of approximately 3,000 men.[4]

Day had not yet broken at Seiver's Ford when Merritt directed Lowell to effect a crossing. Lowell, an officer whom one of Sheridan's aides claimed had "no cooler head or better brain in all the army, no one to be more absolutely relied upon," assigned the task to Captain Theophilus F. Rodenbough's 2nd United States Cavalry. The Regulars deployed dismounted on a rise overlooking the ford and waited for the signal. According to one of the Rebels on the western bank, an unidentified Union officer rode near the creek's edge and shouted across: "We don't want to kill you fellows, and you had better get away; we are coming after you."[5]

Rodenbough's men, as the brash Yankee warned, soon came, spilling down the hillside into the waters. Cochran's Virginians, however, had not heeded the advice, responding with a "galling fire." The Regulars never hesitated, secured a foothold on the opposite bank and then sprinted toward the Rebel line, indicated only by the flashes of their rifles. The Yankees, without hardly firing a shot, overran the Virginians, dislodging them and grabbing some prisoners. Behind Rodenbough's troopers, Lowell sent the 5th United States Cavalry and part of the 2nd Massachusetts Cavalry over as support. A bloody red sun was tinting the eastern sky as the Yankees consolidated their position on the Opequon's western bank.[6]

To the north, three quarters of a mile downstream, George Custer's Michigan Brigade was duplicating Lowell's success at Locke's Ford. "Autie" Custer, as his wife and close friends called him, had already revealed those traits which pulled him toward the Little Big Horn. He, like Emory Upton, coveted military glory and sought any opportunity to acquire the attention of superiors and newspaper reporters. Supremely confident, with a contempt for danger, Custer seemingly took much pleasure in recklessly exposing himself. He believed that he rode under a lucky star, an officer destined for fame. His meteoric rise from last place in the academy's class of 1861 to the leap from first lieutenant to brigadier general had not been bought in blood, however. He did not needlessly sacrifice his men for his own personal glory, and his troopers adored him. His enemies, and they were plentiful, were fellow officers who resented his promotions. Custer and James Wilson, for instance, loathed each other, with Custer describing the manipulating Wilson as "upstart and imbecile," "this court favorite."[7]

Colonel James H. Kidd, commander of the 6th Michigan Cavalry, called Custer "the most picturesque figure of the civil war," while an aide of Meade thought him to be "one of the funniest-looking beings you ever saw, and looks like a circus rider gone mad!"[8] Captain George Sanford of Torbert's staff, penned a graphic sketch of the tall, 24-year-old officer:

> He was scarcely more than a boy in years, but was a man of tremendous energy and immense power. His great height and striking countenance made him a very imposing figure. His blue eyes, blond moustach and great mass of blond curling hair falling almost to his waist gave him the appearance of one of the Vikings of old, and his fancy for startling effects was still farther indicated by his dress which I remember about this time to have consisted of an immensely broad "slouch" hat, a black velvet jacket heavily trimmed with gold lace, riding breeches of the same, and immensely long cavalry boots. . . . One thing I have forgotten and that perhaps the most conspicuous article of his apparel—around his neck, loosely knotted, he generally wore a long flowing ribbon or cravat of brilliant red cashmere or silk. This streamed behind him as he rode, and made him a marked man a mile away.[9]

So the glory-seeking "Autie" Custer, dressed like the darkness in his velvet, deployed his brigade of four Michigan and one New York regiments. The morning's light already bathed the ground when Kidd's 6th Michigan, dismounted, sprinted across a plowed field to a ridge looming above the ford. As the Wolverines raced over the barren ground, the shadowy woods across the creek exploded in flashes of musketry. The concealed members of the 22nd Virginia Cavalry momentarily threw the Union regiment into confusion. Kidd, who was very ill from jaundice, straightened his ranks and, urging his veterans forward, the Yankees secured the crest, peppering the Rebels with their Spencers. Just to the left of the prone Federals, a farmhouse, with outbuildings, nestled close to the stream, separated from the water by a road which turned abruptly west at the house into the Opequon. On the western bank, on both sides of the road, the Confederates shielded themselves behind rail fieldworks.[10]

Kidd's Michiganers and Bowen's Virginians duelled for only a short time before Custer launched a mounted attack with the 7th Michigan and 25th New York Cavalry. Aligned in a column, with the New Yorkers at the head, the Yankees went thundering down the road. As the van reached the shallows, the Southerners laced them with a volley, bringing down horses and riders in a jumble. The entire attack force, in Custer's words, broke in "considerable confusion" and hurriedly retired. The assault amounted to nothing more than a glancing blow before the wall of fire.[11]

With this repulse of an attack which never got untracked, Custer brought up the 1st Michigan Cavalry for a second attempt. This regiment also clattered toward the crossing on the road, with two squadrons under Lieutenant Colonel George R. Maxwell spearheading the thrust. Maxwell, "one of the most dashing and intrepid officers of the service," according to Custer, managed to push his troopers to the creek's edge but could get no farther under the Confederate rifle bursts. Stalled on the bank, Yankees suffered from the fire. An officer of the regiment spurred his horse up the hill where Kidd's troopers were positioned and asked Kidd for more covering fire, shouting that "they are shooting my men off their horses." At about the same time, the 5th Michigan drove toward the creek and, with this support and withering discharges from the 6th, Maxwell's squadrons poured across the stream. The Rebels abandoned their works, withdrawing westward. Custer then followed with his remaining regiments and two batteries of horse artillery. It was probably after six o'clock, perhaps nearer to seven, when the Michigan Brigade halted with the Opequon behind it.[12]

Custer asserted in his report that his men opposed gray infantry at the ford. What he encountered, besides members of the 22nd Virginia Cavalry, probably amounted to no more than the advanced skirmishers of one of Brigadier General Gabriel Wharton's brigade, most likely those of Colonel Augustus Forsberg's. The butternut foot soldiers certainly stiffened the defense but, if Forsberg's entire command had been deployed in the woods, the Federal attack probably would not have succeeded.[13]

When Jubal Early reacted to Wilson's attack at Spout Spring on Ramseur's division by directing Rodes and Gordon to Winchester, he ordered John Breckinridge, with Wharton's division, which had bivouacked at Stephenson's Depot, to guard the army's left and to oppose any Union sorties from the north or east. Early correctly determined that Sheridan's main assault was against Ramseur and there he sent most of his infantry and artillery. Curiously, Old Jube wanted Rodes's and Gordon's veterans, who were surely weary from the forced march on the 18th, at the point of greatest danger, not Wharton's rested troops. The Confederate commander also gave Breckinridge Lieutenant Colonel J. Floyd King's artillery battalion. If Sheridan were to be licked, Early chose the infantry and artillery of the Second Corps to do it.[14]

Breckinridge, then, as Rodes and Gordon strode toward Winchester, moved Wharton's division, approximately 1,800 effectives, toward the Opequon. Forsberg's and Colonel Thomas Smith's brigades tramped eastward toward Locke's, while Colonel George S. Patton's command marched toward Seiver's. Forsberg halted behind some fieldworks a mile short of the crossing; Smith deployed farther back to the right. Patton aligned his veterans on a rise, also crowned with some works, about a mile and a half west of the creek. Forsberg pushed his skirmishers forward to the stream as support for the cavalrymen, while neither Smith nor Patton sent any contingents into the action with the Yankee horsemen. When Custer's brigade dislodged the Rebels at Locke's, Forsberg's skirmishers fell back on their brigade. The two gray cavalry regiments regrouped behind the infantry before moving north to rejoin their brigade along the Valley Pike. Breckinridge held King's artillery battalion near its bivouac, finally dispatching, at eight o'clock, one section of Captain Thomas A. Bryan's Lewisburg Battery as support for Forsberg and Smith.[15]

The Kentuckian's dispositions had been completed well before any Yankee cavalry appeared before the Southern infantrymen. In fact, hours would pass before the Federals pressed the Confederates. Once Merritt secured the crossings, his advance ground to a halt. Neither Merritt nor Torbert, who accompanied the division, acted with any sense of urgency. From daylight until after ten o'clock the Yankees basically stayed put. Lowell kept well back from Patton's line while Devin even remained on the Opequon's eastern bank. Only Custer probed the Rebel works and that primarily with artillery fire from Lieutenant Franck E. Taylor's Batteries K and L, 1st United States Horse Artillery.[16]

Torbert attributed the delay of over four hours to the strength of the Confederate battle line behind stone walls and rail breastworks. Custer described the Southern position opposite him as "a heavy line" of entrenchments with "a formidable cheval-de-frise" in front. The cavalry division's duty was to occupy Breckinridge's attention, to prevent the Kentuckian from shifting his division to Winchester or "at least, if he did send it, to follow closely in his rear and get on the enemy's flank," as Merritt stated it. When Custer reported just before ten o'clock that the Rebels appeared to be withdrawing and that he was advancing, Merritt started Lowell forward. Some minutes short of eleven o'clock Lowell and Custer linked up in the open farmlands west of the Opequon.[17]

Breckinridge, in the interim, shortened his front by pulling back Forsberg's brigade to Smith's position just outside of Brucetown. (Forsberg's withdrawal apparently was the movement reported by Custer.) Bryan's cannon and those of Captain William M. Lowry's Wise Legion Battery bolstered the infantry. The Confederates occupied a ridge line with fieldworks. Before them fields of crops, mostly of buckwheat, lay. To get to the Rebels, the horsemen had to cross the open ground.[18]

About 11:00 a.m. Custer advanced against Forsberg and Smith "to test the strength and numbers of the enemy." As the 1st and 7th Michigan Cavalry and 25th New York Cavalry, supported by the 2nd United States Cavalry from Lowell, spurred forward in the mounted charge, the Confederate artillerists responded. Maxwell and the 1st Michigan again led the assault, galloping straight toward the Southern works. The Wolverines, enduring the musketry and shellfire, pierced the gray line and plunged toward the cannon. But Forsberg's and Smith's men flailed at the flanks of this mounted blue arrow while the gunners scorched the point of the column. The spirited attack crumbled. With the head of the column shattered, the supporting regiments also disengaged. Custer and Merritt learned that Breckinridge's infantry still confronted the Union cavalry and, with this ascertained, the Yankee horsemen resumed a holding action, skirmishing at long-range with the Southerners.[19]

Events on other parts of the far-flung battlefield were now transpiring which would have direct bearing on the duel between Breckinridge and Merritt. At 11:40 a.m., at the very moment Sheridan launched his infantry assault at Winchester, Early scribbled a message to Breckinridge, instructing the major general to withdraw Wharton's and King's commands to a position on the Valley Pike a mile north of Winchester. Secondly, beyond Breckinridge's left flank, toward Bunker Hill, the morning-long engagement between Averell's cavalry division and the mounted brigades of Colonel George Smith and McCausland was moving toward a climax.[20]

Averell, instructed to press enemy forces southward up the Valley Pike, forded the Opequon near Darkesville at 5:00 a.m. Each trooper carried forty to sixty rounds of ammunition, and stringent orders had been issued against straggling. The Federal division, composed of Colonels William Powell's and James Schoonmaker's brigades of seven regiments, approximately 2,000 effectives, encountered almost immediately the 23rd Virginia Cavalry, Colonel Charles T. O'Ferrall commanding. O'Ferrall had had his men in line for hours because, as O'Ferrall recalled, the Yankees were "astir all night." When the Northerners crossed the stream, the Southerners were prepared.[21]

Opposing videttes initiated the action. The Virginians, confronting odds approaching ten-to-one, doggedly contested the Yankees' advance. With many of his veterans mounted on "weak and broken-down horses" and with no other Confederate units at hand, O'Ferrall finally ordered a withdrawal. For the next three hours the Virginians, edging southward, engaged the Yankees, slowing the Northern advance. At Bunker Hill, O'Ferrall, "much to my relief," found his brigade commander, George Smith, and the 62nd Virginia Mounted Infantry. O'Ferrall later asserted that Smith and the 62nd were "a colonel without a superior and a regiment that had never been known to waver under the hottest fire."[22]

The Confederates, soon joined by the 18th Virginia Cavalry, fashioned a line across the Pike. The Federals also deployed into line—Schoonmaker on the right, west of the road, Powell east of the Pike. Supported by Lieutenant Gulian V. Weir's Battery L, 5th United States Artillery, the Yankee horsemen, for the first time this morning, undertook a charge. The Rebels fought "stubbornly," as Averell reported, but only for a brief time. Overlapped on both flanks, the Virginians abandoned their position, racing southward. Averell, however, did not order an immediate pursuit, allowing the Rebels to regroup up the Pike.[23]

This engagement at Bunker Hill occurred close to ten o'clock. An hour later Custer tested the Confederate line near Brucetown and was repulsed. Another sixty to ninety minutes would pass in relative quiescence except for the skirmishing between Merritt's division and Wharton's command, and then McCausland's brigade.

The situation, at approximately 12:30 p.m., on this sector of the battlefield, an area centering upon Stephenson's Depot, was slowing creeping toward a temporary resolution. As for the Federals, Averell's two brigades were deliberating moving south along the Pike toward the railroad station, while brigades of Custer and Lowell lay about two miles east of the depot with Devin still east of the creek. As for the Confederates, the situation had shifted significantly during the preceding hour. Smith's Virginians were deployed across Averell's path; McCausland's regiments, aligned just east and south of Stephenson's, confronted Merritt. Breckinridge, with Wharton and King, had been summoned by Early to Winchester, and were just getting underway. With the battle raging east of Winchester, Old Jube had decided that he needed Breckinridge's command to bolster the Second Corps. The lieutenant general additionally directed Wickham's cavalry brigade, under Colonel Thomas T. Munford, to move from its position supporting Breathed's horse artillery north of Red Bud Run to the army's right flank south of Abraham's Creek. Finally, Early gave Fitz Lee, who was overseeing the action of Breathed's six cannon against the Union XIX Corps, command of all the cavalry north of Red Bud Run.[24]

Early's decision to recall Breckinridge had justification. He had thrown every reserve he possessed into the counterattack against the Union infantry while Sheridan still had not committed Crook's two divisions to the battle. Victory or defeat would be decided on the plateau east of Winchester and, when that critical moment came, Early required every musket and cannon he could gather. If he considered it a gamble, he never spoke to it. His cavalry, under Lee's able direction, would have to secure the army's left flank. Old

Jube simply possessed no more reserves; he could either abandon a field which his men had stubbornly held or he could cover his weaknesses by shifting troops and taking risks. Unfortunately for the Southerners the bringing of Wharton's infantrymen to Winchester resulted in fatal consequences. Captain James M. Garnett of Rodes's division later noted in his diary, with some exaggeration, that "to the withdrawal of this division, though necessary perhaps, may be attributed the loss of the day, for now our disasters commenced."[25]

The Confederates had less than an hour to wait until the "disasters commenced" around Stephenson's Depot. The time neared 1:30 p.m. when Merritt finally ordered a general advance of his division toward the Valley Pike. Devin, who returned to command of his brigade on this morning after recovering from a wound, forded the Opequon with his five regiments and trotted westward on the road to the railroad station. Custer and Lowell moved across country, coming in on Devin's right flank. About a mile short of the macademized highway, Devin's Yankees reined up before McCausland's deployed brigade of five Virginia regiments. The blue-jacketed horsemen formed a front by regiments and prepared to charge across the farmlands.[26]

Two cannon, discharged in rapid succession, signalled the Union assault. The 18th Pennsylvania, under Major Coe Durland, swirled forward in a thundering charge, supported by the shell fire of horse gunners. McCausland's line disappeared before the artillery bursts and the galloping Keystone State volunteers. Mounting up, the Virginians fled "over the cleared fields like so many sheep," averred Sergeant Joseph E. McCabe of the Union regiment. The gunfire, however, alerted Smith, who had his three regiments aligned northward awaiting the approach of Averell. Smith wheeled the 23rd Virginia Cavalry and the 62nd Virginia Mounted Infantry to the right and counterattacked. The two Confederate regiments tore into the Pennsylvanians' exposed flank, stopping the Northerners cold.[27]

As Durland's troopers streamed back, Devin, who Merritt called the "Old War Horse," sent Colonel Alfred Gibbs and his 1st New York Dragoons against Smith's Virginians. The New Yorkers checked the Rebel thrust but lost Captain Alexander Thorp, a well-liked and experienced officer, from a bullet in the forehead. The repulsed Southerners regrouped across a field from the Dragoons. But then Devin swung Lieutenant Colonel George S. Nichols's 9th New York Cavalry in on Smith's flank and, with the Dragoons resuming their frontal attack, the gray colonel's brigade cracked, galloping southward after McCausland's retreating command.[28]

The two Confederate brigades regrouped about a mile up the road in an open pine forest, where they met Fitz Lee. The jovial, thickset officer, the nephew of Robert E. Lee and one of the Confederates best, most experienced horse soldiers, had been of little consequence so far in the day's struggles. He had superintended Breathed's artillery fire on Emory's infantry in their attack on Gordon, but little else. Curiously and inexplicably, Lee had not used either of his two cavalry brigades in the action against Merritt or Averell, a contest in which Smith and McCausland, especially after Breckinridge left, were at a clear disadvantage. Now, Lee had only Brigadier General William H. Payne's brigade with him and upon this seasoned outfit, Lee rallied the splintered units of Smith and McCausland.[29]

Back at Stephenson's Depot, meanwhile, the divisions of Merritt and Averell, who had been a close friend of Fitz Lee at West Point, finally linked up. The five Union brigades wasted little time forming an imposing line across the Valley Pike. With Averell to the west, Merritt to the east and a solid cordon of skirmishers in front, the Yankees clattered south. It was quite a scene, and Custer described it in his report: "The bands playing national airs, presented in the sunlight one moving mass of glittering sabers. This, combined with the various and bright-colored banners and battle-flags, intermingled here and there with the plain blue uniforms of the troops, furnished one of the most inspiring as well as imposing scenes of martial grandeur ever witnessed upon a battle-field. No encouragement was required to inspirit either man or horse."[30]

In the pine woods, Colonel O'Ferrall and his comrades watched the approaching Yankees, whom O'Ferrall described more cryptically as "in a compact mass and powerful in numbers." Lee, however, didn't wait for the storm to break upon his ranks but, as the Federal skirmishers neared, launched an attack. The Confederates burst from the pines, using their carbines and pistols. "Autie" Custer, his brigade next to the Pike, immediately waved his rugged veterans into the charging Rebels. It was sabers against firearms in a "closely contested struggle," with the Wolverines and New Yorkers prevailing. Back into the woodlot poured the Southerners with the Yankees in pursuit. Lee galloped into the fragments only to have his favorite horse, Nelly Gray, killed from under him. Borrowing another mount, Lee again attempted to rally his men. This time a Federal bullet struck him in the thigh and, with blood streaming down his leg, the Virginian joined the retreat.[31]

The impetus of the Northerners' pursuit carried them through the pines into open terrain, where they suddenly came under artillery salvos. When Devin had smashed Smith and McCausland at Stephenson's Depot and the news reached Early, the lieutenant general countermanded his orders to King's battalion and Patton's infantry brigade. The three batteries had only recently unlimbered behind some stone walls when Custer's brigade dismembered Lee's line. Now, as the Federals cleared the woods, King's gunners rammed in charge after successive charge.[32]

Before these cannon blasts, Custer's troopers stalled. The young brigadier attempted a charge, but it dissolved before making any headway. The Confederate discharges were so rapid and intense that Lowry's crews expended all their ammunition. Averell, finally, brought his two brigades into the action. Confronted with these Northerners, King limbered his guns and rumbled southward, behind Patton's deployed brigade. When Custer saw King retire, he sent his men after the prizes. The Yankees, unsuspectingly, galloped into Patton's concealed graycoats, who rose and laced the mounted detachments. Custer temporarily had had enough; Averell, too, halted.[33]

It was approaching three o'clock, midpoint in a sun-basked Virginia afternoon. "The field was open for cavalry operations such as the war had not seen," Merritt stated. Before this occurred, however, the battle—a struggle of ten hours duration so far—shifted back to Winchester, where the Union infantry were undertaking another full-scale assault on the Confederate lines. For the time being, the Yankee horsemen were to be spectators.[34]

Less than two hours had passed since Russell's division slammed the counterattack of Rodes's division to a halt and since Sheridan ordered Crook to bring his two divisions on to the field. In the interim the two bloodied opponents basically clung to the same positions they held when the fighting flickered and then died. Emory's battered XIX Corps, its two divisions still badly mixed, had refashioned a line at the edge of the First Woods. South of these Yankees, Wright had managed to regroup his three divisions along the base and crest of Ash Hollow to Abraham's Creek. Across the cornfields and pastures, where the wounded and dying writhed in pain, Early's Confederates, except for Ramseur's division, maintained their original positions. Gordon's brigades held the Second Woods; Rodes's veterans, now under the command of Grimes, lay in the trees from which they had launched their counterattack; and Ramseur's men, driven back from the Dinkle farm buildings, were aligned on Grimes's right flank. It was a draw, with neither commander willing to renew the costly frontal thrusts and counterthrusts. If the situation remained unchanged, Early, perhaps, could claim victory, one with barren results, however.[35]

With his numerical superiority, Sheridan still retained the initiative. It had been a frustrating, even infuriating, morning for Little Phil. His plans to crush Ramseur before Early could reinforce the North Carolinian had miscarried because of his own mistakes. Funneling 20,000 soldiers through the Berryville Canyon gave Old Jube time to reconcentrate the scattered gray divisions, and directing an attack along the Berryville Pike with its sharp turn to the south created the gap into which Rodes poured his division and nearly wrecked the Union army. The Yankees, except for a few of Emory's units, had fought with discipline, courage and tenacity. Russell's veterans, in their fearful, thirty-minute, stand-up fight with Rodes's men closed the breach in the Union center and saved the army. The Federals were not fought-out, but they needed support. Sheridan might yet salvage his error-plagued offensive with his reserve. That was why at about 1:00 p.m., he turned to his good friend and subordinate, Crook, and directed the Ohioan to bring his troops through the gorge.

The commitment of this final element of the Union infantry and its role in the afternoon's struggle resulted in subsequent controversy. The two antagonists in this feud were the self-serving Sheridan and the embittered Crook. The dispute would have no bearing on these officers' relationship during the campaign, but would occur after the war with the filing of Sheridan's official report in 1866 and the publication of his memoirs in 1888. By then, the renowned hero of the Shenandoah either forgot or deliberately sacrificed a friendship to enhance his own role and to cover his mistakes.

The controversy centered upon two items: the role Sheridan had planned for Crook's divisions and who conceived the turning movement of and attack upon Early's left flank. Sheridan addressed the initial point in his report and then more fully in his memoirs. He stated in his official document that after Russell's attack stabilized the Union center he reluctantly summoned Crook's men on to the field. "I still would not order Crook in," Little Phil wrote, "but placed him directly in rear of the line of battle; as the reports, however, that the enemy were attempting to turn my right kept continually increasing, I was obliged to put him in on that flank, instead of on the left as was originally intended." Expanding on this over two decades later, the Union general argued that he resisted the advice to place Crook on Emory's right because "so strongly had I set my heart on using him to take possession of the Valley Pike and cut off the enemy." Sheridan was counting on Torbert's attack at Stephenson's Depot to free Crook to operate against Early's right but, when Little Phil did not hear from his cavalry commander, he brought the two remaining infantry divisions forward.[36]

If Sheridan originally intended to outflank the Confederate right with Crook, as he averred in his report and memoirs, his orders of the 18th don't specifically spell this out nor does his actions up to 1:00 p.m. support his claim. The commander directed Crook to march to Spout Spring and "be held there as a reserve to be marched to any point required." This could be interpreted to mean that the Union commander planned a flanking movement beyond Early's right flank until the near-defeat of the VI and XIX Corps necessitated that Crook's divisions be brought forward to bolster the Union line. More likely, however, Sheridan had no definite plan for Crook. Little Phil settled upon a headlong, frontal assault to crush Early's Rebels not a heavy demonstration to hold the Confederates in place while Crook overlapped their flank. In the 11:40 a.m. offensive the duty of probing the Southern right fell to Wilson's horsemen. Whatever Sheridan intended for his reserve, he wasted it for the entire morning and half the afternoon. By keeping Crook so far removed from the battlefield—approximately two and a half miles—the Union commander prevented his subordinate from exploiting a breakthrough or from moving with dispatch to the south and west beyond the Confederate lines. The commanding general, then, might have planned to execute a classic envelopment of his opponent's position but, like many other things on this day for the Northerners, tactical designs had a way of becoming unhinged.[37]

Sheridan's other claim—the one which eventually so embittered his former roommate—has even less credibility; in fact, the evidence contradicts his assertion. In his report, he stated that as Crook brought the troops onto the field, he instructed his subordinate "to act as a turning column, to find the left of the enemy's line, strike it in the flank or rear, break it up, and that I would order a left half-wheel of the line of battle to support him." Sheridan, moreover, in his memoirs, wrote that he personally crossed Red Bud Run and told Crook that the Union cavalry was driving the Rebels and that the corps commander should attack as soon as possible. On both counts, the superior erred; he either forgot or deliberately lied to enhance his own reputation.[38]

Crook, conversely, said in his official account, dated October 17, 1864, that his superior simply ordered him to form on Emory's right and rear and "to look out for our right." In the Ohioan's memoirs, written after Sheridan's, he stated it more emphatically, "whereas so far as I know the idea of turning the enemy's flank never occurred to him [Sheridan], but I took the responsibility on my own shoulders." Additionally, as for Sheridan's contention that he personally rode to Crook to begin the attack, the opposite occurred. Crook, when his Second Division was ready to charge, sent Captain William McKinley of his staff back across Red Bud Run, where the future president informed Colonel Joseph Thoburn, commander of the corps's First Division, of the impending advance and then relayed the information to Sheridan.[39]

This argument could simply have been an ascerbic dispute between two former friends except that Captain Henry DuPont, who spent most of the day with Crook, supported his commander's assertion. In his memoirs and in a postwar letter to James Wilson, DuPont recalled Sheridan's orders as Crook reported them and was present when the latter general dispatched McKinley on the aide's mission. The Delaware artillerist, too, believed that Little Phil distorted the record to increase his own fame and consequently ignored his subordinate's contribution to the outcome of the battle. "Crook was clearly a very prominent factor in bringing about the victory at Winchester which had so much to do with establishing Sheridan's military reputation," DuPont argued in his reminiscences. He, like Crook, would not forgive Sheridan for this.[40]

This controversy lay in the future, however; for the moment, on the battlefield, Sheridan needed his academy roommate. Crook, with most of his staff, had watched the Union offensive and its repulse from the knoll on the Eversole farm. When Sheridan turned to his subordinate and ordered forward the latter's two divisions, Crook sent his aides galloping eastward into the Berryville Canyon. Staff officers, at such moments when they dash about delivering instructions, look "like spirits of unrest," according to a veteran. The time had passed noon—Russell's division was slugging it out with Rodes's—when these "spirits of unrest" entered the gorge, riding toward the Opequon.[41]

The aides found Isaac Duval's and Thoburn's infantrymen, numbering approximately 6,000, lying on the creek's eastern bank, opposite Spout Spring. These experienced soldiers grasped the significance of the sudden flurry and soon shifted into marching ranks. Months past they had christened themselves the "Mountain Creepers" or "Buzzards" because of the many forced marches they had endured in the Alleghenies. With Duval's men in the lead, the Army of West Virginia splashed through the waters. Thoburn, receiving instructions to guard the wagons and field hospitals with his smallest brigade, detached Lieutenant Colonel Robert S. Northcott's three regiments for the task. This duty didn't set well with Northcott but, to his West Virginians, the news was "to our not very sorrowful surprise—for the boys had got over being eager for a fight," said one of them.[42]

Entering the narrow defile the Northerners encountered the human and material debris which had hampered Emory's march and had by this hour increased in volume. "We met a steady and strong current of wounded men, and stragglers," William S. Lincoln, 34th Massachusetts, remarked. Besides this flood of the maimed and the cowardly covering the banks, ambulances and ammunition wagons were snarled in one log jam on the roads. Like the XIX Corps, Crook's men groped their way along the ravine's sides. Those Yankees from Wright's and Emory's regiments willingly spread "the most doleful and alarming reports of our disaster at the front," Crook later wrote. "There seemed to me to be as many fugitives as there were men in my command." If this flotsam in the canyon indicated the situation ahead, it appeared that "the forces engaged in the forenoon had been overmatched," argued Rutherford Hayes.[43]

As the "Mountain Creepers" cleared the gorge, Sheridan conferred with Crook, directing the Ohioan to extend Emory's flank along Red Bud Run "and to look out for our right." The passage through the canyon had taken over an hour, and it was nearly two o'clock when the two divisions and Du-Pont's batteries angled northward. Crook detached Thoburn's two brigades, which shortly entered the First Woods behind the XIX Corps. Thoburn was shifting his units into two lines when Emory reined up before the colonel. Emory explained that his center remained weak and asked Thoburn to move deeper into the woods, relieving the brigades of Dwight's division on the corps's right flank. Thoburn complied with the request and Emory, in turn, readjusted his lines in the woods.[44]

Crook, meanwhile, led Duval's soldiers and the artillery on a lane which crossed Red Bud Run at "a very primitive manufacturing establishment" called "The Factory." At this point, across the stream, the column turned to the west, moving behind "an open expanse of comparatively level and treeless tableland." The Yankees soon encountered part of the 9th Connecticut, a regiment from Grover's division which had been lying on both sides of Red Bud Run since mid-morning. The Connecticut men claimed they had not seen any Rebels all day. The blue snake of marching men eventually passed the houses of George Keller, Eveline Moore and Charles Wood before halting near the farmhouse of A. Huntsberry. The Hackwood house lay about 800 yards to the southwest. The Yankees also had passed beyond Early's left flank, Gordon's division lying in the Second Woods.[45]

Crook, surveying the terrain and his fortuitous position, directed Duval's brigades into two lines. Hayes's four regiments of Ohio and West Virginia troops formed the left, Colonel Daniel D. Johnson's four regiments from the same states the right. Just west of the Huntsberry house DuPont unlimbered his three batteries of eighteen cannon. Crook then sent McKinley to order Thoburn forward when the division commander heard Duval's attack. Du-Pont later stated that the time was "precisely three o'clock by my watch" when "with a tremendous shout which resounded along the lines of the Nineteenth Corps, our Second Division rushed forward to the charge."[46]

DuPont's gunners added thunder to the cheers as the Federals stormed down the slope of the ridge toward Red Bud Run. The Yankees came in opposite the Hackwood farm, behind Gordon's ranks in the Second Woods. This Confederate officer, however, had refused his left flank westward, and his troops lying behind the ruined stone Hackwood house, responded with musketry. Farther south, the left units of the division of Rodes/Grimes added their firepower against this new Union attack. Additionally, beyond Grimes's flank and running perpendicularly to it, Wharton's brigades of Forsberg and Smith were deployed. This much-shifted command had arrived at 2:00 p.m. at Winchester, where Old Jube placed it on the army's right flank alongside Ramseur's division. Wharton's veterans had barely settled in, however, before Early, learning of his cavalry's repulse at Stephenson's Depot, ordered them back to the opposite flank. Retracing their steps, they had just filed into position west of Grimes when Crook launched his assault.[47]

The Southerners of these three gray divisions, supported by some of Braxton's cannon, caught Duval's Yankees in a cornfield and a meadow. The Confederate fire sang along the exposed ground as the Yankees went down the slope. Duval caught a minie ball in the thigh almost immediately but stayed with his men. Nearby his one brigade commander, Johnson, also fell from a wound, with Lieutenant Colonel Benjamin F. Coates, 91st Ohio, assuming command of the brigade. The color bearer of the 34th Ohio slumped to the ground, his life ebbing away in a farmer's field. Private Jonathan Harlan grabbed the fallen standard only to be flattened by a spent piece of shell striking his chest. But Harlan recovered and soon rejoined his regiment, carrying the flag through the rest of the battle.[48]

These battlewise Ohioans and West Virginians had endured similar walls of fire before, and they kept coming. At the bottom of the ridge lay Red Bud Run, a deep slough thirty to forty yards wide, with a bottom of soft mud and "a thick bed of moss" for a surface. "No one probably knew of it until its banks were reached," Hayes claimed in his report. What the Confederates could not do, this murky excuse for a stream now did—the Yankees stopped on the banks. But as Hayes told his wife in a letter two days later: "To stop was death. To go on was probably the same; but on we started again."[49]

Into the morass, the blue-clad regiments plunged. All of the Yankees floundered immediately. "Some were almost under the water some waist deep & some knee deep & were pulling each other through," said William S. Wilson, "they all had hold of each other & those on the bank were pulling those in the slough out." A mounted Hayes soon found himself mired in the mud. The colonel managed to pull his horse's front legs "loose from the suction with reports like pistols," but the animal fell on its side, tumbling Hayes from the saddle. He then crawled to the opposite bank, one of the first across. Captain B. F. Stearns of the 36th Ohio evidently made it to the southern side before any other Yankee.[50]

The Northerners, with "almost incredible difficulty," finally popped out of Red Bud Run. Regiment and brigade organization had disappeared; Hayes wrote that "they came flocking, all regiments mixed up—all order gone," while Crook called them "one great throng." But the soaked Federals, as a huge swarm, drove through the grounds of the Hackwood farm. The Confederate ranks burst open like the doors of a blast furnace. A Yankee described their musketry as "an uninterrupted explosion, without break or tremor." Captain Russell Hastings, one of Hayes's aides, recalled that "I never saw the killed and wounded lying thicker on the ground than here."[51]

Gordon's Georgians, Louisianans and Virginians had by now relinquished their hard-fought grip on the Second Woods, having been hit on the flank by Duval and in front by Thoburn. For these rugged men in butternut and gray, this bloody Monday would be one of the longest in their annals. From the forced march to Winchester to the counterattack against the XIX Corps, whatever Early and Gordon ordered or asked of them, they had done, inflicting more casualties than sustained. But caught between the closing jaws of Crook's vise, Gordon's men could no longer stay in the Second Woods. The time had come for a withdrawal, an orderly retrograde movement executed by men of character and intrepidness, who would punish their unrushing foes.

Thoburn's two brigades, under Colonels George Wells and Thomas Harris, emerged from the First Woods moments after the "rousing cheer" from across Red Bud Run announced the charge of Duval. With Wells on the left, Harris on the right, these Federals swirled across the six hundred yards of open field separating the two stands of trees. Gordon's men waited until the line reached the mid-point before unloosing a volley. Some of the Northerners went down, but most, "with deafening yells and cheers," responded in kind and kept going. The Confederates abandoned the Second Woods as the Yankees entered. The impetuousness of the attack and the tangled underbrush in the woodlands disrupted the Union ranks, and the two brigades cleared the treeline as "a victorious throng."[52]

When Thoburn's division reached the undulating farmland beyond the Second Woods, Grimes's Confederates, lying south and west of the "throng" of Federals, raked the Union left with musketry. In front of the mingled Northern regiments, Gordon's receding ranks flailed at their pursuers, and Braxton's gunners unleashed their charges of shellfire. The attack stalled before this "terrible storm of shot and shell."[53]

The situation on this section of the field had become momentarily fluid, with eddies of men in blue and gray flowing in three directions, bringing back some form to this combat. Crook's two divisions, with both their organizations badly disrupted by the penetration through the Second Woods and the crossing of Red Bud Run, finally linked up. Duval and Thoburn began their attacks almost simultaneously, but the latter arrived before the Confederate works ahead of Duval, whose men floundered in the morass. Between these two Union commands and ebbing rearward were Gordon's Rebels. These graycoats' refusal to panic, the terrain's slowing of the converging Yankee wings and the firepower of their comrades on the plateau saved Gordon's veterans from possible destruction. While the Northern divisions touched flanks, Gordon reformed his command between Grimes and Wharton, with his front paralleling Wharton's and perpendicular to Grimes's.[54]

The fusillades did not noticeably abate during this brief sorting out. Confronting this flame, the Yankees, not bothering to reform, "rushed on heedless of the destructive fire of shot, shell, canister and musketry," reported Crook. The Northerners, however, had approximately 800 yards of barren ground to cross to reach the Confederates lying behind stone walls and modest fieldworks on a plateau. An occasional swale in the ground, some rock ledges and a few intervening stone walls offered the only protection for Yankees. It would not be enough.[55]

The five brigades of Gordon and Wharton and the artillery crews scorched the front of the charging Yankees with a furnace of death, while part of Grimes's division riddled the Federals' left flank. "The rebels had the advantage in numbers, position, and cover," reported Wells, "and their fire seemed to increase in intensity every minute." Captain John Suter, 54th Pennsylvania, wrote his wife a week later that the Union advance "was the most desperate of anything I ever saw . . . the ground over which we passed was well marked by a bloody track." William S. Lincoln of the 34th Massachusetts described the moment when his regiment went up the ascent. From the stone wall before the Bay Staters, Lincoln said, "a vivid sheet of fire, like the burning, blinding lightning's glare, ran along the front, and a deadly storm of grape and bullets tore through our ranks. It seemed as if half the regiment went down before that single volley."[56]

Two of those hit in the Massachusetts ranks were Private John Hines and

George Burnham, both struck in the groin by the same bullet. Hines, who was hit first, writhed in agony, shouting to his company commander, Captain Charles Elwell. "I'm kilt, Captain! clean kilt entirely! take care of my money, please." Elwell knelt beside him, retrieved fourteen dollars and gave the private a half pint of whiskey. Hines, who possessed "a keener nose for whiskey than any other man living," gulped down the entire amount. He soon twisted convulsively, screaming to Elwell: "take your pistol, Capt! and for the love of the holy mother, blow out my brains." But the officer could not do it and, leaving Hines to die, moved ahead to rejoin his company. "I never saw him afterwards, as he died that night," Elwell recalled years later, "but those yells of his ring upon my ears, at this distance of time, as loud, and piercing, as when uttered on the plains of Winchester."[57]

Elwell found his command lying in the grass under salvos from two batteries of Napoleons and rifled cannon. One Confederate shell ripped a knapsack off the back of a Bay Stater, spewing the contents into the air. The lucky Yankee no sooner finished saying: "That was a close shave, boys," when another shell demolished his face, scattering "his quivering flesh over his comrades lying near."[58]

To the left of the 34th Massachusetts, on the end of the Union line, the 116th Ohio crouched behind a stone wall, their advance repulsed by frontal and flank fire. The Ohioans fought as clusters of sharpshooters behind the barricade of rocks, except for their color bearer, Corporal Henry T. Johnson. Refusing to stop, Johnson carried the flag beyond the wall into the teeth of the Southern volleys. The corporal, waving the banner, shouted for his comrades to follow him, but none listened. Lieutenant Colonel Thomas S. Wildes, regimental commander, vainly bellowed at Johnson to come back. Wildes then sent members of the color guard forward to bring him in. Sprinting across the exposed ground, they, too, were unsuccessful, returning to the safety of the wall with a message for Wildes. Johnson said: "Tell Colonel Wildes to come on! We can finish this job just as well as not, and capture those d---d rebel flags." Minutes later, the valiant, stubborn color bearer went down with a wound in the arm.[59]

Up and down the line of the two Union divisions, the attack had been brought to a standstill. The musketry still roared; acrid, choking smoke smothered the field. Some of the Northern units attempted to go on again but without any real success. A Georgian on the plateau later admiringly wrote: "It is but just to say that the Federal officers exhibited the greatest gallantry in rallying their men and bringing them up to renew their assaults on the thin gray line, as they were broken and scattered by the deadly fire of the Confederates."[60]

"Every man was fighting on his own hook," was the way Crook described the situation now. For the Yankees, it became exceedingly dangerous to expose themselves, even for a second or two. Captain William S. Wilson, a company commander in Hayes's brigade, wanting a better view of the situation, rose to his knees only to be hit in the chest where his straps crossed by a spent ball. He tumbled backwards with a sudden lurch. "It was the hardest blow I ever received," recounted Wilson, "and I thought the ball went clear through me. . . . I thought I was a dead man sure." Even though painfully bruised, the captain had two of his men carry him along during the final assault.[61]

Near Wilson lay the 23rd Ohio, under Lieutenant Colonel James M. Comly. The regimental commander asserted that "a continual shower of bullets pelted the ground" before his ranks. Two of Comly's men, ignoring this fire, calmly stood up and walked forward between the lines. The pair turned sideways to the Rebel works and, "cool as mules," rifled the pockets of the wounded and the dead. One of them was named Currie, who had his knapsack smashed into shreds by a piece of a shell. Unscathed but furious at losing his loot, Currie "jumped up and down, shrieking and shaking his fist at the enemy and swearing a perfect stream of the most horrible oaths I ever heard," Comly remarked. "The men laughed at first, but the swearing seemed to strike them as unsuitable at the time, and they began yelling at him." Both of the scavengers amazingly returned to their comrades with their spoils.[62]

Others in the 23rd Ohio reacted somewhat differently to the combat. One of the Ohioans turned on his stomach until his feet pointed toward the Southerners. He told the lieutenant colonel that this end "is the proper one to present to the enemy," for that part of his body had no vital organ. Lieutenant Lyman H. McBride, no longer willing to endure the fire of a Rebel battery, picked a squad of his men, who were armed with .71 caliber Saxony rifles. Crawling forward, the sharpshooters quickly shot down the artillery horses, forcing the Southerners to wheel their cannon by hand to a safer position.[63]

The Northerners could achieve limited successes, like McBride's sortie, but little else. The heroic color bearer of the 116th Ohio, Henry Johnson, had been mistaken. The way things stood, "The Buzzards," without help, could not "finish this job"—and George Crook knew it. The major general had ordered the assault, followed Duval's brigades across the slough and now watched as his veterans died before this ridge of fury. The Army of West Virginia still had fight in them but, without support, it would remain stalled in the pastures just west of the Hackwood farm. Crook thus rode southward to find Emory's and Wright's corps.[64]

The Ohioan officer soon encountered the 8th Vermont and 12th Connecticut just beyond the western fringe of the Second Woods. This pair of stalwart regiments, for the past two hours, had maintained their line in the field between the First and Second Woods, duelling with Gordon's men and taking fearful losses. No commands in the XIX Corps had fought more courageously or steadfastly than these New England units. Then, when Thoburn charged into the Second Woods, Colonel Stephen Thomas, commanding the 8th, rode to the colors, exhorted his Vermonters to pray, remember Ethan Allen, "and we'll drive them to hell." "Come on, old Vermont," shouted Thomas. To the Vermonters' right, Captain Sidney E. Clark of the 12th turned to his volunteers and bellowed: "The Eighth Vermont is going to the d---l, but they shan't go ahead of us!"[65]

The New Englanders leaped to their feet at the words, swirling after Thoburn's soldiers into the trees. They got in one final lick at Gordon's retreating Southerners. The Vermonters found Lieutenant Colonel Willoughby Babcock, commander of the 75th New York and a close friend of Thomas, propped against a tree, his life oozing out of him. Thomas picked a detail to carry his comrade to a hospital, where Babcock later died. Brigadier General James McMillan, the regiments' brigade commander, then galloped up, ordered them to halt. But the soldiers of the XIX Corps seemingly possessed a penchant for ignoring commanders' directives and, like Grover's men in the morning assault, the New Englanders swept past McMillan and out of the woods.[66]

Confederates—most likely Grimes's division—unleashed "a most murderous volley." Thomas's and Clark's men recoiled before this concentrated fusillade, edging back into the treeline. Some of the Vermonters sought shelter behind a rail fence. Just beyond the Vermonters, between the two opponents, lay a dead Confederate. Beside the body a small brown dog, shaking with fear, sat in a solitary vigil next to his master.[67]

Most of the men in the two regiments had expended all their ammunition, being unable to reply to the Confederate fire. The regiments occupied this position for only a few minutes when Emory Upton, who had replaced a fallen Russell in command of the VI Corps division, bridled up. Upton instructed Thomas to fire on a battery approximately 150 yards away. The Vermont colonel, believing the guns to be Federal, and his view obscured by the smoke, refused. "Some high words passed between" the brigadier and the regimental commander. Finally the smoke lifted, and the blue-slashed scarlet flag could be clearly seen. Thomas yelled: "Fire on that battery!" A flash streaked from the woods; the Rebel battery fell silent. For numbers in the regiment, it had been their final round of ammunition.[68]

It was about this time that Crook found the two regiments. He met McMillan, who had brought up the 160th New York as a replacement for the 12th Connecticut, which had no ammunition. The major general, "in tremendously strong and emphatic language," urged the brigadier to advance and relieve the pressure on Thoburn's left flank. McMillan, under orders from Emory to halt the attack of his two regiments, refused. Upton then joined the parley, seconding Crook's argument. McMillan, however, would not budge without direct instructions from Emory. Furious, Upton asked Crook to prefer charges against the corps commander, who the young, impatient New

Yorker called "a damned old coward." Crook described Upton as "nearly cry-ing" with rage. Crook then asked Thomas if he would advance his regiment, but the Vermonter, too, declined, with justification. Crook angrily turned away, riding back to his troops; Upton, likewise, rejoined his division, lying to the west of McMillan. The XIX Corps was basically out of the battle.[69]

This heated exchange occurred some minutes before four o'clock. When Upton returned to his command, the VI Corps was aligned in battle forma-tion. Orders, carried by Sheridan's staff, had come down earlier to prepare for an advance. The three divisions, comprised of eight brigades with over 10,000 effectives still in the ranks, sprawled across the center of the battlefield from the eastern fringe of Ash Hollow to Abraham's Creek. Colonel Charles H. Tompkins's six batteries stood at the ready behind the infantry. It had been three hours since their slugging match with Ramseur's and Rodes/Grimes's divisions. At four o'clock the members of the VI Corps stepped out, moving across ground they had held momentarily earlier in this day for warriors.[70]

The front of Wright's corps extended for approximately 1,500 yards, with Upton's division on the right, Ricketts's in the center and Getty's on the left. Ahead, nearly 1,000 yards to the west, the divisions of Ramseur and Grimes, with skirmishers in front, waited, their firepower augumented by the batteries of Nelson and some cannon from Braxton. Nelson's gunners had been flailing the Federal ranks even before the battle line got underway. The shell bursts struck few but, when they did, it could only remind the Northerners of the grisly work ahead. Private John Arnold of the 49th Pennsylvania in Upton's command watched two of his comrades die instantly from one piece of the raining metal. "The sheel," Arnold, a poor speller, wrote his wife four days later, "struck half of Weippards Head off and went through Rhoadses Boath arms and Body." "I feel Sorry for them two Boys," he added, "for the ware two as nice a Boys as ware in our Company."[71]

Tompkins rolled three of his batteries forward to bring counterfire upon the Confederate guns. The Yankee artillerists wrecked two Rebel limbers and killed some horses, but their opponents' fire didn't noticeably slacken. Union infantry dropped with nearly every step. A Northern officer sketched, in graphic words, what a soldier in the ranks witnessed in an advance under such fire. "There is a strange fascination in a scene like this," he averred, "which almost tempts one to suspend duty, and look around him. On your right and left men go down, while you are commending their good fighting, and urging them to keep up to the work. They fall in front of you,—some lapsing heavily to the ground, stricken with instant death; while others settle slowly down, and limp or crawl back as best they may. It is a scene replete with horrors, and ringing with unearthly cries and noises."[72]

Wright's battle-tested soldiers kept "to the work," closing the distance between them and the gray infantry. On the right, it became a resumption of the fierce stand-up fight between the veterans of Russell and Rodes, now under Upton and Grimes, respectively. Earlier, part of Upton's own brigade, commanded now by Colonel Joseph E. Hamblin, 65th New York, had assisted Thoburn in the latter's charge on Gordon in the Second Woods. The 2nd Connecticut Heavy Artillery and the 65th New York entered the action to the left of McMillan's XIX Corps regiments. In their thrust, the two regiments exposed their left flanks and came under enfilading musketry from butternut infantry. It was this situation which propelled Upton, as recounted earlier, to seek some forward movement from McMillan's regiments. When this failed, he ordered Hamblin to wheel his brigade to the right toward Crook's flank.[73]

While the New York colonel executed the movement, Upton's remaining brigades—those of Lieutenant Colonel Edward L. Campbell and Colonel Oliver Edwards—suffering under the Confederate artillery bursts, came up "marching in beautiful order," according to Upton. Grimes's troops began lashing the ranks of the Union division with musketry. "Here," argued one Federal, "was the deadliest spot of the day." Yankees fell in as neat a row as they stood. The ground seemingly possessed life as waves of Rebel canister churned it up.[74]

Casualties mounted in the Union division. Major James P. Rice, 2nd Connecticut Heavy Artillery, was mangled by a shell, his torso nearly severed. Colonel Ranald S. Mackenzie, commanding the Connecticut unit, had his horse cut in two by a solid shot. Mackenzie, who Upton cited in his report for "the fearlessness with which he led his regiment and the ability he displayed in commanding it during the entire action," luckily escaped unharmed. But Upton was not spared as a shell fragment ripped into his right thigh, "cutting out the flesh about three inches in length and one in depth." Bleeding profusely, he reluctantly relinquished his command to Edwards until a tourniquet could be applied and he returned on a stretcher.[75]

South of Upton the divisions of Ricketts and Getty were now fully engaged, applying pressure to Grimes's right and Ramseur's entire front. The brigades of Ricketts, under Colonels William Emerson and J. Warren Keifer, crossing open fields, endured murderous artillery fire but drove forward with a determination. It might have been these Federals, moving in clear view of others, which moved one blue-clad witness to describe them as "those living lines of men like the foaming waves of ocean."[76]

Getty's three brigades on the left of the corps, came to grips, head-to-head, with Dodson Ramseur's Southerners. The Confederates, extending Grimes's right flank, occupied a ridge east of the Josiah Baker house and about 800 yards west of the Dinkle farm. When Getty's division went forward, they initially passed through the Dinkle ground, the area they had seized and then lost in the 11:40 a.m. attack. The Yankees first struck Ramseur's "heavy but somewhat disordered skirmish line" just beyond Dinkle's. The sharpshooters receded before the oncoming battle line as the distance between the opponents narrowed. Captain William H. McCartney's Battery A, 1st Massachusetts Light closely trailed the moving infantry, adding support to their attack.[77]

Ramseur's three brigades, confronting Getty directing and Ricketts along their left front, stood for awhile. Getty reported that "the enemy held his ground with considerable tenacity for some time." But unlike the initial Union attack shortly before noon, this assault was coordinated, in an unbroken front and delivered with a relentlessness. The combat between the veterans of Getty and Ramseur evidently did not reach the same intensity as that between Upton and Grimes. The Confederates might have fought stubbornly, but Frank Wheaton claimed his brigade proceeded "with little difficulty." A Vermonter in the division asserted that the Yankees moved ahead "steadily and deliberately."[78]

The Confederate divisions, whether directly ordered by Early or not, began ebbing westward before the mounting Union pressure. Ramseur, Grimes, Gordon and Wharton soon abandoned their positions in a general constriction of the Southern front. Ramseur and Grimes, fighting as they went, shifted due west. Gordon and Wharton, under renewed attacks from Crook, angled south by west. The time was approaching 5:00 p.m. as the Rebels formed a giant L-shaped line on a plateau just east of town. Wharton and Gordon, facing north, held the base, while Grimes and Ramseur, looking eastward, extended the front. Confederate artillery, some of King's guns, manned a redoubt at the angle, connecting Gordon and Grimes. The butternuts could go no farther without abandoning the field. The proud Second Corps, Army of Northern Virginia and Wharton's Valley fighters steeled themselves.[79]

In a huge crescent—from Duval's Ohioans and West Virginians on the right to Getty's New Yorkers, Pennsylvanians, Vermonters and Mainelanders on the left, the Northern infantrymen pressed forward. The opposing lines blazed in a man-made storm of thunder and lightning. The ripping crackle of musketry mingled with the bellow of artillery discharges. The Confederates benefited from the shelter of stone walls and old fieldworks built two years earlier by Jackson. Along the Union front, the protection varied: Crook's troops crouched behind stone walls they had wrenched from the Southerners; Upton's regiments, after clearing the trees, had little cover, as did Ricketts's pair of brigades beside Upton; Getty's division, fighting on the grounds of the Josiah Baker and John Burgess places, used the buildings for shields, with Keifer's Vermonters manning a "strong paling fence" along Baker's tomato garden.[80]

Regardless of the protection, the toll increased in the Union ranks. Hayes, the Ohio colonel, termed the Rebel fire "destructive," a "storm of grape and musketry." "Officers on horseback were falling faster than others," he informed his wife, "but all were suffering." Curiously, Hayes added that "I certainly never enjoyed anything more than the last three hours" of the battle.

In the ranks of the VI Corps, it was no different. Wheaton reported the Rebel artillery fire as "severe;" Warner called their musketry "withering."[81]

In the midst of the carnage, a Federal officer "took particular notice of a wild looking Irishman who stood near me." The Yankee enlisted man loaded and fired as rapidly as he could. "While loading and reciting some prayers in a jumbling sort of way . . . he would shout, 'Now Jeff Davis, you son of a bitch, take that,' giving his head a twist at the same time and his eyes looking wildly in front he repeated this several times."[82]

On the plain, the Southerners echoed the views of the foes about the intensity of the combat. Virginia artillerist Milton Humphrey noted later in his diary that "the cannonade on all sides was appaling." A member of the 21st North Carolina in Ramseur's division asserted that "at no time during the war was the courage, endurance and discipline of the regiment put to a greater test than in this battle." Captain Henry R. Morrison of the 26th Virginia Battalion told his brother: "I never saw our men act more splendidly." While Morrison's Virginians fought as such, Lieutenant Colonel George M. Edgar, the battalion's commander, shouted to Morrison: "Isn't it glorious to see them [Federals] piled up that way?" Captain James Garnett, an ordnance officer, thought not of the glory when he sat down later with his diary. Garnett, probably speaking for thousands on both sides, confided privately that "I have never experienced such a day in my military life, and God grant that I may never experience such another."[83]

In the midst of this violence rode Philip H. Sheridan. It had not been a good day so far for the army commander; his mistakes had directly contributed to the tardy Union attack before noon and its near ruin. When he thrust, Early deftly parried. But now he was in his element, along a boiling battle line, acting more like a division commander than the leader of an army. Hours before he abandoned Eversole's knoll to be with the troops, offering them encouragement. Little Phil's entire countenance underwent transformation at these times. He looked animated, nervous, impatient, with a confident smile on his face. One of his men thought Sheridan "looked as happy as a schoolboy." When he spoke, the words darted out in strings and, at the mention of attack, he drove his right fist into his left palm.[84]

No other Union general probably could match this short Irishman in his effect upon troops. Captain George B. Sanford, one of Torbert's aides, in his memoirs, wrote of Sheridan and his presence:

> In action, however, or when specially interested in any subject, his eyes fairly blazed and the whole man seemed to expand mentally and physically. His influence on his men was like an electric shock, and he was the only commander I have ever met whose personal appearance in the field was an immediate and positive stimulus to battle — a stimulus

strong enough to turn beaten and disorganized masses into a victorious army. Many of our generals were more warmly loved by the soldiers . . . but none, to the best of my belief, carried such a convincing air of success to the minds of his men, or could get the last drop of strength out of their bodies, when an effort was demanded, in the style of Philip H. Sheridan. They simply believed he was going to win, and every man apparently was determined to be on hand and see him do it.[85]

Sheridan, mounted on his black horse, Rienzi, spurred back and forth several times among his engaged ranks before the Rebel-held works. His location along the front was marked by the cheers of his soldiers; "the troops cheered vociferously," exclaimed Captain Charles R. Paul of the New Jersey Brigade. To some regiments, Little Phil told them "to give 'em h--l; to the 49th Pennsylvania, he said: "Boys the only way we have to Do is to Kill Every Son of a Bitch." These last words brought forth "Such a cheering I never heard Before," John Arnold related to his wife. When a Confederate shell burst under Rienzi, harming neither rider or mount, Sheridan shouted to nearby troops: "D--n close, but we'll lick h--l out of them yet." "The enthusiasm of the men became unbounded," reported a Pennsylvania officer. Finally, Sheridan bridled up next to Getty, informing the division commander that he had dispatched his aides with instructions for Torbert to attack with the cavalry and for Crook to follow. "Press them, General, they'll run," Little Phil exhorted Getty. "Press them, General, I know they'll run."[86]

The Union commander might urge his infantry to "press them," but he left the resolution of the issue to his cavalry. One of Sheridan's biographers has argued that the general was "the last of the great horse cavalrymen."[87] He considered the mounted arm to be a strike force, the cutting edge of an army. As dismounted fighters, the troopers, armed with repeaters, could match infantry—a fact other generals, besides Sheridan, understood. But Sheridan also grasped the shock effect of a mounted charge. He, like no other Union army commander, would use cavalry in the manner of their 20th century counterpart—armor. To him, the mounted arm could be the thunderbolt of battle. And so it would be on this day at Winchester or, as Merritt noted, "the field was open for cavalry operations such as the war has not seen."

The divisions of Averell and Merritt, while the combat raged between the infantry and artillery, had covered the ground between Stephenson's Depot to a point just north of Winchester. Averell's brigades of Powell and Schoonmaker were aligned west of the Pike, Merritt's of Devin, Lowell and Custer on the east. Patton's Rebel brigade and King's batteries had been withdrawn earlier to the main Confederate line when Crook attacked. No organized body of Southerners lay between the blue-jacketed horsemen and Early's works on the plateau. Things had almost come full around—the battle began with Federal cavalry charging with a rising sun and it would end similarly with a setting sun.[88]

The Northern horsemen started forward at a walk, increased it to a trot and then to a gallop. Those who witnessed it or rode within the thundering ranks never quite forgot the scene. An Ohio infantry officer thought it to be "the most gallant & exciting cavalry charge I ever saw." A Vermonter argued that "no man ever saw a more thrilling sight." "It was like a thunder-clap out of a clear sky, and the bolt struck home," stated another Vermonter. One of Custer's men admitted that the charge had to be the "grandest sight I saw during my army life." "Every man's saber was waving above his head," a New York cavalryman recalled, "and with a savage yell, we swept down upon the trembling wretches like a besom of destruction."[89]

On the right of Merritt's front, along the Pike, Custer's Michigan Brigade spearheaded the onslaught, surging into the works held by Wharton's division. "The enemy's line broke into a thousand fragments under the shock," reported Merritt. Lowell's Reserve Brigade soon came in of Custer's left, opposite Gordon's brigades. Devin's regiments, next to Lowell's, "burst like a storm of case-shot" where the Confederate works formed the angle between Gordon and Grimes. What ensued was a furious struggle without form, units, both blue and gray, so badly mingled or disorganized that men fought alone, or in pockets. A Yankee trooper termed it a "carnival of death."[90]

The divisions of Wharton and Gordon disintegrated. The Southerners, who stood and fought, fired a round and then swung their muskets at the sabering Yankees. The Virginia private, John Worsham, claimed that "now the hardest fighting of the day took place." Unfortunately few of Worsham's comrades joined him. Most skedaddled as swiftly as they could. "I never seen any men Run faster then the Rebels Run last Munday after we got them drivin out in the open plaine," a Federal informed his wife, "it was fun To see them Running." Scores of Confederates threw up their hands, pleading: "For God's sakes, Yankee, don't kill me; I surrender." Colonel George Patton, grandfather of the World War II general and his namesake, fell mortally wounded rallying his splintered brigade. Early's artillery commander, Colonel Thomas Carter, in a mission similar to Patton's, went down with a painful wound from a shell fragment. Carter eluded capture and Nelson took over direction of the batteries.[91]

No Confederates, during this battle, fought with more valor and more steadfastness than the artillerymen. When Gordon's and Wharton's veterans broke, the gunners, still at their posts, extricated nearly all the cannon. Lowell's Regulars overran and seized two pieces of the Lewisburg Battery. Captain George Chapman also lost one cannon of his Monroe Battery. Another of Chapman's pieces, under the direction of Milton Humphrey, became plugged as the crew endeavored to fire another round while fleeing. The gunners feverishly worked to clear the barrel. Rebel infantrymen, running past, shouted that it would explode. Moments later, Old Jube rode up, shouting: "Stop that, you damned fools! You'll kill yourself and anybody about you."

One of the artillerists, not knowing Early by sight, thought him to be a farmer. "Go to hell, you damned old clodhopper," the gunner bellowed in reply, "and tend to your own business." Early uncharacteristically grinned and continued on, while the crew pulled the clogged piece southward to safety.[92]

Seven Federal horsemen in the swirling action each captured a Southerner flag, earning for their bravery the Congressional Medal of Honor. Two of them, commissary Sergeant Andrew J. Lorish and Corporal Chester B. Bowen, belonged to the 1st New York Dragoons of Devin's brigade. The pair, galloping into the splintered Confederate ranks, grabbed two flags. When Lorish wrenched a Confederate national flag from its bearer, a Southerner yelled: "Shoot that d---d Yankee! He's got our flag!" About a dozen graycoats aimed at the Yankee sergeant, ordering him to surrender. Lorish, brandishing his saber, galloped into their midst, shouting: "Ground your arms, or I'll send every soul of you to hell in a minute." The Confederates obliged long enough for Lorish to escape with the prize.[93]

The handsome Kentucky soldier, John Breckinridge, plunged into the midst of his wrecked corps, managing to stop clusters of his troops long enough for them to fire another round. He recklessly exposed himself in this vain effort at stemming a flood. Gordon, as fearless as the Kentuckian, somehow found Breckinridge in the maelstrom. "His Apollo-like face was begrimed with sweat and smoke," as Gordon remembered Breckinridge's appearance. "He was desperately reckless—the impersonation of despair. He literally seemed to court death." The Georgian protested to him about endangering himself. "Well, general," replied Breckinridge, "there is little left for me if our cause is to fail." The former vice president said no more, and Gordon took him rearward.[94]

With the collapse of Early's left, the flank and rear of Grimes's and Ramseur's divisions were exposed. Old Jube rushed orders to Grimes, whose division lay next to Gordon, directing the brigadier to refuse his left. Grimes dashed toward the danger. A week later he related to his wife what he saw: "Upon coming into the open field, I perceived everything to be in the most inextricable confusion—horses dashing over the field, cannon being run to the rear at the top of the horses' speed, men leaving their command, and scattering in confusion."[95]

This sight of a headlong flight unnerved many in the North Carolinian's division. Groups of them abandoned the line, running with the beaten elements of Wharton and Gordon. Grimes threatened "to blow the brains out" of those who broke for the rear. Somehow Grimes executed Early's orders, fronting toward the north and offering some resistance to the Yankee cavalry. The brigadier had his horse shot from under him and three of his staff officers went down with wounds. The division, in "tolerable order," according to Ramseur, crossed the plateau, entering the southern portion of Winchester, where Grimes saw women standing in the streets pleading with the stampeding

Rebels to halt. "Our troops did not behave with their usual valor," admitted Grimes the next day in a letter home.[96]

Dodson Ramseur's North Carolinians and Virginians had enough warning to offer a stubborn resistance to the Yankees. Ramseur claimed his organization remained "unbroken" in the deluge. The three brigades withdrew slowly, pausing to deliver a volley into their pursuers. At least one regiment, the 20th North Carolina, perhaps more, formed into a hollow square, the most effective formation against mounted thrusts.[97]

It was fearful, costly work for these butternuts, their ranks subjected to musketry and artillery fire. Brigadier General Archibald C. Godwin, a giant of a man at six feet, six inches tall, died instantly from a shell fragment in his brain. Godwin had just finished commending Captain John Beard of the 57th North Carolina for the regiment's conduct when he toppled into Beard's arms. The color bearer of the 57th, George B. Swink, wounded already, stuck the regimental standard into the ground, grabbed a rifle and died where he stood.[98]

A member of the 12th North Carolina of Robert Johnston's brigade summarized aptly in his own style what had just transpired:

> I thout we could whipe the world we was so well fortifide but I was badly deceived the enemy flanke our cavelery on our left and came up in rearer of us. This was one of the awfull times for us I ever saw and I hope to never to see another such a time with our army. It was a perfect skidaddle every man fore him self I say to you cousin it was god blessing to us it was neare nite or the most of our army the would have ben taken prisoner. . . . they was maney tears shed in giting out from that place.[99]

South of Winchester, the Confederates fashioned a final rear guard position, which saved the wagon trains and some artillery crews. Confederate officers and soldiers, in postwar reminiscences, vied for the honor of having held this post of honor. Parts of Gordon's, Wharton's and Grimes's units, plus some cavalry, could probably justly boast of being in line. Most likely, however, the main component of the rear guard came from Ramseur's organized command. The North Carolinian claimed this in a private letter written a few weeks later. Whoever covered the rear, they repulsed a few feeble thrusts from the cavalry and the VI Corps. The Yankees were probably as nearly spent as the Rebels and the night was settling in.[100]

While Merritt's cavalry and the Union infantry crushed Early's center, the mounted divisions of Averell and Wilson struck the Confederate flanks. Averell had advanced with Merritt, moving west of the Valley Pike against the so-called Star Fort or Fort Hill, north and west of the town. With Schoonmaker's brigade spearheading the charge, the Northerners galloped toward the fort's entrance. Two cannon of Breathed's Horse Artillery and the mounted brigades of Payne and Munford manned the eminence and enclosed work.[101]

Munford's four Virginia regiments arrived from the south as Schoonmaker, supported by Powell, charged. "Things looked very ugly for us," Munford said, but the Southerners repulsed the Yankees' attack, deflecting it to the right. According to Munford, three Union horse batteries then concentrated on the fort. The Virginia colonel ordered Breathed's guns out. Schoonmaker, on the Rebels' left, had regrouped, coming on again with Powell in the Confederates' front. Schoonmaker's Yankees carried the works this time; a brief hand-to-hand melee ensued before the Southerners disengaged. For this attack, Schoonmaker would eventually win the Medal of Honor. Averell directed no pursuit, and Munford and Payne soon joined in their army's retreat.[102]

On the battlefield's southern flank, beyond Abraham's Creek, the action had been a day-long draw. In the morning after the Union infantry cleared Berryville Canyon, Sheridan sent Wilson's mounted division south of the stream to oppose Lomax's horsemen. When the infantry charged at 11:40 a.m., Wilson, too, advanced, striking the gray troopers at the Greenwood Church and school house on the Senseney Road. "Mudwall" Jackson's men withdrew stubbornly and not far, as Wilson only tentatively probbed the opposing line.[103]

In the afternoon the Federals disengaged, swinging south and west coming in on the Millwood Road. Lomax countered this; Jackson's brigade, supported by Bradley Johnson's command, again barred the way. When the VI Corps launched their four o'clock assault, Sheridan instructed Wilson to press the Confederates and "gain the Valley Pike." But, like the earlier movement, Wilson did little more than demonstrate against Lomax. The Federal cavalry officer, perhaps, might have secured the Valley Pike, cutting Early's only avenue of retreat. Instead, he fought so feebly that Lomax could dispatch Munford to the beleaguered Confederate northern flank. After Wilson's swiftly executed sunrise attack through the gorge, his performance deteriorated with possibly significant results.[104]

Darkness, finally, mercifully, ended the combat. On the Valley Pike, the Confederates stumbled through the blackness, most not halting until they passed Newtown. For the first time in the annals of the Second Corps, they had been driven from a field they defended. It was an exhausted, dispirited army which marched under the Virginia stars—"I have never witnessed so complete a licked out crew as Genl Earlys army," a Northerner, who watched them abandon the plateau, exclaimed with exaggeration. The Southerners had "got a hellish licking" but they were resilient and would wait for a chance to even the score.[105]

In the fields rimming Winchester, the victorious Federals built campfires, cooked suppers, and savored their victory, while regimental bands rendered a few songs. About 10:00 p.m. orders came down for a roll call. As sergeants read names, the responses—"Dead," "Wounded," "Killed"—reminded the living and unharmed of the victory's cost. But this would be a night when sleep came easily to these Yankees for they had done what no other Union command before had accomplished—they had won a decisive victory in the Shenandoah Valley. In the words of the army's chief of staff, James Forsyth, they sent the Rebels "whirling through Winchester."[106]

The day's soon-to-be acclaimed hero, Philip Sheridan, had entered Winchester soon after the Confederates fled. Riding with Crook, he stopped to converse with ladies and praise officers he encountered, showing evident satisfaction. Telling Crook he wanted to telegraph Grant, the subordinate directed him to the home of Rebecca Wright. Sheridan thanked the young Quaker woman for her intelligence and then, sitting at one of the desks in her school, he wrote out a message to Grant, briefly summarizing the day's work. Later, the commander established his headquarters in the home of Lloyd Logan. Before Sheridan slept, he issued orders for a 5:00 a.m. march southward, up the Valley, after Old Jube.[107]

The historic village, meanwhile, had been "turned into a HOSPITAL." Every building of any size was crowded with the maimed and dying. Women of Winchester, "in large numbers," moved among the wounded and Southern prisoners, distributing food and comfort. A Northern newspaperman, walking the streets, recounted for his readers the scene. "Nearly every house, along the pathway of battle," as he described it, "contained one and sometimes half a dozen wounded men. Hospital duties were performed in Winchester itself by half the families as well as by rebel surgeons and our own. Lights gleamed from every window, and shadows of moving nurses flickered against the curtains; faint cries of pain sometimes issued from the doors."[108]

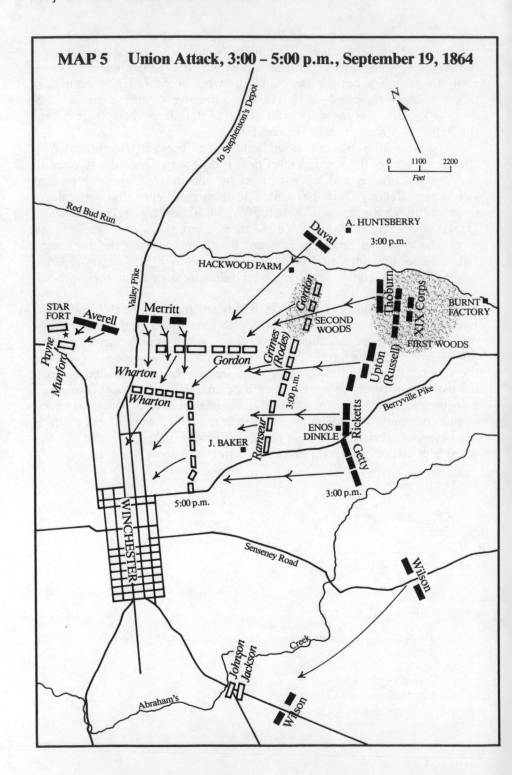

MAP 5   Union Attack, 3:00 – 5:00 p.m., September 19, 1864

6

"First Fair Chance"

James E. Taylor, special artist for *Frank Leslie's Illustrated Newspapers*, arrived at the battlefield of Winchester or the Opequon—as the Federals would come to designate the engagement—on the morning after. A Union soldier until 1863, Taylor possessed both an artist's and a veteran's eye for the scene of combat. Riding through Berryville Canyon, he approached the ground along the route of the Union infantry. What the Ohio native saw, and recorded, was the human wreckage of war, the "gory spectacle" when the fighting ended and the armies passed on.[1]

Taylor moved deliberately—he called it "my stroll"—across the field: through the canyon where Union surgeons worked in field hospitals, to the fieldworks where Robert Johnston's North Carolinians duelled with James Wilson's horsemen, to the Dinkle farm where Dodson Ramseur's division slugged it out with the VI Corps. Turning north, the artist entered the Second Woods. "I paused," he jotted down, "to contemplate a grizzly Old Confederate fully accoutered and wearing a black overcoat, who lay stretched on his back with arms extended, and a bullet through the center of his forehead. The agonized expression of that face haunted me for many a day."[2]

The dead, like the "Old Confederate," drew Taylor's attention. They were all around him in those bloody woods. He looked closely at them and described yesterday's harvest:

> It was curious to note the position of the bodies encountered—a characteristic sight to be observed on all field[s]—nine out of ten were on their backs, with arms outstretched and feet pointing all round. Men shot in the head strike this attitude invariably. Men shot below the neck have one leg drawn up and their fingers are clenched. On few faces is there a look that might be called pain or anguish nor do you find smiles or placidity.

Look into the faces of a hundred men killed in battle and you will find the same general expression, wether [sic] old or young. It is a look of surprise or fear—this look rests on the faces of men killed in their tracks. The mortally wounded man may turn on his side to die, and you may find a man with a smile on his face who has had time to breath[e] a prayer and think of his wife and children.[3]

Two other sights near the Second Woods Taylor recorded. The small, brown dog, which had sat motionless beside its fallen master beyond the line of the 8th Vermont on the previous afternoon, still maintained its sentry post when the artist crossed the ground. Not far from this sad bond between a man and an animal, he witnessed about ten Yankees, whom he described as "likely coffee coolers and cowards certainly," rifling the pockets of a Confederate officer. The Rebel had had both his eyes shot out and, lying blind and helpless, pleaded with the Northerners not to rob him. "Familiar as I had become with the horrors of the Battlefield," Taylor wrote, "this scene capped the climax in my experience. Going through dead men was legitimate, but this passed the limits."[4]

Union soldiers offered similar descriptions of the windrows of the fallen. The battlefield "was a horrid sight," J. S. Lloyd informed his sister. "The dead were scattered in all directions." A member of the 38th Massachusetts claimed that "the dead were horrible dead. It seemed as if the majority had received their death from shells. Most of the bodies were dismembered, and at least half were mangled beyond recognition." An army chaplain asserted that some of the bodies were mutilated during the night.[5]

Isaac D. Best, 121st New York, noted a particularly bloody spot (most likely the open ground where David Russell's Yankees and Cullen Battle's Alabamians, standing elbow-to-elbow, ravaged each other). "The two lines of battle must have stood for some time, steadily firing at each other," stated the New Yorker. "Between two thickets, probably twenty rods apart there was a row of blue clad dead lying close together, and fairly touching each other; and only a few yards in front of them a similar windrow of gray clad dead, lying as closely and straightly aligned as were their opponents."[6]

The grisly duty of removing the corpses and neglected wounded fell to the 82nd Pennsylvania of Colonel Oliver Edwards's VI Corps brigade and the medical personnel. The casualties covered miles of ground. Strings of ambulances waited to unload at the field hospitals along Opequon Creek or in the converted buildings in Winchester. The Union medical corps eventually filled twenty buildings in town with the wounded, erected a tent hospital near Shawnee Spring and expanded a 300-bed hospital at Sandy Hook, Maryland, to accommodate 1,300 patients. Six days after the battle, Surgeon John H. Brinton reported 4,201 wounded still flooded the hospitals.[7]

By the standards of major Civil War engagements, Third Winchester was not notably sanguinary in the total number of casualties incurred. Though

Jubal Early reported slightly higher figures to Robert E. Lee, casualties among the gray infantry and artillery were officially recorded at 199 killed and 1,508 wounded, for a total of 1,707. The lieutenant general also claimed that 1,818 were missing but admitted that many of them had not been captured "but are stragglers and skulkers." His cavalry officers did not list their casualties separately for the battle but reported 60 killed and 288 wounded for the month of September. If the cavalry sustained at least 200 of those at Winchester, Early had between 1,900 and 2,000 men fall in combat or roughly 15 per cent of his army, excluding those missing or captured. If half those listed as not present had been captured, his losses amounted to approximately 23 per cent. This latter figure exceeded Confederate losses at Seven Days, Second Manassas, Fredericksburg and Chancellorsville in the East and Shiloh, Corinth, Perryville and Chickamauga in the West.[8]

More importantly for the Army of the Valley, the killed, wounded and missing incurred by the four infantry divisions and three artillery battalions reached nearly 30 per cent, a staggering figure comparable to Lee's casualties at Gettysburg. Robert Rodes, whose death was the most grievous of the day for Early, and his division suffered more dead and maimed than any other infantry command—686—compared to John Gordon's 396, Dodson Ramseur's 327 and Gabriel Wharton's 217. The casualties among Rodes's four brigades reflected their counterattack into the gap in the Union line and their combat with David Russell's division. At brigade command level Early lost only three—Archibald Godwin and George Patton, dead, and Zebulon York, wounded—while at regimental level, twenty officers fell mortally wounded, wounded or captured at the head of their units. The combat prowess of the army was seriously impaired by Third Winchester.[9]

The Army of the Shenandoah, committed to offensive assaults, counted 697 killed, 3,983 wounded and 338 missing, for a total of 5,018. This loss amounted to approximately twelve per cent of the Union command. Disregarding those listed as missing, the Northerners suffered over twice as many combat casualties as did the Southerners, who maintained a defensive position. In the Civil War, to attack meant to die in disproportionate numbers.[10]

Among units of the Union army, the XIX Corps sustained 40 per cent casualties, or 2,074 men. Cuvier Grover's division, decimated in their 11:40 a.m. charge through the First Woods and counterattack by John Gordon's troops, had 1,527 fall. Losses at regimental level were inordinately high—every regimental commander had been either killed or wounded. Thirteen of twenty-one officers in the 14th New Hampshire of Henry Birge's brigade, for instance, went down. If Philip Sheridan doubted the reliability of the corps before Winchester, the engagement's bloody toll on the command could only weaken its temper in combat.[11]

The dead, maimed and missing in Horatio Wright's VI Corps reached 1,699 and in George Crook's two divisions, 794. Wright's three divisions shared almost equally in the losses, with James Ricketts's command topping the lists. The death of David Russell and the wounding of his successor, Emory Upton, impaired the efficiency of that division. Russell was the equal of Ricketts and George Getty, and no brigade commander surpassed the brilliant Upton. For Crook, the loss of Isaac Duval was mitigated by the appointment of the experienced, capable Rutherford Hayes in his place. In the cavalry corps, casualties amounted to only 451. The battle had not seriously affected the fighting prowess of the Union army.[12]

But for those still in the ranks of both armies, Winchester or Opequon left an indelible mark. A Virginia artillerist admitted in his diary that "this had been one [of] the longest and hardest day's fighting that I have done since this awful war began." The Virginian's chief, Thomas Carter, told another gunner that Winchester "was the hardest stand-up, all-day fight he was in during the war." A Yankee, a Massachusetts veteran, said virtually the same thing, asserting that the battle was "the hardest fight that [I] was ever in." One of George Custer's Wolverines asserted: "One day's experience during my army life which impressed me more than any other was the 19th day of September, 1864." A New York cavalryman, however, perhaps best expressed the sentiments of his army when he described it as "a great and glorious day's work for the Union troops."[13]

This "great and glorious day's work" the Yankees unreservedly attributed to Sheridan. "Our little Sheridan is a trump," one of them told his sister two days after the battle. A member of the XIX Corps claimed that "an unusual confidence was felt in him. We may have had a blinder faith in McClellan, but no such intelligent trust as we now had in Sheridan." Harris Beecher, 114th New York, wrote that "after the battle of the Opequon, our boys had acquired a wonderful confidence in their General, and believed that he was adequate to any undertaking." Other Federals expressed similar views, claiming that the men had "abiding confidence and admiration" for Little Phil and "unbound faith in his leadership and enthusiasm for the man."[14]

The acclaim accorded Sheridan by his men and soon by the Northern administration and newspapers overlooked the flaws in his tactical scheme and conduct of the battle. The Union commander committed a series of blunders which, if there had been a more numerical parity, could have resulted in a disastrous defeat. His plan hinged upon a rapid and overwhelming assault against Ramseur's isolated division and then Wharton's before Early could reconcentrate. His decision to funnel over 20,000 infantry through Berryville Canyon when other avenues of march were available permitted his opponent to bring Rodes and Gordon onto the field well ahead of the Union assault. Then, when the two corps rolled forward, Sheridan's instructions to guide on the Berryville Pike with its sharp turn to the south created the dangerous gap into which Early hurled Rodes's brigades. Russell's counterattack sealed the breach and unquestionably prevented a victory for the

Confederates. The Union army's reserve, Crook's "Buzzards," was placed too far to the rear to be of immediate help.

The Northern victory resulted from little tactical finesse on the part of Sheridan. He fought the battle much in the manner of his personality — aggressive, headlong, with hammering assaults which could crush an opponent. The veterans' shared description of the battle as a "stand-up fight" possessed a considerable degree of truth. The maneuver which brought victory — Crook's attack on Early's left flank followed by the cavalry charge — was implemented by the Ohioan and not the army's leader.

Sheridan, however, could afford mistakes because of his three-to-one numerical superiority. "Sheridan's physical strength was Early's weakness," Confederate cavalry officer Thomas T. Munford later wrote. "There is," the colonel added unfairly, "no evidence of military skill or strategy anywhere shown by the former." Private John Worsham, 21st Virginia, likewise stated that "we were so outnumbered that we could not prevent being flanked by the enemy."[15] The plain east of Winchester lacked the natural strength for the Confederates to repel the Union numbers once they were all brought to bear on the Southern position. The single most important factor in determining the outcome of the battle was "those living lines of men like the foaming waves of ocean," as a Yankee cavalryman portrayed the final Union attack.[16]

Third Winchester nevertheless revealed attributes of Sheridan's generalship which not only contributed to the victory but had an impact on the remainder of the campaign. "All battles have more or less of the accidental and unexpected," the Connecticut officer, John De Forest, asserted, and Sheridan's ability to respond to such circumstances appeared almost instinctive. He possessed a remarkable sense of the ebb and flow of an engagement, grasping the key to changing situations and implementing new tactical arrangements for those circumstances. He rapidly directed Russell into the hole in the Union line and, when Crook launched his three o'clock charge, Sheridan ordered the cavalry forward and coordinated the assault of the VI Corps with that of Crook. All day long he stayed close to the front, his charismatic presence inspiriting the troops and his cool head reacting to the shifting combat. When his opponent erred, Little Phil quickly exploited the advantage. His personal supervision of his army in combat compared with George Meade's battlefield direction at Gettysburg.[17]

The fiery, former cavalry officer stood pre-eminent among army commanders in his use of the mounted arm. "He was the only general of that war," James Kidd, the Michigan colonel, argued subsequently, "who knew how to make cavalry and infantry supplement each other in battle." Another Yankee officer stated: "For the first time during the war the Federal cavalry was really raised to the dignity of a third arm of the service given its full share in the hard fighting, heavy losses, and great victories. . . . Sheridan's mounted force was at once the eye and the mounted arm of his fighting column."[18]

At Winchester, the final charge by the Union horsemen decided the issue, the thunderbolt which disintegrated the Confederate line. Old Jube and others attributed primarily their defeat to the blue-jacketed troopers. "The enemy's very great superiority in cavalry and the comparative inefficiency of ours," Early informed Lee, "turned the scale against us." Though the general's opinion was self-serving, his horsemen paled in numbers and prowess to Sheridan's. But it was the latter's utilization of Alfred Torbert's command in a full-scale, mounted attack against the Rebel infantry which, in George Custer's immodest words, "stands unequaled, valued according to its daring and success, in the history of this war." A Confederate officer expressed it well in his diary: "It is the first time that I have ever seen cavalry very effective in a general engagement." And when the two armies next met, the memory of that whirlwind of mounted Yankees—"the horror of a cavalry charge is indescribable," said a Pennsylvania trooper—affected the Southerners. Credit for this belonged to Sheridan.[19]

For the Northern commander, then, victory stilled much of the contemporary criticisms, but what of the man who lost the battle, how did Jubal Early perform? The most serious indictment of Old Jube's generalship was his deployment of his infantry divisions prior to the battle. Given Lee's orders for a diversion, Early had acted for six weeks with boldness. He understood the exposed position of his army in the lower Valley but maintained his dispositions in fulfillment of his superior's strategy. The movement of Rodes and Gordon to Martinsburg on September 18, however, invited the piecemeal destruction of his army and was unjustified even before an opponent Early viewed as timid. Though the two divisions returned that day in a forced march, the scattered units could not regroup in time to withdraw south of Winchester. Sheridan's advance forced Early to give battle on terrain unfavorable to his outnumbered defenders. Fisher's Hill, not Winchester, should have been Early's chosen ground.[20]

Once the armies joined in combat, Old Jube handled his units with tactical skill and daring, nearly inflicting a stunning defeat on Sheridan. When he determined that the Northern movement was a full-scale advance early on the 19th, he reconcentrated his infantry with rapidity. The lumbering Union march through Berryville Canyon and Ramseur's stalwart defense abetted Early's redeployment. Then, when the Yankees charged, his infantry wrecked one wing of Sheridan's line and repulsed the other with a counterattack. He wisely withdrew instead of needlessly sacrificing his troops. The disruption of the 11:40 a.m. Union assault showed Early at his best, coordinating his units, fighting with all the forces at hand. Though speculative, it can be reasonably argued that had Joseph Kershaw's division been with the army, Early would have won at Winchester.[21]

The repulse of Sheridan's initial offensive committed Early to remain on the field so skillfully and valiantly held. His army might have been extricated with little loss, but that meant turning victory into defeat. So the butternuts stood until the floodtide of Union manpower engulfed their lines. The Confederates then escaped in reasonable order because of the experienced infantry and the service rendered by the artillery. In fact, on this field, the Southern gunners fought superbly, supporting the infantry and cavalry and, at times, erasing Union lines with canister and shell fire. Their performance paralleled their conduct during the "artillery hell" of Sharpsburg. The Federals seized only three cannon during the battle.[22]

Jubal Early nevertheless suffered defeat in a major engagement, the first by a Confederate general in the Shenandoah Valley. That fact was not lost on those serving under him. Private John Casler, 33rd Virginia, reflecting the sentiments of many in Old Jack's Second Corps, asserted that the foot cavalry "never had any confidence in him afterwards, and he never could do much with them." In the view of Casler and his comrades, Old Jube "would fight the enemy wherever he met them and under any circumstances" while not heeding the cost.[23] It was an unfair criticism, written later and based upon Fisher's Hill and Cedar Creek. But Winchester brought doubts to the minds of the troops about Early's generalship with their final judgment reserved until after another test.

The Southerners had not long to wait, for the campaign resumed even as the 82nd Pennsylvania harvested the carnage and before special artist James Taylor forded the Opequon. At 5:00 a.m., September 20, the Yankees departed from Winchester, heading south after the enemy. The mounted divisions of James Wilson and Wesley Merritt clattered in the van of the main army while William Averell's horsemen moved on the Back Road. Wilson's troopers eventually turned off the Valley Pike at Stephensburg, angling southeastward to Cedarville, where they swung east toward Front Royal. Behind Merritt on the macademized highway, came the infantry, wagons and artillery.[24]

The warming day and the spirits of the men speeded the pace. The celebrations of the previous night lingered; "everybody is in high glee," wrote a Massachusetts veteran. The sense filled the ranks that they would not be, like a month earlier, racing back to Winchester, that "half-nice, half-shabby, predominatingly nondescript town." On this morning, adding to the Northerners' satisfaction, some Federal units, while passing through the town, viewed part of yesterday's fruits. In the public square before the court house stood hundreds of Confederate prisoners. "They were in appearance," remarked a Yankee of the Rebels, "able-bodied, active men, with long hair and shabby clothes, and bronzed by exposure to air and sun. They bore their changed fortunes with great stolidity."[25]

The Union columns stretched for miles through the heart of the Valley. It was indeed an imposing array, this Army of the Shenandoah on the move. The ribbons of blue, edging the stream of white-capped wagons, testified to the war's course in the autumn of 1864. Fed from Northern farms, clothed and armed from Northern factories, the Yankees embodied the agricultural and industrial might of their society. This conflict reforged the nature of war and it could be witnessed on this day along the Valley Pike.

The twenty-mile march of Sheridan's army to Strasburg consumed most of the day. Rebel cavalrymen harried Merritt and Averell, but the Northerners swatted them aside as though they were only bothersome gnats. Merritt passed through Middletown, crossed Cedar Creek and halted north of Strasburg. Averell, on the Back Road, stopped south of the creek, beyond the ruins of Isaac Zane's Iron Works built in 1775. (For years Valley residents called the Back Road "Zane's Road.") About 5:00 p.m. Wright's and Emory's foot soldiers replaced Merritt's horsemen, who shifted westward, linking their pickets with those of Averell. The three divisions of the VI Corps filed into position west of the turnpike, strung out their own pickets and settled in for a meal and sleep. To the east of the road, the XIX Corps duplicated the procedures with their front anchored on the North Fork of the Shenandoah River. The wagon train and Crook's two divisions encamped north of Cedar Creek, the infantry staying beyond the view of Rebel signal stations.[26]

Directly in front of Wright's and Emory's bivouacking men and nestling in the shadow of Fisher's Hill lay Strasburg, a "dingy, dilapidated village," said one Yankee; "not much of a town," according to another. Founded between 1747 and 1753 by German immigrants, Strasburg had been noted for its tanneries and six potteries, which led to its nickname of "Pot Town." In October 1854 the Manassas Gap Railroad reached the town, but the war had ceased its operations as early as 1862 with Southern guerrillas wrecking the track as soon as the Federals repaired it. Opposing armies usually just passed through it, unless one halted on Fisher's Hill, as it had on this Tuesday, September 20.[27]

Confederate skirmishers, shielded by Strasburg's buildings, exchanged rifle fire with the Federal videttes, with the staccato popping continuing into the evening. These butternuts and their comrades on Fisher's Hill had been in line most of the day, waiting for the oncoming Yankees. All of them needed a quiet day after yesterday's twelve-hour struggle and the ensuing retreat in the darkness.

The night of September 19–20 stayed in the memory of the Army of the Valley. Embittered by defeat, hungry, exhausted, the graycoats stumbled up the Pike for hours. Remnants around a flag marked those that had maintained some organization. "Lucky was the Confederate private on that mournful retreat who knew his own captain," Gordon recalled, "and most lucky was the commander who knew where to find the main body of his own troops."[28]

Most of the butternuts snatched a couple of hours of sleep, spilling into the fields from Kernstown to south of Newtown. They slept "without molestation," said one, with the retreat resuming well before sunrise. In the column, a carriage held Mrs. John B. Gordon and their six-year-old son Frank. Fanny

Gordon had always made it a point to be as near her husband as possible, regardless of the danger. When the Confederates broke at Winchester, she stood in a street, imploring the fleeing soldiers to reform. One veteran allegedly shouted when he saw her: "Come, boys, let's go back. We might not obey the general, but we can't resist Mrs. Gordon." Her husband found her there and ordered Fanny into a house. A handful of soldiers then hitched up her carriage and, with Frank and one or two wounded officers, she joined the flight, eluding capture. Old Jube, a sour bachelor, never appreciated her constant presence and most likely cursed the fact that the Yankees failed to rid him of Fanny Gordon.[29]

The Confederate commander arrived at Fisher's Hill about daylight. During the night retreat, Early rode part of the time with John Breckinridge. The former vice president had championed in the 1850's the cause of Southern rights in the western territories. Old Jube, an avowed Unionist until Virginia seceded, reportedly said to his subordinate: "General Breckinridge, what do you think of the 'rights of the South in the Territories,' now?" The Kentuckian had no reply.[30]

The sun had passed the meridian by the time the final contingent of Confederates filtered on to the heights of Fisher's Hill. Officers designated positions on the eminence; the men then cooked what rations they had and those that could, slept. Bryan Grimes admitted that he was "sore as a boil all over" and could speak barely above a whisper. Much had been taken out of them in the past twenty-four hours, but they were resilient. Gordon heard a soldier say: "Cheer up, boys; don't be worried. We'll lick them Yankees the first fair chance, and get more grub and guns and things than our poor old quartermaster mules can pull."[31]

Early, as Casler noted, would give battle almost anywhere, and he chose to stand at Fisher's Hill. His decision, he informed Lee, to hold the dominating heights was because Fisher's Hill "was the only place where a stand could be made" with the "hope of arresting Sheridan's progress." The lieutenant general expanded on this later in his memoirs: "To have retired beyond this point would have rendered it necessary for me to fall back to some of the gaps of Blue Ridge, at the upper part of the Valley, and I determined therefore to make a show of a stand here, with the hopes that the enemy would be deterred from attacking me in this position, as had been the case in August."[32]

If Early were to bar the entrance to the upper Valley, then, it had to be here. In the undulating, fertile Shenandoah, Fisher's Hill appeared like a geologic aberration. A Vermonter with Sheridan portrayed it well. The hill "is so formed," he stated, "that it appears a huge, high-fronted billow of earth and rocks, which had some time been rolling down the Valley, and became strangled between these two mountains and held still, with its frowning crest looking northward, where it now sternly faced our advance."[33]

Nestled against the Massanutten on the east and Little North Mountain on the west, the elevation extended for nearly four miles. It was a steep, rock-strewn bluff, creased by ravines, splotched with woodlots. Along its base, Tumbling Run, a "brawling brook," earned its name, while coursing into the North Fork. The Southerners boasted of it as "their Gibraltar;" a Yankee termed it "the bugbear of the valley." If adequately manned, the heights were nearly impregnable.[34]

For the Confederates unfortunately, the circumstances present in mid-August no longer applied. Sheridan, without the restraints from Washington and with an army flushed by Winchester, would give battle. His army, allowing for the casualties and detachments, numbered approximately 35,000. Confronting this force, Early now mustered less than 10,000 effectives. The Rebels, too, would fight, but they were not quite the same command of a month earlier. Early needed every musket in the works and that still might not be enough. His position was, in the words of a perceptive Union officer, "too big for his enfeebled army."[35]

Old Jubilee compounded this error in judgment by his unwise dispositions, which were completed on the 20th. His right, where the face of the bluff was the steepest and a bend in the North Fork confined the area of attack, was virtually unassailable. Additionally, the "Three Sisters" or peaks towered 1,365 feet above the floor, giving Early a natural watch tower with an unparalleled view of any Union force preparing an attack. Here the commander stationed Gabriel Wharton's infantrymen, supported by J. Floyd King's artillery battalion. A brigade or two of his cavalry and a horse battery would probably have been sufficient.[36]

Aligned on Wharton's left, across the turnpike, Gordon's veterans held the works. Next came Dodson Ramseur's three brigades, now under the command of John Pegram, a thirty-two-year-old Virginian, West Pointer, who had joined the division in August. Pegram assumed direction of the command because Early transferred Ramseur to the division of Rodes. Earlier in the day, Major Greene Peyton, Rodes's chief of staff, met with Early and requested Ramseur. The North Carolinian had led a brigade under Rodes for over a year until he secured Early's old division. The army commander acceded, most likely preferring to have his largest infantry division in the hands of an experienced officer. The veterans of the command welcomed Ramseur back but, to them, no man could replace Rodes.[37]

Ramseur's four brigades lengthened the infantry front to the so-called Middle Road, where the bluff sloped down into a small valley before butting against Little North Mountain. Part of Pegram's center brigade, Robert Johnston's, and his left brigade, Godwin's under Lieutenant Colonel William S. Davis, 12th North Carolina, bent south along the brow of the hill, with Ramseur's units angling south by west. The latter's troops occupied a well-timbered section of the crest which limited their view. The artillery battalions of William Nelson and Carter Braxton were positioned among the infantry units.[38]

Ramseur's line terminated in the swale along the Middle Road near the residence of A. Funkhouser. To the west the dismounted brigades of Lunsford Lomax's cavalry division were deployed in the low ground and on "a kind of hog-backed" ridge which paralleled Fisher's Hill and slightly south of the main heights. This elevation also was wooded, restricting the view of the defenders. Most of the infantry blamed Lomax's command for the disasters at Winchester. The horsemen were undermanned, poorly armed, seriously demoralized and without the guidance of Fitz Lee, who was in an ambulance rolling toward Staunton and out of the campaign. Early had no confidence in them at all, yet he placed them—without explanation then or later—at the vulnerable key to his army's position. He further reduced Lomax's strength by moving John McCausland's brigade across the North Fork in the shadow of the "Three Sisters." For an officer of Early's experience and ability, the disposition and location of the cavalry was a tactical blunder of the highest order.[39]

From the floor of the Valley, however, the Southern works appeared just as formidable as they had in August. One of "Upton's Regulars" claimed that Fisher's Hill was "one of the strongest positions I have ever seen." An engineer officer stated that "if they have prolonged their left sufficiently, they are inattackable." A member of the Vermont Brigade concurred, writing: "It was evident that a direct assault must fail. Bravery alone could never gain us the upper Valley."[40]

Sheridan, while his infantry encamped, reconnoitered the works on the heights. The views of the engineer and the Vermonter were accurate, but September was not August. The Union general was not to be deterred, if an acceptable scheme could be fashioned. He called a council of war for that night.[41]

Sheridan, Wright, Emory and Crook met at army headquarters, a wall tent pitched beside the turnpike south of Cedar Creek. This meeting, like the question of who proposed the flank attack at Winchester, subsequently generated controversy. From the available evidence, the four officers unanimously dismissed the idea of a frontal assault. The army commander then proposed a flank movement beyond Early's right, where Fisher's Hill butted against Massanutten. No Union attack force, forming under the noses of enemy signalmen, required to cross the North Fork and then assail almost a sheer bluff and mountainside, could accomplish the task. The coterie of officers rejected this plan.[42]

Crook, who also had examined the terrain, suggested a turning movement beyond the opposite end of Early's line, at Little North Mountain. Wright and Emory didn't like this idea either, but Sheridan believed Crook's proposal had a chance of success. He then summoned Joseph Thoburn and Rutherford Hayes, Crook's division commanders, to headquarters. Little Phil wanted their views of the plan's feasibility. According to one version of the conference, the pair seconded the proposal.[43]

The details of the operation consumed the remainder of the meeting. Success depended on the critical element of surprise, the ability to march Crook's command to Little North Mountain without detection by Early's signal station. It was decided to move the "Buzzards" forward into concealed positions only at night so, when the meeting broke up, Crook, returning to his camps, shifted his troops into a stand of timber north of the creek. As a secondary phase, Sheridan instructed Torbert to take Merritt's division and join Wilson at Front Royal. From there the cavalry could sweep up the Luray Valley, cross the Massanutten at New Market Gap and form a barrier across the Valley upon which Little Phil could destroy the Southern army. Crook would attack on the 22nd and, if the plan succeeded, Sheridan would have Early and the Army of the Valley bagged by September 23. With this decided, Sheridan adjourned the meeting.[44]

The controversy surrounding this council resulted from a statement of Sheridan in his official report, filed in February 1866. "I resolved to use a turning column again," he wrote. Like his reconstruction of the events on the afternoon of the 19th regarding Crook's movement, this assertion, to a lesser degree, skirted the truth. If he meant that he took responsibility for the proposed movement against Early's left, he was indeed correct; if however, he meant that he conceived the idea, then he wanted credit for something he did not deserve. From the accounts of those present, Crook unequivocally broached the proposal. Crook was not "the brains of this army," as an admiring Hayes claimed, but the Ohioan surely deserved better of an old friend. Sheridan commanded the army; he, alone, was ultimately responsible for what it did or did not accomplish. But to the hero of the Shenandoah, credit and fame, like responsibility, need not be shared.[45]

The Union movement commenced on the 21st, again at five o'clock in the morning when Merritt's troopers splashed across Cedar Creek, riding northward. The division commander stopped at army headquarters for final instructions before detaching Thomas Devin's brigade as protection for the army's rear. Proceeding, the brigades of George Custer and Charles Lowell forded the North Fork at Buckton's Ford and cantered toward Front Royal. Merritt, with Torbert personally accompanying the command, halted short of the town about midday. While the troopers ate, an unidentified enlisted man had his head shaved for "killing a pig."[46]

Torbert found his Third Division, James Wilson's, already in possession of Front Royal. For the past twenty-four hours Wilson had been engaging Williams C. Wickham's two mounted brigades, plus horse artillery, in the area between Cedarville and Front Royal. Directed by Torbert on the 20th to occupy a "good position" between the two villages, Wilson—the only officer from Grant's staff ever promoted to line command—had initially encountered Wickham's units after noon on the 20th across the Cedarville-Front Royal road at Crooked Run, which flowed into the Shenandoah River. The Yankees, outnumbering the Rebels about two-to-one, drove their opponents across the North Fork. Wilson then bivouacked for the day.[47]

At daybreak, September 21, Wilson took the initiative. Shielded by fog, his brigades of George Chapman and Lieutenant Colonel George A. Purington, who had replaced the wounded John McIntosh, "with a terrific yell," charged Thomas Munford's brigade of Virginians. Wilson also sent the 1st Vermont and 1st New Hampshire Cavalry via Kendrick's Ford to swing in on the enemy's flank. The Virginians, positioned between the South Fork and Front Royal, held momentarily before the two Yankee brigades. A civilian described the firing as "incessant." When the two detached regiments came in, the Confederates broke, with part of the 2nd Virginia Cavalry having "to cut our way out." Munford regrouped south of town on William Payne's brigade, and Wickham pulled back four miles from the village.[48]

The Union pursuit developed slowly. When Merritt arrived at Front Royal, Wilson's advance had stalled at Gooney Run, six miles south of the town. Desultory artillery fire from Confederate horse batteries marked the extent of the action. When Wickham learned of Merritt's approach, he ordered another withdrawal. The Confederates waited until after nightfall and then rode south, halting at Milford, approximately a dozen miles from Luray. The Union cavalry encamped north of Gooney Run.[49]

At Fisher's Hill, meanwhile, the day passed with relative inactivity. The infantrymen of Wright and Emory rose at sunrise, cooked breakfast and relaxed for hours, while Crook's troops stayed hidden in the trees north of Cedar Creek. Sheridan, with Wright, resumed his examination of the Confederate lines. On the heights, the Confederates strengthened their entrenchments; a gun crew occasionally arced a round toward the Union camps. Desultory skirmishing characterized the morning's action.[50]

Shortly before noon, the units of the VI and XIX Corps formed into marching columns. Before the infantrymen started, officers read telegrams from Abraham Lincoln, Edwin Stanton and Grant, congratulating them on their victory at Winchester. "Have just heard of your great victory," said the president. "God bless you all, officers and men. Strongly inclined to come up and see you." The assembled learned that one hundred cannon had been fired in the capital and by the Army of the Potomac at Petersburg in honor of their achievements. Stanton's wire also reported the promotion of Sheridan to brigadier general in the Regular Army and his permanent assignment to the Middle Military Division. The Army of the Shenandoah responded with three cheers.[51]

Minutes later, Wright's divisions began Sheridan's swing around Strasburg. Emory's troops followed the VI Corps. From Fisher's Hill, Early's men caught glimpses of the movement across the wooded Valley floor. Occasionally a cannon boomed in defiance and gray-clad sharpshooters engaged in some long-distance sniping. The operation consumed most of the afternoon;

Wright halted his command about four o'clock west of where the Manassas Gap Railroad bent south toward the heights.[52]

Wright's front overlapped the ruined roadbed. His veterans piled fence rails along the line. Ricketts's two brigades manned the right; the three brigades of George Getty extended the former's left to the railroad. Across the tracks, Russell's two brigades, under Brigadier General Frank Wheaton, connected with Emory's deploying corps. Wheaton had formally replaced Russell and his successor, Emory Upton, earlier in the day. A Rhode Islander by birth, Wheaton was thirty-one years old, a horse soldier before the war and the son-in-law of Confederate Samuel Cooper, the ranking general officer in that service. He had been transferred from Getty's division, with Colonel James Warner switching from the Vermont Brigade to replace Wheaton. His third brigade, Oliver Edwards's, had remained in Winchester as provost guards.[53]

Skirmishers from each division stepped out, drawing fire from their gray counterparts. Captain William H. McCartney's Battery A, 1st Massachusetts Light soon added its firepower, eventually expending 57 rounds. This brought a renewed response from Nelson's and Braxton's batteries on the heights.[54]

While the duel heated, Sheridan and Wright surveyed the ground. To the right front of the VI corps, butternut skirmishers held a knoll, which, according to Sheridan, would give him an "unobstructed view" of the lines on the heights. He ordered Wright to seize the rise, known locally as Flint Hill.[55]

The 126th Ohio from Ricketts's division and the 139th Pennsylvania from Getty's drew the assignment. With the Ohioans on the right, the two regiments cleared their sheltering woods and drove across an open field. The Confederate defenders—most likely from Pegram's division—unleashed a "galling fire" into the ranks. The 126th Ohio volleyed once before its companies on the right broke under the musketry, carrying the rest of the regiment back into the trees. The Pennsylvanians, in turn, stood only momentarily before the fire. Major Robert Munroe, their commander, went down with a wound, and they followed the Ohioans into the woods. The Southerners had repulsed the sortie in less than ten minutes.[56]

Ricketts then directed a second regiment from J. Warren Keifer's brigade, the 6th Maryland, forward. Captain Clifton K. Prentiss led his Marylanders, moments later, into the meadow. This third regiment got nowhere, even though Prentiss "displayed great gallantry in this action," according to Ricketts. Getty, meanwhile, was hurrying Warner's brigade to the front.[57]

The former commander of the Vermont Brigade brought his new units—veterans from Pennsylvania and New York—into line 150 yards from Flint Hill. Reforming ranks and fixing bayonets, the four regiments swept across the field and up the hillside, wrenching the crest from the outnumbered Confederates. Warner lost 38 officers and men in the swiftly-executed attack. His soldiers immediately dug rifle pits and Sheridan had his "unobstructed view" of Early's position.[58]

It was past sundown; the Union front stretched, with few breaks, from Strasburg westward to near the Amos Stickley farm, a distance of close to two miles. Emory's divisions of Cuvier Grover and William Dwight blanketed the ground between the North Fork and the railroad, just south and west of "Pot Town." Dwight's right connected with Wheaton, whose brigades still lay east of the tracks. Getty was closed on Wheaton's right and Ricketts terminated the lines. Videttes dotted the entire front; artillery batteries braced the rear.[59]

Evening brought a breeze from the south and east. For the members of the 116th New York of the XIX Corps on picket duty along the river bank, the light wind carried to them the sound of "some very fine music" from a Confederate band. The pleasant notes were an ironic twist from the Yankee music enjoyed by a Virginia cavalryman across the Opequon on the night before Winchester.[60]

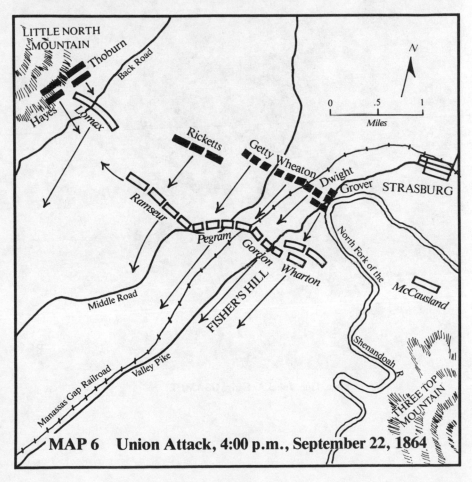

MAP 6   Union Attack, 4:00 p.m., September 22, 1864

Lieut. Gen. Jubal A. Early. USAMHI.

7

"Old Jube Early's About Played Out"

The Federals slept little during the night of September 21–22. The capture of Flint Hill by Ricketts necessitated an adjustment by Getty and Wheaton. Begun well after dark, the shift to the west took most of the night to complete because of the broken ground and dense woodlots. Getty moved only one brigade—Colonel George P. Foster's Vermonters—marching it from his left flank to the opposite end, where Foster aligned on Ricketts's flank. Wheaton, in turn, started about midnight and led his three brigades westward nearly the length of a full division to conform with Getty's redrawn line. Colonel Charles Tompkins massed the corps's artillery behind Flint Hill. By daylight the front of the VI Corps, marked by freshly spaded rifle pits, formed a semi-circle south and east of the Amos Stickley farm, in whose house Wright established his headquarters.[1]

The sidle by Wright required a similar realignment by Emory's XIX Corps. "Old Brick Top" ordered the movement for first light, but Dwight, whose First Division connected with Wheaton, began his march at 4:30 a.m., at least thirty minutes before daybreak. He assigned a staff officer to superintend each of his two brigades and, consequently, his shift went smoothly and swiftly, completed by five o'clock. Grover's Second Division followed, halting about 200 yards to the left and rear of Dwight between the railroad and the river. Emory's artillery was posted with Grover's four brigades.[2]

The final element of Union infantry, Crook's pair of divisions, crossed Cedar Creek. Well-rested after spending the 21st hidden in woods, the soldiers advanced shortly after dark into another tract of trees located north of Hupp's Hill, an eminence a mile from Strasburg. Crook's men then lay down for a few hours of rest and, in the words of John Young, a West Virginian, were "all ready for a fight, in the morning—the boys confident of victory." After two days of quiet, these seasoned fighters were scheduled to bear the brunt of the day's operation.[3]

The Union maneuver—except for Grover's adjustment—had been completed by dawn. The morning's light brought the inevitable testing from gray-clad skirmishers. The Confederates had slept on the ground they held, the fields and woods between the Yankees and Tumbling Run. They rimmed the entire Union front, utilizing every advantage the terrain provided—knolls, large trees, fences and buildings. On the rises and on the side of Fisher's Hill, groups of five or six Rebels fired from "bull pens," as the Federals called them. A "bull pen" was "a structure of rails hurriedly thrown together and covered with earth, scattered along at intervals of ten or twelve yards."[4]

The Southerners went about their work "quite earnestly," noted Jedediah Hotchkiss. Their counterparts offered counterfire, and the exchanges lasted all morning. Intermittently, a cannon discharged a round, but the duty was more annoying than deadly for both sides.[5]

Sheridan, nevertheless, ordered pressure applied while Crook marched to Little North Mountain. He had been in the saddle early, examining his and the enemy's lines. A member of the Vermont Brigade of Getty's division claimed that Sheridan, Wright, Emory, Crook and Averell, using a telescope mounted on a tripod, scanned Early's works from a field near the Vermonters. Sheridan definitely rode back and forth along his ranks. He was anxious about whether the Confederate signalmen would discover Crook's movement and foil the Union plan. Early had to be convinced that the Yankees might attempt a frontal assault. For this reason the action escalated around midday.[6]

About 11:30 Emory, in his words, received an "intimation" from Sheridan "to press the enemy." The Southerners held a string of "bull pens" about 400 yards in front of Dwight's and Grover's lines; Emory described the rifle pits as "strongly barricaded and strongly manned." At 12:15 p.m. he sent in some infantry, who overran the "bull pens" and repulsed two Confederate counterattacks. Emory now had a continuous line of fieldworks approximately 500 yards short of the base of Fisher's Hill.[7]

At the opposite end of the Union line, Wright directed Ricketts to shift farther to the west, opposite the left front of the Confederate infantry works manned by Dodson Ramseur's division. It was between one and two o'clock when Ricketts attacked with two brigades. Before this force, the Confederates fled. The infantry of Getty and Wheaton remained stationary, but Wright had his corps where Sheridan wanted them.[8]

From Fisher's Hill, Jubal Early watched carefully and with concern these various Federal sorties. Ricketts's attack, in particular, convinced him that Sheridan, indeed, might be preparing for an assault on the Confederate works. What had been true for Early two days earlier—Fisher's Hill was "the only place where a stand could be made"—no longer washed. He sent instructions down the chain of command for a withdrawal after dark. His decision, he told Lee on October 9, resulted from the fact that "my line was very thin, and having discovered that the position could be flanked, as is the case with every position in the Valley, I had determined to fall back on the night of the 22d." In his memoirs, Early reasoned that "I knew my force was not strong enough to resist a determined assault.[9]

Early's rationalizations, of course, came after the fact, after Sheridan's army swept the Confederates off Fisher's Hill in a flank and frontal attack. As things stood by mid-afternoon on the 22nd, Early had witnessed only indications. He possessed no intelligence that his left flank was endangered. If the latter were true, he displayed even more tactical myopia than was the case.

For two days, his veterans, though not severely tested, stood well; morale, except among Lomax's horsemen, remained fairly high, despite the defeat at Winchester. Few in the ranks of infantry must have believed that the Yankees could take such a position from them in a head-on charge—their works were even stronger than they had been in August.

If anything detracted from the prowess of the army, it was the loss of John C. Breckinridge. On the 21st Early received orders recalling Breckinridge to the Department of Southwestern Virginia, a post he still officially retained. For weeks Lee and the War Department had wrestled with what was described as "a bad state of affairs in West Virginia and East Tennessee." On September 10, the Kentuckian offered his own views of the situation to the War Department. A week later the authorities in Richmond directed Breckinridge to resume his command. The orders reached the major general four days later and, with his staff, he departed that same day. "I lost the benefit of his services," Early subsequently wrote. "He had ably co-operated with me, and our personal relations had been of the most pleasant character." In three days the Confederates lost the services of Rodes, Fitz Lee and Breckinridge.[10]

Early, then, correctly surmised Sheridan's intentions; he miscalculated when the attack would occur and from where it would come. The lieutenant general, too, evidently worried little about the two-day absence of Crook's command. He did not—then or later—explain this oversight. He ordered a withdrawal, sent caissons and ammunition chests to the front to expedite the retreat, and then waited for darkness. Old Jubilee had never before been so completely surprised.[11]

When Early issued his orders for a nightime retreat (probably between two and three o'clock), Crook's "Mountain Creepers" were nearing the base of Little North Mountain, still north of the Confederate left flank. The two divisions of Rutherford Hayes and Joseph Thoburn had been enroute since early morning. They had marched slowly, circuitously, a snake of men winding through ravines and woodlands. Crook, dressed in a plain blouse with no insignia of rank and wearing a slouch hat, rode at the head of the long column. "I led the way in person," he wrote, "following my way up a succession of ravines, keeping my eyes on the signal station on top of the mountain, so as to keep out of their sight, making the color bearers trail their flags so they could not be seen."[12]

The Union force struck the Back Road at St. Stephen's Church, over a mile and a half from Lomax's lines. Between the church and the enemy, William Averell's pickets formed a screen. The horsemen had been duelling with Lomax's troopers since daylight, eventually connecting their left flank videttes with those of Ricketts. Crook conferred with Averell, requesting the support of one cavalry brigade in the attack while the second one protected the infantry rear from suspected guerrillas and secured any men and equipment seized by Crook's soldiers.[13]

At St. Stephen's the infantry entered the green expanse of the mountain. Crook proceeded but a short distance before halting his units. He brought Thoburn's trailing division up alongside Hayes's to form two parallel columns. The soldiers discarded knapsacks and arranged canteens and bayonet scabbards so that no clinking of metal could reveal their presence.[14]

His march up and along the mountainside then resumed, a creeping, difficult ascent because of precipitous slopes intersected by numerous ravines. Rocks, huge boulders, thick underbrush, too, impeded their progress. The route passed through a cleared swath of the mountain which exposed the Federals to the Southerners. A pocket of gray videttes, stationed on the mountain, fired a ragged volley and disappeared; down in the Confederate lines, Captain Thomas J. Kirkpatrick's Amherst Battery lobbed a few shells toward the clearing. A short time later Crook's van stumbled into the Rebels' reserve picket post, which also fled into the forested mountainside. Again, Kirkpatrick's gunners probed the area with shells, making a racket among the trees but hurting few of the Yankees. The cannon fire then ceased almost as quickly as it had started.[15]

If Confederate officers guessed the extent of the Union force, they made no adjustments to meet it. Bryan Grimes, the North Carolina brigadier, in a letter to his wife four days later, stated that he saw two columns of Federals at 3:00 p.m. moving along the mountainside. Grimes reported this to Ramseur, urging his superior to shift one or two brigades to support Lomax's cavalry. Ramseur declined until he communicated with Early. "During that hour I suffered more than I've ever done in my life," Grimes confided to his wife. "My anxiety for the fate of the army was intolerable."[16]

The assertion of Grimes has support in a diary entry of Private Robin Berkeley, a member of the Amherst Battery. Berkeley evidently jotted this down at the time he witnessed it. "We can see them plainly climbing up the side of North Mountain," scribbled the artillerist. "Gen. Early knows this and has troops there to meet them, and unless he has, we will have to get from this position, and very quickly."[17]

The statements of the general and the private cannot be dismissed out of hand—both were written within minutes or days of Crook's attack. Berkeley's conjecture about Early's knowledge of the Federals could be nothing more than that. Grimes's letter, however, was unclear whether Ramseur relayed the intelligence to army headquarters located beside the Valley Pike. It was un-characteristic for the experienced, capable Ramseur not to have forwarded Grimes's observation. The division commander, more importantly, should have personally attempted to verify the assertion of his brigade commander, an officer with a proven record and one not prone to exaggeration or wild speculation. That Ramseur evidently did not reconnoiter himself or ask Lomax for intelligence does the North Carolinian no credit. A storm was brewing on Little North Mountain, a whirlwind in blue which threatened the entire Rebel army and, somewhere along the line, the Confederate chain of command failed.

Crook, meanwhile, halted his columns about 200 yards beyond the gray picket post, faced the men to the east and brought Thoburn in on the left of Hayes. The divisions formed in two lines, one brigade behind another, sepa-rated by only fifteen to twenty yards. The four brigades, numbering over 5,500, deployed under a renewal of Confederate artillery fire. Crook passed instructions down the ranks not to yell until he gave the signal, but these men of Illinois, Ohio, West Virginia, Pennsylvania, New York and Massachusetts had their fighting blood up. With the artillery charges rattling above their heads, the Northerners emitted a tremendous shout. "And unless you heard my fellows yell once," boasted their commander, "you can form no conception of it. It beggars all description." The time neared 4:00 p.m.[18]

Down the eastern slope of Little North Mountain went the Yankees, "like a western cyclone," in the words of an Ohio officer. The steep descent, the rocks and "almost impenetrable cedar thickets" instantly disrupted the organ-ization of the attack force. Coordination evaporated; the Federals, sensing the surprise they had accomplished, scrambled individually toward the bottom, the swifter, braver men leading the way. "The men rushed on," as Hayes pictured the scene as his veterans reached the foot of the mountain, "no line, no order, all yelling like madmen."[19]

The swarm of "madmen" cleared the woodline, seeing before them the Confederate works. "The sight of this," reported Colonel George D. Wells, "instead of checking the men, seemed to inspire them with new ardor. Every man yelled, if possible, louder than before, and each regiment strove to be the first in with its colors."[20]

The Yankees crashed into Lomax's cavalrymen like a rolling boulder. The brigades of Bradley Johnson, "Mudwall" Jackson and George Smith were no match for the Federals. The stunned defenders — "They were thunderstruck; swore we crossed the mountain," Hayes said — scattered at impact. Most sprinted for their mounts or disappeared into the woods to the south. A Confederate infantryman put it this way: "Our cavalry rushed down like the swine with an overdose of devils." The 1st Maryland Battalion, under Captain Gustavus W. Dorsey, launched a counterattack to save their comrades and horses, but the Northerners easily repulsed the thrust, with Dorsey falling with a grievous wound. Old Jube had not trusted the mettle of these horsemen, and they didn't disappoint him.[21]

Ramseur, on Lomax's right, reacted swiftly to the onslaught. He shifted his closest brigade, Cullen Battle's Alabamians, from their earthworks to a "prominent ridge" paralleling the Union advance. The Alabamians knelt behind some stone walls and unleashed a volley. At the end of Battle's line at the main works, Kirkpatrick's Virginian gunners hand-wheeled their cannon to the left, with the pieces exploding in sheets of double canister. The momentum of the Federals temporarily slowed, particularly Thoburn's division which followed the Rebel works. The butternuts, Crook wrote, "were making the ground hot for us." Some of the Northerners turned back toward the wooded mountain only to meet their commander who began pelting them with rocks. Given the choice between a furious Crook and his armful of rocks or the Confederates, most of the skulkers picked the graycoats.[22]

Battle walked behind his roaring line, branishing a cedar stick, clubbing anyone within reach who turned and ran. His hardened fighters could only hope to buy time for the artillerymen to get out their pieces and for Ramseur to redeploy his other brigades. Colonel Thomas Nelson, the battalion artillery commander, wheeled Captain John L. Massie's Fluvanna Battery into line behind the Alabamians. This added metal still couldn't stem the flood of Crook's surging men. Thoburn's soldiers had closed to within sixty yards, and Hayes's jumbled ranks were overlapping Battle's left flank.[23]

The Confederate brigade relinquished its grip on the stone walls to the Federals, who were "gallantly charging with irresistible impetuosity." On Battle's right the 3rd Alabama stood long enough for Kirkpatrick to escape with three of his four cannon. When the blue-bloused soldiers stormed off the mountain, the battery's chaplain, Reverend Thomas W. Gilmer, volunteered to go to the rear and bring up the horses. Gilmer arrived barely in time; the gunners discharged one more round and then limbered up with the drivers whipping the horses into a gallop. Nelson, who earlier had his horse shot from under him, was with the battery, "the old game cock seated on a caisson, wounded," said an Alabamian, "waring his bee-gum (cap) in salute as he passed the regiment." With duty done, the 3rd Alabama followed the cannon.[24]

Ramseur, meanwhile, pulled William R. Cox's brigade out of the main works and sent it toward Battle's left. Cox, like Ramseur and Grimes, was a North Carolinian, thirty-two years old, an attorney by training, former colonel of the 2nd North Carolina. In an army of unkempt men, he was a man after fashion, always "dressed up to date." He wasn't vain and diligently looked after the needs of his soldiers. He would, in combat, if the circumstances required, soil his spotless uniform. Cox had earned his brigade in places like Chancellorsville and Spotsylvania and, before the war ended, the brave Tarheel suffered at least eleven wounds.[25]

On this day, however, Cox committed a serious blunder. While marching his six North Carolina regiments toward the sounds of battle, he became confused and then lost in the wooded terrain. He obliqued his command toward the southwest, passed unseen beyond Hayes's charging troops and eventually stumbled upon Lomax and some of his men. The cavalrymen "kindly conducted me by the nearest route to the turnpike," remarked the errant brigadier. His brigade reached the Pike at "full dusk," in time to act as a part of the rear guard.[26]

Cox's mistake allowed Hayes's division to penetrate far beyond Battle's left and to enfilade the ranks of the retiring Alabamians. The Southerners had enough, scattering "pell-mell" across the countryside. They threw away their rifles and gear in their flight. Nelson's redeployed gunners were still by their pieces, scalding the onrushing Yankees once more before galloping farther east to make another stand.[27]

The ground before Crook's men was a series of timbered ridges with intervening bottoms parallel to their advance. Upon one of these slight prominences Grimes had posted three of his regiments—the 32nd and 45th North Carolina and the 2nd North Carolina Battalion. The Tarheels lashed the Union ranks with musketry, slowing what Grimes described as "an avalanche" of Federals. The "Buzzards" returned the fire, a knee-buckling punch which levelled many North Carolinians. But the three regiments held on in a valiant defense. To their right, in the entrenchments on Fisher's Hill, their fellow Tarheels, however, were abandoning the crest under another wave of Northerners. Horatio Wright's VI Corps was storming "Gibraltar."[28]

The three divisions of the Union corps attacked en echelon from the right to the left, with Ricketts initiating the assault. While Crook's units moved into position on the mountain, Ricketts's skirmishers kept up a rattling musketry with the sharpshooters of Ramseur's division. The Federals' demonstration might have distracted Ramseur and, perhaps, have contributed to the Confederate officer's reluctance to accept Grimes's observation. The 126th Ohio, under orders from Keifer, even feinted a charge when it appeared some of Ramseur's troops pulled out of the entrenchments.[29]

Ricketts launched his attack moments after he heard the sounds of Crook's assault. His skirmishers preceded Emerson's and Keifer's brigades with orders to concentrate on Rebel cannoneers. The crest of heights exploded in response—Philip Cook's Georgians and part of Grimes's North Carolinians, supported by Captain John Milledge, Jr.'s Georgia Regular Battery and part of Carter Braxton's battalion. The Union brigades obliqued to the west under what Emerson described as "heavy artillery fire." Tompkins, however, rolled four of his batteries into line, blanketing the crest of the hill with shell fire. The eleven Union regiments, temporarily sheltered by woodlots, reached the base of the heights and then clambered up the steep face.[30]

The Yankees, "with wild and victorious shouts," engulfed the Confederate works. The scene at the crest and beyond was one of roaring confusion, its elements very difficult to reconstruct because of the conflicting Union accounts and the paucity of Confederate reports and reminiscences. Crook and Ricketts, for example, disputed each other's claims as to whose troops captured which cannon. Crook, in his memoirs, asserted that as he rode behind his line he encountered approximately fifty soldiers removing Rebel artillery pieces from the earthworks. He "pitched into them for not being at the front," thinking that they were his troops. The soldiers replied that they were there under orders from Ricketts, who just then rode up and, in Crook's retelling, "looked as though he was stealing sheep." Ricketts, however, noted in his report that his division should be credited with four seizures. Emerson, in support, credited the captures to the 151st New York and 10th Vermont. Nelson's battalion lost four pieces—one from Kirkpatrick and three probably from Milledge. The 116th Ohio of Thoburn's division unquestionably overran Kirkpatrick's cannon; as for the other three, the evidence remains contradictory.[31]

A major factor contributing to the dispute is the scarcity of Confederate versions. In particular, what was the contribution of Cook's Georgians; how long did the brigade stand; had it already abandoned their trenches before Ricketts closed on the crest? The Georgians, according to Jedediah Hotchkiss's map of the battle, were aligned between Battle and Cox. When Ramseur turned Battle to meet Crook and then pulled Cox out, Cook evidently kept his position, confronting Ricketts. The Georgians, however, most likely only remained in the trenches until Battle was routed on their left flank and rear. Hit by what would have been an enfilading fire from Thoburn's troops, the Georgians probably scampered southward between Crook's closing line and the ridge upon which Grimes had placed his three regiments. It had to have been a narrow escape, with Ricketts's men pouring over the works in their rear.[32]

What is certain, when Crook and Ricketts converged, is that only the North Carolinians of Bryan Grimes were left of Ramseur's division to meet the wave of Yankees. Grimes had kept the 43rd and 53rd North Carolina in the main works when he shifted his other three regiments against Crook. The Tarheels now found themselves in a cauldron of fury, laced with musketry from three sides. The 43rd and 53rd regiments went first, spilling out of the trenches as Ricketts's shouting fighters spilled in. Ramseur rode to Grimes and ordered the brigadier to save his command—Crook's Federals were only 100 yards away. But it was unnecessary; the North Carolinians had taken all they could and were streaming eastward toward John Pegram's division. Pockets of Tarheels turned and fired; most sought safety. Dodson Ramseur now commanded three broken brigades and a lost one.[33]

One North Carolinian who barely escaped was Bryan Grimes. Slowed by a sprained ankle caused by an earlier fall in the trenches, he hobbled into a hollow, where he had left his horse. Someone, however, had removed it and

Grimes could not possibly elude the Yankees with a bad ankle. He then saw a cannon, abandoned because two of the team had been killed. Members of the crew were cutting the other horses out of the traces so Grimes limped to them—it "was a matter of life and death with me." Mounting one horse, he asked a gunner to cut him loose, but the artillerist, figuring the horse was his, turned and ran. Grimes tried to free the animal but couldn't. Another cannoneer, with a freed horse, then severed the traces for the brigadier. The Northerners were only fifty yards away when Grimes galloped after his troops. Enroute he found Colonel John Winston, 45th North Carolina, and swung him up on the horse. The pair escaped under a shower of minie balls. "Grimes seemed to possess a charmed life," admitted an officer, "always to be seen in in the most exposed positions."[34]

Jubal Early reached this section of the field as the North Carolinians scattered. The Southern commander had sent staff officers to bring Wharton's division from the right flank, but the rout of his largest infantry division was probably worse than he expected. Furious, and most likely cursing, Old Jube shouted at the 13th Virginia, which held the left edge of Pegram's works, to shoot the cowardly Tarheels. The Virginians refused and joined in the flight.[35]

The retreat of the 13th Virginia merely anticipated the disruption of Pegram's entire line. With their left flank uncovered, Pegram's three brigades, like Ramseur's, confronted an assault from three directions. Getty's VI Corps troops were coming in beside Ricketts's veterans toward Pegram's entrenchments.

Getty hit the crest of the heights after Ricketts, his advance having been slowed by Confederate fire and the terrain. The division, after clearing a "belt of dense woods," were subjected to immediate fire from Pegram's command and the batteries of Braxton. Bidwell's brigade, on the left, momentarily broke under the fusillades and tumbled back into the trees. On Bidwell's right, Warner's regiments, passing through an orchard, kept going while Bidwell reformed his ranks. The third brigade, Foster's Vermonters, lagged even farther behind, their advance hampered by the fire of gray sharpshooters who still gnawed at the Federals. Ten or twelve of the Rebels fought from the branches of a large tree until a Rhode Island gun crew sent a solid shot whistling into the perch. The snipers dropped to the ground and bolted up the hillside.[36]

The Confederate fire caused surprisingly few casualties, and Getty's Yankees kept coming. Reaching the foot of the heights, the Northerners splashed through Tumbling Run and a race which provided power for a grist mill owned by David Fisher for whose family the hill was named. At this point, the defenders on the crest "poured in one tremendous volley . . . then broke and fled in the wildest disorder," reported Getty. The Federals, grabbing bushes and rocks, scrambled up the hillside.[37]

The men of Bidwell, Warner and Foster poured over the works "in a confused delirious mass." A mad scramble ensued. "Guns were fired wildly into the air," recalled a Vermonter, "and re-loaded as the soldiers ran." Years later the veterans argued who planted their colors first upon the trenches and which guns they seized. There were as many candidates for the honor as there were regiments. The Northerners captured several cannon, including Captain John C. Carpenter's four-gun Alleghany Battery. Soldiers of the 43rd New York and 61st Pennsylvania turned a pair of the artillery pieces on the fleeing Southerners. Another member of the 43rd New York, Private James Connors, grabbed a Rebel flag, earning a Medal of Honor for the feat. Color-bearer William Smith planted the banner of the 93rd Pennsylvania on a caisson which then exploded, ripping a leg off Smith.[38]

To the east of Getty, meanwhile, Wheaton's two brigades had wrenched the earthworks from Gordon's troops. These Federals scaled the heights minutes before or minutes after Getty's men burst over the crest. Lieutenant Colonel Edward L. Campbell's brigade of New Jerseymen spearheaded the division's charge. "So rapidly did the men dash up the hill," Campbell reported, "that the enemy had no time to fire their pieces, after the first discharge, before our men were upon them." Wheaton's men, like Getty's, bagged some of Braxton's cannon and scores of Gordon's men.[39]

The entire Confederate line west of the Valley Pike had been smashed into pieces. Several gray units maintained their organizations, but most of the intrepid Second Corps ran. A Yankee boasted that "the rebel army could have been no more easily held than a whirlwind." Jedidiah Hotchkiss, one of Early's aides, bringing Wharton's division across the turnpike, groused that "our men came back in a perfect rout." Wharton's infantrymen and King's artillerists got caught in this gale of a broken army and were swept south with it. Grover's division of the XIX Corps had stormed over Wharton's vacated lines, captured one of King's cannon, helping to propel this part of Early's army up the Pike.[40]

The scene in the fields and woodlots south of Fisher's Hill now beggared for a description; for those who had been at Manassas, it must have looked like First and Second Bull Runs, only in reverse. The Yankees were barely more than an amorphous mass of cheering, shooting men—"our men seemed wild with excitement," admitted a Union lieutenant. Crook's, Wright's and Emory's units had become so intermingled that they defied separation. But some officers tried, yelling: "This way, Eighth Corps!" [Crook's former designation]. "Sixth Corps, this way." The men of the two corps, in turn, cheered each other.[41]

For the routed Confederates, it became a matter of eluding capture or getting shot. Hundreds went up the side of Massanutten to elude the Yankees; most, however, followed the turnpike. Numbers ran as far as they could, fell to the ground in exhaustion and then waited to be captured. Some even surrendered willingly, telling their captors that they had had enough of poor rations and sound lickings.[42]

These latter were the exception — most of the graycoats wanted no part of a Yankee prison. But the Federals bagged hundreds of Southerners. Colonel Edmund M. Atkinson, a brigade commander in Gordon's division, would have made it had he not stopped and tried to get a bogged cannon underway again. He begged passing soldiers to assist him, but only one did and he fled as the Federals neared. Atkinson was still clinging to the wheel when he surrendered. A Virginia officer, who had been captured, encountered his son, a member of the 13th West Virginia, while being escorted to the rear. The father and son shook hands, embraced and then returned to their separate paths.[43]

One butternut, "a ragged, dejected, unkempt 'Confed'," halted by the Pike, built a fire and, crouching and shivering, sang a song. A group of passing officers overheard one distinctive line:

"Old Jimboden's gone up the spout,
And Old Jube Early's about played out."[44]

The stampede of Early's army continued for miles. "The rout of wagons, caissons, limbers, artillery, and flying men was fearful as the stream swept down the pike toward Woodstock," as Hotchkiss described it, "as many thought the enemy's cavalry was aiming to get there by the Middle Road and cut us off." On a hill near Mount Prospect, Gordon, Ramseur, Pegram and staff officers rallied a remnant and fashioned a rear guard. A firefight ensued in the enveloping darkness with a small contingent of Union pursuers.[45]

The clash amounted to little and might have passed without remark in most accounts, except that Lieutenant Colonel Alexander S. Pendleton fell mortally wounded with a bullet in the abdomen. Sandie Pendleton, son of Lee's artillery commander, was Early's chief of staff as he had been Jackson's. Stonewall had watched Pendleton grow up in Lexington and placed him on his staff before the young man was twenty-one. For two years Pendleton served the eccentric warrior with dedication and skill. Once, when asked about the record and capacity of certain officers in his command, Jackson said: "Ask Sandie Pendleton. If he does not know, no one does!" Now, like his beloved boss earlier, he was being attended in his final moments by Dr. Hunter McGuire. Sandie Pendleton died in Woodstock the next evening, September 23, five days before his twenty-fourth birthday. Comrades buried him in Woodstock, but a month later his remains were reinterred in Lexington, where Stonewall rested. He left behind a wife, the former Kate Corbin, who was bearing their child. This campaign was not only tearing apart the body of Old Jack's Second Corps, it was killing its soul.[46]

The Confederate retreat continued throughout much of the night. The fatigue and despair probably surpassed that of the night after Winchester. "All the army was nearly exhausted," said Private G. W. Nichols of the 61st Georgia. "I was so fatigued till I spit blood." The main body of the army bedded down for a brief rest south of Woodstock at the Narrow Passage. The wagon train, under the direction of Hotchkiss and Major John A. Harman, a cursing maestro who could handle recalcitrant mules like no other wagonmaster, halted beyond Mount Jackson, an additional dozen miles south of Woodstock.[47]

The lieutenant general commanding informed Lee of the defeat in a message dated 4:00 a.m., September 23. "Late yesterday," Early reported, "the enemy attacked my position at Fisher's Hill and succeeded in driving back the left of my line, which was defended by the cavalry, and throwing a force into the rear of the left of my infantry line, when the whole of the troops gave way in a panic and could not be rallied. This resulted in a loss of twelve [14] pieces of artillery, though my loss in men is not large. I am falling back to New Market, and shall endeavor to check the enemy if he advances. Kershaw's division had better be sent to my aid, through Swift Run Gap, at once," he concluded.[48]

In this matter-of-fact message, Early alluded to what became for him, then and later, the source of all his and the army's defeats. "The enemy's immense superiority in cavalry and the inefficiency of the greater part of mine," he told Lee on the 25th, "has been the cause of all my disasters." In his mind, Winchester and Fisher's Hill resulted from the unjustifiable conduct of his outnumbered, ill-disciplined horsemen. But Old Jube possessed a remarkable ability to overlook his own faults or mistakes—to not see his faulty dispositions at Fisher's Hill, to disregard the mysterious absence of one third of Sheridan's infantry and to defend a position too lengthy for his reduced numbers. The performance of Lomax's cavalry and some of the infantry units deserved censure but, as Gordon argued in his reminiscences, "it is not just to blame the troops." "There are conditions in war," the Georgian wrote, "when courage, firmness, steadiness of nerve, and self-reliance are of small avail. Such were the conditions at Fisher's Hill." Early, unlike at Winchester, was beaten by superior generalship.[49]

Southern casualties amounted to only 30 killed and 210 wounded. Early reported an additional 995 missing but, of that figure, he estimated only half were captured by the Federals. His artillery, which in his words "behaved splendidly," lost fourteen cannon. (In a postwar letter, Early stated that Braxton reported the loss of his seven cannon "with tears in his eyes.") The Confederates, though routed, had been spared because of the advent of darkness, the outburst of a howling thunderstorm near the conclusion of the battle and the confusion in the Union ranks. The Army of the Valley lived to give battle again, but for now it needed time to heal, so the army marched most of the night, putting distance between it and its pursuers, heading toward a haven in the Blue Ridge.[50]

Back at Fisher's Hill, the exultant Army of the Shenandoah reveled in self-congratulation while trying to extricate its mingled commands and undertake a vigorous pursuit. The Federals scored a victory which surely exceeded most sanguine predictions. Reverend John R. Adams, chaplain of the 121st New York, returning to the scene weeks later, boasted to his wife in a letter that "I was surprised to see how much Nature had done to fortify the place; my wonder and amazement are that we ever took the place. *But we did."* Rutherford Hayes, in a letter of the 28th, said: "we have whipped the flower of the Rebel army; they are scattered in all directions." Wright, in his report, was even more effusive, stating that "the annuals of the war present, perhaps, no more glorious victory than this." And it had all been achieved at a human cost of 36 killed, 414 wounded and 6 missing.[51]

No one in the Union army could have been more elated and satisfied with the outcome than its commander. Sheridan, his aides believed, was never in better humor than when in combat and, when he won, the Irishman reminded them of a frolicking schoolboy. Little Phil again had been seemingly everywhere along the surging lines. When he heard the gunfire signaling Crook's attack, a staff officer heard him shout: "By God, Crook is driving them!" and then sent his aides scurrying with orders for an immediate advance by Wright's corps. Sheridan trailed the VI Corps up the heights, hollering to the men to "Run boys, run! Don't wait to form! Don't let 'em stop!" One winded Yankee yelled back that he was too tired. Sheridan replied: "If you can't run, then holler."[52]

Sheridan wired Grant of the spectacular news within hours. "I have the honor to report," the telegram read, "that I achieved a most signal victory over the army of General Early at Fisher's Hill to-day." He briefly recounted the day's movements which terminated in Crook's sweeping attack. He could not yet give his superior an accounting of casualties or of prisoners taken but, he told Grant, "only darkness has saved the whole of Early's army from total destruction." If his secondary plans went as formulated, Old Jube would be finished. "The First and Third Cavalry Divisions," Sheridan stated, "went down the Luray Valley to-day, and if they push on vigorously to the main valley, the result of this day's engagement will be more signal."[53]

Annihilation of the Rebels, that had been Sheridan's goal since Grant unleashed him. Perhaps with another day's sun, maybe two, the Southerners would be crushed by an anvil of cavalry and a hammer of infantry and artillery. The quarry had been crippled, now it had to be pushed into Torbert's expected barrier of horsemen.

An organized pursuit took time to form amid the jumbled units, celebrations, rain and darkness. Various commands or parts there of had chased the Confederates up the Pike. It was one of these groups of Federals which mortally wounded Sandie Pendleton. When the officers managed to straighten things out, Emory's command, with Grover's division in the forefront, led the pursuit. Wright's corps followed, while Crook's soldiers, after their day's work, guarded prisoners and bivouacked on the battlefield.[54]

Grover's troops marched southward through the "intensely dark" night in "great confusion at times." Regiments overlapped the turnpike, stalking through the fields, ferreting out Southerners who had given it up. Occasionally the Federals stumbled into an ambush prepared by pockets of opponents. Flashes of rifles suddenly ignited the dark before the Rebels stole away to repeat it farther up the road. At times the Federals mistakenly shot into one of their own regiments. It was deadly, numbing work, and the ranks thinned with each successive mile. A member of the 12th West Virginia recalled that "our men had been dropping out of the ranks all along the road to rest or sleep; and as the Twelfth passed along, it looked as though there was a string of those dropped out soldiers all along the 12 miles from Strasburg to Woodstock. When our regiment reached this latter town there was not more than the equal of a company left in the ranks." Many of the Northerners, falling to the ground near another soldier, discovered in the morning that they had slept beside a Southerner, who then surrendered.[55]

The van of the pursuit force entered Woodstock about 3:30 a.m., on the 23rd. The Yankees passed through the village, encamping on its outskirts. Emory estimated his loss during the night at 210; Grover reported his men captured approximately 200 Confederates and found six burned, abandoned wagons. The VI Corps frittered in throughout the morning, followed by supply wagons from which the victors drew their first rations in four days and more ammunition.[56]

The army commander, with his staff, clattered into Woodstock in the morning rain. Sheridan must have been ebullient over the day's prospects. He also must have been anxious, anticipating the distant sound of gunfire which indicated that Torbert had sealed Old Jubilee's escape path. In a house he waited, probably pacing nervously while outside the infantry and artillery rested in the drizzle. Where was Torbert? Had the two mounted divisions succeeded? Was Early truly "about played out?"

The divisions of Merritt and Wilson—as Sheridan soon learned via a courier—were miles from their objective; in fact, the Union cavalry were marching north, not south. The day before, on the 22nd, in the secondary— to Sheridan, vital—action in the Luray Valley, Torbert had failed his chief. The army commander would be so disappointed by events beyond the Massanutten that he never could justify Torbert's performance, even quite understand it.

Torbert had part of his command in the saddle hours before daylight on September 22. "Autie" Custer's brigade marched shortly after midnight from Front Royal, following the South Fork to McCoy's Ford, where it recrossed the river with the morning's light. Wilson, his division lying north of Gooney Run, had been instructed by Torbert to attack the Rebels behind the stream when Custer appeared on his right flank. Custer arrived on schedule and Wilson moved forward only to find that Williams C. Wickham's horsemen had withdrawn during the night.[57]

Wilson, with Custer and the rest of Merritt's division and the horse artillery, undertook an immediate pursuit. The Yankees found the Confederates about seven o'clock in a position behind Overall's Run at Milford. The Southerners had been fortifying a line, using stumps, trees, rocks and fence rails, since daybreak. The butternuts were deployed on a bluff above the stream with their left flank anchored on the South Fork and their right on a spur of the Blue Ridge. William Payne's brigade edged the river, Thomas Munford's the ground between Milford and the mountain. James Breathed's Stuart's Horse Artillery had unlimbered on a knoll to the rear. When Charles Lowell, Jr. crawled forward for a better look at the enemy position, he just shook his head. A Michiganer with Custer jotted in his diary: "Johnnys in a strong position."[58]

Wilson, upon contact, brought forward his artillery, initiating the combat. Dismounted Yankee skirmishers soon added the crackle of carbines to the bellows of cannon, with the Southerners responding with "a ringing fire," in the words of Munford. So it went for hours; Torbert being unwilling to launch a charge against the strong position. Late in the afternoon, he feinted an attack against Payne, while trying an envelopment of Munford's right flank. Munford, who directed the division because Wickham had ridden to confer with Early, learned of the Union movement while standing with Breathed. The colonel asked the artillery officer if he thought his cannon were safe. "If 'Billy' [Colonel Payne] can hold that bridge—and it looks like he is going to do it—I'll put a pile of cannister [sic] near my guns, and all h--l will never move me from this position."[59]

Munford countered Torbert's maneuver by sending a squadron of the 4th Virginia Cavalry to support of the 2nd Virginia Cavalry which defended that flank. The Virginia officer also sent along three buglers, who, spacing themselves apart the distance of three regiments, sounded the charge at a given signal. The ruse and the fire from the Virginians stopped the feeble Union probe. Torbert then disengaged, retiring northward down Luray Valley. He explained his timid efforts in his report: "Not knowing that the army had made an attack at Fisher's Hill, and thinking that the sacrifice would be too great to attack without that knowledge, I concluded to withdraw to a point opposite McCoy's Ferry."[60]

Torbert's retrograde march resumed on the morning of the 23rd. Wilson's division crossed the South Fork at McCoy's, proceeding toward Buckton's Ford on the North Fork. The wagon train and Merritt followed the Luray road to Front Royal. Just south of the village, a body of Lieutenant Colonel John S. Mosby's Partisan Rangers struck the wagon train. The Rebels believed the prize was unescorted, but Merritt quickly counterattacked, routing the guerrillas and capturing six of them. In a brutal act of vengeance—which will be detailed in Chapter Nine—the Yankees executed the prisoners. About 4:00 p.m. Torbert learned of the victory at Fisher's Hill and received orders to move up the Luray Valley. After "vociferous cheering," the horsemen retraced their fresh trail, bivouacking at Milford, which the Confederates had abandoned when they learned of the outcome of the battle and withdrew to beyond Luray. The Northerners bedded down at the same place they had been thirty-six hours before.[61]

Sheridan learned of the dispiriting news from the Luray Valley before noon on the 23rd. He raged at what he viewed as Torbert's ineptitude. Little Phil never forgave the cavalry officer, making public, in his report and in his memoirs, his "extreme" disappointment. "Had General Torbert," he stated officially, "driven this cavalry or turned the defile and reached New Market, I have no doubt but that we would have captured the entire rebel army." Expanding on this in this postwar book, Sheridan accused Torbert of "only a feeble effort." He admitted that Munford manned a formidable position "but Torbert ought to have made a fight." "To this day," he stated twenty years later, "I have been unable to account satisfactorily for Torbert's failure."[62]

An immediate victim of Sheridan's wrath on the 23rd was not Torbert but William Woods Averell, who reported to headquarters at Woodstock just before noon. The furious Irishman had also been expecting Averell and his cavalry division for hours and, when the tardy brigadier finally arrived, Little Phil erupted. "We had some hot words," in Sheridan's retelling. The commander wanted to know where Averell had been and why the subordinate had not pursued the fleeing Rebels during the night. Averell replied that he had received no information or instructions from headquarters. The exchange worsened as Sheridan said he could not locate Averell, with the horse officer rebutting by asking if Little Phil had tried. The major general then described the Confederates as "a perfect mob" which would scatter under a forthright pursuit. "The tone, manner, and words of the major-general commanding," Averell wrote in his report, "indicated and implied dissatisfaction. I did not entertain the opinion that the rebel army was a mob." But Sheridan was basically correct—Averell had been more interested in rounding up the spoils in the wake of Crook's attack than driving a beaten foe into the ground.[63]

Sheridan, nevertheless, gave Averell another chance. Thomas Devin's cavalry brigade, Little Phil told him, was presently pursuing the enemy and the commander wanted Averell to assist "Uncle Tommy." Wright's and Emory's commands would trail the cavalry. Averell followed orders, finding Devin engaged with gray infantry north of Mount Jackson. Neither cavalry officer pressed an attack on the two Confederate divisions of Wharton and Ramseur. Eventually the skirmish trickled to a close, and the horsemen encamped on the ground. The Union infantry never reached Devin and Averell, halting for the night at Edinburg.[64]

Sheridan's foul mood of the morning got no better by nightfall, especially after he learned of Devin's and Averell's inconclusive action. It had been a bitter, infuriating day for the army commander, his high expectations wrecked first by Torbert and then by Averell. The latter officer had done about all he could in the afternoon, but it didn't matter given Sheridan's frame of mind. Neither Sheridan nor Grant ever retained much confidence in Averell and now Little Phil lashed out. Between 11:00 p.m. and midnight a staff officer arrived at Averell's campsite at Hawkinsburg, with orders relieving the brigadier and naming Colonel William Powell as his replacement. Sheridan offered no explanation for the dismissal in his report but argued in his memoirs that "I therefore thought that the interest of the service would be best subserved by removing one whose growing indifference might render the best-laid plans inoperative." The next morning Averell bid farewell to his assembled men. He then, to "prolonged cheers and regrets," rode out of the campaign. His greatest flaw might have been that he was an outsider, an officer not associated with the Cavalry Corps of the Army of the Potomac.[65]

First Sergeant Henry Keiser, 96th Pennsylvania, scribbled in his diary for September 23 that the Confederates were "on a full skedaddle." But the sergeant's assertion was really not accurate. The butternuts spent the day around Mount Jackson, regrouping, waiting for stragglers to return. The Southerners were unquestionably demoralized—"I don't see why they [the Yankees] don't go home and leave us alone," Virginia gunner Robin Berkely confided to his diary. "That is all we ask"—but Early had the infantry in battle ranks and the artillery posted. Wharton and Ramseur held a position north of the town; Gordon and Pegram acted as a close reserve, aligned between the North Fork and the village. The army's train was parked south of the river at Rude's Hill, while Lomax's horsemen patrolled to the west. If pressed, Early would have retired across the river, but Wharton and Ramseur handled Devin and Averell easily. After nightfall, the four infantry divisions filed into new lines on Rude's Hill, a favorite defensive position of Jackson.[66]

Saturday, September 24, was a day of movement. The Yankees departed from Edinburg at daybreak, the infantry of Wright and Emory striding along the sides of the Pike as the artillery and wagons rumbled on it. Crook's divisions, moving from Fisher's Hill to Woodstock on the 23rd, followed from the latter place. About ten o'clock the Federals cleared Mount Jackson and halted before the Confederates on Rude's Hill. Sheridan probed with a few artillery rounds, before sending Devin's brigade along the river to turn the Southern right flank and Powell's division westward toward Timberville to envelope the left of Early. Blue-bloused infantry skirmishers then filed across a bridge to engage the Rebels.[67]

The Confederates, on Rude's Hill, had an unobstructed view of the Union movement. Early ordered a withdrawal of the infantry and artillery, for the wagons had already departed. The odd-numbered brigades in each division went first, retiring a mile up the turnpike, and redeploying. Bugles then sounded and the even-numbered brigades relinquished their hold on Rude's, filing through the newly formed line to refashion their own two miles farther south. In this method—"every movement made very slowly and deliberately and with perfect order," said Berkeley—the graycoats retreated through New

Market to Tenth Legion Church, where a full battle line was formed. "It was a grand sight," Berkeley exclaimed, "and I never expect to see its like again."[68]

The Federals dogged the Confederate rear. Chaplain Alanson Haines of the 15th New Jersey, watching all this and sharing Berkeley's sentiments, later sketched the scene more fully:

> This advance was one of the magnificent sights of the war. From the tops of hills we could see the enemy's long lines of battle stretching across the valley, and moving away from us. Passing over cleared fields or plowed fields, their lines could hardly be distinguished from the ground, save by the flashing of their musket-barrels in the sun. Before their lines of battle were their skirmish lines, which were continually attacked by a line of our cavalry skirmishers. Behind the cavalry skirmish line was an infantry line of skirmishers, and when the first line was checked, the second immediately came up, and the enemy moved on.[69]

Sheridan halted his units south of New Market about 5:00 p.m. The ranks were broken, campfires built and the Northerners settled in for a meal and sleep. It had been an unusually warm autumn day, causing much straggling. Sheridan had tried before the halt to lure Early into an attack, using Devin's troopers as bait. When the wily Confederate didn't bite, Little Phil knew that he could not engage his foes before dark.[70]

Across the Massanutten Merritt's and Wilson's mounted divisions duelled with Wickham's troopers. The Confederates had to hold New Market Gap, which they did with a stint of fighting and Torbert's caution. Late in the day Wickham's troopers disengaged and rode southward, encamping along the South Fork. The Yankees bedded down at the foot of the gap.[71]

Even as the Union campfires flickered south of New Market on Saturday night, Early's infantry and artillery were marching. They halted at midnight, slept until daylight and then continued via Port Republic. By sunset on the 25th the foot soldiers were bivouacked in Brown's Gap of the Blue Ridge, while Lomax's cavalrymen picketed the South Fork at Port Republic. Wickham brought his division in during the night. Joseph Kershaw's division, ordered back to the Valley, came through Swift Run Gap, joining Early later in the morning.[72]

The Union army did not trail the Confederates, marching instead to Harrisonburg. By late in the afternoon the commands of Wright, Emory, Torbert and Powell covered the fields surrounding this village, which was ten miles almost due west of Port Republic. Crook's corps halted for the day at the intersection of the Pike and Keezletown road. The Pennsylvania sergeant, Henry Keiser, described the situation well in his diary: "The Rebels are scarce in the Shenandoah Valley just now."[73]

8

In The Upper Valley

The irony could have only made the defeats more embittering. Two years, plus three months, ago, in June 1862, the foot cavalry of Old Jack camped on these same grounds in the shadow of Brown's Gap. Then the Virginians, Louisianans and Georgians—there were so many of them in that spring—rested and basked in the afterglow of one of the most remarkable and brilliant military achievements of the war. Now those few that still remained were hungry, shoeless, half-naked, beaten, with little spirit. Then it had been the mid-morning of their country. Now it was its evening. The Second Corps, Stonewall's "army of the living God," had never seen worse.

The reports of inspector generals, filed September 29 and 30, detailed the extent of the toll exacted by Winchester and Fisher's Hill. The divisions of Gordon, Ramseur and Pegram mustered barely over 6,000 effectives, while Wharton could place another 1,200 in the ranks. Thomas Carter's three artillery battalions had only 23 cannon left, served by 850 officers and men. Figures for the cavalry were not reported at this time, but the mounted commands of Wickham and Lomax could not have totaled much over 3,000 troopers in the saddle.[1]

The numbers alone do not encompass the damage done to the combat quality of the Army of the Valley. Inspector generals for Ramseur's and Wharton's divisions filed fuller accountings, which specifically discussed the efficiency and discipline of the two commands. Ramseur's four brigades, formerly Rodes's, had lost their "best and efficient" officers. No field officer remained among Cox's five regiments, with the 4th North Carolina under the direction of a second lieutenant. In the other three brigades it was only slightly better: Grimes and Cook had two field officers each, while Battle counted three for five regiments. Some of the nineteen regiments did not average an officer per company. "Under these circumstances," Major H. A. Whiting of Ramseur's staff reported, "it is impossible that discipline should be kept unimpaired or even efficient. Comparatively, the discipline of the division is fair, but much impaired by the recent disaster." Whiting suggested that the empty slots be filled with temporary appointments in attempt to restore the command's discipline and fighting prowess.[2]

The crippling casualties among officers in Wharton's three brigades even surpassed those of Ramseur. Colonel Thomas Smith was the only field officer in his brigade while captains headed the other two brigades. The late George Patton's brigade numbered 2,150 in May; it now counted only 266 present for duty. "This great and almost unprecedented reduction in five months," noted the inspector, "is due exclusively to the casualties of war." Smith's inspector, First Lieutenant Henry G. Cannon, reported "the men are much worn and exhausted by the fatigues of the campaign, and the regimental and company organizations are very much broken and are quite imperfect." Cannon then added: "In many of the companies there are neither commissioned nor non-commissioned officers. The brigade discipline and general efficiency would manifestly be much improved if time and opportunity sufficed for a thorough revisal and reorganization of its several regiments and the companies belonging to them."[3]

Though neither Gordon nor Pegram had such detailed inspections completed or the reports were either not filed or subsequently lost, the situation in those units, in general, mirrored that of Ramseur and Wharton. Early, in his September 25 message to Lee, admitted that "my troops are very much shattered, the men very much exhausted, and many of them without shoes." A North Carolinian with Pegram said they were poorly fed, poorly clothed and "miserably shod." An Alabamian claimed the army's morale "was at a low ebb." A staff officer of Wickham argued that "we never witnessed a worse situation of affairs or worse demoralization among our troops."[4]

The twin defeats and the conditions at Brown's Gap brought the inevitable criticisms of Early's generalship. In one week his army had been beaten at Winchester, routed at Fisher's Hill and nearly shoved out of the Valley. No Confederate general, directing operations in the region, had ever suffered comparable setbacks. Fisher's Hill became a turning point in the troops' judgment of Old Jube's leadership. A Virginian, recalling this time in his postwar memoir, stated that after the second engagement "I always felt like giving a groan when I had to fight under Early."[5]

The censure of the lieutenant general was not confined to the army, however; it spilled over into the corridors of government and the press. Early's foremost adversary was one of his former brigade commanders, William "Extra Billy" Smith, now governor of the Old Dominion. Smith had resigned from the army following Gettysburg, after having demonstrating his own military limitations. His criticisms were not unbiased for the two men cared little for each other personally, the governor describing it as "some little unfriendliness in my relations with General Early."[6]

The state executive based his fault-finding upon correspondence from a member of Early's army, "an officer who has my entire confidence," Smith said. Writing directly to Lee, "Extra Billy" quoted from the letter. "The impression among the men," Smith's confidante informed him, is that Early "has no feeling for them, his appearance along the line of march excites no pleasure, much less enthusiasm and cheers. No salute is given. He is not greeted at all by private or officer, but is allowed to pass, and passes, neither receiving nor taking notice. The Army once believed him a safe commander, and felt that they could trust his caution, but unfortunately this has been proven a delusion and they cannot, do not, and will not give him their confidence." The critic in the ranks went on to claim that Old Jube "was surprised at Winchester . . . and Fisher's Hill was the terrible sequence."[7]

This scathing indictment, with its bleak picture of the relationship between Early and his men, Smith used to recommend that his former commander be replaced by John Breckinridge. The governor conceded that Early was brave and patriotic but, he averred to Lee, Old Jube "has no other qualities for independent command, none whatever." In a second letter to Lee, Virginia's chief executive wrote that Early's Valley campaign was "from its commencement to this hour . . . a most disastrous failure." Smith cited seven reasons for his conclusion, with their reliability supported by the views, information and opinions supplied to him "from a variety of sources" in that region. "The good of the service, by which I am governed, requires that he should be relieved," the governor concluded.[8]

Robert Lee responded promptly to Smith's charges. The Confederate chieftain, too, had received intelligence from the Valley, but his sources relayed a somewhat different version. Breckinridge, whom Lee cited, thought that Early's dispositions at Winchester were, in Lee's words, "judicious and successful until rendered abortive by a misfortune which he could not prevent and which might have befallen any other commander." Lee preferred not "to enter into any argument on these points." "The utmost caution," believed the general, must be exercised in this matter which "involves the safety of the army and the defense of the country." From his information and to his thinking, "General Early has conducted his operations with judgment, and until his late reverses rendered very valuable service considering the means at his disposal. I lament those disasters as much as yourself, but I am not prepared to say that they proceeded from such want of capacity on the part of General Early as to warrant me in recommending his recall." If a more competent officer could be found, Lee would assign him to Early's post, but the general had none in his estimation at this time. Early would stay.[9]

This exchange between the governor and the general occurred in private, but the sentiments expressed by Smith were held by thousands of civilians. Not since the reorganization of the Army of Northern Virginia after the Seven Days had one of Lee's top lieutenants been subjected to such public outcry than that which now fell upon Early. The Richmond *Enquirer*, on September 27, in a typical editorial, stated that "there seems to have been bad management in these affairs in the Valley." The newspaper, like the governor, called for Early's dismissal, suggesting that James Longstreet, who was still convalescing from his Wilderness wound, be given the command. But the *Enquirer*, endeavoring to buoy sagging spirits, argued that Sheridan's ultimate fate would be the same as Hunter's. "Neither party can permanently hold the Valley," the paper read. "Thus the events of the Valley are mere episodes of the war."[10]

Jubal Early, as we have seen, warranted censure for his bad dispositions and judgment at Fisher's Hill. He earned, in part, his veterans' doubts about his capacity for directing an army. For two months, Early had growled about his cavalry, often blaming the mounted arm for his reverses, but did little to rectify the command and discipline problems among the horsemen. His entire handling of this segment of his army seemed awkward, hesitant, with a misunderstanding of their proper role. He did not trust their reliability in battle, yet he placed the cavalrymen at the vulnerable key to his position at Fisher's Hill, which contributed significantly to the engagement's outcome.

But the critics lacked an understanding of and an appreciation for the burdens and the achievements of Early. Much of the stridency of the disapprobation resulted simply from the fact that the pair of defeats shattered the aura of Southern invincibility in the Shenandoah. Coupled with this, of course, was the memory of Stonewall Jackson rampaging through the Valley, whipping three Union forces and tilting the strategic balance in the crucial spring days of 1862. Neither Early nor any other general could hope to compare favorably to the fallen hero of the Confederacy. Old Jack had brought glory to their arms in the Valley; Old Jube had brought dishonor.

The gamble undertaken by Lee and Early in June was grand strategy in the order of two years earlier. For three months Old Jube accomplished Lee's risky designs with a combination of hard marching, tough fighting and daring bluff. In the end, it was not enough because of the long odds against the Confederates and Philip Sheridan was neither Nathaniel Banks, John Fremont nor James Shields. The Army of the Valley fulfilled much of Lee's plan, draining Union troops from Petersburg, while rekindling the expectations of a brighter time. Until Winchester and Fisher's Hill, the Confederate strategy succeeded under Early's leadership and execution. Brown's Gap then led to a crossroads in the campaign—it was a time of decision for both Southerners and Northerners.

The architect of Confederate strategy, Robert Lee, could not abandon the worn fork. It was the gambler of Second Manassas and Chancellorsville who had dispatched a fourth of his infantry to the Valley in June and supplemented the force with an infantry division, an artillery battalion and a cavalry division he could not spare. He altered the balance in Virginia to refashion his old strategy along the Blue Ridge. Lee sought victory in the Shenandoah, hoping—probably believing—that the Union military and political leadership would react as they had done when George McClellan threatened Richmond two years earlier. Grant, unlike McClellan, however, would fight with what he had at hand; besides, the diversion of Sheridan's thousands to the Valley only hindered Union operations around Petersburg, it did not cripple them. This then was the classic Lee of history, the general of the spectacular. Unfortunately for the magnificent warrior, less, not more, was required in the autumn of 1864.[11]

A crucial factor contributing to Lee's strategy was his unwillingness to accept or comprehend the powerful weapon confronting Early. The gray chieftain had always faced an opponent with superior numbers but never at such a numerical disadvantage as his Valley commander. On September 25 Early accurately informed his superior that "the enemy's force is very much larger than mine, being three or four to one." Yet two days later, Lee stated that Sheridan's "force cannot be so greatly superior to yours. His effective infantry, I do not think, exceeds 12,000 men" when, in fact, the Union foot soldiers totalled more than double that figure. His strategy, his orders, his expectations in the Valley rested, to a significant degree, upon this erroneous estimation of Federal strength.[12]

Consequently, when Lee learned of the "reverses" at Winchester and Fisher's Hill, he reacted swiftly to augment Early's army because, as he wrote, "one victory will put all things right." On the 23rd, Lee ordered Joseph Kershaw's infantry division and Wilfred Cutshaw's artillery battalion back to the Valley. For over a month the Southern general had basically misused this command, wrestling with the prospects of a victory against Sheridan and the need for every musket and cannon in the trenches at Petersburg. When Lee recalled this detachment—with Early's acquiescence—Sheridan attacked at Winchester. Old Jube suffered defeat and Lee, committed to the audacious in the region, returned Kershaw and Cutshaw to Early, abandoning his own offensive plans at Petersburg. Lee had shuffled the cards in June, raised the ante in August and, as September neared October, refused to fold, with almost fatal consequences for his own force at Petersburg.[13]

The instructions for the two units' countermarch reached Richard Anderson and his command at Gordonsville. Anderson and his staff were to continue on, while the infantry and artillery moved via Swift Run Gap into the Valley. At early light on the 24th, "in a blinding rain," Kershaw and Cutshaw started west again, reporting to Early before noon on the 26th. Kershaw's 3,100 veterans and Cutshaw's three batteries of twelve cannon increased Early's infantry strength by over forty per cent and his artillery pieces to 35.[14]

Lee additionally promised another cavalry brigade—Thomas Rosser's—and called out "all the troops in the Valley." These latter troops, reserves, numbered probably only a few hundred, under the command of Brigadier General Edwin G. Lee at Staunton. Lee also requested reinforcements, if they could be spared, from Brigadier General Raleigh E. Colston at Lynchburg and from Breckinridge's department. To the Kentuckian, with headquarters at Abingdon, Lee wired that "if possible, re-enforce Early so that I can recall Kershaw; the necessity is urgent." But Breckinridge could not release any of his units; in fact, he requested troops from Early. Only Edwin Lee moved toward Old Jube, but "my little command," as he described his reserves, participated only in one minor action.[15]

The commitment of vital manpower and more shoes, clothing and arms to Early meant that, despite Winchester and Fisher's Hill, Lee held firm to his gambling strategy. What he wanted, what he expected, he outlined in a September 27 letter to his subordinate. The commander regretted deeply the defeats, he told the lieutenant general, "but trust they can be remedied." Lee then counseled Early: "You must do all in your power to invigorate your army. Get back all absentees; maneuver so, if you can, as to keep the enemy in check until you can strike him with all your strength." From his perspective at Petersburg, the Virginian thought that Early's major error was that the latter fought his divisions piecemeal, not in concentration. "Circumstances may have rendered it necessary, but such a course is to be avoided if possible," Lee advised.[16]

Continuing, the senior officer admonished that "it will require the greatest watchfulness, the greatest promptness, and the most untiring energy on your part to arrest the progress of the enemy in his present tide of success." "I have given you all I can," added Lee, "you must use the resources you have so as to gain success. The enemy must be defeated, and I rely upon you to do it." The chieftain then suggested that Lomax's brigades be separated, with one brigade assigned to Wickham and another to Rosser when he arrived. Near the close of the letter, Lee reminded his irreverent subordinate that "we are obliged to fight against great odds. A kind Providence will yet overrule everything for our good."[17]

Lee then had done all he could to arrest the Union "tide of success"—the reversal of Confederate fortunes rested with Jubal and Jehovah, a most unlikely pair. But that river of blue, running bank full, now engulfed most of the Shenandoah, threatening not only Early's legions but Lee's lifelines and the storehouse of the Confederacy. Philip Sheridan and Ulysses Grant, more than the defeated and the divine, governed circumstances in the region.

The Army of the Shenandoah, bivouacked around Harrisonburg, had shifted, in one week, the scene of operations from near the Potomac River eighty miles southward. In the North, the news of Fisher's Hill, coming so closely after Winchester, electrified the populace. The Yankees dealt, what appeared to be, a lethal blow to a symbol of an unconquered Confederacy. Or, as Grant put it to Sheridan, the pair of victories "wipes out much of the stain upon our arms by previous disasters in that locality. May your good work continue is now the prayer of all loyal men."[18]

Republicans in the region exulted in the growing prospects of the reelection of the president. First Atlanta, then Winchester, now Fisher's Hill—a drumbeat sounding the apparent death knell of the Confederacy. It had been just a short time ago, on August 23, when Abraham Lincoln predicted his own electoral defeat, but new eddies had formed, recoursed and created a stream rushing toward triumph at the polls. And men and groups joined the flow. Gold prices plummeted after Winchester and Fisher's Hill, an inverse indicator of Union outlooks; Horace Greeley's New York *Tribune* announced support for the president; Radical Republicans rendered stump orations on behalf of Lincoln. Major General James A. Garfield, a future candidate for the office, wrote his wife that "Phil Sheridan has made a speech in the Shenandoah Valley more powerful and valuable to the Union cause than all the stumpers in the Republic can make—our prospects are everywhere heightening." A lesser soldier, a Connecticut private with Little Phil, told friends back home in a letter to their newspaper that "the 'hero of the seven days retreat' is fast becoming unpopular in the army."[19]

The outcome of the most crucial presidential election in American history was settled then on the battlefield. Atlanta turned the tide for Lincoln; Winchester and Fisher's Hill insured that it stayed the course. The victories guaranteed for the Confederacy that grim-visaged war would be even grimmer.

With his victories, Sheridan became an enormously popular hero throughout the North, with his picture adorning the walls of many households. He laid to rest the questions and concerns about his age and experience, vindicating Grant's judgment of and trust in the fiery, youthful Irishman. Brigadier General John A. Rawlins, Grant's chief of staff, addressed this in a letter. On September 25, while on temporary leave from the army, Rawlins wrote to Ely Parker, another staff member:

> One of the best military moves Grant has made since his appointment to the command of all the armies, is that of putting Sheridan in command of Washington, Baltimore and the Maryland and Penn borders. The fruits of it are our recent brilliant victories in the Shenandoah. But for the Generals persistency in having all the country contiguous to Washington put under one man Early today would have been raiding in force in both Md. & Pa., and I will venture an opinion still further, that had General Grant attempted to communicate his recent order to Sheridan to move, through Halleck, instead of going himself, he would have failed and Early would still have held his old position near Winchester. I may be mistaken in this, but I dont think I am. The fact is, Grant and Halleck have never looked through the same military glasses.[20]

Like Early and Lee, Sheridan and Grant faced strategic choices in the Valley. Little Phil, from his own observations and from his intelligence network, possessed an accurate estimation of conditions in the Rebel army at Brown's Gap. He informed Grant that every town from Winchester to New Market had Confederate hospitals, "all containing a number of wounded." The material losses incurred by Early were seen along the route of march in abandoned wagons, ambulances and accouterments. Daily between two and three dozen Southerners gave up the cause, coming through the lines and surrendering. "From the most reliable accounts," Sheridan stated, "Early's army was completely broken up and is dispirited." Union spies also reported the departure of John Breckinridge for southwestern Virginia and the arrival of Joseph Kershaw's division within days of their occurrences.[21]

For Grant, at City Point, the dispatches of Sheridan, specifying the casualties and demoralization in Early's ranks, presented the Federals with a splendid opportunity to accomplish what the General-in-Chief had sought for months. The Rebel army initially, then the region's harvests and finally the iron sinews which bound Lee's besieged troops to the supplies—these had been the Illinoisan's unwavering targets since he placed Sheridan in command. Grant wanted—expected—his subordinate, with Early's ranks shattered and disspirited, to destroy all the foodstuffs the Yankees did not consume, while advancing eastward on Charlottesville and the Virginia Central Railroad, eventually linking up with George Meade's army. Such a movement could perhaps result in the fall of Richmond and its outpost, Petersburg, within a month. Grant relentlessly reached for the vitals of his opponent.[22]

As soon as the General-in-Chief learned of Fisher's Hill, he prodded Sheridan toward this line of operations. "Keep on, and your work will cause the fall of Richmond," the lieutenant general wired on the 23rd. Three days later he followed with: "Your victories have created the greatest consternation. If you can possibly subsist your army to the front for a few days more, do it, and make a great effort to destroy the roads about Charlottesville and the canal [the James River and Kanawha] wherever your cavalry can reach it." On the 27th Grant informed Henry Halleck to have railroad repair crews ready to reopen the Orange & Alexandria tracks as he "expected" an advance by Sheridan on Charlottesville.[23]

In order to assist Sheridan and to freeze Lee's troops in their Petersburg defenses, Grant moved a scheduled offensive ahead one week. He initially thought that after Little Phil's victories Lee might bring Early eastward in a concentration against him, but he soon dismissed this, guessing that the Confederate general might detach even more troops to the Valley. On September 29, to prevent such a countermove, Grant launched the so-called Fifth Offensive, a sequential north-south strike against Lee's works at Richmond and Petersburg. The Federal assaults continued until October 2, resulting in a few limited successes. But the Confederates refashioned new lines behind those lost, and the seige resumed its deadly monotony. If Sheridan succeeded, however, a sixth offensive at Petersburg might be the final, fatal thrust.[24]

From his headquarters at Harrisonburg—the Abe Byrd residence on Red Hill—Sheridan viewed the strategic landscape somewhat differently than his fellow Westerner and superior officer. The aggressive tactician became the cautious strategist. He hinted at his thinking as early as September 24, when in a dispatch to City Point, he stated that he found it "exceedingly difficult to supply this army." "The engagements of Winchester and Fisher's Hill broke up my original plan of pushing up the Valley with a certain amount of supplies and then returning. There is not sufficient in the Valley to live off the country."[25]

Five days later, on the 29th, after reading Grant's proposals, he expanded on his considerations and views. It was still "exceedingly difficult" for the army to cross the mountains and to strike at the Virginia Central. "I cannot accumulate sufficient stores to do so," he explained, "and think it best to take some position near Front Royal, and operate with the cavalry and infantry." Sheridan planned to stay at Harrisonburg "a few days," while the work continued of making the region "a barren waste." "The destruction of the grain and forage from here to Staunton," he added, "will be a terrible blow to them." All the foodstuffs around Staunton had been retained for Early's troops, while those in the upper Valley were awaiting shipment to Richmond and Lee. He finished by stating that "the country from here to Staunton was abundantly supplied with forage and grain, etc."[26]

The Union general's argument against a descent on Charlottesville and the railroad rested then on his inability to "accumulate sufficient stores." But, when Grant, Halleck and Edwin Stanton moved to reopen the Orange & Alexandria Railroad for his use, Sheridan still demurred. He opposed this, as he wired Halleck, because "if the Orange and Alexandria Railroad is opened, it will take an army corps to protect it" from guerrillas, and Sheridan could not reduce his army with such a detachment and expect success. The Yankees lacked the wagons necessary for hauling the supplies required by such numbers of soldiers on the march. "I am ready and willing to cross the Blue Ridge," he told the Chief of staff, but it was beyond "my present means."[27]

The best policy, Sheridan believed, "will be to let the burning of the crops of the Valley be the end of this campaign," as he put it in an October 1 telegram to Grant, "and let some of this army go somewhere else." This was not what the Illinoisan wanted to hear, but Grant refused to impose officially his own predilections. The lieutenant general accepted his subordinate's argument, informing Halleck on October 2 that the railroad construction crews should cease their work on the Orange & Alexandria and turn to the Manassas Gap line. The Army of the Shenandoah, by implication, would be moving on Front Royal and not Charlottesville.[28]

Sheridan's views prevailed, but Grant's instincts were probably the correct ones. The subordinate's army lay where David Hunter's had in June, but it was a much more powerful weapon under much more superior leadership than the latter's. In a day or a day and a half of good marching the Union infantry and artillery could have been at Charlottesville. Early, if he contested the advance, would have had to do it at Waynesborough, with his outnumbered army with its back against the mountain and its escape route through one narrow gap. Sheridan had the chance to strike a mortal blow to the Confederacy, most likely shortening the war in the East by months. Instead, he responded with excuses and rationalizations. He evidently did not consider abandoning his supply lines and living off the fertile land, which by his own admission was "abundantly supplied." His cavalry, for instance, collected 3,000 head of cattle and sheep just in the area between Staunton and Mount Crawford.[29] The enterprise required daring—Sheridan chose to end the campaign. He was not the Grant of Vicksburg or the Sherman of Georgia.

Sheridan implemented his resolve to "clean out the Valley" while he and Grant shuttled messages regarding future operations. Beginning September 26, the day after their arrival at Harrisonburg, and lasting for ten days, the Federals were engaged in "devastating crops and devouring cattle." This phase of the campaign resembled the fortnight of movement and countermovement before the Winchester engagement. The Union cavalry performed most of the tasks, scorching the lush region.[30]

The destruction wrought by the Yankees encompassed the area from Port Republic, through Staunton, to Waynesborough. A Rhode Islander described the ten days as a period when "the fire demon reigned supreme." Barns, factories, mills, tracks of the Virginia Central Railroad were burned, while livestock and foodstuffs were seized by the roaming Union horsemen. The fires glowed day and night, the devastation widening with each passing day. Losses reached into the tens of thousands as civilians watched their livelihoods put to the torch. It was, however, only a precursor of more systematic destruction to come.[31]

Early, with his army encamped near Brown's Gap, endeavored with little success to restrict the limits of the Federals' handiwork. He had not the cavalry to match Sheridan's and, though he twice used the infantry against the mounted enemy, Old Jube could do little more than watch the smoke and flames rising from the countryside. On September 28, he sent his command to Waynesborough, where the Southerners routed some of Torbert's troopers and closed Sheridan's most direct route to Charlottesville. Three days later, the Confederates marched to Mount Sidney, outside of Staunton, and encamped until October 5.[32]

During this period James Wilson left the Union army. On September 25, Grant had asked Sheridan to send either Torbert or Wilson to Georgia to command Sherman's cavalry. Little Phil waited until the 30th and then selected Wilson, replacing the cavalry officer with "Autie" Custer. Wilson had not been a notably popular commander with his troopers, while Custer—the two brigadiers despised each other—proved an instant favorite. The men, said a Vermonter, "welcomed the change, though they knew it meant mounted charges, instead of dismounted skirmishing, and a foremost place in every fight." A New Yorker wrote that "the boys liked General Custer, there was some get up and get to him." For James Wilson, whose finest moment had been in the early hours at Winchester, the popular acclaim he, too, sought awaited at Selma, Alabama.[33]

Four days after Wilson's departure, Custer and his new command received orders from army headquarters for "the most heart-sickening duty we had ever performed," according to one of them. During the previous night, October 3, Lieutenant John R. Meigs, Sheridan's engineer officer, and two assistants, while conducting a military survey, encountered three Confederates on a scout outside of Dayton. What then transpired in the dusk is open to dispute. Meigs either did or did not draw his pistol, and was shot in the head by either F. M. Campbell, B. Frank Shavers or George Martin, Virginia cavalrymen. One of the assistants escaped, galloping back to headquarters, where he related the young officer's killing to Sheridan.[34]

The Union general listened to the chilling account with stunned rage. Meigs, the first son of Union Quartermaster General Montgomery C. Meigs and an 1863 graduate of West Point, ranking first in the class, had been a favorite of Little Phil. The commander liked the bright, young officer as well or better than any other on his staff. Sheridan blamed the "murder" and "atrocious act" on Rebel guerrillas and the civilians who harbored them. He wanted revenge and issued orders that all houses in Dayton and in a five-mile area surrounding the town be burned. Sheridan was determined, as he later said, "to teach a lesson to these abettors of the foul deed—a lesson they would never forget."[35]

The reprisal started that night with the burning of Noah Wenger's barn. Meigs's body had been found where it had fallen—in the road adjoining Wenger's farm. Then, with the daylight, Custer's troopers came. Though the veterans did not like the duty, they did their work well. Seventeen houses and five barns, plus some outbuildings, were destroyed. Some residents were given time to remove furnishings from their homes, others were not. One of the victims described it as a "holocaust of fire," and the area became known as the "Burnt District." Before the Yankees applied the torches to Dayton, Sheridan countermanded his instructions. Colonel Thomas F. Wildes, commander of the 116th Ohio, which occupied the community, had successfully interceded with Sheridan, convincing the latter that the residents were loyal Unionists, for the most part, and innocent. Sheridan's fury had subsided and he acceded to the request. When the Ohioans departed on the 6th, the grateful people gave them many provisions and delicacies.[36]

Sheridan, as noted, attributed the killing or murder of Meigs to Confederate guerrillas. Since the outset of the campaign, groups of these irregulars plagued Union operations, attacking wagon trains, capturing or killing stragglers. Of these commands, none was more effective and deadly than the guerrillas of John Singleton Mosby. In the midst of this decisive campaign for the Valley, another more bitter, more vicious one was fought. And some of its wounds took generations to heal.

Lieut. Col. John Singleton Mosby. USAMHI.

9

Mosby

During the last week of August, while the Army of the Shenandoah occupied the Charlestown-Halltown line, about a dozen members of Company B, 23rd Ohio, swinging their hats, shouted: "See the prisoners! Mosby a prisoner!" Soldiers nearby spread the electrifying news and it raced through the camps like a prairie fire. All activities ceased as Yankee after Yankee sprinted toward the Ohioans. "The thing took," Rutherford B. Hayes, former commander of the 23rd, related to his wife, "and the whole camp clear to army headquarters a mile off or more, perhaps ten thousand men, followed their example. Officers of course ran, major-generals and all. Then the 'sell' was discovered, and such laughing and shouting I never heard before."[1]

The Ohioans' practical joke illustrated the hold Lieutenant Colonel John Singleton Mosby and his Partisan Rangers had achieved in less than a month on the Union army. "A more harrassing enemy could not well be imagined," a New Yorker asserted of Mosby's guerrillas. Daily, in daylight and in darkness, the Rangers, like a body of apparitions, appeared suddenly, causing alarm, striking at Union outposts, pickets and wagon trains, grabbing prisoners and supplies. They were a constant presence — "a most dangerous element," to one Yankee — a factor in the campaign, which affected Union operations. Though no band of Southern guerrillas, even one as lethal as Mosby's Rangers, altered the campaign's ultimate outcome, their existence exacerbated the wounds created by the struggle for the Shenandoah. Success was measured in fleeting encounters, while reprisal came to characterize much of the combat.[2]

By the summer of 1864 Mosby and his 43rd Virginia Battalion operated with impunity east of the Blue Ridge in the four Virginia counties of Loudoun, Prince William, Fairfax and Fauquier, the area known as "Mosby's Confederacy." Since their formation in February 1863, when J. E. B. Stuart, Lee's cavalry commander, detailed Mosby and fifteen men to serve within

Union lines in northern Virginia, the Partisan Rangers frustrated every Federal effort to eradicate their command. Within a month of the unit's formation, Mosby stunned the Yankees by capturing Brigadier General Edwin H. Stoughton at his headquarters in Fairfax, Virginia. Mosby and his Rangers soon became the most effective and feared guerrilla command in the Confederacy.[3]

In the classic fashion of irregulars, the Rangers relied upon a sympathetic populace to shelter and sustain them. They had no camp or fixed quarters, no supply line to protect, no vulnerable base, for the young Rangers resided with Confederate sympathizers. Mosby's unofficial headquarters were near Piedmont, at the farm of Joseph Blackwell, a huge man whom the Rangers affectionately called "The Chief." When Mosby planned a raid, oral messages, passed from farmhouse to farmhouse, summoned his men to a rendezvous. They functioned without bugle calls and rare roll calls. The "personality" of Mosby held the command together.[4]

Mosby was thirty years old in 1864, a lawyer by profession, who would throughout his life be an "aginner," a man who sailed against the prevailing winds. Sparse, physically inconspicuous, he was "restless, hatchet-faced, with sandy hair, a high-pitched voice, a hawk-like nose and a piercing eye." He possessed unquestioned bravery, an iron mettle and with those luminous blue eyes he could scald a man's soul. He did much of his own reconnoitering, sometimes alone, usually with one or two others. "Mosby was the fastest 'scouter' I ever knew," claimed Ranger John Munson. The guerrilla chieftain confided in no one. Once, when an inquisitive Munson asked about Mosby's plans and objectives, the superior replied: "Munson, only three men in the Confederate army knew what I was doing or intended to do; they were Lee and Stuart and myself; so don't feel lonesome about it."[5]

Mosby sought youthful, fearless, superb horsemen, who "haven't sense enough to know danger when they see it, and will fight anything I tell them to." Many of the guerrillas came from the ranks of Lee's army and, if they would or could not adapt to the commander's standards and discipline, he returned them to Lee. Altogether slightly over 1,000 officers and men served in the 43rd Virginia Battalion, with approximately 800 being the maximum number at any time in the unit's existence. These rough riding daredevils had a particular fondness for fine clothes and young ladies. Their uniforms meant generally "something gray," but most had gold braid, buff trimmings on their coats and ostrich plumes in their hats. Mosby preferred a red-lined, black cape and an ostrich feather in his slouch hat. One Ranger described them as "a lot of dandies;" Mosby called them his "Tam O'Shanter Rebels."[6]

The lieutenant colonel believed that cavalry should be employed not as a powerful weapon of offense, but as a pestiferous body of scouts who hampered an opponent's plans and harried his outposts and supply lines. Mosby adhered to the classic tactics of swift movements and surprise attacks. "If you are going to fight, then be the attacker," he explained to one of his men. "That is an old principle, and it is also my own principle." He early on discarded the saber as useless—"My men were as little impressed by a body of cavalry charging them with sabers as though they had been armed with cornstalks." Instead, each Ranger carried a brace of muzzle-loading .44-caliber Colt army revolvers in belt holsters, with some having another pair in saddle holsters or in their boots. In close, swirling combat, Colts were deadly weapons against a foe armed with sabers and carbines. Mosby boasted after the war that "I think we did more than any other body of men to give the Colt pistol its great reputation."[7]

Daily three or four Ranger detachments, after meeting at a previously designated rendezvous, rode out to harass the defenses of Washington, D.C., or Federal units in the Shenandoah Valley. When the guerrillas trotted westward into the Valley, they usually crossed the Blue Ridge at Snicker's Gap and forded the Shenandoah River at Castleman's Ferry, Berry's Ferry or Rock Ford. Scouts circled each detachment, guarding against an ambush. When a Union target was located, the Rangers, rising from the mists like specters, charged in a swarm, with blazing Colts. Each Confederate attacked the Yankees on his own, in a "helter-skelter race" for the front. More often than not, the Northerners fled upon contact, offering little resistance. With their prisoners and booty—which the members divided equally among themselves—the apparitions vanished into the secluding swales of the Blue Ridge, before disbanding in Loudoun County until summoned again.[8]

When Sheridan and the Army of the Shenandoah were coming together outside of Harpers Ferry during the first week of August, Mosby had six companies in his battalion, adding an artillery company later in the month. For the Virginian, "the main object of my campaign was to vex and embarrass Sheridan and, if possible, to prevent his advance into the interior of the State." He also accelerated his excursions toward the Union capital, with the intent of preventing troops from that garrison being sent as reinforcements to Sheridan. The tenacles of the Rangers then increasingly extended beyond the Blue Ridge, against the Union host gathering for battle with Early's Confederates.[9]

The guerrillas' campaign against Sheridan's troops began on August 8, the day after Little Phil officially assumed command, and continued weeks after Early's defeat at Cedar Creek. The Rangers were a constant presence in the Valley. No Union supply train or small detachment of troops were safe from a surprise attack. On August 9, for example, Mosby and a handful of men attempted to kidnap Sheridan from his headquarters, but a Yankee picket sounded the alarm. Three days later, on the 12th, 330 Rangers intercepted a wagon train near Berryville, routing the guard, burning 75 wagons and hauling off over 200 prisoners and between 500 and 600 horses. Within a span of less than a week, Mosby had demonstrated to the Federals the danger his command could wrought.[10]

Sheridan ignored the Ranger depredations while he formed his army and undertook the first advance up the Valley. His superior, Ulysses S. Grant, suggested in two telegrams of August 16 that Sheridan commit an entire cavalry division to the destruction of Mosby's base in Loudoun County and the imprisonment of all its male residents. As for the Rangers, Grant added that "where any of Mosby's men are caught hang them without trial." Little Phil, however, was reluctant to lose the services of a mounted division for a period of time. He complied, in part, with Grant's wishes by issuing a circular to all his commanders directing them to arrest "all able-bodied male citizens under the age of fifty who may be suspected of aiding, assisting or belonging to guerrilla bands." The Southerners would be treated as prisoners of war and confined in Fort McHenry, Maryland. "A written statement should be forwarded in every case," Sheridan stated in conclusion.[11]

Instead of following Grant's suggestion of using a cavalry division, Sheridan created a unit with the sole mission of eliminating Mosby's band. The sequence of events in the formation of these Independent Scouts is unclear, but the suggestion for such a command came evidently from George Crook. Months earlier Crook had established an irregular body of 100 picked soldiers from his Ohio and West Virginia regiments to gather intelligence and suppress bushwackers. Captain Richard Blazer had led this outfit and he probably proposed to Crook that his veterans be given the new task. Sheridan approved the proposition and wired Washington, D.C., on August 20: "I have 100 men who will take the contract to clean out Mosby's gang. I want 100 Spencer rifles for them."[12]

Richard Blazer, a native West Virginian, enlisted in the 91st Ohio in September 1862, earned his captaincy while serving in the Shenandoah Valley and in the Allegheny Mountain region. A Confederate described him as a "hardened Indian fighter," who had record of capability, resourcefulness and composure in tight spots. Blazer looked like just the officer to snare the elusive Mosby.[13]

The Independent Scouts, known familiarly in the army as "Blazer's Scouts," adopted the hit-and-run methods of their opponents. Their leader understood that to engage Mosby successfully he, too, had to strike unexpectedly and swiftly. Throughout the existence of the Scouts, Blazer camped only late at night, returning to the saddle before daylight. His forays, characterized by stealth and celerity, usually lasted three or four days. The Scouts went into action upon information supplied by spies or Union sympathizers, the discovery of fresh trails or reports of a Ranger attack. They followed up any lead and operated occasionally in "Mosby's Confederacy."[14]

The duel between the Scouts and Rangers lasted from the final days of August until late in November. The Union captain and his band proved to be a formidable adversary. The Scouts gave as good as they took. On a number of occasions the Yankees surprised Ranger detachments, routing the Southerners. At the end of September Blazer and some Scouts ransacked houses in Upperville in "Mosby's Confederacy," searching for the guerrilla commander. Mosby abided the Scouts for they never seriously hampered his operations until the middle of November when a contingent of Scouts ambushed a Ranger company returning from a raid. Mosby ordered Captain A. E. Richards to take about 100 Rangers and "Wipe Blazer out! go through him." Richards's command found the Scouts on November 18 outside of Myerstown. The Rangers charged, and a running gunfight ensued into and through the village. The Southerners prevailed, bagging all but 29 of the Yankees. Blazer was among the prisoners and, with his capture, the unique three-month mission of the Independent Scouts ended. Blazer was sent to Libby Prison in Richmond, but he had earned the respect and admiration of his nemeses, a rare feat for a Union officer.[15]

While Blazer harried Rangers west of the Blue Ridge, detachments from the garrison at Washington, D.C. operated east of the mountains. Sheridan had hoped that Major General Christopher C. Augur, commander of the capital defenses, could carry the burden of operations against Mosby. Little Phil directed Augur on August 25 to picket Snicker's Gap and burn "all wheat, hay, and fodder in Loudoun County." Augur replied that day, stating that "to get information from Snicker's Gap would require a force able to manage Mosby and to apply the torch to the region" which Augur did not possess. "I will do all I can, however," the garrison commander concluded.[16]

Augur assigned most of the scouts and forays to the 13th New York Cavalry and the 8th Illinois Cavalry, commanded by Colonel Henry S. Gansevoort and Major James D. Ludslam, respectively. The two Union regiments, however, were outmatched by the intrepid Rangers. Neither could operate for any extended period of time in "Mosby's Confederacy." The Federals clashed frequently with the guerrillas, who daily harrassed the capital works, in order, as Mosby said, to "keep Augur in remembrance of his duty to guard the Capital." But, overall, Augur's cavalrymen were inadequate to the task. Henry Halleck informed Grant on September 4 that "the two small regiments under General Augur have been so often cut up by Mosby's band that they are cowed and useless for that purpose."[17]

The only real clash between Mosby's men and a sizeable body of the Army of the Shenandoah occurred on September 23, at Front Royal. Approximately 120 Rangers, under Captain Samuel Chapman, attacked a Union wagon train rumbling down Luray Valley toward Front Royal. Chapman, believing the wagons were unescorted, divided his command to sweep in on both flanks of the train. But, as he led his contingent over a rise, they encountered Colonel Charles Lowell, Jr.'s Reserve Brigade in an unbroken column of fours. The Federals, the leading unit of two divisions, were enroute from Milford following their action of the previous day.[18]

Chapman, realizing that his entire command could be trapped, ordered his detachment to Chester's Gap and galloped toward the other wing, led by Captain Walter E. Franklin. Chapman was too late as Lowell's rawhide tough Regulars stormed into the startled Rangers. "They came up like a flock of birds when a stone is cast into it," averred a Southerner. Chapman and Frankland rallied the shattered band, directing them toward the gap. The Yankees swarmed after the fleeing Rebels. "A few of Mosby's men," stated a witness, "turned occasionally and fought bravely but hopelessly against the overpowering odds." Much of the fighting swirled around in the bottom land of Perry Criser's "Oak Hall" farm near the gap road. The raiders bolted for the defile only to have their escape barred by more of Lowell's troopers, who had circled east of Front Royal. The two adversaries blasted each other with pistols and carbines, but the momentum of the Southerners pierced the Union ranks, opening an avenue of escape. In the rear of the Rangers, Lieutenant Charles McMaster, 2nd United States Cavalry, lay fatally wounded with a bullet in his head. McMaster's bridle rein had been clipped in the exchange, and his frightened horse plunged into the midst of the Confederates. In the excitement and confusion, some of the Northerners believed that the lieutenant had been gunned down after he surrendered.[19]

The pursuit spilled into the mountain hollows, where the Federals overtook six of the Rangers. In Front Royal, meanwhile, the mistaken report about the circumstances of McMaster's wounding had infuriated the Union cavalrymen. One of Custer's Wolverines said that when he arrived he "found the town in an uproar." Lowell's men soon entered the village with the six prisoners, one of them a terrified teenager bound between two horses. The Yankees—their command had been notably victimized by Mosby—clamored for revenge. Merritt, Custer, Lowell and probably Torbert were all present. Though some accounts blame Custer or Lowell, Merritt ordered the immediate executions of the Rangers. Lowell, who regretted his role in the affair, told his wife in a October 5 letter that "it was all by order of the Division Commander." Torbert probably concurred with the order.[20]

A group of Yankees then grabbed two of the captives, David Jones and Lucian Love, and shot them in the yard behind the Methodist Church. Other Federals, meanwhile, led a third Ranger, Thomas E. Anderson of Markham, Virginia, to Perry Criser's farm, stood him under an elm tree and shot him, too.[21]

The fourth prisoner was not a member of the 43rd Virginia Battalion but a 17-year-old resident of the town, Henry C. Rhodes. When Frankland's men passed through the village enroute to their attack point, young Rhodes, who dreamed of becoming a Ranger, borrowed a neighbor's horse, which broke down in the swift retreat. The teenager was now nearly unconscious, facing execution. His widowed mother, learning of her son's capture from friends, ran to the Northerners, pleading for his life. One callous trooper, drawing his saber, threatened to behead both mother and son. Men from Custer's brigade then led the youth to a field at the foot of "Rose Hill," the Richardson family residence. A screaming, helpless Mrs. Rhodes followed. A Wolverine untied Rhodes's hands, ordering him to stand up. The dazed boy staggered forward, and the cavalryman emptied his pistol into him. From a shuddered window of "Rose Hill," Sue Richardson, watching in horror, described what followed. "We could see the crowd assembled around him," she wrote, "then we had the pain of seeing the stock passing over him before his body could be removed. His poor mother is almost crazy." A Michigander admitted that it was a "hard war."[22]

The remaining two prisoners had been taken to the local wagon yard, where their captors interrogated them about Mosby's headquarters. The Federals offered them their lives for the information, but the pair—one a large Georgian, William Thomas Overby, and the other named Carter—refused. Men from McMaster's troop led them to a large walnut tree north of the town, while a band played "Love Not, The One You Love May Die." Given one more chance to betray Mosby, both again refused. A weeping Carter prayed and a defiant Overby told his executioners that "Mosby'll hang ten of you for every one of us." Two whips cracked, and it was done.[23]

Before the Northerners departed, one of them hung a placard on Overby. It read: "Such is the fate of all of Mosby's men." With the Union horsemen gone, the townsfolk walked into the streets, staring at the victims. "The sight was the most ghastly incident our citizens had ever witnessed," exclaimed one of them. Another, a young girl, called it the "dark day of 1864," a nightmare which "clouded my childhood." The residents of Front Royal never forgot and, thirty-five years later, on September 23, 1899, they and about 150 surviving Rangers dedicated a monument to their comrades and townfolk. The twenty-five-foot granite shaft still shadows the graves of four of the Confederates in Prospect Hill Cemetery.[24]

Mosby learned of the executions on September 29. He blamed Custer for the cold-blooded acts and determined, in his words, "to demand and enforce every belligerent right to which the soldiers of a great military power were entitled by the laws of war. But I resolved to do it in the most humane manner, and in a calm, judicial spirit." "It is my purpose," Mosby informed Lee a month later, "to hang an equal number of Custer's men whenever I capture them." Lee authorized the retaliatory executions, forwarding Mosby's letter to Secretary of War James A. Seddon, who concurred.[25]

The Ranger commander did not subordinate his operations to his desire for retaliation. During October, with the Federals scorching the upper Valley around Harrisonburg, Mosby concentrated more of his operations against Sheridan's extended supply and communication lines and the re-opened Baltimore & Ohio Railroad. Union supply trains, moving from the depot at Martinsburg to the front, became particularly inviting targets. Sheridan detached entire brigades as wagon guards. The railroad, in turn, was protected by troops from Harpers Ferry. But Mosby penetrated this latter screen and, early on the 14th, derailed a westbound express. The Confederates seized some Union officers, including two paymasters, carrying $173,000 in greenbacks. The Rangers, as was their custom, divided the spoils equally in $2,200 shares. The operation was dubbed the "Greenback Raid."[26]

Three weeks after this brilliant exploit, during the early days of November, the battalion settled the score for Front Royal. Mosby assembled his command at Rectortown on the 6th, after two detachments, operating along the Valley Pike, brought in 26 members of George Custer's division. Mosby, disregarding conflicting information, blamed Custer for the executions—in fact, he never doubted Custer's role nor questioned the justification for his act of reprisal. The assembled prisoners, standing before Mosby in an irregular line, laughing, swapping stories, were two officers, twenty-two troopers and two drummer boys. They had no suspicion of their fate until the battalion's adjutant walked to their front and calmly informed them that seven—Union Colonel William Powell had recently hanged Ranger A. C. Willis—were to be selected for execution.[27]

The stunned Northerners then passed slowly from hand to hand a worn hat containing 26 slips of paper with seven marked with the sentence of death. A number of them mumbled prayers; one cried frantically. One of the drummer boys, as the hat approached, became hysterical. "O God, spare me!" he sobbed. "Precious Jesus, pity me!" But, when he secured a blank piece, he leaped into the air, shouting: "Damn it, ain't I lucky." Six troopers and the other drummer boy picked the slips of death.[28]

The spared cavalrymen huddled, talked quietly until one of them, approaching Ranger Sergeant Guy Broadwater, requested a redrawing to replace the drummer. Broadwater relayed the request to Mosby, who readily assented. The Federals reenacted what Mosby called "the painful scene," with one of the officers choosing the marked slip.[29]

The guerrilla chief assigned Lieutenant Ed Thompson the duty of execution. Thompson's detail then rode westward, through Ashby's Gap, where they met Captain R. P. Mountjoy and Company D returning from a raid with more of Custer's men. Mountjoy was a handsome, fearless Mississippian who dressed fastidiously and always wore a Masonic emblem. The condemned Union officer, recognizing a fellow Mason, signalled Mountjoy with the lodge's distress sign. The Mississippian convinced Thompson to swap the officer for one of the former's prisoners. When Mosby learned from Mountjoy of the exchange, he angrily reminded the captain that the 43rd Virginia Battalion "was no Masonic lodge."[30]

Thompson's men carried out the sentences in Beemer's Woods near Berryville. The Rangers hanged three Yankees but, then through carelessness or a lack of fervor for the duty, shot two more, killing neither. The sixth and seventh prisoners, one of whom was G. H. Soule, 5th Michigan Cavalry, escaped after punching a guard. The identities of the three lynched Federals are unknown. Before the Rebels departed, Thompson pinned a note to one of the corpses; it read: "These men have been hung in retaliation for an equal number of Colonel Mosby's men hung by order of General Custer, at Front Royal. Measure for Measure."[31]

On November 11 Mosby wrote personally to Sheridan. In it the Confederate recounted Custer's and Powell's executions of his men, explained his reprisal and concluded: "Hereafter any prisoner falling into my hands will be treated with the kindness due their condition, unless some new act of barbarity shall compel me reluctantly to adopt a course of policy repulsive to humanity."[32]

The hangings in Beemer's Woods and Mosby's message ended the feud. The Union cavalrymen still harbored a bitter hatred for the Confederate irregulars, but the "dark day" at Front Royal was not duplicated again. Mosby, for his part, had maintained a policy of treating captives as prisoners of war, sending them on to Richmond for imprisonment. The Rangers definitely gunned down Yankees, who were engaged in burning barns and ransacking houses. The deep animosity between the antagonists resulted considerably from the embarrassment and the victimization of the Northerners by the Rebels. It could have resulted, in part, from erroneous reports claiming that some Federals were murdered after they surrendered, like Charles McMaster. It was simply, as the Michigan trooper noted, a "hard war."

Finally, with the rout of Early's army at Cedar Creek and the elimination of Blazer's Scouts, Sheridan sent his cavalry into "Mosby's Confederacy." From November 28 to December 3, Wesley Merritt's division implemented Sheridan's instructions to "consume and destroy all forage and subsistence, burn all barns and mills and their contents, and drive off all stock in the region" between the Bull Run Mountains and the Shenandoah River on the east and west, and the Potomac River and Manassas Gap Railroad, north and south. But these six days of smoke and flame did not eradicate the 43rd Virginia Battalion. No Union commander ever succeeded in this. Mosby's Rangers eventually disbanded on April 21, 1865, twelve days after Lee surrendered at Appomattox.[33]

The impact of Mosby's operations on the Shenandoah Valley campaign is difficult to assess. A Union staff officer claimed that the Rangers "caused perhaps more loss than any single body of men in the enemy's service." They and other guerrilla bands—irregulars under John McNeill, John Q. Winfield and John W. Mobberly—were a constant presence in the Union rear and along blue-clad picket posts. One Yankee asserted that after Third Winchester, Confederate guerrillas were "as thick as *Fiddlers down below.*" Sheridan, conversely, believed that Mosby served a positive good for the Union army. "I had constantly refused to operate against these bands," he stated in his report, "believing them to be substantially, a benefit to me, as they prevented straggling and kept my trains well closed up, and discharged such other duties as would have required a provost guard of at least two regiments of cavalry."[34]

No other Confederate partisan command operated with the prowess of Mosby's Rangers. The 43rd Virginia Battalion repulsed all attempts at their elimination, terrorized Union outposts and wagon trains, embarrassed Union soldiers and their military and civilian leaders and cost the North hundreds of thousands of dollars. Mosby's most important contribution might have been instilling in Sheridan the belief that his army could not sustain their supply line for an advance on Charlottesville. If this were the case, Mosby and his redoubtable band delayed the fall of Petersburg and Richmond. But, in the end, the struggle for the Shenandoah was decided by the veteran fighters with Little Phil and Old Jube. In the heart of the Valley, not in "Mosby's Confederacy," was the true drama.

10

The Rebels Are "Disposed Of"

The Civil War was America's great convulsion. Begun with stirring rhetoric and antiquated, romantic notions of warfare, the conflict slid the nation — inexorably — into an abyss. The searing furnace of battle soon shattered the illusions with appalling casualties. Obscure places, rechristened in carnage — Shiloh, Antietam, Gettysburg, Cold Harbor — transformed Americans' perceptions and values. By late summer and early autumn of 1864 the war had gone too far; too many families, in the North and in the South, had mourned in the long sadness of night. For the Union, retreat could never be called again — the war had to be won.

Ulysses Grant grasped this reality as did none of his predecessors. An uncompromising "hard-war man," the General-in-Chief suffered from few illusions about the act of making war. His spring offensive of 1864 brought unrelenting pressures against the Confederacy, a war of attrition. It also became a conflict of staggering human and material cost, but the fall of Atlanta and the victories at Third Winchester and Fisher's Hill justified the sacrifices. The Confederacy reeled under these blows in Georgia and in the Shenandoah Valley, and Grant wanted to insure that the Southern nation never recovered.[1]

For the General-in-Chief, Sheridan's campaign in the Valley of Virginia had a two-fold purpose: the defeat of the Rebel defenders and the destruction of the lush region. Once Grant understood that his soldiers could probably not attain victory in the Old Dominion without the reduction of the Shenandoah, he made it an integral part of Federal operations. His initial order to Sheridan reminded that officer that "in pushing up the Shenandoah Valley, as it is expected you will have to go, first or last, it is desirable that nothing should be left to invite the enemy to return." The Illinoisan then admonished: "Take all provisions, forage, and stock wanted for the use of your command; such as cannot be consumed, destroy."[2] No longer, in Grant's reckoning, would the Valley's fertile limestone soil, its tanneries, its mills feed the Confederates, give them leather for shoes and harness and supply them with mounts.

Sheridan, as we have seen, implemented Grant's instructions with increasing severity as the campaign progressed. For the first seven weeks of operations, Early limited the incendiarism, barring the gateway to the upper Valley, and the larders of the granary brimmed. The Union victories at Winchester and Fisher's Hill unhinged the gate, however; the torch-bearing Yankees poured into the heart of the region. What had been generally sporadic became daily from September 26 to October 5 in the Harrisonburg-Port Republic-Staunton area. "The burning of the crops," as Little Phil expressed it, should be the termination of the campaign and part of his army should "go somewhere else." On October 5, then, he issued orders for a full-scale retrograde movement down the Valley. He intended to leave in his wake an ashen ruin, "a barren waste."[3]

From Thursday, October 6, through Saturday, October 8, Union cavalrymen methodically blasted, burned, slaughtered and devastated nearly everything which could sustain Early's legions between the Alleghenies and the Blue Ridge. The destruction was systematic and purposeful, ravaging the upper Valley with a fury and power no natural force had ever brought. The withdrawal was a deeper slide into the abyss, another inevitable step away from the past. Chaplain John Adams, 121st New York, wrote home on October 4 that "war is terrible in its effects, but the Rebels should have anticipated this before they ventured to test its scathing scourages."[4] But no Confederate soldier or Valley resident could have foreseen the destruction which occurred—Americans had never before seen such demolition, executed with this skill and thoroughness.

"Clouds of smoke marked the passage of the Federal army," noted a Michigan cavalry officer. "The march from Harrisonburg was memorable on account of the sight of burning barns, mills, stacks of hay and grain," a Vermont infantryman remarked. "Pillars of smoke surrounded us through all of the three days." To a Pennsylvanian, "the blackened face of the country from Port Republic to the neighborhood of Fisher's Hill bore frightful testimony to fire and sword." "The Valley is all ablaze in our rear," as another Keystone State volunteer portrayed it.[5]

To trailing Confederates, the scene differed little from Federal descriptions. "On every side, from mountain to mountain," wrote a Virginia trooper, "the flames from all the barns, mills, grain and hay stacks, and in very many instances from dwellings, too, were blazing skyward, leaving a smoky trail of desolation to mark the footsteps of the devil's inspector-general." Another cavalryman remembered that "as it grew dark, the whole horizon in the line of Sheridan's retreat was one bright sheet of flames." "In every direction," he continued, "were visible marks of the fiery ordeal with which the country had been scourged—the most terrible it had ever been subjected to. It was almost literally reduced to ashes." "The very air is impregnated with the smell of burning property," a graycoat scribbled in his diary. He found a plank left by the Yankees, who printed "Remember Chambersburg" on it.[6]

Sheridan assigned the primary responsibility to Torbert and his three divisions. While the infantry, artillery and wagons followed the Valley Pike, the cavalry formed a cordon across the army's rear. Merritt's division covered the Middle Road and the Pike. Westward, on the Back Road, Custer's horsemen rode. Finally, Powell's division, across the Massanutten Mountain, guarded Sheridan's flank in the Luray Valley.

The mobile horsemen ravaged the entire area from Harrisonburg to Strasburg. The amount of property damaged was staggering; one historian of the area calculated the loss at twenty million dollars based on the value of depreciated Confederate currency in 1864. Powell, for example, destroyed Peter Borsk's tannery and stockpile of unfinished leather, which was "used for the exclusive benefit of the rebel army," assessing its value at $800,000.[7]

Merritt reported that his division in ten days, with most of it concentrated between the 6th and the 8th, burned 630 barns, 47 flour mills, 4 saw mills, 1 woolen mill, 3 iron furnaces, 2 tanneries, 1 railroad depot, 1 locomotive and 3 boxcars. His cavalrymen also torched nearly 4,000 tons of hay, straw and fodder, about a half of a million bushels of wheat and oats, 515 acres of corn and 560 barrels of flour, while driving off 3,300 head of livestock. Merritt computed the damages at $3,304,672.[8]

During the evening of October 7 Sheridan telegraphed Grant summarizing their handiwork. Little Phil reported that his men burned over 2,000 barns filled with grain and implements and over 70 mills laden with wheat and flour. The army confiscated over 4,000 head of livestock and killed not less than 3,000 sheep for meat. Additionally, a large number of horses were confiscated. "This destruction," Sheridan informed Grant, "embraces the Luray Valley and Little Fort Valley, as well as the main valley." Concluding, the army commander stated that "when this is completed the Valley, from Winchester up to Staunton, ninety-two miles, will have but little in it for man or beast.[9]

Sheridan's accurate assessment ignored the human hardship his figures entailed. The Union policy eliminated the Valley as "a great magazine of stores for the Confederate armies" for the duration of the war, but at a staggering cost of suffering for the residents of the Shenandoah. A food panic in Rockingham County ensued in the wake of the Union withdrawal. "The condition of things in Rockingham County is most deplorable," a Confederate official reported to Richmond on October 12. The citizens of Rockingham and Shenandoah counties remembered the time simply as "The Burning."[10]

Thousands of residents chose to abandon their scarred land. Most of the refugees were slaves, Dunkers and Mennonites, a category of people an Ohioan soldier called "counter-Bands." The Dunkers, remarked a Northerner, "universally seemed scared almost to death when they saw us coming." From the vicinity of Harrisonburg over 400 wagons, loaded with people and possessions, joined the Union retreat. "The people here are getting sick of the war," Sheridan wired Grant, "heretofore they have had no reason to complain, because they have been living in great abundance." Though many of the Dunkers and Mennonites had been conscripted into Confederate service and left for this reason, their exodus testified to the region's ruin.[11]

Sheridan's systematic and purposeful devastation of the Valley sur- passed—except for Sherman's March to the Sea—any Union operation. The granary of the Confederacy lay smoldering in ruin. The pillars of smoke which wafted skyward—the symbols of a scarred land and a waning cause—marked, the Union commander believed, the final defeat of the Confederates in the Shenandoah.

The conflagration hung as a darkening cloud over Early's camps. The recuperating Southerners lacked the strength and prowess to prevent the burning by Sheridan's horsemen. Old Jube's most pressing need remained his lack of disciplined, well-armed and well-mounted cavalry. After Fisher's Hill Early implored Lee for additional mounted units, and the Confederate com- mander sent the brigade of Brigadier General Thomas L. Rosser. Leaving the lines at Petersburg on September 28, Rosser's veterans arrived at Early's posi- tion around Mount Sidney on October 5, the day before the Federals started northward, commencing their burning.[12]

Thomas Rosser, who reported to Early two days before his command arrived, would be twenty-eight years old on October 15, a native Virginian who grew to manhood in Texas. He had resigned from West Point in April 1861, two weeks before graduation, and entered Confederate service. A handsome giant of a man, Rosser became a favorite of J. E. B. Stuart and, at Stuart's instiga- tion, he rose to the colonelcy of the 5th Virginia Cavalry and then to com- mand of the so-called "Laurel Brigade." The Texan's assignment to Early was a reunion of the two officers. During the winter of 1863–1864 Rosser had served under Old Jube, but an incident had strained their relationship. The young brigadier, unable to endure separation from his wife, managed to have her join him at Staunton. Early, neither understanding nor appreciating the love- sick officer's needs as a husband, reacted characteristically, harboring a preju- dice against Rosser. What the cavalry officer did to displease Early remains unclear, but the latter groused to Lee that "the affair I mentioned to you of his coming here after his wife." Rosser's raid on Moorefield in January–February 1864 somewhat redeemed his reputation with his caustic superior and now, months later, Early evidently overlooked the incident in his need for Rosser's proven ability.[13]

The Valley commander immediately assigned the horse officer to com- mand of Williams Wickham's division. Except for the engagement at Milford, Wickham had not done notably well at the head of his two brigades, and he was waiting to take his seat in the Confederate Congress. With Rosser's arrival, Wickham left the army, finally resigning his commission on Novem- ber 9. Wickham's departure also placed his former brigade in the hands of Thomas Munford, who had been directing it for the past few weeks. But this brought Munford under command of Rosser, a man the Virginia colonel despised. Rosser's rise, under Stuart's prodding, had been at the cost of a deserved promotion for Munford, who naturally blamed the Texan. "I always had a contempt" for Rosser, Munford said in a postwar letter. "We were in the same Brigade for years but he never was in my tent or I in his." Munford conceded that Rosser fought gallantly in combat, but the brigadier "lacked other *qualities* which made it incompatible with my feelings ever to associate with him." Munford never submitted a report while serving under Rosser and, when the colonel came to pen his reminiscences years later, he rendered a scorching indictment of his former commander.[14]

More importantly for Early and his army, Rosser's 600 horsemen, many of them natives of the Valley, brought strength and confidence to the cavalry. The "Laurel Brigade" had their flags trimmed in laurel, and the men wore badges of three to five laurel leaves. Veteran cavalrymen, with many past victories over Union horseflesh, the general and his troopers boasted of their fighting prowess and their ability to purge their beloved Shenandoah of the Northern menace. Rosser, or someone else, began describing the cavalry officer as the "Savior of the Valley." It proved to be a heavy burden.[15]

When Early learned of Sheridan's march northward, he directed his cavalry "to pursue the enemy, to harass him and to ascertain his purposes." Rosser's division followed the retiring Federals along the Back Road while Lunsford Lomax's division rode northward on the Valley Pike. From the 6th, through the 8th, the Southerners harried the Union rear guard units, clashing frequently with Northern cavalrymen. By nightfall of the 8th, Rosser's troopers lay south of Tom's Brook, opposing George Custer's division; Lomax held Woodstock which was south of Wesley Merritt's Yankees positioned north of Tom's Brook, extending Custer's left flank. The Confederate infantry and artillery, meanwhile, were encamped over 20 miles south of Rosser and Lomax, well beyond immediate support. Early and the two cavalry officers had combined to place their mounted units in grave danger, facing an old horse soldier noted for his aggressiveness.[16]

Sheridan had every intention of teaching the Confederates a lesson. That night he sent for Torbert. "Mad clear through" with Rosser's and Lomax's annoyances, Sheridan tersely told his cavalry commander to "start out at daylight and whip the rebel cavalry or get whipped." He added that he wanted Torbert to "finish this 'Savior of the Valley.'" The Union boss wanted all of the cavalry officer's two divisions thrown into the attack, no reserves, no details guarding led horses or wagons. Before Torbert, who "seemed to be in a brown study," departed, Sheridan informed the subordinate that he would ride to Round Top Mountain and personally witness the destruction of the brash Rosser.[17]

Torbert's approximately 4,000 troopers stirred early. Merritt, along the Pike, initiated the action by forcing a crossing of the brook. Charles Lowell,

Jr.'s brigade of Regulars advanced on the left, while Thomas Devin's brigade moved in the center, his right connecting with James Kidd, who had deployed to support Custer on the Back Road. Lomax countered Merritt's deployment with William Jackson engaging Lowell and Bradley Johnson blunting Devin's tenative moves. The Confederates successfully impeded the Federals, but both Merritt and Lomax seemed content to await developments on the Back Road.[18]

Custer's troopers had been in the saddle before Merritt's for they had to ride farther. The 5th New York, under Major Abram H. Krom, led the Union advance and directly beyond Mount Olive encountered pickets of the 4th Virginia. Krom's skirmishers easily pressed the Virginians back on their main position at Tom's Brook. Krom's troopers halted before this line of dismounted cavalry deployed behind a stone fence and a barricade of rails and logs. Custer rode forward and, after surveying the Confederate position, ordered Captain Charles H. Pierce's 2nd United States Artillery, Batteries B and L, to the right of the road, with the gunners soon shelling the crossing.[19]

Munford, meanwhile, on the south side of the stream, notified Rosser of Custer's advance and aligned his brigade. The Southern position rested on a high ridge of hills which covered the crossings of Tom's Brook. Munford posted the 4th at the base of the ridge where the road crossed the creek. He then moved the 1st and 2nd Virginia upstream to the left, deploying them on the ridge. The 3rd Virginia secured Munford's right and rear east of the road. Richard Dulany's brigade moved downstream on Munford's right while William Payne deployed as a reserve, his regiments overlapping the road. Behind Munford and Dulany six cannon responded to Pierce's distant shelling.[20]

The fire from Rosser's horse artillery forced Custer to deploy Colonel Alexander C. M. Pennington's leading brigade. With the 2nd Ohio on the left, the 3rd New Jersey in the center and Krom's 5th New York on the right, Pennington's men advanced as mounted skirmishers. Pierce's gunners limbered up and trailed the troopers, redeploying once more. Neither Pennington nor Pierce could go much farther against the enemy artillery and rifle fire. Colonel William Wells's brigade, to Pennington's rear, remained inactive, unable to assist Pennington's regiments on the narrow front.[21]

Rosser's "stubborn resistance" had succeeded in keeping Custer, an old friend, at bay for two to three hours. Stalemated, Custer ordered the 18th Pennsylvania, supported by the 8th and 22nd New York regiments, to the right in a flanking maneuver. The three regiments encountered rugged ground and numerous fences before finally reaching a point opposite the Confederate left. The Pennsylvanians formed in front with the 8th New York directly to their rear, aligned in three columns. Custer ordered the charge sounded and the entire Federal line surged toward the ridge.[22]

The flank attack of the Pennsylvanians and New Yorkers burst upon the

1st and 2nd Virginia. On the road, Custer—a "terrible demon" in combat, according to one of his men—personally led the assault, riding beside Sergeant John Buckley, color bearer of the 5th New York, in the very forefront. "Our Regt. made one of the most splendid charges they ever made," bragged Trooper Charles R. Farr of his 1st Vermont Cavalry. Munford's and Dulany's line dissolved before these combined charges. The Confederate gun crews joined the flight, endeavoring to overtake the wagon train which was also stampeding southward. Payne's brigade, whose left crumbled under the flank attack, offered no resistance. The exultant Federals, their commands badly mixed, pursued for two miles to Pugh's Run, where the Confederate artillery and Munford's brigade checked the van of Custer's column. Wells and Pennington hastily deployed the disorganized units and, with Kidd advancing on their left and Pierce's artillery support, dismembered the patchwork front.[23]

The pursuit now became a race for the seizures of prizes, with individual troopers displaying reckless daring. Most of the Yankees rode toward the guns and wagons. Private Samuel Fry, 18th Pennsylvania, galloped alone toward a fleeing caisson and gun, sabered the driver and forced him to turn around. Private Smith Allen, of the same regiment, though shot in the neck, duplicated Fry's feat. Another Pennsylvanian, Lieutenant J. R. Winters, leading a detachment, galloped with drawn saber into a woods filled with Confederates. Winters's bravery cost him his life but secured a number of wagons and ambulances. Corporal Charles A. Miner, 5th New York, also dispersed some Southerners in a solitary charge, securing a wagon and six mules as his reward. One of Miner's officers, Lieutenant M. Strait, personally captured Rosser's headquarters wagon and the general's saddle. When the wild pursuit ended, the Confederates had lost their entire wagon train and six cannon.[24]

Only "the most gallant of this affrighted herd," according to Custer, tried to stop the jubilant Northerners. Many of the Confederates halted at Columbia Furnace, where Rosser and Munford assembled only a remnant of the command. "A more discomfited body I never imagined. . . . He had had not even a clean shirt—wagons and all were gone," wrote a disgusted Munford. Custer echoed these sentiments when he boasted that "never since the opening of this war had there been such a complete and decisive overthrow of the enemy's cavalry."[25]

Merritt, on the Pike, equalled Custer's victory. When the division commander heard the firing to the west receding southward, he ordered Lowell and Devin forward. The Confederate line lay on both sides of the road among trees and on a series of knolls. Johnson's horsemen manned Lomax's left while Jackson's troopers faced Lowell's brigade on the right. Supporting the Rebel cavalry was Lieutenant John McNulty's four cannon of the 2nd Maryland Baltimore Light Artillery, unlimbered on a hill outside of Woodstock. Lomax offered a bold front but his troopers lacked sabers and pistols, being armed with only Enfields. "The consequence is," Early wrote Lee, "that they cannot fight on horseback, and in this open country cannot successfully fight on foot against large bodies of cavalry; besides, the command is and had been demoralized all the time." The Confederate commander even considered turning them into infantry but, he concluded, "if that were tried I am afraid they would all run off."[26]

When the Yankees advanced, Lomax, also knowing what the distant gunfire meant, slowly withdrew his two brigades onto the open country near Woodstock. No longer protected by the favorable terrain, they deployed to meet the oncoming Federals. Suddenly, galloping up the Pike, came the 1st United States Cavalry, supported by the 5th United States Cavalry and the 2nd Massachusetts Cavalry. The Union charge severed the Southern line in its center and Jackson's ranks broke. Devin's troopers, cantering across the fields, crumbled Johnson's left and the entire Confederate cavalry front evaporated. Only McNulty's cannon, firing grape and canister through the streets of the town, opposed the Union advance. But with gray horsemen galloping through and around the town, McNulty had no choice but to retreat, abandoning one disabled piece.[27]

The Confederate retreat quickly turned into a rout. "I was unable to rally this command," Lomax admitted. "The success of the day," Merritt reported, "was now merely a question of the endurance of horseflesh." For 20 miles the two forces engaged in a galloping race. Unlike Rosser's men, Lomax's offered only "fitful" resistance. "Each time our troopers came in view," added Merritt, "they would rush on the discomfited rebels with their sabers, and send them howling in every direction." A Southern witness stated that his mounted comrades came fleeing up the Pike "some without arms, some without hats, some without jackets, and some without sensibility."[28]

The pursuit ended when Lomax's demoralized troopers reached Early's infantry lines at Rude's Hill. Tom's Brook lay 26 miles to the north. In between the Union cavalry division counted its booty: 42 wagons, 3 ambulances, 4 cannon, 4 caissons, 5 forges, 25 sets of harness, 68 horses and mules, 52 prisoners and 1 wagon loaded with Enfield rifles. Private Edward R. Hanford, 2nd United States Cavalry, displayed the flag of the 34th Battalion Virginia Cavalry which he captured and for which he earned a Congressional Medal of Honor.[29]

The Battle of Tom's Brook was, as Sheridan said, "a square cavalry fight," which resulted in a smashing Federal victory. At a cost of 9 killed and 48 wounded, his cavalry routed the Confederates "beyond my power to describe." Everyone in the corps rejoiced in the thrashing of the "Savior of the Valley." Torbert described it as "the most decisive the country had ever witnessed," while Merritt claimed that "never has there been, in the history of this war, a more complete victory." The entire Union army enjoyed the success. "When the trophies began to come in," Captain John Suter, 54th Pennsylvania, told his wife, "it caused a regular laugh for it was the most fantastic parade I ever saw in military style."[30]

In the Confederate camps, despair gave way to later recrimination. Quick-witted butternuts soon referred to the "Laurel Brigade" as the "Pumpkin Vine" brigade in honor of their running from Tom's Brook. Most of the castigation naturally fell upon Rosser, the anointed "Savior of the Valley." Major Ferguson, Fitz Lee's former aide, confided to his diary that "the misfortunes of the day are, I think, to be attributed to the injudicious orders from Early, rashness on the part of Gen. Rosser and the misbehavior of the 1st and 3rd [Virginia] Regts. Rosser's [Dulany's] Brigade was so located as to be unable to render any very efficient service in checking the advance of the enemy when first breaking our lines." The commanders of the Virginia regiments— Colonel Richard Carter and Major Henry Carrington, respectively—were relieved.[31]

The most scathing and bitter indictment of Rosser's performance came from Munford in his postwar writings. The colonel attributed the rout, in part, to the fact that "Rosser's head seemed to be completely turned by our success" on the three days preceding the engagement. Expanding on this, Munford asserted that at Tom's Brook "we suffered the greatest disaster that had ever befallen our command, and utterly destroyed the confidence of the officers of my brigade in his [Rosser's] judgment—they knew that he could fight and was full of it, but he did not know when to stop, or when to retire." In another piece of writing, Munford claimed that at Tom's Brook his command "lost more in that one fight than we had ever done before, in all of our fights together."[32]

Rosser's injudicious rashness certainly placed his undermanned command in a precarious position against a formidable opponent. Early, likewise, by permitting his cavalry to be so removed from infantry support, has to share some of the blame for the rout. A New York cavalryman offered an interesting argument about the Southern horsemen's penchant for boldness and derring-do. "It did seem," the Yankee avowed, "as though nearly every Rebel cavalry officer had been touched with a magic wand which filled him with the most weird and romantic views of warfare."[33] But by this date in the war, firepower and numbers in the saddle had replaced knightly thrusts by horsemen in gray, and Tom's Brook epitomized the Confederate cavalry's descent from the glorious days of 1862 to this autumn of attrition and blighted dreams.

So decisive did the Confederate defeat at Tom's Brook appear that on the day of the engagement Captain Peter Eltinge of the 156th New York wrote his father of the latest camp gossip racing through the army's ranks. "It has been the current report here for the past day or two," Eltinge informed his father, "that this army of Sheridan was ordered to be in Washington by the 15th of this month."[34]

This speculation was propelled by the Yankees' nearly universal belief that the Confederate Army of the Valley had been whipped beyond redemption. The Northerners considered their foes to be "thoroughly and permanently broken, dispirited, and disposed of." A member of the XIX Corps scribbled in his own phonetic style a letter to his sister stating that "i dont think that our regiment will ever be in any fight agane they talk of sending us back to loisanna agane this winter."[35]

No member of the Union army adhered to this belief with firmer assurance than its commander, Philip Sheridan. To him the campaign had concluded and, as he argued to Ulysses Grant while at Harrisonburg, saw his duty now as dispatching, segmentally, units of his army "somewhere else." With the "Savior of the Valley" routed, Sheridan thus directed a resumption of the retrograde movement northward. On October 10, his infantry and artillery abandoned their bivouacs at Strasburg and proceeded down the Valley. The commands of William Emory and George Crook halted north of Cedar Creek between the stream and Middletown. The VI Corps of Horatio Wright, however, kept going, through Middletown and eastward on the road to Front Royal. The victors of Tom's Brook, the mounted divisions of Wesley Merritt and George Custer, meanwhile, pulled back to the vicinity of Fisher's Hill. The army's third cavalry division, William Powell's, held Front Royal.[36]

Wright's advance on Front Royal was, to Sheridan's thinking, the first leg of a return to Petersburg, from where the bulk of the corps had departed three months ago to the day. But, on the morning of the 11th, Sheridan received, through Henry Halleck, instructions from Grant, dated the 9th. "General Grant," the Chief of Staff stated, "directs me to say that you had better, at all events, retain the Nineteenth Corps, and that the time of sending the Sixth Corps and a division of cavalry must be left to your judgment." Halleck added that supplies were still to be funneled through Martinsburg and repair work on the Manassas Gap Railroad continued unless Sheridan decided against using it as a future supply line.[37]

Sheridan's response to the lieutenant general's proposals was to delay Wright's march or, as he expressed it in an 8:00 p.m. telegram to Halleck, he "will hold on to the Sixth Corps for a day or two, to watch the developments." Sheridan postponed the corps's return, but he had no intention, at this time, of cancelling it. This the major general made clear to "Old Brains" in the message. Little Phil advised that work on the railroad be stopped, because Wright's veterans were coming to Washington, D.C. by foot and not by rail.[38]

Sheridan additionally informed Halleck that he would comply with Grant's desire for an operation against Gordonsville and Charlottesville and the lines of Orange & Alexandria and the Virginia Central. It would not be a full-scale movement of the army, as the General-in-Chief so much wanted, but a raid by William Powell's two cavalry brigades. Sheridan had ridden to Front Royal on the 10th and personally issued the orders to Powell. The cavalry colonel was to move via Chester Gap, Sperryville and Madison Court House toward the rail centers. As Little Phil told Halleck, Powell "may make a ten-strike." "At all events," he added, "it will spread consternation, and may force everything out of the Valley and onto the railroad [Virginia Central]. If I do not have to send a division of cavalry to Petersburg, I probably can keep the enemy running from the Valley to the railroad and from the railroad to the Valley."[39]

The Army of the Shenandoah then paused in its northbound movement, awaiting "the developments." Wright's divisions stayed near Front Royal throughout the 11th and 12th. At Cedar Creek, the cavalrymen of Merritt and Custer joined the troops of Emory and Crook, pitching their tents north of the stream. It was a pleasant, quiet interlude. Ohio soldiers in the army voted in state and county elections, with Sheridan and Crook, a pair of Ohioans, casting their votes at the polls of the 36th Ohio. The season's first heavy frost iced the morning ground, a sure indicator of winter. But many of these veterans believed that this was the war's final winter.[40]

During this two-day respite, Powell undertook his raid toward Gordonsville and Charlottesville. The expedition lasted for four days, from the 11th through the 14th. The two brigades and an horse artillery battery penetrated as far east as Amissville and as far south as Sperryville, a full 35 miles short of Gordonsville. Powell's troopers crossed the trail of John McCausland's cavalry brigade but never made contact, collected all the livestock they found and burned the house, barn and outbuildings of a reputed member of Mosby's Rangers. Confederate guerrillas rimmed the column throughout the raid but refused battle. The Yankees captured Ranger A. C. Willis, who was hanged on Powell's orders on the 12th. Willis, as noted earlier, became the seventh Ranger which Mosby sought reprisal for. By October 14, Powell had recrossed the Blue Ridge. If Gordonsville and Charlottesville were to be taken as Grant desired, it required more than a small division of cavalry supported by a battery.[41]

Sheridan evidently considered Powell's insignificant thrust as a satisfactory substitute for an operation he had opposed since Grant had broached the idea. Little Phil steadfastly maintained that his battlefield victories had wrecked Early's army beyond repair and his destruction had ruined the granary for the duration. He differed markedly from most Civil War army commanders for, instead of clamoring for more men, he would willingly break-up his independent command when circumstances no longer justified its existence. The Sixth Corps could be spared; the Rebels had not shown themselves since their whipping at Tom's Brook—in fact, Early's infantry had not been seen in a week. Sheridan, consequently, directed Wright to resume his march eastward on the 13th.[42]

Old Jube and his butternuts were coming, however. The gray infantrymen and artillerists had trailed their cavalrymen northward since October 6, halting on the 7th at New Market, where they remained in bivouac until the 11th. Throughout their march down the Pike, the Confederates were greeted by throngs of cheering, crying Valley folk. "This is a time of great trial," Dodson Ramseur admitted to his brother-in-law on the 10th. "We are all called on to show that we are made of the true metal. Let us be brave, cheerful and truthful. Remembering that Might is not Right."[43]

For Jubal Early, this "time of great trial" was worsened by the uncertainties he and his men confronted. He believed that Sheridan would not remarch southward up the Valley again for the Northerners had burned all the bridges in their wake. As Old Jube told Robert Lee in an October 9 message, "the question now is, what he intends doing." By Early's reckoning, his opponent had three options: move across the Blue Ridge, operating along the Piedmont; dispatch part of his army to Petersburg; or ensconce himself in the lower Valley, protecting the Baltimore & Ohio. Early thought that if Sheridan relocated east of the mountains, he could thwart Union movements and "defeat his infantry." "But what shall I do if he sends re-enforcements to Grant or remains in the lower Valley?" Early asked. The ravaged Shenandoah could no longer sustain his legions for any length of time, and "I will have to rely on Augusta for my supplies, and they are not abundant there." Early concluded his message by stating that "my infantry is now in good heart and condition." A special messenger was enroute to get Lee's views as expeditiously as possible.[44]

Early did not wait for Lee's response before testing Sheridan's intentions. The Army of the Valley marched at sunrise on October 12. The bulk of the army encamped for the night around Woodstock, while Rosser's regrouped division bedded down at Columbia Furnace on the Back Road and Lomax's troopers in the Luray Valley. At 6:00 a.m., on the 13th, the infantry and artillery again filed onto the Pike. Over Fisher's Hill, through Strasburg, the column proceeded. John Gordon's leading division finally halted at ten o'clock at Hupp's Hill, a mile and a half short of the Federal camps beyond Cedar Creek. Gordon shifted his troops into a stand of trees, while the divisions of Ramseur, Gabriel Wharton, John Pegram and Joseph Kershaw formed a line under the brow of the hill.[45]

Confederate gun crews rolled their pieces forward, rammed in the charges and sent shells howling toward the Federals, like a familiar greeting from an old acquaintance. The shells exploded in the camp of the XIX Corps, and startled Yankees scrambled for cover. William Emory called for counterfire from his own batteries. George Crook soon joined Emory, and the pair ordered Joseph Thoburn's division of Crook's corps forward in a reconnaissance.[46]

The brigades of Colonels George Wells and Thomas Harris soon filed down the slope to Cedar Creek and crossed the stream. As the Federals advanced across the Abram Stickley farm, about 1000 yards south of the creek, Brigadier General James Conner's brigade of Joseph Kershaw's division charged. The two battle lines exploded at contact. For the next hour or so, the foes hammered each other. Conner went down with a wound, and George Wells suffered a mortal wound. Finally, Conner's South Carolinians, supported by additional troops, cracked the Union line, routing the Federals.[47]

The Confederates pursued to the Stickley farmhouse, where they came under fire from Union batteries across Cedar Creek. This ended the action. Southern losses amounted to 22 killed and 160 wounded; Northern casualties totaled 22 killed, 110 wounded and 77 captured. Emory and Crook learned that most, if not all, of the Rebel army was present. Early ascertained that an advance toward Cedar Creek would be opposed. Late in the afternoon, the butternuts withdrew through Strasburg and settled into their old works on Fisher's Hill.[48]

This engagement at Stickley's farm and another telegram from Halleck altered Sheridan's plans. The Confederates' arrival at Hupp's Hill and Early's show of fight convinced the Union commander that he might still need the VI Corps. That night he recalled Wright, who started back before light on the 14th, marching across country to Newtown, then on the Pike to Middletown, arriving about noon. Sheridan stated in his memoirs that he planned an offensive when the VI Corps returned, but Early's withdrawal to Fisher's Hill cancelled the undertaking.[49]

The second factor affecting the Union general's operation was the wire from the Chief of Staff. Halleck once more relayed Grant's fixation on a movement against the Virginia Central Railroad and the James River canal. "General Grant wishes," in Halleck's words, "a position taken far enough south to serve as a base for future operations upon Gordonsville and Charlottesville. It must be strongly fortified and provisioned. Some point in the vicinity of Manassas Gap would seem best suited for all purposes."[50]

But Sheridan, as he had for most of three weeks, "would not indorse" this strategy. The lieutenant general, likewise, would not issue a direct order for the movement to his subordinate. The debate thus remained stalemated, with both officers convinced of the correctness of their opposing views. Grant, if he believed so firmly in the merits and value of such a movement, should have imposed his will by a clear directive. The General-in-Chief refused to do this, while prodding Sheridan to adopt the course. The subordinate, for his part, tried placating Grant by sending Powell in that direction. It was an impasse which halted the Union army in its tracks.[51]

On October 13 Secretary of War Edwin Stanton entered into the strategic disagreement. "If you can come here," he telegraphed Sheridan, "a consultation on several points is extremely desirable. I propose to visit General Grant, and would like to see you first." The major general received Stanton's request on the 14th. He hesitated initially to comply because of Early's reappearance, but Stanton's proposal for a conference offered a resolution of the conflicting views. Sheridan finally decided on the 15th to go to the capital, but only after he had satisfied himself that "the enemy at Fisher's Hill could not accomplish much."[52]

Reconnaissances by units from Custer and Emory on the 14th revealed that the Confederates had retired to the heights south of Strasburg, about five miles beyond Cedar Creek. Rosser's and Ramseur's division sallied forth to counter the Union probes, but both sides withdrew to their respective lines after some minor skirmishing. Emory told an officer that "I think we learned as much as they did."[53]

This sequence of events—at Cedar Creek, Washington and City Point—brought the entire Army of the Shenandoah, except for Powell's cavalry division, into position between Cedar Creek and Middletown by October 14. Middletown, situated on an elevated plain, was founded as early as 1786 and lay twelve miles south of Winchester. The village had achieved renown in the region for its quality clocks and compasses. The Valley Pike, the macademized conduit of commerce and now of war, passed through Middletown. The highway bridged Cedar Creek at a point one and three-fourths of a mile south of the center of the village.[54]

"Cedar Creek," said artillery captain Henry DuPont, "is a comparatively small stream of steep banks and tortuous curves." The creek, about thirty yards wide, flowed rapidly in its convoluted course into the North Fork of the Shenandoah. The turnpike bridge lay approximately a mile to the west of the confluence of the two streams. A dozen fords, some with names and some without, dotted Cedar Creek from its mouth to where its skirted the Back Road. Less than 3,000 feet beyond its merger with the North Fork, two additional fords—McInturff's and Bowman's—sliced the river's deeper water. The natural waterways offered only a modest barrier for an opponent to cross.[55]

The camps and works of the Union army sprawled across a series of ridges between the creek and the village. The nature of the terrain, with wooded crests, steep-banked ravines and the "tortuous curves" of Cedar Creek, governed the dispositions. The infantry units and artillery batteries manned the successive ridges en echelon running from east-to-west. Torbert's two cavalry divisions patrolled the more even ground extending toward the Back Road. The Union line extended five miles from flank to flank.[56]

Wright's VI Corps manned the infantry's right on "a mass of hillocks and hollows" between the cavalry and Meadow Brook, a tributary of Cedar Creek whose course paralleled the Valley Pike emptying into the larger stream about three quarters of a mile west of the turnpike bridge. The Union commander placed Wright's three divisions along this sector of the line, believing that if the Southerners attacked it would be against the Union right. If the Confederates assailed the opposite end, however, Wright would have difficulty in shifting his veterans across the deep ravine carved by Meadow Brook.[57]

Across the gorge, to the southeast, Emory's two divisions of the XIX Corps occupied a crest which towered 150 feet above Cedar Creek. The crescent-shaped line extended from above the mouth of Meadow Brook to the bridge. Emory's veterans had dug a trench along the peak, piling the ground to a height of about three feet. The corps's artillery commanded the bridge and two fords and the approaches south of the stream. The bivouac sites covered the plain behind their works which sloped downward toward the ravine of Meadow Brook. Emory's command could shatter any frontal attack which had to cross the creek and scale the "precipitous" slope.[58]

Crook's Army of West Virginia and Colonel J. Howard Kitching's Provisional Division occupied the ground east of the Pike. This latter command, an amalgam of regiments from the VI, VIII, and XIX Corps, numbering 6,000 men in three brigades, had just joined Sheridan's army as reinforcements. Kitching was a 26-year-old New Yorker, who had been making arrangements for a leave when Stanton revoked it, sending Kitching to the Valley. The assignment thoroughly displeased the colonel who told his father that "it puts me in the position of a man who tried to get out of the service, but could not." Though the Provisional Division added 6,000 muskets to the army—a figure comparable to the Confederate Second Corps—its and Kitching's reliability in combat was suspect.[59]

Sheridan placed Kitching's brigades with Rutherford Hayes's experienced fighters on a barren ridge approximately 400 yards from the highway and due east of Emory's camps. Because the Northerners considered this position the least vulnerable, the troops of the two divisions did not construct earthworks. It was more of a campsite than a battle line. The tents paralleled the Pike, with Kitching lying north of Hayes. On the level ground between these two units and Emory, the Yankees parked most of their ambulances and ammunition wagons.[60]

Crook's other unit, Joseph Thoburn's First Division, occupied a knoll, "a sort of bastion," over one half of a mile south of Hayes and nearly a mile south-by-southeast of the left of Emory's corps. Thoburn's position was the eastern and southern terminus of the main Union line. His soldiers had erected "a heavy abatis of timber" and Captain Frank C. Gibbs's Battery L, 1st Ohio Light Artillery bolstered the infantry firepower. Henry DuPont's remaining two batteries were unlimbered on a backbone of ground between two ravines. This reserve of cannon lay a few hundred yards to the right and rear of Thoburn, paralleling the latter's line, but perpendicular to the Kitching-Hayes axis of tents. Trees and undergrowth covered the ground between DuPont and Thoburn. If a Confederate assault overran Thoburn's works and dislodged DuPont's artillery pieces before infantry reserves arrived, the flanks of both Hayes and Emory would be exposed to an enfilade attack. The First Division's isolated position was the vulnerable point in the Union line.[61]

"Cedar Creek," remarked a Massachusetts soldier, "was a good place for water, but a bad place for a fight." The position had natural strengths, particularly in front of Wright and Emory, but the terrain—slices of ridges and ravines—segmented the infantry commands. "It was not the handiest field in the world in which to fight a battle," a historian has stated. Reserves could not be shuttled swiftly, with organization, to an endangered sector because of the carved-up ground. A successful frontal assault by the Southerners was impossible but, if they launched a surprise attack against a flank, especially the Yankees' left, it held the possibility of rolling up the entire Northern line, piece by piece. For this to occur, however, the Rebels had to cross both the creek and the river and march to a point opposite Thoburn's outer works without being detected. As long as Union pickets vigilantly watched the fords, such a movement was almost precluded. Sheridan oversaw the dispositions, laboring to make the position secure against an attack. It still resembled more an encampment than a battlefield alignment, with some critical flaws.[62]

By Saturday, October 15, however, Little Phil had dismissed the idea of an offensive movement by Early. He probably viewed the action of two days previous as little more than the final crowing of an old rooster. To him, the ongoing disagreement with Grant over the army's future operations was the pressing concern. He wanted it settled, so he accepted Stanton's suggestion for a conference in the capital. Entrusting the army to Wright, Sheridan, with four staff officers, departed late in the evening for Front Royal. He also took with him Merritt's cavalry division, which, with Powell, were to undertake another horseback raid toward the Virginia Central Railroad while Sheridan met with Stanton.[63]

The major general spent the night at the house of a Mrs. Richards, where a courier from Wright found him the next morning. While Sheridan had ridden to Front Royal, a Union signal station at Cedar Creek intercepted a Confederate message wigwagged from the peak of Massanutten to Early's headquarters on Fisher's Hill. Lieutenants Edward L. Halsted and Charles F. Cross, using a captured Rebel code book, deciphered the intelligence: "Lieutenant-General Early: Be ready to move as soon as my forces join you and we will crush Sheridan. LONGSTREET." Wright forwarded it with the courier, adding a cover note, expressing his concern over the security of the infantry's right flank with the absence of the cavalry. "I shall hold on here until the enemy's movements are developed," concluded the corps commander, "and shall only fear an attack on my right, which I shall make every precaution for guarding against and resisting."[64]

Sheridan considered the dispatch "a ruse," a design to frighten him out of the Shenandoah. He had confidence in Wright, "but on reflection," as he stated in his report, "deemed it best to abandon the cavalry raid and give to General Wright the entire strength of the army." He also wired ahead to Halleck, requesting verification from Grant of Longstreet's continual presence at Petersburg. Sheridan, before resuming his trip, scribbled a note to Wright. He suggested that the subordinate "make your position strong," close Powell's division on the army's left flank and "look well to your ground and be well prepared." "Get everything that can be spared," he admonished. He thought that he would be back at Cedar Creek by Tuesday, the 18th, at the latest.[65]

If Little Phil harbored any misgivings about the situation at Cedar Creek, he kept them to himself as he resumed his eastward trip. While Merritt returned to the army, the army commander, escorted by the 2nd Ohio Cavalry, crossed the Blue Ridge and met Christopher Augur and a contingent of troops at Rectortown, where Sheridan, Augur and their aides boarded a train for Washington. The party arrived in the capital at eight o'clock the next morning, breakfasted at Willard's Hotel before going to the War Department. In the meeting with Stanton and Halleck, Sheridan's views basically prevailed. The bulk of his army would rejoin Grant while engineers laid out a defensive position east of the Blue Ridge in the neighborhood of Manassas Gap. Sheridan, his aides and two engineers were on board a westbound Baltimore & Ohio train shortly after noon, clanging toward Martinsburg. The coterie of officers spent the night at the supply depot. Escorted by 300 cavalrymen, Sheridan rode the next morning, the 18th, to Winchester, where he decided to stay for the night. Nothing urgent required his immediate return. All was quiet in the camps at Cedar Creek, Colonel Oliver Edwards, Winchester's Provost Marshal, told Sheridan. The responsibilities of directing an army could wait for another day, Wednesday, October 19.[66]

Sheridan had been correct in his evaluation of the validity of the Longstreet dispatch, a plant designed to prevent the detachment of troops to Petersburg. The Union officer's miscalculation, however, was his belief that Old Jube would not attempt another thrust. The aggressive Confederate never accepted his adversary's view that the campaign had ended with the defeats and the destruction. To the crippled old warrior, his army still retained its lethal prowess. "I was now compelled," Early explained in his memoirs of the situation before him at Cedar Creek, "to move back for want of provisions and forage, or attack the enemy in his position with the hope of driving him from it, and I determined to attack."[67] One dramatic, decisive victory could retrieve the campaign and, in the process, refurbish a tarnished reputation.

If Early needed additional justification for a gambling offensive, he got it from Robert Lee. In a lengthy dispatch, dated October 12, the Southern chieftain reminded his subordinate that "I have weakened myself very much to strengthen you. It was done with the expectation of enabling you to gain such success that you could return the troops if not rejoin me yourself." Lee, too, regretted the defeats but did not blame Early for them. The commanding officer offered numerous suggestions on morale, discipline and the cavalry. What Lee wanted was a victory, a battlefield success which would compensate for the sacrifices he had made in Early's behalf. If Sheridan detached a part of his army to Grant, "you had better move against him and endeavor to crush him," Lee advised.[68]

From his perspective at Petersburg, Lee believed that the Union tide could be reversed if only Early utilized his entire army in a coordinated offensive. "With your united force it can be accomplished," he wrote. Lee, moreover, still viewed with skepticism Early's figures of Federal strength: "I do not think Sheridan's infantry or cavalry numerically as large as you suppose." For two months Lee had adhered to this mathematical calculation, using it as a basis for his strategy along the Blue Ridge, and, at no other time in the war, was he so in error. In the end, a strike at the Union host could succeed if Early relied upon his judgment, ability and the cooperation of his officers and men.[69]

For Jubal Early, it was now a matter of fashioning a flank operation. On October 17, he directed Gordon, Clement A. Evans, a brigadier under Gordon, and Jedediah Hotchkiss, the army's topographical engineer, to conduct a thorough examination of Sheridan's dispositions and works from the summit of Massanutten's "Three Sisters." Early's arthritis prevented him from scaling the steep, brooding mountain, so he entrusted it his best subordinate and the experienced Hotchkiss.[70]

The trio of officers, along with Gordon's chief of staff, Major Robert W. Hunter, ascended the "Three Sisters" during the afternoon. From the peak they could see miles of the majestic valley, burnished under the sun and the leaves of autumn. "It was an inspiring panorama," recalled Gordon. The officers, with field glasses, examined every section of the Union line, counting cannon, noting the distinctive trimmings of the infantry, artillery and cavalry. Hotchkiss sketched a map for use at their meeting with Early. Gordon and the mapmaker concurred on a plan, discussing the details as they clambered down the mountainside. Returning after dark, Hotchkiss dined with Gordon before reporting "the state of things to General Early."[71]

Tuesday, October 18, was "such a day as few have seen who have not spent an autumn in Virginia." The Yankees were stirring before daylight, standing at arms "as usual till sunrise." After breakfast, many units had an hour of drill, with a dress parade for some commands. But most of the Northerners spent the day similarly to the preceding four—cooking, washing, mending, letter writing and gossiping. Crook sent Thomas Harris's brigade to Hupp's Hill on a reconnaissance, but the colonel found no Rebels and returned. Some regiments drew their pay; others voted in the national elections, but the highlight of the day was the arrival of mail, the first they had in a week. Home, the end of the war, it was a good time for such thoughts, made easier by this "superb specimen of an autumn day." Before Wright turned in for the night, however, he ordered another reconnaissance by units of the XIX Corps for "first dawn" of the 19th.[72]

For the Northerners, it was a day of the routine, the pleasurable and of thoughts elsewhere; for the Southerners, it was a time for decisions and warmaking. Early in the morning, John Pegram reported to army headquarters and presented his own plan for an attack on the Union right flank. After the handsome Virginian had finished his proposal, Hotchkiss, who was present, briefly outlined Gordon's scheme, pointing to the map he had drawn. The army commander deferred, summoning his other senior officers to headquarters.[73]

Soon Gordon, Ramseur, Kershaw, Wharton, Rosser, Tom Carter and William Payne joined Early, Pegram and Hotchkiss. The erect, thin Georgian did much of the talking as he proposed a night march by the Second Corps around the exposed Union left flank, followed by a concerted assault by the entire army. Pegram objected and he, or another, questioned Gordon on how he could pass an entire corps between the sheer northern face of Massanutten and the North Fork of the Shenandoah River flowing along its base. It was a sound inquiry, because the Federals had evidently accepted the view that it was an impracticable route as they considered the opposite flank to be the most likely target. A way would be found, Gordon rebutted, and he would accept full responsibility for failure.[74]

The assembled officers unanimously endorsed the Georgian's scheme—a brilliantly conceived gamble unparalleled in the war. The remaining commands were then assigned their roles. While Gordon led the Second Corps over the river and along the mountain, Kershaw would advance to Bowman's Mill, a ford of Cedar Creek downstream from the Bowman family's Mount Pleasant home, and attack Thoburn at the designated hour. Wharton, with the artillery, was directed to follow the turnpike to Hupp's Hill, crossing the stream after Gordon and Kershaw charged, pressing his attack down the Pike toward Middletown. Rosser, fording at Minebank Ford, would initiate the offensive by engaging the Union cavalry. Payne, meanwhile, would precede Gordon, capture any Federal pickets and then dash toward Belle Grove, an imposing limestone house which served as Union headquarters, and try to grab Sheridan. All units were to be in position by 5:00 a.m.[75]

The council then adjourned. Gordon, Ramseur and Hotchkiss rode to the mountain to examine and select a route. Pegram, who still had misgivings about the plan, climbed Massanutten, conducting his own reconnaissance. He returned after dark, sought Early and once more argued against the enterprise. Old Jube dismissed his objections, ordering him to his post with his division. The soldiers completed their preparations—cooking two-days' rations and removing their canteens to avoid the clinking of metal on metal. The veterans did not know the details, but they knew it meant fighting. A chaplain took this opportunity to conduct services for Robert Johnston's North Carolinians. It was an opportune time for the Lord's work.[76]

At 8:00 p.m., the Second Corps descended Fisher's Hill, marching eastward—"something important is about to ensue," a Tarheel jotted in his diary. The column forded the North Fork at George Hupp's, two miles south of Strasburg. Once over, the foot cavalry passed through some fields before striking the base of Massanutten. Turning north, they followed Gordon's route, a "pig's path," marching single file. Couriers from the corps were stationed at every fork along the path, insuring that the troops turned in the right direction. A bright moon, three days past full, dimly lit the narrow trail. For Gordon it was a march he never forgot: "with every man, from the commanders of the divisions to the brave privates under them, impressed with the gravity of the enterprise, speaking only when necessary and then in whispers, and striving to suppress every sound, the long gray line like a great serpent glided noiselessly along the dim pathway above the precipice."[77]

The Southerners reached the end of the mountain opposite the house of Andrew Pitman, turned eastward and proceeded to the lane running down to Bowman's Ford. The van lay down, waiting for the column to close up. Ahead a blanket of fog already hugged the river and the banks, but the Rebels could see mounted videttes from Colonel Alpheus S. Moore's brigade of Powell's division guarding the shallows. When all his infantry had arrived, Gordon ordered Payne forward. The Virginia horsemen plunged down the bank into the water; gunfire crackled in the stillness, and the stunned blue-jacketed pickets were overrun. Payne's cavalrymen then kept going on their assigned mission.[78]

Behind the Virginians, the foot cavalry slipped silently into the chest-deep, icy river. The butternuts struggled up the slippery bank in their wet clothes. Officers hurried the units forward as the men "trotted up" the country road. The quick pace, however, "was very agreeable after the cold water of the river," said one of them. At the J. Cooley house, a mile and a half due north of the ford, Gordon formed his battle line and wheeled it to the left. A dense fog enveloped the field, limiting vision to feet. But the silence in the mists indicated that their commander, as promised, had brought them undetected beyond the Union flank, and on schedule. It would be another thirty minutes before they went in, so these veterans waited, alone with their private thoughts.[79]

Less than a mile away, on a knoll overlooking Bowman's Mill on Cedar Creek, Old Jube, too, was waiting. Around him, Kershaw's troops were poised for their thrust over the stream. Rosser, Wharton and Carter's artillerymen were also at their assigned positions. Early must have felt fresh, having napped until midnight. He must have sensed the moment, the time of redemption and revenge for Winchester and Fisher's Hill. It could be the masterstroke of the war, surpassing even the great Stonewall's day at Chancellorsville. For Jubal Early, the minutes of anticipation must have seemed like hours.

11

"Hell Carnival"

The members of Company A, 128th New York sensed something was brewing, beyond them, in the blackness of the pre-dawn hours of October 18–19, 1864. From their vantage point—the advanced picket line of the XIX Corps, dubbed the "Stonewall Post," south of Cedar Creek along the Valley Pike—the signs indicated that the "Johnnys" were unusually active. The company's officers, Lieutenants Benjamin T. Benson and Theodore A. Krafft, shared the enlisted men's concerns. Three times Krafft hailed the picket post of the Army of West Virginia but received no response. The wary officers then ordered the men to shoot at any moving objects. Minutes later some of the New Yorkers reported that the woods ahead seemed alive with "Johnnys."[1]

A short time later Lieutenant Colonel Alfred Neafie, brigade officer of the day, visited the "Stonewall Post." Neafie asked the usual questions of Benson and Krafft, and the junior officers expressed their uneasiness. The lieutenant colonel seemed unmoved by their report, informing the pair that if they heard firing to the east, they should be unconcerned. Horatio Wright, acting army commander, had directed a reconnaissance in force by a brigade, supported by two more, of their division, Cuvier Grover's Second, for first light. Any musketry, Neafie stated, was the advance of the force. With this assurance, Neafie remounted, turned back toward the main works and disappeared into the fog. It was only minutes before day broke through the heavy mist.[2]

Downstream from Company A, 128th New York, on the opposite side of the creek, the Second Battalion, 5th New York Heavy Artillery was performing a similar duty. The foremost picket post of Joseph Thoburn's division of George Crook's corps, the battalion had been hearing disturbing sounds to the east, toward the base of Massanutten, since midnight. Convinced that something was astir, Captain Frederick C. Wilkie, battalion commander, reported this to brigade headquarters of Lieutenant Colonel Thomas F. Wildes. Then about four o'clock, the New Yorkers distinctly heard the exchange of carbine and rifle fire at Bowman's Ford when William Payne's Virginians overran the mounted videttes of Colonel Alpheus S. Moore. Wilkie personally went back to headquarters to express his concerns. Meanwhile, Lieutenant Colonel Luther Furney of the 34th Ohio and Crook's officer of the day undertook his own investigation. Furney rode to the river shallows and into the hands of the Virginians.[3]

The New Yorkers naturally knew nothing of Furney's fate but, at approximately 4:45 a.m., a party of Payne's horsemen brushed into some of the Empire State volunteers, who unleashed a ragged blast toward the Confederates. The cavalrymen disappeared; less than thirty minutes later, however, the right wing of the battalion glimpsed a column of infantry fording the creek. The Yankees again fired through the fog, bringing, as in the first instance, no response from the enemy. Wilkes, during this time, made a second visit to headquarters, where Wildes already had started stirring his men and putting them in the fieldworks. The New York captain returned to his post. It could not have been too many minutes before 5:40 a.m. and the arrival of daybreak.[4]

The column of foot soldiers, sniped at by Wilkie's New Yorkers, was the division of Joseph Kershaw, moving toward its final attack position. These four Confederate brigades were to initiate the charge of Jubal Early's infantry. The command numbered 3,000, veterans from South Carolina, Georgia and Mississippi under Kershaw's reliable leadership. The major general was a 42-year-old, dignified, religious South Carolinian, an officer of little military training who had earned his position on battlefields. So far in this campaign, he and his men had accomplished little, but their recall to the Valley after Fisher's Hill allowed Early to undertake this daring offensive. If these dependable fighters and their comrades in the army beat the odds on this October Wednesday and achieved victory, however, Robert Lee's decision to detach them from Petersburg would be justified.[5]

The Georgia brigade of Colonel James P. Simms led the advance of the division. Behind Simms's troops came the brigades of Brigadier General William Wofford and Benjamin G. Humphreys and Major James M. Goggin, who had replaced Brigadier General James Conner after the brigadier went down with a crippling wound in the fight at Abram Stickley's farm on October 13. Simms moved his Georgians downstream a short distance, faced them left and brought them into battle formation. While the Georgians stepped forward into a clump of trees, the other three brigades started deploying. Wofford swung his command to the right or eastern flank of the division. Humphreys shifted his Mississippians into the gap between Simms and Wofford, while Goggin formed his ranks on the division's left beside Simms. Each man carried sixty rounds of ammunition, but Kershaw had issued orders for no firing until the brigades reached the works of Thoburn's division.[6]

Kershaw assigned Simms's 520 Georgians the duty of silencing Thoburn's pickets and spearheading the charge. These veterans evidently began their assault before the other brigades had been completely deployed. Clearing the trees, the Georgians angled slightly to the left, bringing them directly in front of the Union lines. The Rebels marched steadily forward, shielded by the thick blanket of fog. The advanced pickets of the battalion of the 5th New York Heavy Artillery soon saw the serried ranks of shadows coming, triggered a round and fell back on their reserve post. The Georgians pressed the New Yorkers and, before the battalion could withdraw, the Southerners over-whelmed the unit. Simms's men captured 4 officers and 305 enlisted men; only about 40 New Yorkers escaped, including Wilkie.[7]

Morning light was creasing the eastern sky as the Georgians drove ahead toward the isolated works of Thoburn's two brigades. The Confederate battle line closed to within paces of the Union line and then exploded in a roar of musketry. The volley "seemed to wake the stillness from one end of the valley to the other."[8] Screaming their yell, the Rebels poured over the entrench-ments, rushing in at a gap in the line between the brigades of Wildes and Colonel Thomas M. Harris. The Georgians turned left and right, raking the trenches with an enfilading fire.[9]

What ensued in the fog along the breastworks, said a Union officer, "was a blind, confused, feeble scuffle."[10] The Georgians spilled over the portion of the line assigned to the 54th Pennsylvania of Harris's brigade. But this regi-ment had not reached its position when the graycoats attacked. The Pennsyl-vanians came up only to be shattered and sent reeling back through their camp. Captain John Suter, the 54th's commander, rallied his troops in a skirt of woods before they retreated across the Valley Pike.[11]

Harris's remaining three regiments, in turn, were outflanked and rolled up one by one. The 15th West Virginia, aligned next to the breach in the works, broke initially, offering little resistance. Colonel Milton Wells of the 15th took a bullet in his left hip but still hobbled along with his splintered ranks. The 10th West Virginia dissolved next; its commander, Lieutenant Colonel Moses S. Hall, also suffering a wound. Hall was lucky, for the bullet, striking his chest, followed the rib cage and did not hit an organ. Harris's final regiment, the 11th West Virginia, gave way by companies from the left. Two regiments of Goggin's oncoming brigade, the 2nd and 3rd South Carolina, assisted the Georgians in the attack on the 11th West Virginia. Harris, who was not at the front when the Confederates struck, described his brigade's flight as a "confused rout." The Union brigade's casualties amounted to 176, of which 103 were captured, an indication of the feeble defense by the four regiments.[12]

The Georgians and Humphreys's arriving Mississippians, likewise, wrecked Thoburn's second brigade—a Massachusetts and two Ohio regi-ments under Wildes. Captain Andrew Potter's 34th Massachusetts, positioned on the brigade's right, next to the gap in the works, had no chance. Simms's butternuts were ten rods in the rear of the Union regiment before the Bay Staters saw them. The Rebels unleashed "a perfect shower of lead," and Potter's command disintegrated. The Federals "left there mighty quick," musician Joseph Ward admitted in a letter.[13]

The Massachusetts men ran rearward, completely disorganized. In the midst of this headlong flight, one of the regiment's men, Ezekiel P. Kempton of Company K, suddenly stopped and turned back toward the enemy. "Old Zeke," as his comrades called him, was the unit's character. Dressed in a long swallow-tailed, black dress coat, he always carried a staff for walking and went nearly everywhere with "his diminitive little mule." Kempton looked, according to the regimental historian, "for all the world like Joseph journeying into Egypt, as pictured in school books of former days." A devout man, "Old Zeke" read the Bible daily and, often at night during the campaign, he visited Southern houses, seeking to share religious devotions for a meal. Now, as he led his mule toward safety, "Old Zeke" remembered that he left behind his knapsack. After tying the mule to a tree, Kempton went for his knapsack, shouting: "I want my Life of Christ! I must have my Life of Christ." He then disappeared into the fog.[14]

Wildes's final two regiments, the 116th and 123rd Ohio, like the 34th Massachusetts, were swamped in a deluge of gray, blasted in front and on both flanks. The four Mississippi regiments of Humphreys overlapped the left flank of the Ohioans while the Georgians, after dislodging the Bay Staters, ripped into the opposite end of the Federal line. The 116th and 123rd surprisingly extricated themselves from the closing gray ranks in reasonable order. The limited vision—"The mist and fog was so heavy that you could hardly see the length of a regiment," noted Wildes—probably spared the Ohioans. They tumbled back into the woods rimming the rear of Thoburn's entrenchments and momentarily regrouped. The Confederates, however, pressed the pair of regiments, soon sweeping them out of the trees. The Ohioans then followed the remainder of Thoburn's wrecked division westward toward the turnpike and the position of the XIX Corps.[15]

The rout of Thoburn's division had been easy and swift for Kershaw's men. Though difficult to ascertain precisely, the Southern victory evidently took only about a quarter of an hour to achieve. The momentum of the assault, moreover, was sustained. Even as the final eddies of the Federal command flowed westward, the butternuts, clearing the treeline, surged toward the artillery reserve of Crook's corps.[16]

Captain Henry A. DuPont's batteries were positioned on two ridges north-northwest of Thoburn's fieldworks. Battery D, 1st Pennsylvania Light and Battery B, 5th United States Artillery occupied the first rise, a "crescent-shaped ridge," while Battery L, 1st Ohio Light held the western tip of the second rise with its cannon covering the turnpike bridge over Cedar Creek.

The six 3-inch rifled guns of the Regulars and the six 10-pound Parrotts of the Pennsylvanians were 400 yards apart, with the latter pieces on the left, farther east on the ridge and closer to the oncoming Confederates. DuPont had ordered the crews to their posts when he heard the picket fire preceding Kershaw's assault.[17]

Because of the fog, the gunners had no indication of the outcome of the infantry struggle until the smashed remnants of the Federal division appeared out of the mists. Since Simms's Georgians so closely pressed the fleeing Yankees, the Pennsylvania artillerists had no time to react when the butternuts came into view, a scant twenty yards from the muzzles of the cannon. Lieutenant William Munk, the battery commander, who was not with his crews but in camp, subsequently reported that his gunners fired fifteen rounds of canister into the Georgians. DuPont, however, stated that the battery never touched off a round before being overrun. The few Southern accounts support DuPont's assertion.[18]

The Pennsylvanians, in brief, never had much of a chance against the overwhelming numbers of Georgians. The gunners fought bravely with their sponge staffs, but the Rebels bayoneted or clubbed them to the ground. Lieutenant James Boyle, senior officer with the cannon, sabered one Georgian before being flattened by a musket butt. Six Pennsylvanians were killed, six wounded and eighteen captured in the melee. "The heavy casualties in the Pennsylvania battery," DuPont wrote, "were due to the bravery and determination with which Lieutenant James Boyle and the cannoneers of that battery stuck by their guns to the very last moment." The Pennsylvanians had fought with "admirable courage," but the half dozen Parrotts belonged to the Georgians.[19]

Four hundred yards to the west, on the ridge, the gunners of Battery B, 5th United States Artillery had their charges of canister loaded but with no target. DuPont, the 26-year-old scion of the Delaware family fortune, was with the Regulars, listening to the thunder of the unseen combat, figuring out how to extricate his cannon. An experienced, highly capable artillery officer, DuPont had had apprehensions about the dispositions of Crook's divisions and the artillery reserve. "It seemed to me," he recounted in his memoirs, "that our left flank was very inadequately protected. My anxiety was all the more keen because I realized that if our left were turned it would be extremely difficult, if not impossible, to withdraw the pieces. Upon discussing this matter with others, the invariable reply was that our left was protected by Powell's cavalry division, which was not at all satisfactory to me as nobody seemed to be informed as to its exact position. I even went so far as to ride out beyond our left to try to locate it but returned after going some distance and seeing nothing."[20]

DuPont, mounted on a gray mare, looking into the dense fog, knew that his fears had now been fulfilled—the Confederates had stormed into the unguarded Union flank. The Regulars were already under long-range musketry, so their commander, First Lieutenant Henry F. Brewerton, asked DuPont: "At what shall I fire?" The captain, as uncertain of the Rebels' location as Brewerton, replied: "Fire to the left in the direction of the sound." Crews of the two center pieces wheeled the 3-inch rifled guns toward the east and blasted the mists with canister. DuPont told Brewerton to hold the position until he could see the Confederates through the fog and then run the cannon down the hill into the ravine, where the captain would have the limbers readied. DuPont repeated the instructions, before spurring his horse down the slope into the gorge.[21]

The captain found the battery's drivers harnessing and hitching the teams, "making extraordinary efforts," in his words. DuPont stayed long enough to start Munk's caissons rearward and to have Brewerton's limbers placed at the foot of the ridge. He then rode to Captain Frank C. Gibbs's Battery L, 1st Ohio Light deployed on the second rise. The Ohioans, at DuPont's order, commenced firing with two of their four Napoleons on a Rebel skirmish line—indicated only by rifle flashes—south of the creek. The shell bursts drove back the Confederates, who belonged to Gabriel C. Wharton's division. DuPont, in turn, withdrew the other section of Napoleons about 300 to 400 yards, directing the fire eastward toward Kershaw's troops. The artillery commander still did not know the scale of the Confederate offensive or how long his two batteries could stand against a charging opponent concealed by the fog.[22]

Brewerton probably started abandoning the southernmost ridge even as DuPont oversaw the redeployment of Gibbs's one section. The Regulars had stood by their pieces, ramming in one charge after another, until the Georgians closed to within 25 yards of their position. Brewerton ordered a retreat, and the crews hand-wheeled the rifled guns down the slope to the limbers. One cannon became entangled in bushes and was abandoned, but only after a crew member spiked it. Under "a heavy musketry fire" from the Southerners on the crest, the Yankees escaped with five cannon, whipping the teams westward through the ravine to the turnpike. Brewerton, who waited until the final moment, was captured, along with DuPont's staff surgeon and quartermaster. Second Lieutenant Samuel D. Southworth, whom DuPont described as "one of the most promising young officers in the service," was killed. Altogether, DuPont lost half of his dozen commissioned officers.[23]

The Ohio battery soon followed, retiring under DuPont's personal direction. The captain had hoped that by shifting a section of the command, he could hold the second ridge until units of the XIX Corps fashioned a defensive line east of the turnpike. But the Ohioans, like the Regulars, were assailed by the Confederates before Union infantry support arrived. The battery also came under fire from the left units of John Gordon's Second Corps which had smashed into the divisions of Rutherford Hayes and J. Howard Kitching. It was at this point that DuPont realized "the extensive scale upon which the Confederate movement was being carried out" and "the vigor with which it was being pressed." Caught between the converging attackers, both sections of the battery limbered up and raced down the Pike. The graycoats swarmed over the works as the gunners extricated the last Napoleon.[24]

Crook's right flank—Thoburn's infantry division and DuPont's artillery brigade—now had been swept several hundred yards to the rear. Of Thoburn's nine regiments, all but two—116th and 123rd Ohio—had been wrecked beyond temporary repair, while the Pennsylvania battery and another cannon—seven pieces in total—were captured. Except for the valiant stand of the Regular and Ohio batteries, Crook's flank was blown away like leaves before an autumn gale. DuPont and the gun crews, for an indeterminate number of minutes, acted as the only breaker against the gray storm on this section of the field. The young Delawarean could have withdrawn as soon as Thoburn's fugitives ran past his position, but he chose to stand, intending to delay the Southern assault, buying time for the XIX Corps to enter the action east of the turnpike. DuPont directed his batteries skillfully, using his experience and instincts on the fog-shrouded field. The artillerists stood until the final moment, escaping with the loss of only one cannon. If these two batteries had been seized, the Rebels could have brought the firepower of sixteen pieces immediately upon the position of the XIX Corps. DuPont later described the battle as "by far the most momentous episode of my whole military career." His performance earned him the brevet of lieutenant colonel in the Regular Army and eventually the Congressional Medal of Honor.[25]

Several factors contributed to the escape of the Federal batteries. The fog, which obscured the Confederates, likewise, prevented the attackers from seeing the isolated position of DuPont's cannon. More importantly, however, Kershaw charged piecemeal, with Simms's Georgians outpacing the other brigades and bearing almost entirely the struggle against Thoburn and Du-Pont. The division commander, perhaps, wanted to insure a surprise and sent the Georgians ahead before Humphreys and Goggin were fully deployed. Kershaw's purpose is difficult to ascertain for, if he filed a report, it is not included in the *Official Records*. The result was that after the Georgians crushed the Union infantry line and overran the Pennsylvania battery, the momentum of their attack slackened. Most likely, only a small portion of the brigade continued along the ridge toward the Federal cannon. They drove the Regulars off the crest but captured only the spiked piece left behind by the Yankees.

Simms, then, halted his assaults, explaining in his report that "there being no troops either on our right or left, I thought it prudent to fall back to the captured works and await the arrival of other troops." His brigade surely must have required a reorganization because of the limited visibility and the nature of the attack. The few Confederate accounts indicate that not only the command of Simms but those of Goggin and Humphreys were having difficulty maintaining cohesion. "Our ranks soon became almost as much disorganized as those of the enemy," recalled Captain D. Augustus Dickert of the 3rd South Carolina. The captain blamed part of the breakdown on Goggin, whom he described as "a lamentable failure" and "seldom seen during the day."[26]

Dickert also asserted that the South Carolinians, leaving the ranks, engaged in plundering the Union camps—a claim supported by a Mississippian with Humphreys. The kettles of cooking coffee, the stacks of rations and clothing were too inviting targets for the Rebels to ignore. Captain H. H. Stevens, 17th Mississippi, noted that members of his brigade were "eating, drinking, and feeling big and brave."[27] This statement might explain why Humphreys, whose troops participated in the dislodgment of Wildes's Federals from the works, did not support the charge of the Georgians on the Union artillery. The plundering thus began at the outset of the battle, draining away strength from units which needed every musket in the ranks.

Though Kershaw's advance stalled temporarily because of the fog, the poor coordination and the confusion, the fact remained that the southeast anchor of the Union line had been erased, uncovering the left flank of the XIX Corps located nearly a mile away to the north and west. Even as the Confederate officers rectified the lines, some of the Georgians turned around the captured 10-pound Parrotts and opened fire on this second Union infantry position across the turnpike. Kershaw then sent his three brigades toward the Yankees. The fog hugged the field, but the division commander could have heard the roar of combat to the north, where the army's Second Corps was charging. The South Carolinian did not know it yet, but Gordon's command had duplicated the former's success and was also moving against the XIX Corps.[28]

The major component of the Confederate army, the Second Corps under Gordon, launched its assault on the divisions of Hayes and Kitching in conjunction with Kershaw's advance upon Thoburn. Gordon had formed his three divisions in the woods and fields west of the J. Cooley farm, approximately one half of a mile from the Union camps. The Georgian's old division, directed by Clement A. Evans on this day, held the left front of the corps. Behind Evans's three brigades, John Pegram deployed his two brigades of North Carolinians and one of Virginians. Alongside Evans, extending the battle front northward, Stephen Dodson Ramseur aligned the corps's largest division, four brigades of Alabamians, Georgians and North Carolinians.[29]

Ramseur, particularly, was in fine spirits this morning. Three days ago he learned that his wife had given birth to a child and both were fine. The young North Carolinian knew not whether the child was a boy or a girl but, in its honor, he pinned a small bouquet of flowers to the lapel of his uniform coat. When Gordon rode up, checking the formation, Ramseur exclaimed to his friend: "Well, general, I shall get my furlough to-day."[30]

A short time later—just minutes before daylight—Gordon sent the corps forward. Though the accounts of combatants in both armies conflict as to the precise time of the Southern attacks, the preponderance of evidence indicates that the moment of contact occurred at daylight or 5:40 a.m. Moreover—and again some versions disagree—Kershaw struck before Gordon, but only by a handful of minutes. The Second Corps, then, allowing for the march of a half mile, moved toward its target at approximately the same time James Simms's Georgians were overrunning Thoburn's advance picket post of the 5th New York Heavy Artillery.[31]

The foot cavalry came on "in solid lines of battle, without skirmishers." Gordon issued strict orders to the file closers to shoot any soldier who fell out of the ranks during the charge. A Georgian, given this duty, remarked later that "we took this position, but of course had no idea of obeying such order, nor was there any occasion for it."[32]

As the battle line—seven brigades abreast—neared the Union camps on a ridge, the soldiers started running and shrieked their fearsome "Rebel yell." A Yankee once described the latter as "that hellish yell;" another compared it to "a regular wildcat screech." It chilled the spines of many Federals. "You have to feel it," wrote a blue-clad veteran, "and if you say you did not feel it, and heard the yell, you have *never* been there." Stonewall Jackson, however, called it "the sweetest music I ever heard."[33]

The three brigades under Clement Evans, emerging from the mists, stormed into the sector of the Union position occupied by the division of Rutherford Hayes. The Ohio colonel, moments earlier, learned from Lieutenant Frederick L. Ballard of Thoburn's staff that their division was being driven back by a Confederate force. Hayes, who was joined by Horatio Wright and George Crook, immediately sent instructions down the chain of command, ordering his two brigades into line. Because of detachments, the division counted only 1,445 muskets. Only Hayes's left brigade, three regiments and a battalion of Ohioans and West Virginians under Colonel Hiram F. Devol, were under arms and in some sort of a combat formation when the Southerners hit. Lieutenant Colonel Benjamin F. Coates's command, reduced by the detachments to the 14th West Virginia and forty men of the 34th Ohio, were still among the tents. Compounding Hayes's deployment problems were the broken ranks of Thoburn which, in the Ohioan's words, "came pouring past and through the right of my line."[34]

The ill-prepared Union division crumbled rapidly before the fury in gray and butternut sweeping in from the east. Devol's troops replied with musketry, but the Virginians of Brigadier General William Terry and the Louisianans, probably led by Colonel Edmund Pendleton of the 15th Louisiana and ranking officer of the brigade, blasted the brigade with frontal and flank fire. Devol ordered a retreat, but it mattered little. The Ohioans and West Virginians cracked under the onslaught and streamed toward the rear.[35]

On the left of the Louisianans and Virginians, the Georgia brigade, probably under Colonel John H. Lowe of the 31st Georgia, engulfed Coates's understrength unit. "We were shooting them as fast as we could to see them run," G. W. Nichols of the 31st remembered. "It was the worst stampede I ever saw." A number of the Yankees sought shelter in a tree-covered ravine. The Georgians pressed after them and, as one of the Southerners stated, "it looked like murder to kill them huddled up there where they could not defend themselves, while we had nothing to do but load and shoot." The Northerners finally scrambled up the opposite bank, their knapsacks making targets for the Georgians.[36]

In the midst of the wreckage of his division, Hayes, galloping to the rear, had his horse instantly killed under him. The sudden fall briefly knocked him unconscious and injured his right ankle. Some of his men, passing by his still body, spread the report that their commander had been killed. But Hayes regained consciousness and, seeing the Rebels closing, hobbled toward the turnpike. The Confederates shouted at him to stop; "the names they called me," Hayes said later, "reflected disrespect upon my parentage." The colonel luckily found an aide, who relinquished his mount, and Hayes escaped.[37]

Farther north on the ridge, meanwhile, Dodson Ramseur's crack division was routing the 6,000-man command of J. Howard Kitching. Because of the scarcity of accounts of this action, it is extremely difficult to assess accurately the readiness of the Federals or their resistance. Neither Kitching nor any subordinate officer of the unit, for instance, submitted an after-battle report. Of the few Southern reports, moreover, only one briefly describes the combat, stating that the Yankees fled "in great confusion."[38] The lack of accounts—contemporary or postwar—suggest that Kitching's untested regiments scattered and ran before the charging Rebels.

Cullen Battle's Alabamians, on the division's right, spearheaded Ramseur's assault, sweeping into and around the Union left flank. Close behind the Alabamians came the Georgians of Philip Cook and then the North Carolinians of William Cox and Bryan Grimes. The butternuts caught many of the Federals half-dressed or still in their tents. E. Ruffin Harris, 14th North Carolina, recalled capturing three Northerners, "who were nearly scared to death." Harris's prisoners offered him everything they had; the Tarheel settled for their new rifles and ammunition.[39]

An island of Union resistance formed around Frank Gibbs's Battery L, 1st Ohio Light which, after withdrawing before Kershaw's attack, DuPont redeployed east of the Pike, behind the center of Kitching's position. The 6th New York Heavy Artillery of Kitching's Second Brigade, coming in from the wagon camps, supported the artillerists, who blasted the Rebels with case shot. The battery and the solitary regiment endured "a tremendous musketry fire;" fortunately, the Confederates, standing on higher ground, overshot their targets. But the four Napoleons and the infantrymen could not stem the tide, and

DuPont ordered them back. Gibbs retreated across Meadow Brook, where he again unlimbered for a third time. Ramseur's casualties in the whirlwind attack must have been minimal, but they included the capable Cullen Battle, who went down with a crippling wound which incapacitated him for further field service during the war. Lieutenant Colonel Edwin Hobson of the 5th Alabama assumed command of the brigade.[40]

The fog obscured the magnitude of the Union defeat and rout which occurred in the span of less than thirty minutes. On the plain west of the turnpike, from Middletown to the XIX Corps position overlooking Cedar Creek, the shattered remnants of three Federal divisions, over 9,000 soldiers, were pouring westward toward Meadow Brook. Some officers rallied portions of regiments, which turned around and offered battle. Most, however, had had enough and were finished as fighters for the day. A New Yorker in the VI Corps, which lay across Meadow Brook, subsequently averred that the fugitives "were simply insane with fear." A Vermonter in the same command described them as "a disorganized, routed, demoralized, terrified mob." As an explanation, the Green Mountain state volunteer argued: "That these men were brave no one doubts; their previous brilliant conduct had amply shown it; but a night surprise, total and terrific, is too trying for the *morale* of the best troops in the world to survive."[41]

A staff officer of the XIX Corps, Captain John DeForest, riding into the midst of the fugitives, described them differently. DeForest called them "a widespread swarm . . . utterly without organization and many of them without arms," but added that "they were not running, not breathless and looking over their shoulders, but just trudging tranquilly rearward like a crowd hastening home from a circus." Unlike the Vermonter, DeForest "never could understand why Crook's usually spirited veterans went to pieces so quickly." He stopped the first officer he met, asking what it meant. "Why, I suppose it means that we are retreating," shot back the captain. DeForest then inquired if Thoburn had been driven from his position. "His men have," replied the other.[42]

Crook, Thoburn, Hayes, Kitching and subordinate officers regrouped fragments of the three divisions around army headquarters, the Belle Grove mansion, which lay approximately one half of a mile west of the original Hayes-Kitching position. For George Crook, the sight of his usually redoubtable "Buzzards" fleeing before the Confederates must have brought both anger and disbelief. He had galloped from headquarters at the initial volley, but he, too, could not prevent the disintegration of Hayes's and Kitching's ranks. Swept back with his men, Crook and the others rallied, by one officer's estimate, 1,500 of the fugitives, aligning them between Belle Grove and the turnpike. A stand had to be made here, or much of the army's wagon train would fall into Southern hands.[43]

The park of wagons extended from Middletown, along the plain by Belle Grove, to the camps of the XIX Corps. At the explosion of musketry, the teamsters and their escorts started the teams northward. As the Union lines broke and the infantrymen spilled across the Pike onto the plain, the teamsters evidently panicked. Some Yankees claimed that numbers of wagons overturned in ditches and were abandoned while the teams seemed crazed in what must have been temporary bedlam. Sections of the train parked near Middletown escaped with little difficulty. The 2nd West Virginia Cavalry brought off a section without incident. The 91st Ohio, guarding the army's cattle herd near the town, repulsed a charge by William Payne's cavalry brigade on a string of wagons. The Ohioans were assisted in this action when the 5th and 6th Virginia Cavalry mistakenly shot into each other's ranks. The 91st, commanded by Major Lemuel Z. Cadot, then drove the cattle west of the town, eventually reaching Kernstown and safety.[44]

Scores of wagons and ambulances remained, however. Some of the battle's first real combat now ensued as the patchwork Union line bought time for the safe passage of the vehicles. Cook's Georgians and Cox's North Carolinians, aided by some of Payne's Virginians, opposed the Yankees. For the next thirty minutes the opponents blasted each other in the fog. "I think the very hardest and most stubborn fighting of the day took place here," claimed Thomas Wildes. Many Union officers grabbed muskets and stood in the ranks with the enlisted men, as a Rebel thrust was met by a Federal counterthrust.[45]

The slugfest took its toll, notably among officers. Lieutenant Colonel James R. Hall, acting commander of the 13th West Virginia, died where he stood when struck by two minie balls. Captain Philip G. Bier, Crook's assistant adjutant general, suffered a fatal wound, dying the next day. But the command's most grievous loss was that of Joseph Thoburn. A physician before the war, Thoburn had fought in twenty-four battles or engagements, rising from regimental to divisional command. A few days earlier he told Surgeon Alexander Neil that "he only wanted to fight one more great battle and then he would be satisfied." He got his wish on this day, but he had none left. Thoburn went down with a mortal wound, dying an hour and a half later.[46]

Cook's and Cox's tough fighters pressed ahead with a seeming relentlessness, and the Union line finally buckled, then broke through the fields, down and across the Meadow Brook ravine. The Southerners secured some ambulances and wagons, but the stalwart defense saved most. The teamsters escaped by driving their teams into the gorge and over the small stream. The Union infantrymen rallied on the high ground beyond the run.[47]

While this struggle raged from Middletown to Belle Grove, the Confederate divisions of Evans and Kershaw assailed the only Union command still remaining east of Meadow Brook, William Emory's XIX Corps. Occupying the bluffs overlooking Cedar Creek from the run to the turnpike, Emory's troops had been up and about, fed, under arms and in their works before daybreak. One of the corps's brigades, supported by two more, were preparing for the previously ordered reconnaissance-in-force when Kershaw, then Gordon, launched their attacks on Crook's and Kitching's units. The veterans of the Louisiana campaigns heard the thunderous rolls of musketry, followed by "scream on scream of the Rebel yell." "To say it was a startling sound," remarked Francis Buffum, 14th New Hampshire, "is to feebly describe the effect upon the men." As the roar of combat increased "no one knew what to do, and the battalions stood motionless and expectant."[48]

"Old Brick Top" Emory, "coatless and hatless and uncombed," was saddling his horse when the Southerners attacked. He immediately told Captain John DeForest to inform Wright of the attack on Crook and then spurred toward his troops. DeForest claimed in his memoirs that he overheard Emory grumble: "I said so; I knew that if we were attacked, it would be there."[49]

Emory rode in those early minutes, like many others of rank, not knowing the scale of the offensive because of the fog. But he knew that if Thoburn and/or Hayes and Kitching broke under the attacks, his flank and rear were exposed to the Confederates. Additionally, neither of his two divisions were under the command of experienced officers. For the better part of a month, Emory had tried unsuccessfully to resolve a petulant dispute between his top-ranking subordinates, Cuvier Grover and William Dwight.[50]

The quarrel between Grover and Dwight began late in September when the latter filed his report on Winchester. In it, Dwight accused Grover's Second Division of "flying in so much disorder" before Gordon's men in the First Woods. Emory requested modifications in the controversial draft from Dwight, but the commander of the First Division refused. On October 6, Grover retaliated, drawing up two charges—one with seventeen specifications, the other with two supplementary charges and four specifications—against Dwight, primarily accusing his antagonist of eating lunch while the corps fought the Southerners. Emory tried again on the 9th to have Dwight rewrite the report, but the subordinate demurred, attaching three letters from officers in his division supporting his assertions. Five days later Emory relieved Dwight of command. Grover was not at his post, either, on this morning of battle because of "wounds" suffered at Winchester. Brigadier General James W. McMillan now had Dwight's three brigades; Brigadier General Henry W. Birge, Grover's four.[51]

Emory found his troops behind the breastworks, "motionless and expectant," as Buffum said. The fog obscured the fury beyond their left flank, but the sounds, ebbing closer, indicated that the Southerners were coming. Since Birge's brigades held the trenches next to the highway, "Old Brick Top" directed McMillan to bring one of his brigades—McMillan had only two because Colonel Leonard D. H. Currie's had been detached, guarding wagons—from the right to the endangered left. McMillan selected his own brigade, now under Colonel Stephen Thomas of the 8th Vermont, and, at Emory's instruction, sent it across the Pike, straight into the probable path of the Confederates. The corps commander also started shifting part of his artillery and some of Birge's regiments into a line parallel to the turnpike. Emory needed time, and it would be up to Thomas's men to buy some.[52]

Thomas counted approximately 800 effectives among three regiments— 8th Vermont, 12th Connecticut and 160th New York. Exactly a month ago to the day, at Third Winchester, these veterans from Vermont and Connecticut had been thrown forward into that bloody field between the First and Second Woods on a similar mission. But on this day Thomas was leading them into a fury even worse—into a "slaughter pen," said one; into "that vortex of hell," claimed another.[53]

The three regiments crossed the Pike, moved through a hollow and fashioned a battle line in a thick copse of woods. Soon, through the fog and shadowy light, the Yankees saw the enemy coming in "their yellowish suits"— the foot cavalry of Evans's division. The woods roared in anger, in a savagery equaling that found on some of the bloodiest battlefields of this war. "Men seemed more like demons than human beings," said a Northerner, "as they struck fiercely at each other with clubbed muskets and bayonets." A Southerner called such madness a "hell carnival." And, in those woods, for a few frenzied minutes, the devils in men ruled.[54]

Hand-to-hand combat was the order of the "hell carnival." The opponents raked each other at point-blank range, swung their muskets or lunged with bayonets. Some of the fiercest combat raged around the Federal battle flags. In the 8th Vermont, for example, carrying a flag meant death or maiming. Corporal John Petrie, a color bearer, was one of the first to fall with a wound in the thigh which caused his death that night. Petrie, lying on the ground, shouted: "Boys, leave me; take care of yourselves and the flag." Corporal Lyman F. Perham picked up the standard and lived but a few seconds more. Corporal George F. Blanchard then took it and died. Nearby, Lieutenant A. K. Cooper yelled: "Give it to them, boys!" He never spoke again.[55]

Others stepped forward. Corporal Leonard C. Benis grabbed the banner and went down with a wound. Three graycoats lunged toward the colors, but Sergeant Ethan P. Shores bayonetted one of them and Sewall Simpson shot another while the third retreated. All along the 8th's ranks officers and men fell. Major John B. Mead, regimental commander, suffered a flesh wound in his side, while Captain S. E. Howard was hit twice. Captain Edward Hall was less fortunate, taking a bullet in the abdomen which proved mortal. Captain G. O. Ford crumpled to the ground with a minie ball through both legs, but he still escaped. Sergeant Seth C. Hill, clubbing a Confederate, had his torso opened to the spine by another Southerner. Falling, Hill feigned death, waiting until the Confederates swept past, and joined in. When the Rebels encountered opposition and stopped, Hill sprinted into Federal lines. Altogether, of the 175 Vermonters who answered the call, 106 were either killed, wounded or captured in the woods.[56]

It was no different in the other two Union regiments. Though the 160th New York lost only 66, the 12th Connecticut sustained casualties of 192, including 93 captured. At one point in the searing, blind melee, a Connecticut officer, believing that some of the Vermonters were firing at his men, bellowed: "What the devil are you firing this way for?" "Surrender you d---d Yankee!" was the reply. It was over in ten minutes as the "nearly annihilated" brigade fled back over the macademized highway. Their sacrifice amounted to over one third of their number.[57]

While Thomas's soldiers bled in their "slaughterhouse," Horatio Wright joined Emory. The acting army commander, like Crook, had ridden from Belle Grove at the explosion of the Confederate offensive. When the mounting musketry and yells indicated a full-scale enemy assault, Wright sent instructions to James Ricketts, commanding the VI Corps, to send two divisions "at once." The major general briefly joined Crook behind the divisions of Hayes and Kitching, watching those commands shatter under the charges of Evans and Ramseur. He then spurred southward, met the 116th and 123rd Ohio from Wildes's brigade of Thoburn's division, turned the regiments around and personally led them back across the Pike in a counterattack. The Ohioans charged gamely, but the Confederates—most likely troops from Evans—repulsed the counterthrust. Wright was clipped between his lower lip and chin by a minie ball, staunching the blood with a handkerchief. A Union officer stated later that "all officers say that Wright made prodigious exertions and rode along all parts of the line in the hottest fire."[58]

When Wright bridled up beside Emory, he suggested that "Old Brick Top" shift two more brigades across the roadway as support for Thomas. But the corps commander opposed this, believing that it was too late with the flight of Hayes's and Kitching's divisions. Emory wanted to make his fight west of the Pike, convinced, as he reported, that his remaining five brigades could hold their position. Emory's post-battle assertion was curious, considering that he knew that his left flank and rear had been uncovered by the repulse of Crook's corps and Kitching's division. His determination to stand fast was in the tradition of warriors but, defending an untenable position against superior numbers, could result in the possible decimation of his command. Wright evidently concurred in his subordinate's decision.[59]

Emory countered the approaching gray battle lines by redeploying all five of his brigades. Colonel Daniel Macauley, whose brigade held the extreme left of the works, closest to the Pike, shifted two of his regiments—156th and 176th New York—perpendicularly to the original line and parallel to the highway.

Colonel David Shunk's four regiments, aligned next to Macauley, were pulled out of the trenches, marched eastward and positioned on the left of the New Yorkers. Between these two commands, Lieutenant Frederick Chase unlimbered his Battery D, 1st Rhode Island Light. Birge's remaining two brigades—Colonels Thomas W. Porter's and Edward L. Molineaux's—were ordered to the reverse side of the works, facing north. Molineaux, as directed, detached two regiments as support for Battery A, 1st Maine Light, which was formed north of Porter's troops and west of Shunk's and Macauley's regiments. Birge's command was now L-shaped with the base parallel to the direction of the charging Rebels. Finally, Colonel Edwin P. Davis's brigade of McMillan's division crossed over the entrenchments, extending Molineaux's left to Meadow Brook.[60]

These dispositions were completed under artillery fire from Confederate batteries located south of Cedar Creek and from the captured pieces of Battery D, 1st Pennsylvania Light to the east. For the first time in the battle, the gun crews of William Nelson, Carter Braxton, William McLaughlin and Wilfred Cutshaw entered the action, sending solid shot and shells—called "iron pots & canned fruit" by the Federals—into the works and camp of the XIX Corps. A number of the "canned fruit" exploded between the cannon of Battery A, 1st Maine Light, but the discharges caused few casualties.[61]

The battle was probably not yet an hour old—approximately fifteen minutes past sunrise—when the gray infantry closed on Emory's corps. From the south and east came the brigades of Goggin, Simms and Humphreys of Kershaw's division. From the east came the brigades of Lowe, Pendleton and Terry of Evans's division. Kershaw's troops were moving toward a head-on collision with the base of Emory's "L" line, while Evans's were kniving in at angle, beyond the tip of the "L."[62]

Macauley's New Yorkers and the Rhode Island gunners first glimpsed the enemy through the smoke and fog at a distance of 150 yards. The Union line flamed with musketry and cannon blasts. Kershaw's line stretched beyond both flanks of the 156th and 176th New Yorkers, and the Southerners kept coming, supported by the six captured cannon served by Simms's Georgians. The Rhode Island pieces belched canister into Humphreys's South Carolinians; the 17th Mississippi lost five color bearers, four wounded and one killed. A member of the regiment termed it "a hot place."[63]

The butternuts, replying with "a terrible fire," engulfed the Federal position and were met by musket-swinging, bayonetting New Yorkers. Another hand-to-hand slaughter ensued, with Confederate numbers prevailing. The New Yorkers fled—"I had to run till I was nearly exhausted to escape capture," admitted Captain Peter Eltinge of the 156th. The Yankees passed through a slicing crossfire. Macauley, cheering his men, toppled from his mount with a severe chest wound. Minutes earlier the colonel sent his aide, Lieutenant H. E. Macomber, to the left rear with orders to stop the firing. Macomber soon returned, reporting that Southerners, not Northerners, were doing the shooting. The aide "did not tell them to stop firing, for he didn't think they would care a d--n." Macauley then fell, and Macomber carried him off the field.[64]

Macauley's last regiment, the 38th Massachusetts, joined the retreat. The Bay Staters, occupying the original works, facing south, were enveloped when the 156th New York broke. Many in the regiment huddled in the trench under the crossfire before bolting to the rear. The brigade's casualties amounted to slightly more than 200, with 115 captured.[65]

As Kershaw's men routed Macauley's regiments, Evans's veterans hammered Shunk's command, wrecking it, too. This second Confederate division, like the first, overwhelmed the Union brigade with sheer numbers. The fighting was fierce for a few minutes as Shunk's Iowans and Hoosiers stood while Frederick Chase's Rhode Island artillerists brought off their pieces. Lieutenant Colonel Alexander J. Kenny, commanding the 8th Indiana, dropped with a grievous wound, and Lieutenant Colonel John Q. Wilds, commanding the 24th Iowa, suffered a fatal wound. Chase's gunners extricated all but one cannon as Shunk's line crumbled. The battery lost another piece as it and Shunk's brigade retreated across Meadow Brook.[66]

The destruction of the base of the "L" placed Emory's three remaining brigades in an untenable position. One by one the commands abandoned the field works, moving into the direct path of the Southerners. And one by one they were swept off the field by the two gray divisions.

The Rebels initially struck Lieutenant Eban D. Haley's six-gun Battery A, 1st Maine Light. Positioned a few hundred yards behind Macauley's troops, the artillerists served their pieces until ordered back by one of Emory's staff officers. The Southerners, closing fast, blistered the Federals with musketry, killing 49 horses in harness. But Haley's men, suffering three killed and seventeen wounded, including Haley, extricated the other five pieces, though two of the cannon were soon abandoned.[67]

The 22nd Iowa and the 3rd Massachusetts Dismounted Cavalry, dispatched from Molineaux's brigade as supports for Haley's battery, arrived as the Maine gunners were retiring. The butternuts welcomed the two regiments with a blizzard of minie balls. The volley splintered the ranks, and the Yankees tumbled back in disorder. The Iowans and Bay Staters rallied on their brigade, which Molineaux had brought into line farther west on a rise.[68]

Between Molineaux's regiments and the Confederates stood the brigade of Thomas Porter. These four regiments and two battalions—all New Englanders except for a regiment of New Yorkers—were Birge's brigade, now under Porter's temporary command. The graycoats charged to within a dozen rods when the two battle lines locked in combat. The numerically superior Rebels ripped the Union brigade apart, killing or wounding over 150 and capturing 169. Porter's soldiers fled. One of the Yankees, who escaped, remembered seeing part of a Southern unit halt at a sutler's tent which had been recently stocked. "Even the color-bearers went into help clean it out," wrote the Federal. "That was one case, certainly, where the sutler was of great benefit."[69]

Most of Kershaw's and Evans's veterans stayed in the ranks and pursued closely the broken Union command. It was not long before they collided with Molineaux's regiments aligned on the hill. Once more the opponents raked each other at point-blank range. "In this stand," reported Colonel Harvey Graham of the 22nd Iowa, "the enemy were so close to our ranks that their fire burnt the clothes of our men." Molineaux's outnumbered units, like Porter's, melted before the furnace of musketry and flowed westward toward Meadow Brook. Union casualties approached 300, with nearly 100 as prisoners.[70]

Incrementally, brigade by brigade, the veterans of Kershaw and Evans had smashed apart the XIX Corps until now only the regiments of Colonel Edwin P. Davis of McMillan's division maintained an organization. McMillan earlier had divided the brigade, placing the 30th Massachusetts and 114th New York in an advance position while Davis formed his other four regiments, supported by Captain Elijah D. Taft's 5th Battery, New York Light, on a knoll to their rear. When Molineaux's troops retreated, the Bay Staters and New Yorkers faced the Southerners. Captain James Fitts of the 114th later recalled that moment: "We who commanded companies walked up and down their front, exhorting the men to stand firm to the fiery shock that was approaching. There is, at such times, a dead weight of suspense at a soldier's heart, which is perhaps harder to bear than the fury of battle itself."[71]

The Federals, nervously clutching their rifles, looked through the curtain of mists. When they finally saw the gray ranks, they triggered "a withering volley." The Confederates staggered but came on. It was a "hopeless" struggle, wrote a New Yorker, as the butternuts swarmed around the two blue-clad regiments, shouting: "Surrender! you sons of b-----s!" Back streamed the Yankees, rallying on their comrades who waited for the "fiery shock."[72]

Davis's men offered a fierce resistance, but they, too, broke under the onslaught stinging them from three directions. The Southerners raked the Northerners, again yelling at the "d----d Yankees" to surrender. Davis's casualties approached a staggering 500, with only 49 as prisoners. Taft lost three cannon as his battery withdrew.[73]

The scene, at this point, defied any kind of concise description. The remnants of Emory's corps poured across "thigh deep" Meadow Brook. The command's disorganization ran from solitary soldiers escaping on their own to regiments still formed around the colors. A few units made one last stand before wading through the run. The 14th New Hampshire, for instance, shook out a line at Hottle's Mill, where the Brook entered Cedar Creek. The New Hampshiremen lashed at their pursuers, but the Rebels shoved them across the stream, capturing the 14th's commander, Major Theodore A. Ripley, and others.[74]

Scores, perhaps hundreds, of the Yankees, crazed with fear, ran; most retired "with curious deliberation." Captain Ezra Farnsworth of the 26th Massachusetts met one Northerner standing on a narrow footpath at the edge of Meadow Brook. Farnsworth said: "Move on." The soldier replied: "I am afraid I shall wet my feet." "I'm dead sure you will," rebutted Farnsworth as he shoved the man into the water.[75]

Emory, who had his white horse killed under him, erected a line around the batteries of Taft and Chase on Red Hill near the home of a Dr. Shipley, approximately 1,200 yards west of Belle Grove. Grover, riding an old mule, brought his depleted brigades in on the left of the artillery while McMillan formed on the right. Behind them and to the east, the sturdy VI Corps was awaiting its turn. The time neared 7:30 a.m.[76]

Across Meadow Brook, the Union camps and fieldworks were blanketed with Confederates. In the span of less than two hours the Southerners, hitting like "a terrific thunderbolt," had driven five enemy divisions from the plain between Middletown and Cedar Creek and captured over 1,300 prisoners and eighteen cannon. Partial disarray, worsened by those absent, plundering the camps, characterized some of the victorious units. Their work was not finished, but a bright October sun, like their fortunes, was ascending.[77]

Cedar Creek, Va., September 1885. View of the hill occupied by Sheridan's Left, October 19, 1864, from "Kershaw's" Ford. USAMHI.

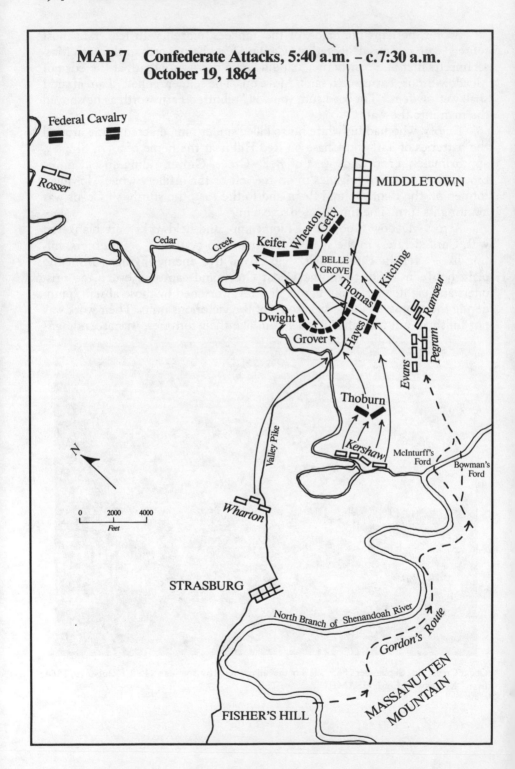

MAP 7 Confederate Attacks, 5:40 a.m. – c.7:30 a.m. October 19, 1864

Federal Cavalry

Rosser

MIDDLETOWN

Cedar   Creek

Keifer

Wheaton

Getty

BELLE GROVE

Kitching

Thomas

Ramseur

Dwight

Hayes

Pegram

Grover

Evans

N

Thoburn

Kershaw

McInturff's Ford

Bowman's Ford

0   2000   4000
Feet

Valley Pike

Wharton

STRASBURG

North Branch of Shenandoah River

Gordon's Route

FISHER'S HILL

MASSANUTTEN MOUNTAIN

12

"The Sun of Middletown"

Jubal Early rode onto the battlefield as the veterans of Joseph Kershaw and Clement Evans mopped up against the XIX Corps. Crossing Cedar Creek at the turnpike bridge, the army commander climbed the hillside and soon met John Gordon. The pair likely exchanged salutes. Early's abrasive nature and his jealousy of Gordon's rise still strained their relationship, but Old Jube could only have been well pleased with his subordinate's work. The day, so far, belonged undeniably to the ramrod-straight Georgian. The bold plan had been Gordon's; he had accepted responsibility for its outcome; and, now, he had delivered.[1]

The acting commander of the Second Corps briefly summarized the situation. Two Union corps had been swept from the field, Gordon stated, resulting in the seizure of numerous cannon and hundreds of captives. The divisions of Kershaw and Evans were pursuing toward the camps of the VI Corps, while the divisions of Dodson Ramseur and John Pegram were aligned along the turnpike north of where Early and Gordon conferred. Gordon had just ordered Pegram forward against the remaining Union corps. With this reported, the Georgian departed to resume direction of his corps.[2]

Old Jube saw little of the dispositions outlined by Gordon because of the smoke and the fog which hung, like a thick curtain, in low places. The roar of musketry and artillery indicated that the gray infantry had collided with the VI Corps. He needed to see for himself, so the stoop-shouldered Virginian spurred his horse down the Pike. Behind Early, filling the macademized road-bed, came the division of Gabriel Wharton and the artillery battalions of Tom Carter. These fresh infantrymen and ordnance might be required in the operation against the rugged VI Corps.[3]

This latter Union infantry command, the bedrock of the Army of the Shenandoah, was already deployed in a defensive position beyond Meadow

Brook when Early headed northward toward Middletown. With Horatio Wright commanding the army, James B. Ricketts, the senior brigadier, directed the corps, and he had had his veterans, numbering over 9,000, stirring before daylight. The corps members were cooking coffee and shivering in the morning chill when the Confederates attacked George Crook's units. A New Jerseyman claimed that he and his comrades "did not pay much attention" to the musketry until the long roll of drums sounded through the camps. Officers ordered their men under arms and into ranks. Columns formed, details flattened tents — "bullets were wizzing over our Head Quarters from three diferant directions wen we was packing the wagons" — and, within twenty minutes of the beginning of the Southern offensive, the VI Corps, marching by the left flank, moved east toward the sound of battle.[4]

Ricketts hurried his units as Wright had called for two divisions "at once." The corps advanced en echelon by the left flank: George Getty's division in the van, then Frank Wheaton's, and finally Ricketts's, under Colonel J. Warren Keifer. The fog seemingly rained bullets — the result of overshooting by the Confederates. As the divisions approached the Meadow Brook ravine, they encountered the first signs of the disaster unfolding across the gorge. "I am utterly unable to describe the universal confusion and dismay that we encountered," grumbled a Vermonter with Getty.[5]

Getty's troops reached the western edge of Meadow Brook ravine first and came under fire from gray skirmishers in a woodlot on the opposite plain. Two regiments and a battalion from Brigadier General Lewis A. Grant's Vermont brigade shook out a skirmish line, went down the slope, through the run, and dislodged the enemy. Getty brought his three brigades across, behind the Vermonters, and formed a line approximately 1,000 yards north of Belle Grove and 500 yards from the southern limits of Middletown. On his right Wheaton divided his division, placing Colonel William H. Penrose's three New Jersey regiments east of the sluggish stream about 200 to 300 yards from Getty's flank. Keifer, in turn, halted his two brigades behind Wheaton's right brigade, while shoving three Ohio regiments from Colonel William H. Ball's brigade across the run as a strong skirmish line. The Ohioans deployed directly behind the Belle Grove mansion. These dispositions were completed well before 7:30.[6]

Wright — "seeing that no part of the original line could be held," as he reported — countermanded his orders to Ricketts, directing that the corps should form a defensive position west of Meadow Brook. Wright's instructions, however, took time filtering down through the chain of command. The delay was lengthened when the reliable, steady Ricketts fell with a serious wound in his chest and right shoulder. Consequently, the divisions pulled back incrementally with Keifer initially, then Wheaton and finally Getty.[7]

Keifer began his retirement toward the hills behind the command's original campsite as the final units of William Emory's XIX Corps poured across

Meadow Brook before the divisions of Kershaw and Evans. The fugitives caused disorder in Keifer's ranks. "So great were the number of broken troops of the other corps," he reported, "that for a time the lines had to be opened at intervals in order to allow them to pass to the rear." Ball's brigade, in fact, was severed as the fleeing soldiers temporarily prevented the three Ohio regiments from recrossing the stream. The 122nd and 126th Ohio managed to rejoin their command after the fugitives passed but, in the confusion, the 110th Ohio moved in the wrong direction, found Wheaton's troops and fought with them.[8]

The division's officers had barely rectified the disrupted lines when part of Kershaw's command, pursuing Emory's men, ascended the hillside. Colonel William Emerson's six regiments, deployed in two lines, responded with a volley. On Emerson's left, Captain James McKnight's Battery M, 5th United States Artillery added their firepower along with Ball's veterans on the left of the cannon. The Southerners staggered and then turned. Ball's command, followed by Emerson's, counterattacked, driving the Rebels across Meadow Brook. The 6th Maryland and 126th Ohio pursued nearly to the camps of the XIX Corps until stopped.[9]

The repulse of the Confederates allowed for a refashioning of the division's front on a crest north of its abandoned camps. The infantry deployed again in two lines, with Emerson on the right and Ball on the left. McKnight's cannon remained between the brigades. On Ball's left, Captain George W. Adams's Battery G, 1st Rhode Island Light covered the approaches on that flank. To the right and rear of Emerson, Lieutenant Orsamus R. Van Etten's 1st New York Independent Battery unlimbered. Colonel Charles H. Tompkins, corps artillery commander, personally directed the batteries. Farther to the west on Red Hill, Emory was reforming his battered units, but Keifer could not rely upon these soldiers when the Confederates returned.[10]

While Keifer stopped Kershaw's pursuit and then regrouped, Wheaton brought his two brigades into position approximately 250 yards east and slightly north of Keifer's left flank. Colonel Joseph Hamblin's brigade of four regiments manned a ridge paralleling and overlooking the Meadow Brook ravine. At the base of the high ground lay the so-called Hite Road, a country lane which followed the defile from Hottle's Mill on Cedar Creek to the Samuel Sperry home, where it turned west. Hamblin's left flank was 500 yards south of the Sperry place. The colonel counted 1,356 officers and men in his ranks, plus the guns of Lieutenant Jacob H. Lamb's Battery C, 1st Rhode Island Light, which anchored the infantry line's northern end.[11]

Wheaton's second brigade, the New Jersey regiments under Penrose, covered the division's southern front. With Confederate forces to the east and south, Wheaton formed an inverted "L," by placing this unit, numbering 626 effectives, perpendicular to Hamblin's command. This configuration put Penrose on a line parallel with Keifer's ranks and 250 yards east of them.

Wheaton finished his redeployment only a short time before Kershaw and Evans launched attacks on the two VI Corps divisions.[12]

Kershaw's three brigades — from left to right: Goggin, Simms and Humphreys — struck first. Debouching from Meadow Brook ravine, the Confederates, crossing the same ground they had earlier in pursuit of the XIX Corps, passed through the abandoned Union campsite of the VI Corps and drove toward the knolls occupied by Keifer's Yankees. The blue-clad line blazed. To the west, from Red Hill, Emory's reorganized elements laced the left flank of the attackers. It was too much for the Southerners and, for a second time, they went back.[13]

The Union division counterattacked under direct orders from Horatio Wright, who had joined Keifer during the assault. But the Rebels had not been broken by the repulse and were prepared. When Keifer saw that Humphreys's brigade overlapped his left flank, he suspended the advance. The Northerners returned to their position on the crests.[14]

There was, on this day, a seeming undeniability about the South Carolinians, Georgians and Mississippians of Kershaw, however. They had accomplished all that had been asked of them. When a Yankee command stood in their path, they had shredded it. But Keifer's seasoned fighters, argumentatively, were cut from a different bolt and twice these Federals held. A third time settled it.

The Southerners returned for the decision in the wake of the abortive Union counterattack. The batteries of Van Etten, McKnight and Adams greeted the renewed offensive and, then as the Confederates closed, the opposing lines exploded. The foes stood at the top and bottom of the slopes pounding each other with a steadiness which ignored the hellishness surrounding them. These men in blue and butternut shared the "common experience" that "when a soldier is once engaged in conflict, his nerves, if before afflicted, become steady, and danger is forgotten."[15]

"The battle raged with great fury," reported Keifer. Casualties mounted; every officer in the 87th Pennsylvania battalion went down, with a sergeant major assuming command. Emerson brought his second line forward as Goggin's South Carolinians, shifting westward, overlapped his brigade's right flank. (For reasons not explained, Emory's troops evidently abandoned Red Hill between the Confederate attacks, allowing Goggin to turn Emerson's line.) Caught in a scissors of musketry, Emerson ordered a withdrawal. The brigade relinquished their grip on the crest but retired fighting.[16]

The South Carolinians swarmed onto the hill, overrunning McKnight's battery, which was limbering up when the infantry fell back. When Emerson saw the Rebels among the cannon, he ordered the 10th Vermont to retake the guns. The Vermonters, numbering slightly more than 250, stepped forward into "a terrific storm of lead and iron." They marched through it and were joined on their left by the 6th Maryland from Ball's brigade. Sergeant William

Mahony, color bearer of the 10th, reached the crest first and, jumping on a cannon, waving the flag, shouted: "They is taken, Kurnel." Around Mahoney, his comrades and the Marylanders clubbed and bayonetted the South Carolinians in hand-to-hand combat for the prizes. The Yankees prevailed long enough to bring off three cannon; the others were disabled. Now, nearly surrounded, the two Union regiments got out. The Vermonters lost approximately forty per cent of their members.[17]

At this point, Ball's regiments, aligned on the left or east of McKnight's battery, were abandoning their hilltop. When Emerson withdrew, he not only left the cannon unsupported but exposed Ball's right flank. Goggin's troops, in turn, according to a member of Ball's command, "came down on our right with them cat-like yells, that sounded more like demons than men." The 6th Maryland, occupying the right front of the line, had already started rearward when Ball sent it back with the 10th Vermont. Like Emerson's men, these Northerners could not stand before musketry from the front and flank. The Marylanders went first and the other five regiments followed as the South Carolinians, joined by Simms's Georgians, wrenched a second crest from the Yankees.[18]

Ball rallied his units on another knoll 200 yards farther north. The Southerners, however, pressed their assault and, with Emerson's brigade still retreating, Ball's veterans, under a "very severe" fire, again fled. As they streamed down the slope, Wright rode into their midst, stopped Major James W. Snyder, commander of the 9th New York Heavy Artillery, and told the regimental officer to take his command back and hold the crest until the brigade regrouped. Snyder turned his men around, leading them up the slope. The "Heavies" cheered, climbed to the top and lashed the Southerners with a volley.[19]

The New Yorkers—400 of them were recruits in their initial battle—fought alone and valiantly. The Confederates sliced their ranks with a galling crossfire. "Here one of our boys, Anthony Riley, was shot and killed," recalled a member of the regiment. "His father [Charles E. Riley] was by his side; the blood and brains of his son covered the face and hands of the father. I never saw a more affecting sight than this; the poor old man kneels over the body of his dead son; his tears mingled with his son's blood. O God! what a sight."[20]

Captain J. P. Dudrow of Ball's staff galloped through the fury with orders for Snyder's withdrawal. When Dudrow informed the major of his instructions, Snyder pointed to Wright, who was in sight, and said: "The general ordered me to hold this crest, and I shall obey his orders." Minutes later Snyder received word that the brigade had reformed. Some of the Confederates were closing in on the regiment's rear when Snyder pulled his New Yorkers back. Charles Riley, still kneeling by his son's body, leaned down, kissed Anthony's cheek one more time and then joined his retreating comrades.[21]

The dislodgment of Ball's brigade left the Rhode Island battery of George Adams unsupported. Before the artillerists could escape, the Confederates were among the pieces, "howling like devils." Less than 200 yards to the east was the New Jersey brigade of Wheaton's division. When its commander, William Penrose, saw the battery in Confederate hands, he changed front to rear and led his three regiments toward the Rebels. Wheeling to the left, the Union brigade charged up the slope.[22]

The graycoats—most likely, Georgians—stung the New Jerseymen. Penrose's horse was killed and, as he continued on foot, another bullet ripped into his right arm, splintering a bone. He turned back with Lieutenant Colonel Edward L. Campbell of the 15th New Jersey replacing him. The Federals kept coming, reached the brow and drove the Southerners down the opposite slope. Members of the brigade started pulling the cannon away, but the Georgians counterattacked and reclaimed the pieces.[23]

Campbell rallied his veterans at the base of the rise and led them up again. The musketry roared; Campbell took a bullet in his left arm, shattering a wrist bone. Major Lambert Boeman, commander of the 10th New Jersey, was killed, and Captain Baldwin Hufty, commander of the 4th New Jersey, was wounded. But the New Jerseymen prevailed, retook the guns and stood on the crest while the gunners dragged them to safety. An order from Wheaton arrived, directing them rearward by "right of battalions." As they started back, Sergeant John Mouder, carrying the unfurled state flag of the 15th New Jersey, was killed. No one in the regiment noticed, and the banner was left behind on the ground beside Mouder.[24]

Wheaton recalled the New Jersey command because his other brigade, Joseph Hamblin's, had been badly broken. Hamblin's four regiments—more than double the strength of Penrose's command—manned the ridge above the Hite Road, facing the Meadow Brook ravine, on a line perpendicular to the front of the New Jersey brigade. On the brigade's left, Lamb's Battery C, 1st Rhode Island Light was deployed. Hamblin's men came under attack at about the same time Kershaw's division engaged Keifer. The Southerners charging the ridge above Hite Road, according to Union accounts, belonged to the division of Clement Evans.[25]

These final two points—the time of the assault and the composition of the Confederate force—exemplify the difficulty of presenting an accurate description of the combat on this field. All Civil War battles, to one degree or another, were, by the nature of the combat, struggles of inordinate confusion. The chess set-piece maneuvering often portrayed by generals dissolved in a cauldron of hellish noise and blind, choking smoke. Subordinate officers and the enlisted men in the ranks saw only the fury around them, generally remembering only those comrades who fell or performed bravely and the particular viciousness of the combat. Few rarely knew whose command was on their left or right and few rarely checked their watches. Certain battles, or

phases of them, thus defy neatness of description. The one fought at Cedar
Creek belongs in this category.

A number of factors specific to this major engagement compound the
problems of historical inquiry. Nothing affected the initial three hours of
combat more than the fog, which thickened because of the smoke from
discharged black powder. The blanket of mist shielded the charging Southerners, reduced their casualties and increased the confusion in Northern
ranks as the Federals fashioned patchwork lines against an unseen opponent.
A Yankee later addressed this point: "The enemy pushed so furiously that he
seemed to arrive first at every place which we wished to occupy."[26] This blind
struggle, conversely, spared Federal units from probable annihilation, gave
them a curtain of protection as they fled and hampered the coordination
among the attackers.

Cedar Creek, thus, during the early hours of combat, was a battle of
sounds. Union officers, particularly, shifted units toward the thunder. Rebel
commanders, however, drove their men westward until they collided with
another defensive line. The Valley Pike served as a guide for the Southerners,
an axis perpendicular to their advance which marked a specific location on
the field.

Descriptions of the engagement reflect the uncertainty, caused by the
fog, of unit locations on the field. The Federals benefitted from fighting a
defensive battle at spots at or close to their pre-battle dispositions, and their
reports and memoirs are fairly reliable. The accounts of Crook's and Emory's
officers and men, however, increase in vagueness when they discuss positions
beyond Meadow Brook. The Northern writings nevertheless are far superior
to the handful of Southern versions. The Rebels usually named only their
opposing units and noted only two main spots—the turnpike and Meadow
Brook—placing their commands either east or west of them. The most reliable guide for the Confederate commands, their dispositions and attack
routes is Jedediah Hotchkiss's maps in the atlas accompanying the *Official
Records*. But the topographer's fine work does not clarify some conflicting
descriptions.[27]

A second factor hampering a reconstruction of this fluid, two-to-three-
hour segment of the battle is the dearth of Confederate accounts. Of Early's
five division commanders, only one—Bryan Grimes, writing for a mortally
wounded Dodson Ramseur—had his report published in the *Official Records*.
If Kershaw, Evans, Pegram and Wharton filed summaries, their reports were
either lost or destroyed. Of the seventeen brigade commanders, three—two
from Kershaw's division and one from Ramseur's—had their accounts published in the records. Gordon, in his reminiscences, stated that he had submitted a report on the operations of the Second Corps. Why it was not published,
the Georgian did not know, describing its absence as "unexpected and unex-
plained."[28] Gordon, an acerbic critic of Early, wanted the reader to infer that

Old Jube deliberately got rid of the report to protect his reputation.[29]

Regardless, this lack of official after-battle reports of Southern commanders leads to unresolved questions. The duel along the Hite Road between Hamblin's Northerners and Evans's Southerners illustrate the uncertainties: What was the attack path of the Confederates? Did the gray division strike the Union brigade's right front and then, sidling northward, overlap the Federal left, the flank which was turned according to Northern statements? But how could the Rebels turn Hamblin's left and capture part of Lamb's battery when Getty's division was only 300 yards from that flank? Did the fog conceal Evans's veterans from Getty though this Union general stated in his report that he could see "heavy lines of rebel infantry" advancing as Hamblin's brigade fled "in confusion?"[30]

What of Pegram's division, the command Gordon told Early that he had committed to the attack? Did this division envelope Hamblin's left and capture the cannon, as the veterans of the command later asserted? If Pegram charged around 7:30, how could he have avoided Getty's troops? In fact, what was and had been the role of the Virginian's three brigades during this phase of the battle? Had Pegram's 1,600 troops been wasted so far and whose fault was it?[31]

Not all these questions can be answered with assurance. But, from the sources available, it appears that Evans, perhaps marching his three brigades en echelon, hit Hamblin along the latter's right front and, then shifting northward, assailed Lamb's battery, collapsing Hamblin's left. Getty, in turn, reacted only after Hamblin had been routed by withdrawing across Meadow Brook at about eight o'clock. The gray battle line moving toward Getty probably was Pegram's, whose troops would soon attack Getty west of the stream. Why Pegram was not seriously engaged until nearly three hours after the initial Confederate assault remains unknown. It was a critical mistake on someone's part.

Evans's infantrymen, therefore, moving through and up the western slope of Meadow Brook ravine, charged Hamblin's troops about the same time Kershaw attacked Keifer, or at approximately 7:30. Coming in from the southeast, across the fields north of Belle Grove, the Confederates hit the right front of the Union brigade, occupying the ridge behind the Hite Road. For the next thirty minutes—and for the first time on this day—the Southerners had all they wanted. When the Rebels pressed toward the ridge, the Yankees pounded them back. The country lane must have seemed to the Southerners like a boundary of hell.[32]

The defenders fought tenaciously, but at a dear price. Hamblin was wounded along with a dozen other officers, while three more were killed, including Lieutenant Colonel Thomas H. Higinbotham, commander of the 65th New York. Finally, when Penrose's New Jersey brigade was driven back on the right by Kershaw's men, Colonel Ranald S. Mackenzie, Hamblin's successor, ordered a withdrawal. As the Federals retired, the graycoats stormed up the ridge, pressing their advantage. Lamb's Rhode Island gunners lost three of their cannon to the Confederates. The 139th Pennsylvania, detached from Getty's division, was supporting the battery and covered the retreat of the remaining pieces.[33]

Mackenzie reformed the line on another crest a few hundred yards to the west, but the enemy gave the Yankees no relief. The gray fighters swarmed around the left of the Federal line, collapsing it. Mackenzie had his mount killed and took a bullet in the heel, forcing him to relinquish command to Lieutenant Colonel Egbert Olcott. What had been an orderly retirement from the first ridge now became a rout. Pockets of Federals fought rearguard actions, but the command had been temporarily wrecked. Its casualties amounted to over a quarter of its strength.[34]

The time now neared eight o'clock; two divisions of the VI Corps — Keifer's and Wheaton's — and the organized remnants of the XIX Corps were streaming northward over the farmlands west of Meadow Brook. These commands soon regrouped, approximately three-fourths of a mile from the hills and ridge from which they had been driven. The only Union infantry command still remaining on the field south of Middletown was the third and largest division of the VI Corps, that of George Washington Getty. It, too, was retiring, not back with these other infantry units, but to a better defensive position. Getty was one of the best commanders in the army and his men were some of the finest soldiers. They had no intention of leaving the field without a fight.[35]

Getty began his retrograde movement from east of the run after Keifer and Wheaton had been forced back. The retreat of these latter two commands placed Getty in an untenable position with Kershaw and Evans beyond his right flank. Getty was 45 years old, experienced in both artillery and infantry, one of those bedrock-steady officers, "a splendid soldier" to Henry DuPont. When he saw Wheaton's ranks tumbling rearward "in confusion," he directed his three brigades back about 300 yards to "a strong crest, semicircular in form and partially wooded." With its natural strengths, it was the best defensive position on this section of the field. The men in the ranks also noticed that it was the site of Middletown's cemetery.[36]

James M. Warner's brigade of one New York and three Pennsylvania regiments — the 139th Pennsylvania had been detached from Warner — held the division's right, facing "nearly south." On Warner's left, in the center, Getty placed Lewis Grant's Vermonters. Daniel D. Bidwell's command of three regiments and three battalions — men from Maine, New York and Pennsylvania — covered the left front, "parallel to and bordering the run." Skirmishers from Bidwell's 1st Maine and 43rd New York completed the alignment by connecting with the videttes of Thomas Devin's cavalry brigade. Getty's line resembled the arc of a circle or "a horse-shoe." Most of Bidwell's regiments and half of Warner's were sheltered by trees while Grant's units occupied open ground. A handful of regiments erected some crude breastworks, but most lay down behind the crest line. Skirmishers rimmed the entire front, an early warning system in the fog. Approximately 500 yards behind the infantrymen, Lieutenant Franck E. Taylor's Batteries K and L, 1st United States Horse Artillery provided ordnance support.[37]

The "heavy lines" of approaching Confederate infantry which Getty saw before his withdrawal to the crest most likely were those of Pegram's division. The Yankees, consequently, were deployed around the cemetery but a short time before these Southerners attacked. Accounts place the initial assault on Getty at about 8:30. One of the mysteries of this battle, which the sources don't resolve, is why Pegram's command was not seriously engaged until nearly three hours after the engagement opened.[38]

When Evans and Ramseur dismantled the Union commands of George Crook and J. Howard Kitching, Pegram's three brigades acted as a reserve, trailing the two front divisions. The troops of Evans and Ramseur bore the fighting, including the sorties against the fleeing Union wagons. When Evans swung southwestward and joined Kershaw in the offensive against the XIX Corps, Ramseur's four brigades stopped along the turnpike between Middletown and Belle Grove. Skirmishers from the North Carolinian's regiments fanned out toward Meadow Brook and secured Middletown. Ramseur did not press farther west, according to the report of Bryan Grimes, because the division was under artillery fire from Federal cannon beyond the run, and he decided to wait until Confederate artillery arrived to offer counterfire. Grimes thought this delay lasted "perhaps half an hour," but it most likely was longer.[39]

Pegram's command, meanwhile, filled the gap in Ramseur's line between the brigades of Philip Cook and Cullen Battle, now under Edwin Hobson. Ramseur and Pegram had, by seven o'clock, about 4,000 veterans at hand. But the fog and smoke limited their vision and, without orders from Gordon, who had followed Evans's attack, the pair of generals hesitated. Dodson Ramseur was one of the most aggressive combat officers in the Army of Northern Virginia, but he chose a safe course. He learned between 7:00 and 7:30 that his skirmishers had been driven back by Union infantry—Getty's division crossing the run. This may have convinced him that a blind assault against Federal cannon of uncertain numbers and infantry of unknown strength would be rash without artillery support. So, for over an hour altogether, two Confederate divisions stood idle.[40]

This inaction, attributable to the fog and a lack of command direction, became a critical factor, if not decisive, in the outcome of the battle. Perhaps, at no other point in the engagement, did the concealing mists abet the Union forces more than at this time. Ramseur and Pegram held the key to the battle—the Valley Pike—and did not know it. If they had been able to view the dispositions of the VI Corps, Ramseur could have held Getty in place while Pegram marched down the turnpike and through Middletown. Pegram would not only have been beyond the left flank of the Union army, but he would have secured the highway, which commanded the area. The Yankees could not have used the road either as an escape route or a point of rallying as they subsequently did. Getty, in turn, could not have attacked Ramseur, with Kershaw and Evans assailing Keifer and Wheaton behind his right and rear. The Union infantry, pressed by the three Southern divisions, could only have retreated westward across the countryside toward the Back Road and not northward toward the Pike as they did.[41]

This, of course, was beyond the view of Ramseur or Pegram or Gordon. Would it have been different had the Georgian not accompanied Evans but remained with Ramseur and Pegram? Unlikely, except, perhaps, he would have committed Pegram sooner. Gordon only knew that the rugged VI Corps lay west of Meadow Brook and, once Kershaw and Evans found part of it, he sent Pegram searching for the rest of it. The Second Corps commander also knew that final victory meant defeating this Federal command. A splendid opportunity slipped unseen past the Confederates.

Gordon's orders to Pegram, then, reached the Virginian probably between 7:30 and 8:00. He responded promptly. His 1,600 Virginians and North Carolinians marched across the plain "as if on dress parade." Though the sources conflict, Edwin Hobson's Alabamians apparently advanced with Pegram, going in beyond the latter's right flank, closer to the southern edge of Middletown. At least one Southern battery covered the infantry. It was these serried ranks that Getty must have seen when he retired across the run to the crest at the graveyard.[42]

The Confederates soon emerged from Meadow Brook ravine, climbing toward the waiting Yankees. Pegram's three brigades — those of Brigadier General Robert Johnston, Colonel John S. Hoffman and Lieutenant Colonel William S. Davis — passed on both sides of the Samuel Sperry house on an attack path leading to Warner's and Grant's brigades. Hobson's Alabamians, marching almost due west, headed for a collision with Bidwell's Northerners. The Yankee skirmishers disappeared into the lines as the gray ranks ascended the hillside. Getty's men, numbering nearly 4,000, rose to a kneeling position. The division commander issued instructions prohibiting firing until the Southerners closed to within thirty yards.[43]

The Federals aimed; knuckles whitened; grips tightened. The Rebel yell, "ringing out above all other sounds," rolled up the ascent. When the butternuts crossed Getty's boundary, the crest flashed death; a volcano of musketry drowned out the fiendish screams. The attackers replied with lightning of their own, but the Federal wall of flame stopped the Rebels where they stood. Captain Samuel Buck of the 13th Virginia of Hoffman's brigade remembered seeing a Captain Richards of the regiment, "to the surprise of all," in the line. Richards, however, was crawling on all fours behind the ranks and, when a bullet hit him, he "yelled like an indian." Buck laughed in the wounded officer's face.[44]

The kneeling defenders, protected by trees and some breastworks of rails and stones, blasted the attackers "with terrible effect." The gray-clad ranks began receding down the slope. Warner launched a counterattack against Pegram with the 93rd and 102nd Pennsylvania, while Bidwell hurled his skirmishers against Hobson's Alabamians. The thrusts drove the Confederates across Meadow Brook, completing the repulse. Warner's and Bidwell's troops returned to their position on the crest.[45]

As the four Southern brigades retreated across the plain, a number of Confederate batteries concentrated on Getty's men. The Federals hugged the ground under "a terrible fire." During this firestorm, Getty learned of Ricketts's fall and his assumption of corps command. He turned over the division to Grant and then rode northward, searching for Keifer's and Wheaton's commands.[46]

Lewis Addison Grant was a 36-year-old native of Vermont, where he practiced law before the war. Commissioned major of the 5th Vermont, he assumed command of the brigade of Green Mountain state volunteers at Fredericksburg in December 1862 and led it with distinction throughout the next year and a half. Evidently absent on leave during August and September 1864, he had rejoined the command after Fisher's Hill. Grant had a proven combat record but, among the Vermonters, he had "a reputation for old-maidishness." The brigadier, wrote a member of the brigade, "had, by diligent study, made himself so thoroughly acquainted with the red tape of the Regulations, that he became a martinet in his disposition to require the performance of many of its absurdities, which were especially ridiculous in a field campaign." Grant was, groused the enlisted man, "constitutionally a Regular" in his concern for details. He took especial care with his skirmishers in battle.[47]

The fussy, new division commander, however, had little time for fretting before his videttes announced the approach of a second attack force. The oncoming Southerners belonged to the North Carolina brigade of Bryan Grimes—the 2nd Battalion, the 53rd and parts of the 43rd and 45th. With the repulse of Pegram and Hobson, Ramseur ordered his good friend and best subordinate forward. Grimes, a plain, unassuming man, was an exceptional, inspirational combat officer, but now he had been asked to accomplish with an understrength brigade what four did not. Dodson Ramseur committed a cardinal mistake of generals—charging piecemeal against an entrenched, numerically superior opponent.[48]

The Tarheels, skirting Middletown, advanced under a preceding blanket of Confederate artillery salvos toward the section of line held by Bidwell and the Vermonters, under Lieutenant Colonel Amasa S. Tracy. As they went up the rise, they, too, screamed their yell. The crest once more flashed with fire from hundreds of rifles. The North Carolinians kept coming and, in the words of a Vermonter, "pressed us harder and harder, the lines being but a few yards apart." The 61st Pennsylvania and the 77th New York on Bidwell's right started falling back, while the 6th and 11th Vermont on Tracy's left nearly panicked. Bidwell, "a man of remarkably large frame," galloped toward the breach. A Confederate shell burst above him, its shrapnel tearing away his shoulder and puncturing a lung. The 45-year-old brigadier died that night, saying at the end: "I have tried to do my duty."[49]

Lieutenant Colonel Winsor B. French, 77th New York, rallied his men and the Pennsylvanians; the Vermonters steadied; and, together, they resealed the gap. What the North Carolinians so valiantly took, they could not hold. The Federals raked the Tarheels from three sides, pounding them off the crest "with great slaughter." A Confederate officer stated in his report that the brigade "lost many good and gallant men." Grimes reformed the regiments east of Meadow Brook.[50]

At this point in the action, Jubal Early, riding down the turnpike, found Ramseur and Pegram. Though two of his brigades and Pegram's division had been checked, Ramseur remained buoyant. When the North Carolinian saw Major Henry Kyd Douglas, one of Early's aides and an old friend, he exclaimed: "Douglas, I want to win this battle, for I must see my wife and baby."[51]

If Old Jube overheard Ramseur's remark, he ignored it; his concern was the business at hand. He inquired about the situation—fog and smoke still obscured parts of the field—and the division commanders briefly summarized, stating that they opposed part of the VI Corps and "there was a vacancy in the line on their right which ought to be filled." "I ordered Wharton's division forward at once," the army commander later stated, "and directed Generals Ramseur and Pegram to put it where it was required."[52]

It was, on Early's part, a hasty decision, a critical mistake. He permitted two subordinate officers, who admittedly knew the conditions on this sector of the field and were reliable, to commit the army's final infantry division to a third attack on a position which had defied two previous attempts. Wharton's assignment for the day's operations was, after crossing Cedar Creek, to "press up the pike."[53] As discussed earlier, the Valley Pike, commanding the battlefield, was the key, the avenue of Confederate victory. Wharton, at this time, between 9:00 and 9:30, still could have secured the roadway north of Middletown, for the Union cavalry, in force, had not yet reached it. But Early, by redirecting Wharton on the request of Ramseur and Pegram, missed this second opportunity for an envelopment of the left flank of the Union army.

Captain Benjamin W. Crowninshield, a member of Sheridan's staff, subsequently termed Early's judgment as "worse than folly." Captain Henry DuPont, in his memoirs, called it "his fatal error." Expanding on this, DuPont argued: "The battle in any event was lost to the Confederates from the moment that Wharton was ordered to support Ramseur and Pegram in their assault upon Getty's division, not only for the reason that it then and there became apparent that the morale of Getty's troops was still unimpaired and that his men could not be driven an inch farther by frontal attacks, but also because the very heavy casualties in the three hostile divisions seem to have made Early much more circumspect."[54]

Southern accounts—those that praise Early and those that condemn him—curiously ignore the use of Wharton. The bulk of these writings dwell on the hours of inaction from approximately 11:00 a.m. to 4:00 p.m., attributing Confederate defeat to Old Jube's failure to press the Federals. Historians, likewise, have neglected it. Douglas S. Freeman in his *Lee Lieutenants*, which remains the fullest version of Southern activities, does not address this issue. Freeman, like the participants, sought an explanation for the reversal of Confederate fortunes in those hours of delay. These arguments rest upon one major premise: the Union army, reeling under a succession of Rebel blows, would have dissolved under a final, vigorous pursuit which never came because of Early.[55]

Why this absence, concerning Wharton, in the Confederate versions? Did Early misuse that command and why? It would seem that the Rebels, then and later, did not realize the importance of holding the turnpike north of Middletown. When the Confederate commander joined Ramseur and Pegram, he knew virtually nothing of Union dispositions and the situation beyond the town. Understandably, Early listened to the pair of division commanders and accepted their assessments of their tactical needs. A personal reconnaissance on his part might have altered his decision but the limited visibility prevented this. Early, through Ramseur and Pegram, was drawn into another frontal assault on the Federal division.

The lieutenant general, thus, reached his decision based upon the best information available at the time. Should he, in turn, warrant censure? Was it "worse than folly," "his fatal error?" From the perspective of hindsight, with the knowledge of what transpired, the diversion of Wharton denied the Confederates their final opportunity of altering, by maneuver, the events of the afternoon. The remarkable success of the Southern offensive, up to this time, had been achieved with a brilliantly executed movement. They negated Federal numerical superiority by maneuver, not with battering, headlong assaults. If Wharton's original assignment—"press up the pike"—meant proceeding through Middletown, holding the Yankees' main retreat route, then Early blundered by reassigning that division before personally checking the situation north of the village—it would have taken only a handful of minutes. The sources, unfortunately, don't clarify what "press up the pike" entailed. Regardless, Old Jube did not reconnoiter; he ordered Wharton forward without support. Once he concurred with Ramseur and Pegram, the army commander should have hurled all the available troops at hand—Pegram's division and, at least, the brigades of Philip Cook and William Cox from Ramseur's. Instead, he permitted another piecemeal attack.

Wharton's three brigades, approximately 1,100 effectives, went in gamely. Behind the infantry, Captain Thomas A. Bryan's Lewisburg Battery unlimbered 300 yards from the Federal position and opened fire. Following the attack path of Pegram, these Virginians drove toward the Union right center. But Warner's and Tracy's soldiers ripped apart the attacking ranks, repulsing them "in the wildest confusion." Bryan, in turn, pulled back his cannon. Wharton personally reported the outcome to Early while his men reformed near the turnpike.[56]

"The fog soon rose sufficiently," Early wrote, "for us to see the enemy's position on a ridge to the west of Middletown, and it was discovered to be a strong one." The commander concluded, from a visual inspection, that a fourth assault from the Pike could not succeed. Finding Tom Carter, he ordered a concentration of artillery on Grant's Federals. While Carter aligned the batteries, Early also dispatched Major Mann Page, with instructions for an attack by Gordon and Kershaw. Additionally, Old Jube learned that a force of Union cavalry was closing on Middletown, threatening his right flank. He countered by sending Wharton's division and William Wofford's brigade of Kershaw's division, supported by some artillery, toward the village.[57]

Wofford's command of Georgians had been on this sector of the battlefield for an indeterminate amount of time. When Kershaw charged Joseph Thoburn's command at 5:40, Wofford, swinging east of the Union works, marched straight ahead, instead of wheeling leftward. The Georgians, consequently, moved through the camps of Hayes and Kitching in the wake of the assault of the Second Corps. Wofford finally halted east of the turnpike, behind Ramseur and Pegram. While the latter officers were engaged, the Georgians must have rested, perhaps rummaging through the camps, for at least two hours. Why no one thought of utilizing this unscathed unit remains a mystery, an indication of Confederate command problems on this part of the field.[58]

Carter, meanwhile, had deployed eighteen or twenty guns, which began shelling Grant's men on the crest. A trooper in Devin's brigade, located behind the infantry, stated that "the enemy's guns seemed to fill the air with cast iron all about us. Several shells passed through our company's ranks but with little damage. One cut half of a Co. C boy's head off which stood next to us." Grant, seeing that Kershaw and Evans overlapped his right flank, ordered, with Getty's approval, a withdrawal. Early believed that the cannon fire drove the Yankees back, but Union reports clearly affirm that the presence of the two Confederate divisions on their flank necessitated a retreat.[59]

It was a few minutes past 9:30 when the Northerners abandoned the shell-swept hilltop and cemetery. For over an hour they had stood, like a breaker against a tide, repelling three assaults, slowing the momentum of the

Southern offensive. No Union troops rendered greater service on this day than these men from New York, Pennsylvania, Vermont and Maine. Staff officer Crowninshield subsequently asserted that their defense "was the turning-point in Early's attack, and but for this the final success could not have been possible, for it gave a breathing spell, most necessary, to our disorganized troops."[60]

Jubal Early, however, could not know the implications of this stand; from his vantage point near the turnpike, he saw only another Federal retirement. He directed Ramseur and Pegram to occupy the vacant crest but soon shifted Pegram's division north of Middletown as reports kept coming in of the advance of Union horsemen. Additionally, Mann Page returned. The major informed his commander that neither Kershaw nor Evans could advance at this time. "They [Kershaw and Gordon] stated in reply," as Early put it in his October 21 report to Robert E. Lee, "that a heavy force of cavalry had got in their front, and that their ranks were so depleted by the number of men who had stopped in the camps to plunder that they could not advance them." But Gordon, at least, never told Page this, because the major did not encounter the Georgian. The aide, seeing Evans's troops reforming, concluded that the command was as badly scattered as Kershaw admitted his troops to be.[61]

The lieutenant general, judging by his memoirs, accepted Page's intelligence with little concern. Let Kershaw take Pegram's place in the line beside Ramseur, Early concluded. With this done, he spurred his mount toward Middletown. He was uncharacteristically buoyant—victory seemed imminent. Captain S. V. Southall, a staff officer, remembered seeing the grizzled old warrior earlier react to some good news. "His face became radiant with joy," Southall noted, "and in his gladness he exclaimed, 'The sun of Middletown! The sun of Middletown!'"—a reference to Napoleon Bonaparte's words at Austerlitz.[62]

Early entered Middletown after ten o'clock. He found Pegram's and Wharton's divisions and Wofford's brigade, positioned on the northern edge of the village, already engaged with Union cavalry. A number of Carter's batteries were deployed behind the infantry, adding their metal to the brisk exchange. The Yankees, dismounted and mounted, bolstered by horse artillery and pieces from the Union infantry corps, kept the Rebels at bay and, in Early's view, threatened the right flank.[63]

Temporarily, then, the Confederate offensive stalled, checked by enemy horsemen. Neither Early nor anyone else in the army knew it yet, but their tide had crested before a barrier of Yankee cavalry. Ironically, if the Southerners had not sent the bogus message about James Longstreet reinforcing their army, Wesley Merritt's troopers, the largest contingent of Federal horsemen, would not have been on the field. Fortune ignored Jubal Early.

Horatio Wright had requested the recall of the cavalry because of concern for his right flank. When Alfred Torbert returned with the division of

Merritt on the 16th, the cavalrymen reoccupied their old camps between the bivouac site of the VI Corps and the Back Road. Merritt's tents were pitched a mile north and west of the VI Corps, while George Custer's lay about a mile and a half west of Merritt's. Like the infantrymen, the troopers relaxed on the 18th; a reconnaissance that day by some of Custer's regiments uncovered no Confederates in their "immediate front." The 7th Michigan Cavalry of Merritt's command drew picket duty along Cedar Creek for the night.[64]

Before daylight on the 19th—Union reports time it as 4:00 a.m.—the Michiganers were attacked by Southern cavalry. The 100 Wolverines stationed south of the stream were nearly cut off but escaped in the fog. The Confederate force consisted of two brigades, some 900 Virginians, and horse artillery under Thomas Rosser. Early's orders for the day specified that Rosser should "occupy the enemy's cavalry" while the infantry charged the opposite flank. It was an enormous burden for the officer, whose command was outnumbered by about eight-to-one. Rosser, consequently, acted cautiously, beginning with this initial contact. He pushed the two brigades across the creek at Minebank Ford—three and a half miles, as a crow flies, from the turnpike bridge—halted them, planted the artillery on the opposite bank and waited until first light.[65]

But the brush between the Wolverines and the Virginians alerted the Union camps. Custer and Merritt aroused their men as a precaution. The 7th Michigan belonged to James Kidd's brigade, so Merritt ordered that command toward the creek as support for the videttes. For the next hour or so neither side, because of the darkness and fog, advanced. At daylight Rosser's horse artillery began shelling the Union bivouacs while his skirmishers probbed forward. For the Yankees, however, the more ominous sound was the rumble of heavy musketry coming from the east, where the infantry bivouacked.[66]

Alfred Torbert, when he heard the thunder of the Confederate offensive, reacted at once. He ordered tents struck, troopers to their saddles and wagons loaded and sent rearward. Details worked feverishly, flattening tents, piling them into the wagons. Within minutes his headquarters campsite was cleared, except for one tent. Torbert, mounted on a "beautiful gray," dashed toward it and demanded of a sergeant standing beside it why the tent had not been taken down. "Capt. (John J.) Coppinger is taking his bawth, sir," replied the non-commissioned officer. "I thought Torbert would ride him down as he screamed, 'Cut those tent ropes. Cut the ropes, I say,'" remembered Captain George B. Sanford, Coppinger's tent mate. Out spilled a wet and embarrassed Coppinger and down went the canvas.[67]

Torbert guessed correctly that the intensity of the fighting on the left indicated a full-scale engagement, but he hesitated, at first, in shifting most of his command in that direction. He also did not know the strength of the Rebel cavalry force on his right, which Custer was engaging with his horse batteries. But he shortly learned of the disaster unfolding to the east when hundreds of the most frightened of Crook's, Kitching's and Emory's men came running across the fields. Torbert directed his escort, the 1st Rhode Island Cavalry, and Merritt's, the 5th United States Cavalry, "to check this stream of stragglers." Merritt also gave Thomas Devin's brigade the dual duty of moving eastward and assisting in the rallying of the fugitives.[68]

A New Yorker with Devin wrote later that for his regiment this task of stopping the infantry was "the most difficult and most distasteful duty it had ever been called upon to perform, and one almost impossible to accomplish." Many in the herd of fugitives eluded the mounted troopers by darting under the horses. Devin reported that he checked the rout—"it being necessary in several instances to fire on the crowds retiring, and to use the saber frequently." According to a member of the brigade, Devin shouted at one soldier, leading a squad, to halt. "I'll be hanged if I'll halt for any d---d cavalrymen," rebutted the infantryman. "Uncle Tommy" shot him dead where he stood.[69]

This distasteful business occupied the two regiments and Devin's brigade for the better part of two hours. By the time the Confederates assaulted Getty's division on the cemetery knoll, Devin had brought his three regiments to a position north of the infantry division, with his two batteries, under Franck Taylor, supporting the foot soldiers. Part of Devin's skirmish line, as noted previously, connected with Bidwell's brigade while another segment stretched to the turnpike, where it linked with skirmishers from Alpheus Moore's brigade. Moore, after his pickets had been driven back from Bowman's Ford by William Payne's Rebels, regrouped his units, retired northward and now had his three regiments, about 600 troopers, covering the fields east of the highway, north of town. Opposing Moore's men were Payne's some 300 Virginians, who, after grabbing some wagons, swung east of Middletown and engaged the Yankees. The action amounted to fitful skirmishing.[70]

Shortly after nine o'clock, Horatio Wright, with only Getty's division still holding, instructed Torbert to move his entire corps to the left. "This I was opposed to," the cavalry officer stated in his report, "but proceeded to obey the order, but on my own responsibility I left three regiments to picket the right." The brigade of Colonel William Wells of Custer's division drew the assignment of frustrating Rosser, who had really done very little in the ensuing period. Though Torbert disagreed with Wright's order, it was the single, most important decision made by the acting army commander on this day.[71]

The march of the cavalry across the fields north of Middletown, in Merritt's words, "was done with the precision and quietness of troops on parade." As the columns neared the village, Tom Carter's artillerists unleashed a "terrific" fire. One shell, exploding above the 6th Michigan Cavalry, erased an entire set of fours; those behind just closed up and proceeded.[72]

Merritt, in the van, deployed his brigades between the roadway and the right of Moore. Devin, who preceded the division, held the ground abutting the Pike; on his left, Kidd brought in his Wolverines; finally, Charles R.

Lowell, Jr.'s Reserve Brigade linked with Moore. Devin's and Kidd's troopers stayed in the saddle while Lowell's veterans, dismounting, manned some stone walls. Behind these units, Custer, wearing a red necktie as a badge, placed his remaining brigade, commanded by Colonel Alexander C. M. Pennington. Five batteries of horse artillery anchored the position, which lay entirely east of the turnpike. The Federals completed the dispositions by ten o'clock. Torbert counted upwards of 7,500 troopers in the ranks.[73]

A few minutes later, the infantrymen of Gabriel Wharton and William Wofford, clearing the village, engaged Merritt's troopers. Wharton's troops charged Lowell's men behind the stone walls but were repulsed. Many of the Northerners carried Spencer repeaters, and this weapon gave them a decided edge in firepower. The action continued as a brisk skirmish. Opposing gun crews duelled, adding a deep bass to the treble of carbine and musket fire. Pegram's command soon added its firepower but the Southerners, outnumbered and overlapped on their right, stayed put.[74]

This, then, was the situation Jubal Early found when he rode into Middletown after ten o'clock. After examining the enemy position, he concurred with the reports that the blue-jacketed cavalry might envelope his right flank, guarded only by Payne's understrength brigade located east of Wofford. Wright or Torbert had no intention of implementing such a movement but Old Jube could not have known this. To his view, the army needed help on that flank before it could attempt another advance.[75]

Early's poor understanding of the role of cavalry haunted him now. The army's largest mounted command, Lunsford Lomax's division of 1,700 troopers, was miles away, beyond Front Royal, proceeding toward the Valley Pike. The commanding general had detached Lomax from the army on a vague mission against the rear of the Federal army, whom Early hoped to rout. It was a plan borne of optimism, but it constituted a major blunder by the Southern commander. By removing his numerically strongest cavalry division from the field, Early decisively crippled his army. If Lomax's division, not Payne's understrength brigade, had charged with the Second Corps, it may be reasonably argued that the Confederates would have secured the Valley Pike north of Middletown, enveloping the Union left flank. Moore's Yankees, facing odds of three-to-one, could not have been expected to shatter Lomax's deathgrip on the turnpike. Merritt and Custer, additionally, could not have attacked Lomax frontally with Rebel infantry and artillery on their right flank.[76]

Instead, the Yankee cavalry held the vital highway, threatened the Rebels' right flank, and Lomax was too far away to be of help. But Early had no other choice, so he sent Lomax orders, "requiring him to move to Middletown as quickly as possible." The courier never reached the cavalry officer, and Lomax kept moving farther away from the field.[77]

During this period in the battle—between 9:30 and 10:30—John Gordon joined Early. It is impossible to time precisely this famous encounter but, from the sequence of other events, the two could hardly have met before ten o'clock. The exchange, which Gordon restructured in his reminiscences, has been quoted many times since by historians. Gordon's account of the conversation has become a cornerstone of the case against Jubal Early at Cedar Creek.[78]

According to Gordon, when he met Early for a second time, Old Jube greeted the Georgian, exclaiming: "Well, Gordon, this is glory enough for one day. This is the 19th. Precisely one month ago to-day we were going in the opposite direction."

"It is very well so far general," replied the Second Corps commander, "but we have one more blow to strike, and then there will not be left an organized company of infantry in Sheridan's army."

Gordon then pointed toward the Union VI Corps, adding that he had ordered a movement against it. "No use in that," rebutted Early, "they will all go directly."

"That is the Sixth Corps, general. It will not go unless we drive it from the field."

"Yes, it will go too, directly."

Gordon, in his memoirs, then described his reaction to Early's words, writing: "My heart went into my boots. Visions of the fatal halt on the first day at Gettysburg, and of the whole day's hesitation to permit an assault on Grant's exposed flank on the 6th of May in the Wilderness, rose before me. And so it came to pass that the fatal halting, the hesitation, the spasmodic firing, and the isolated movements in the face of the sullen, slow and orderly retreat of this superb Federal corps, lost us the great opportunity, and converted the brilliant victory of the morning into disastrous defeat in the evening."[79]

These words by one of the Confederacy's finest combat officers form the primary indictment against Early. The "fatal halt"—Douglas Freeman termed it a "fatal delay"—entered Civil War history.[80] Had Old Jube frittered away "the great opportunity?" Would a vigorous pursuit have finished the Union army? Were Early's stated reasons for the delay—plundering in the camps and the threat posed by Union cavalry—valid? Could the Southerners, in other words, have launched one more massive attack at the time the two generals met? Was this the moment, in fact, which doomed the Rebels?

The facts or events, placed in their proper sequence, destroy this assertion of a "fatal halt." What must be kept in mind is that this alleged exchange occurred near ten o'clock, maybe closer to 10:30. In Gordon's own words, the VI Corps was retreating "sullen, slow and orderly." This withdrawal by the Union corps to its so-called third or final position on a ridge about a mile and a half north of Middletown, near the farm of David Dinges, transpired between 9:30 and 10:30. Additionally, Gordon's description of the march is supported by a Union soldier, who said the command "went leisurely."[81]

If this famous conversation occurred then at this time, what could Gordon have meant by his claim that he had ordered a movement which "I felt sure would compass the capture of that corps—certainly its destruction?" To whom did Gordon issue the order? It certainly could not have been Pegram and Wharton and probably not Ramseur, for they had been under Early's direct command. If the Georgian meant Kershaw and Evans, why had Kershaw told Mann Page a short time before that he could not advance because of the condition of his command. Page, as noted previously, also described Evans's brigades as similarly disposed. Perhaps, Gordon's memory failed him regarding such a directive or, perhaps, he lied. His statement, however, lacks credibility.[82]

What was the situation in the Confederate army at 10:30 a.m.? The divisions of Pegram and Wharton and the brigade of Wofford had all they wanted with the Federal cavalry. Ramseur, sent by Early to occupy the crest held by Getty, was moving forward to or had just arrived at his subsequent position alongside Pegram. Kershaw, too, most likely was enroute but behind Ramseur, while Evans was even farther back. Early, if he had listened to Gordon, then, had not the troops present, nor a favorable tactical situation—with the Union cavalry so located—for such a movement. At best, the Southerners could not have launched Gordon's spectacular assault before eleven o'clock, and then possibly without Evans. A more reasonable time would have been well after that hour.

Not only were the infantry divisions not in place, but Early contended in his report and in his memoirs that the commands' ranks had been seriously depleted because of those absent, plundering. Gordon, conversely, vigorously disputed this allegation of pillaging, quoting letters from fellow officers as support for his argument. Gordon numbered the culprits as few and mostly disabled soldiers.[83]

The men in the ranks, then and thereafter, admitted that plundering occurred on a wide scale. A member of the 4th North Carolina jotted in his diary on this day that "many of our soldiers, to their shame be it told, left ranks and commenced collecting plunder. This depleted our ranks very much." A Virginian claimed later that his comrades secured shoes and clothing which "weakened our lines considerably." A South Carolina officer in Kershaw's division, describing the scene after his troops defeated Keifer's division, wrote: "I looked in the rear. What a sight! Here came stragglers, who looked like half the army, laden with every imaginable kind of plunder—some with an eye to comfort, had loaded themselves with new tent cloths, nice blankets, overcoats, or pants, while others, who looked more to actual gain in dollars and cents, had invaded the sutler's tents and were fairly laden down with such articles as they could find readiest sale for."[84]

Federal accounts support the charges. Though one Yankee cavalryman argued later that he saw the Rebels engaged in plundering, most based their assertions after viewing how many of their dead and wounded comrades had been stripped. One Northerner asserted that hundreds were left entirely naked; he counted 63 while crossing part of the field on the 20th. Another, writing home on the 23rd, believed that the Southerners simply "captured too much" and they "got to plundering the camps."[85]

Some of the Confederates explained the pillaging by stating that the vast supplies were "too tempting" and "we just couldn't resist all them good things."[86] Private John Worsham, a veteran of many campaigns with the 21st Virginia, offered a justification for the breakdown of discipline, writing:

> The world will never know the extreme poverty of the Confederate soldier at this time. Hundreds of men who were in the charge and who captured the enemy's works were barefooted. Every one of them was ragged. Many had on everything they had, and *none* had eaten a square meal for weeks. As they passed through Sheridan's camp, a great temptation was thrown in their way. Many of the tents were open, and in plain sight were rations, shoes, overcoats, and blankets. The fighting continued farther and farther, yet some of the men stopped. They secured well-filled haversacks and, as they investigated the contents, the temptation to stop and eat was too great. Since most of them had had nothing to eat since the evening before, they yielded. While some tried on shoes, others put on warm pants in place of the tattered ones. Still others got overcoats and blankets—articles so much needed for the coming cold. They had already experienced several biting frosts to remind them of the winter near at hand.[87]

That the plundering drained away hundreds from the fighting ranks for a period of time is incontrovertible; that Early and his commanders lacked officers for controlling it is also evident. Moreover, for those who remained in line—and most did—physical exhaustion began slowing them. The Second Corps, for instance, had been marching or fighting, without eating, since 8:00 p.m. on the 18th while Kershaw's and Wharton's men a few hours less. That the Rebels had enough left for a full-scale assault at this time remains dubious. A North Carolinian remarked that the members of his regiment slept from fatigue during the afternoon lull.[88]

This halt, contrary to what Gordon pictured it, was thus neither fatal nor because of Early's satisfaction with the day's outcome to that point. When the pair met, the advance elements of the Army of the Valley—the commands of Pegram, Wharton and Wofford—had already stopped because of the Union cavalry. Without Ramseur, Kershaw and Evans closed up, those units were going nowhere against the rugged Yankee horsemen. By the time the Confederates could have executed the movement envisioned by Gordon, the tactical situation favored the Federals. Gordon was correct and Early wrong when the Georgian told Old Jube that the VI Corps would not leave "unless we drive it from the field." That the Southerners could have accomplished this after eleven o'clock with a frontal attack across open fields and with both flanks overlapped by Union cavalry and horse artillery defies reason. The conclusion of Early's biographer seems valid: "The whole planning of the Cedar Creek attack shows Old Jube's daring, and he could be expected to press on as long as there was any chance for success. That he did not do so must be due to the fact that his army was in no position to continue the attack."[89]

One other factor—which neither Early nor Gordon nor any Confederate knew—tipped the balance in favor of the Federals. Philip Sheridan was on the field.

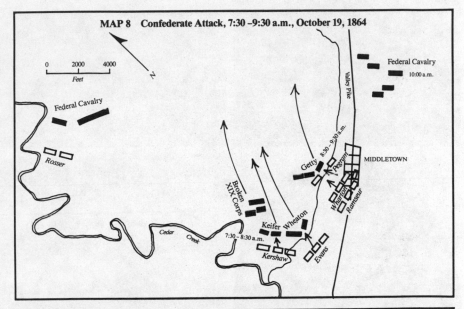

MAP 8   Confederate Attack, 7:30–9:30 a.m., October 19, 1864

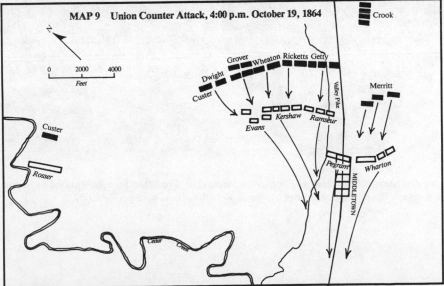

MAP 9   Union Counter Attack, 4:00 p.m. October 19, 1864

Four Confederate Major Generals: Top Left: Fitzhugh Lee; Top Right: John Brown Gordon; Bottom Left: Joseph Brevard Kershaw; Bottom Right: Robert Emmett Rodes. USAMHI.

13

"Put a Twist On 'Em"

The distant rumble, like the whisper of a giant, sounded ominous. For the Yankees on picket duty along the Valley Pike near the southern edge of Winchester, the muffled noise indicated artillery fire. The men were veterans, members of Colonel Oliver Edwards's VI Corps brigade, and they had spent the past month garrisoning Winchester. While the Army of the Shenandoah marched to Fisher's Hill and Harrisonburg and back to Tom's Brook and Cedar Creek, Edwards's soldiers stayed behind, performing routine post duty. Little of the fighting seemed near, except for the almost daily reports of excursions by John S. Mosby's Rangers. The dull thunder, which the pickets now heard at daylight on October 19, was unusual. It had to be reported, especially with Philip Sheridan in town.

An officer with the pickets rode to post headquarters, a large brick residence owned by tobacco merchant Lloyd Logan, located at the southwest corner of Braddock and Piccadilly Streets. Arriving before six o'clock, he was escorted to Sheridan's room. The officer submitted his information to the army commander, describing the fire as irregular. Sheridan, who was in bed, reassured him that it was only a scheduled reconnaissance by Cuvier Grover's division, which Horatio Wright had informed Sheridan of during the previous night. Though awake, Little Phil did not get up until, a short time later, another officer entered his room and stated that the firing continued. Sheridan finally dressed, walked downstairs and requested breakfast and his horse saddled.[1]

The major general left the Logan home between 8:30 and 9:00 and mounted Rienza, an "animal of immense strength and endurance." Rienza was a favorite of Sheridan, a present to him from officers of the 2nd Michigan Cavalry while he served in the West. The horse was six years old, black and possessed a peculiar gait between a trot and a walk which often drew silent curses from Sheridan's aides. Standing seventeen hands high, Rienza dwarfed his owner, and the soldiers joked that Little Phil mounted Rienza by shinning up his saber. Sheridan probably looked even smaller atop the big horse on this day, because he had become "as thin as a greyhound during the campaign."[2]

Riding east on Piccadilly for a block, Sheridan turned south onto Loudoun Street or the Valley Pike. With him were Lieutenant Colonel James W. Forsyth, his chief of staff, two other aides and a pair of engineer officers from the capital. As the party reached the town limits, the five heard firing "in an unceasing roar." Placing his head near his pommel to hear better, Little Phil spurred Rienza up the roadbed. At Mill Creek, slightly more than one half of a mile out of town, the escort, the 17th Pennsylvania Cavalry, filed into column behind the officers.[3]

A short distance south of Mill Creek the horsemen, crossing a rise, encountered the first evidence of the disaster occurring at Cedar Creek—a stalled jumble of wagons. "Part of the wagons faced one way, part the other," said Major George A. "Sandy" Forsyth. "Others were half turned round in the position to swing either way, but were huddled together, completely blocking the road." The brigade of Colonel William Curtis of George Crook's command guarded the train, which had been rolling toward the army when fugitives, bearing "terrible tales of rout and ruin," caused a temporary panic. Curtis's West Virginians were untangling the mess and moving the wagons off the highway when Sheridan approached.[4]

The general ordered "Sandy" Forsyth (no relation to chief of staff, James Forsyth) forward to "find out the trouble here, and report promptly." The aide learned from a quartermaster officer that the Union army had been defeated. Forsyth quickly relayed this information to Sheridan. Moments later, another officer, who had been on the field, confirmed the news, stating that army headquarters had been captured and the troops dispersed. It was staggering intelligence, a calamity whose implications jeopardized the entire Federal campaign.[5]

Sheridan reacted at once. "I felt," he recounted, "that I ought to try now to restore their broken ranks, or, failing in that, to share their fate because of what they had done hitherto." In rapid-fire succession he issued a spate of instructions: he, with "Sandy" Forsyth, Captain Joseph O'Keefe and a trimmed-down escort would proceed immediately to the front; James Forsyth and the engineer officers would form a cordon across the turnpike to stem the flood of fugitives, using the cavalrymen, Curtis's men and Edwards's troops, which were summoned from Winchester. With this done, Sheridan, Forsyth, O'Keefe and the escort (sources placed its number at 12, 20, or 50) spurred up the road. As Little Phil passed the wagons and stragglers, he shouted: "Boys if you don't want to fight yourselves, come back and look at others fighting. We will whip them out of their boots before 4 o'clock." He was ten miles away.[6]

Sheridan set a swift pace on Rienza and, with the horse's peculiar gait, the rest of the party found it "most distressing" in keeping up with the mount. At one halt, Sheridan, who broke a rowel on his spurs, had Forsyth bring him a switch, which he used on Rienza's shoulder. Each successive mile brought further signs of a defeated army. The highway teemed with wagons and fleeing soldiers, and the horsemen abandoned the roadway for the fields. Many of the men, according to a member of the escort, "did not appear panic-stricken, seeming scarcely to know why they were going to the rear. Groups were halted preparing rations or getting coffee." Though impossible to determine, scores of the Yankees were skulkers, those ever-present soldiers who at the first sound of battle departed the field—those who stayed and fought derisively called such types "a regular *bullet-barometer*."[7]

The commanding general paused beside these clusters of soldiers, telling them that they should return to the battlefield. To one group, he exclaimed: "Boys turn back; face the other way. I am going to sleep in that camp to-night or in hell." His bravado, his cocksure manner inspirited many, who cheered and started back. Not all listened, however. While skirting Newtown, whose streets were so congested he could not pass through, Little Phil met a chaplain, halted and inquired about the situation. "Everything is lost," blurted the minister, "but all will be right when you get there." With that assessment, the chaplain continued on his way northward.[8]

South of Newtown, Sheridan crossed the Pike into the fields west of the thoroughfare, whose bed remained clogged with wagons, ambulances and caissons. To the right and to the front, he saw organized groups of infantry. Major William McKinley of Crook's staff, recognizing the approaching horseman, rode among the troops, spreading the news that Little Phil had arrived from Winchester. Sheridan, Forsyth and O'Keefe finally bridled up behind the line of Lewis Grant's division, lying on the farmland of David Dinges. The VI Corps veterans, when they saw their commander, jumped up and hollered. Sheridan removed his hat in response and then rode a short distance to the rear, where a line of regimental flags "rose up out of the ground, as it seemed, to welcome me." The banners belonged to what was left of Crook's corps. The major general proceeded to a hillside between Crook's and Grant's men, found Horatio Wright, Crook, William Emory, Alfred Torbert and others. He dismounted from Rienza, joining his top subordinates. It was approximately 10:30; the fabled "Sheridan's Ride" had ended.[9]

Wright, looking "tired and a little disspirited," greeted his boss, saying: "Well, we've done the best we could." "That's all right; that's all right," replied Sheridan. Emory then reported that his troops were reorganized and could cover the retreat to Winchester. "Retreat-Hell!" flashed Little Phil, "we'll be back in our camps tonight."[10]

With this settled, Sheridan asked for a summary of the situation and dispositions of the Federal units. The army, he learned, was dispersed, but in reasonable order. The divisions of Frank Wheaton and J. Warren Keifer and Emory's regrouped commands lay to the right and rear of Grant's ranks, strung out for a distance of two miles. Torbert's horsemen, skirmishing with the Confederates, guarded the army's left flank, east of the turnpike. As he listened, Sheridan decided then and there—or, so he claimed in his memoirs—to attack the left flank of the Southern army. He "suggested" to Wright that "we would fight" on Grant's line and that the infantry of Wheaton, Keifer and Emory should be formed on this front. He directed that Custer be transferred from the left to the right flank. "I then started out all my staff officers to bring up these troops," he wrote in his report, "and was so convinced that we would soon be attacked that I went back myself to urge them on."[11]

The Confederates, however, did not attack, and the redeployment was completed, except for Emory's troops, between eleven o'clock and noon. During the hour, Sheridan formally reassumed command of the army, with Wright taking direction of his corps and George Getty supplanting Grant at the head of the division. He also spent much of the time surveying the enemy line from a point near the turnpike. He still anticipated a Southern assault at any moment but, except for the skirmishing between Southern infantrymen and Northern cavalrymen, nothing developed. About midday "Sandy" Forsyth suggested to the general that he ride along the entire line so the men could actually see for themselves that he had rejoined the army. William McKinley, who was present, added that he should remove his overcoat and hat that he might be more readily identified—no other general in the army possessed his unmistakable, bullet-shaped head.[12]

What occurred next has no equal in the annals of the Civil War—except possibly for the response given George B. McClellan by the Army of the Potomac as it streamed toward Washington in the wake of Second Bull Run. A renewed spirit, an intangible sense that all would be righted flashed across the length of the Army of the Shenandoah, gripping each member like an electric shock. This diminutive general, brimming with energy and confidence, possessed a presence, a charisma which could not be reasoned, only felt. He had taken an amalgam of commands and made of them an army. Where others before him failed, he brought victory. Winchester, Fisher's Hill and Tom's Brook tempered them as an army. They attributed it to him, and now they reciprocated.

As he passed in front of each successive unit, holding his hat in his hand, speaking to them, the men thundered their approval. "A deafening cheer" cascaded through the woods where the line stretched. He told them to cheer up, promising that the army would sleep tonight in its old camps. To a New York regiment, he boasted: "Never mind boys—G-d D--- it, we'll lick them like Hell before night." Francis Buffum of the 14th New Hampshire argued afterwards that "we believe that not another man in America could have got that victory out of that army." It was this bond—fused at Winchester and Fisher's

Hill—between Little Phil and the men in the ranks which caused their response to his appearance. Sheridan possessed neither exceptional tactical nor strategic skill, but he could inspire men in battle like no other Union commander at this date in the war. He had a battlefield presence of inestimable worth.[13]

To the south, across the pastures and stubbled grain fields, divided by stone walls, lay the morning's victors. If the Southerners, from their position, heard the vociferous welcome given Sheridan, they made no mention of it in their accounts. The Confederates' main line extended through the fields for three miles, from the Abram Stickley farm on the west to beyond the angle of the Cedarville and Buckton roads on the east. Topographer Jed Hotchkiss, in his journal, timed the formation of this line at ten o'clock, but this was not possible, if he meant the completion of the front, because of the sequence fully explained in the previous chapter. His map for the battle shows this line as of eleven-thirty. The Confederates, therefore, were probably settling in as Sheridan ordered Custer's division to the right flank and closed the Federal infantry on the Getty/Grant position at the David Dinges farm.[14]

William Payne's cavalry brigade patrolled the army's right flank beyond the Cedarville-Buckton roads. From this point to the turnpike, the ground was occupied by Gabriel Wharton's three brigades and William Wofford's brigade of Joseph Kershaw's division. These units manned a sunken road roughly perpendicular to the Pike, with an indeterminate number of sharpshooters using some houses as vantage points. John Pegram's division, connecting with Wharton's left brigade at the highway, stretched the front to the eastern edge of Meadow Brook. Across the stream, in succession from right to left, came the division of Stephen Dodson Ramseur, the remaining three brigades of Joseph Kershaw and the division of Clement Evans, whose left flank reached Middle Marsh Creek at the Stickley place. Tom Carter's dozen artillery batteries were interspersed among the infantry units.[15]

The position lacked natural strength, but it had not been selected with a view of defending the terrain. Its location resulted from the collision of the Confederate infantry with the Union cavalry shortly after ten o'clock. As Wofford and Wharton, then Pegram became engaged with Torbert's units east of the turnpike and their advance stalled, Jubal Early, as noted previously, ordered Ramseur, Kershaw and Evans up. As each of these latter commands arrived, the line stretched westward from Pegram's left flank to Middle Marsh Creek. Evans's brigades, closing last, filed into line sometime around eleven o'clock.

It was here, then, that the Confederate offensive stopped. The Southerners could go no farther, at least temporarily, in the view of Jubal Early, until the threat posed by the Federal cavalry had been removed and the plunderers returned to the ranks. "I determined, therefore," he stated in his report, "to content myself with trying to hold the advantages I had gained until all my troops had come up and the captured property was secured."[16] He planned a pursuit of the defeated Federals, but only once everything was ready to his satisfaction. Conditions on the field precluded such a full-scale advance, as envisioned by John Gordon, before at least eleven o'clock, probably eleven-thirty. When Confederates again rolled forward at one o'clock, however, only Evans, Kershaw and Ramseur went in, and the thrust lacked vigor. Most importantly, it had little or no chance of success by then.

During this phase of the battle, from ten to one, something evidently happened to Jubal Early. Douglas Freeman, writing of this, argued that "as the forenoon passed, the thought of the wreck of his Divisions by absentees began to sap Early's soldierly vigor. His state of mind changed subtly and progressively from one of confidence to one of concern." Freeman added: "By successive stages, then, the triumphant Early who had acclaimed the 'sun of Middletown' was reduced to confusion and perplexity of mind."[17]

A strong indictment, to be sure, but was it accurate? Unfortunately, Early, in his postwar statements, offered only hints and excuses, not explanations. The thoughts which gripped him during these hours, a historian cannot know. But, by judging his subsequent actions, it would appear that he concluded his army could achieve little more. His legitimate "concern" over the safety of his right flank, the plundering and the fatigue of his men provided the justifications for his conclusions. Perhaps, too, as John Gordon alleged— though not at ten, but later—Early became satisfied that the victory had been won. Regardless, the martial fire evidently went out in him; the earlier general of daring became the general of caution, not of confusion and of perplexity.

The most telling evidence of Early's frame of mind was the advance of Evans, Kershaw and Ramseur at one o'clock. The commanding general claimed subsequently that he ordered it "for the purpose of driving the enemy from his new position." Early, however, clearly expected less. He wanted the distant Federal line, concealed from Confederate view by the woods in which it lay, tested for its strength and composition, but his instructions to Gordon, who directed the movement, affirmed his doubts about success. "As the enemy's cavalry [Custer] on our left was very strong," he explained later, "and had the benefit of an open country to the rear of that flank, a repulse at this time would have been disastrous, and I therefore directed General Gordon, if he found the enemy's line too strong to attack with success, not to make the assault."[18]

At one o'clock, then, the three divisions stepped out. Skirmishers preceded the battle ranks, which stretched across the fields for upwards of a mile and a half. Behind the foot soldiers rumbled artillery batteries as close supports. For the waiting Yankees, watching the Rebels cross the autumn landscape, it must have been an impressive sight. Sheridan had expected such a movement for two hours and, seeing that the Southerners were heading toward his right and right center, manned by Emory's reorganized corps and

Wheaton's division, he shifted the Vermont brigade from Getty to the threatened point.[19]

What ensued when the Confederates came into musketry range is open to dispute. Southern accounts of the battle, except for Early's, virtually make no mention of this movement and firefight. Old Jube, in his memoirs, stated that only the skirmishers became engaged and, confronting the prepared Northern ranks, Gordon did not press the assault. By contrast, Union writings described the action as a blazing, roaring struggle. "Sandy" Forsyth, who was with Emory at this time, later wrote that the Rebels "with a piercing yell poured in a heavy volley, that was almost instantly answered from our side, and then the volleys seemed fairly to leap from one end to the other of our line, and a steady roar of musketry from both sides made the woods echo again in every direction." An unidentified Federal, in a postwar newspaper reminiscence, asserted that they repulsed the sortie with only three or four volleys. The enemy, in his view, lacked "dash."[20]

In any event, the Confederate thrust, which, in reality, amounted to nothing more than a spectacular reconnaissance-in-force, was easily repulsed. By this time, the Union line, lying "in the midst of magnificent great trees," was too strong for a frontal attack. The Yankees enjoyed numerical superiority, a compact front and the protection of crude fieldworks. Gordon, consequently, disengaged without needless sacrifice, withdrawing the divisions to a new line approximately midway between their original position and the Union line. Most of the units deployed behind stone walls. Ramseur's right stopped at the D. J. Miller residence, one thousand feet west of the Pike while Evans's left was a mile farther west on some wooded hills.[21]

With the repulse and retirement of Gordon's troops, the fighting subsided. Except for some probes by Union cavalry on the flanks, no further action ensued until the final Union assault at four o'clock. During this lull, the soldiers on both sides eased the fatigue and hunger by munching on any available food, filled canteens and/or slept. Many Northerners might have gathered that, with Little Phil back, their work remained unfinished; to the Southerners, it must have looked the opposite, with a brilliant victory achieved and with the prospects of a pleasant night's sleep.[22]

Jubal Early reached the latter conclusion—no other explanation seems reasonable. Though Gordon's sortie revealed that the enemy remained in strength in the woods, the army commander evidently dismissed the idea of a possible Union counterstroke. He appears contented with the day's work. "I determined, therefore," as he said later, "to try and hold what had been gained."[23] He issued orders starting the 1,300 prisoners, the captured stores and cannon southward. The tactical situation prevailing on the field during the afternoon justified his assessment. But, why, then, did he not pull back the divisions of Evans, Kershaw and Ramseur to the position they held before one o'clock? Why maintain an alignment which invited disaster when, in his own words, he had ceased offensive operations? Did he ignore a string of warnings from John Gordon of the mounting danger? Could he, once more, have underestimated his opponent?

These questions, like the many others regarding phases of Confederate operations on this day, have few certain answers. The primary chronicler of events on the Southern side during the lull and the chief witness against Early was John Gordon. In his reminiscences, the Georgian claimed that he learned of the Union counterattack against his left flank through wigwagged messages from signalmen atop Massanutten and oral or written messages from Thomas Rosser. The problem with this allegation is that the only Yankees on that portion of the field visible to the signalmen and Rosser were George Custer's cavalrymen. The Union infantry were not, as Gordon pictured them, "coming closer and massing in heavy column on the left" — they remained stationary in the woodland until the assault. All of the blue-bloused foot soldiers were concealed, except for a small portion of the XIX Corps at the edge of the treeline. The detail on the mountain might have seen these troops, but Rosser certainly could not have.[24]

That Gordon used Rosser as a supplier of information about enemy infantry critically weakens the Georgian's case. Rosser's two brigades, in fact, were at least a mile and a half, as the crow flies, from the right flank of the Union infantry with Custer's division barring the way. The Confederate cavalry officer probably knew less of the situation than Gordon. Additionally, probably about three o'clock, Custer charged Rosser's right flank. The surprise attack threw the Rebels, in Custer's words, "into the utmost confusion." Rosser retired to Minebank Ford, but Custer did not pursue because of "the wide gap existing between my left and the right of the Nineteenth Corps." By the time Sheridan advanced his infantry, Rosser was basically out of the battle. If he warned Gordon of any buildup, it could have only been about Custer, who now completely overlapped Gordon's left flank.[25]

Gordon's second contention, however, has more substance. With or without the alleged series of messages, the major general knew that his left flank was dangerously weak, unsupported and with "a long gap" between his westernmost brigade and the main line. The division of Clement Evans, positioned on some wooded knolls, held this section. Though Gordon offered no explanation for the disposition, he apparently extended his flank with the intention of linking his skirmishers with those of Rosser. This placed Colonel John Lowe's Georgia brigade nearly a fourth of a mile from Colonel Edmund Pendleton's Louisianans. Gordon had, in his words, "scarcely a vidette to guard" the gap between Lowe and Pendleton. Lowe, in turn, trying to establish contact with Rosser's cavalrymen, sent three companies of the 31st Georgia farther to the left. The three companies never found the horsemen, so the Georgians formed their own line, with about thirty steps between each man.[26]

Gordon concluded then that if the position had to be maintained he needed reinforcements. As the afternoon lengthened, his concern increased; a sentiment shared, as he said, with "every Confederate commander of our left wing." "One after another of my staff," he continued, "was directed to ride with all speed to General Early and apprise him of the hazardous situation." The aides returned with "no satisfactory answer," so Gordon personally rode to army headquarters near or in Middletown. The Georgian, in his retelling of their third meeting, urged that Early "reenforce the left and fill the gap, which would prove a veritable deathtrap if left open many minutes longer; or else that he concentrate his entire force for desperate defense or immediate withdrawal. He instructed me to stretch out the already weak lines and take a battery of guns to the left. I rode back at a furious gallop to execute these most unpromising movements. It was too late."[27]

That an officer of Early's ability and experience ignored the arguments of his most reliable subordinate, maintaining the divisions in an untenable, isolated position, defies logic. Their placement served no purpose, since, in Early's belief, his army could not assume offensive operations. But Gordon's account seems creditable, for his duty and responsibility required him to warn his superior of the inadequacy of his position. The army commander should have, at least, ridden to his advanced line and examined the dispositions for himself, but there is no evidence that he conducted a personal reconnaissance. At best, once the signs mounted of a Federal movement, he should have pulled back the divisions to their original position. The Yankees then would have had to charge across a mile and a half of relatively open ground, subjected to barrages from Confederate artillery. Yet the Southern commander did not retrench; he ignored the warnings; and he committed an inexplicable, an inexcusable blunder that lost for him and his army all that they had gained.

Time ran out for Jubal Early and his Army of the Valley at four o'clock when Philip Sheridan launched his counterattack. The Union commander, almost from the moment he arrived on the battlefield, when he sharply told William Emory that "Retreat—Hell—we'll be back in our camps tonight," had thought of a counteroffensive. His redeployment of Custer from the left flank to the right, between eleven and noon, was an initial step. Then, when the Confederates advanced at one—a movement he had expected for two hours—and were repulsed, Sheridan had the tactical initiative. He probably wanted to attack shortly afterwards, but he decided to wait until more of the stragglers came in.[28]

The delay, however, lasted for nearly three hours, because Sheridan received reports that another Confederate force, identified as infantry belonging to James Longstreet, was moving toward Winchester. The Union scouts apparently mistook Lunsford Lomax's horsemen for foot soldiers. But the intelligence, Sheridan wrote, "caused me great anxiety for the time, and although I could not fully believe that such a movement would be undertaken, still it delayed my general attack."[29]

In an effort to confirm the presence of Longstreet's additional divisions on the field, Sheridan ordered Wesley Merritt to charge a Rebel battery located outside of Middletown and to capture some prisoners. Merritt, in turn, assigned the duty to Charles Lowell, Jr.'s brigade, supported by Thomas Devin's and James Kidd's commands. Lowell's troopers thundered across the farmlands, scattering gray pickets and forcing the battery back. The Yankees bagged a handful of Southerners, who admitted that only Joseph Kershaw's division was on the field. Merritt relayed this to Sheridan, who, a short time later, received word from William Powell that Longstreet was not in the area of Newtown or Winchester. Powell's courier arrived about 3:30 and, with Merritt's information, cleared the way for Sheridan's "general attack."[30]

A Massachusetts veteran, writing years later in his regimental history, perceptively noted that Sheridan "never waited for the rebs to get ready. When he was ready he would fight." Such a moment now had come, and Little Phil planned to throw everything he had at his old nemesis. Staff couriers scurried up and down the waiting ranks, reminding unit commanders to keep closed on their adjoining commands. When Sheridan saw "Old Brick Top" Emory, he admonished the subordinate to charge "boldly and energetically." "And I want you to see to it General," he added. "Send a trustworthy officer there to overlook the movement. Have those men told to go in like good fellows. Tell them victory depends on it."[31]

Minutes before four o'clock, from one end of the Union infantry line to another, buglers blared the charge—one account placed the number at 200. Even as the notes peeled skyward, the ranks emerged from the trees. On the right the battered XIX Corps stepped out; beside them moved the VI Corps and, on its left, across the turnpike, was what remained of George Crook's command. Sheridan's plan called for the XIX Corps to turn the left flank of John Gordon's position while the VI Corps, supported by Crook's troops, hammered the front. It was warfare reflective of the army commander— simple, headlong and powerful. For the soldiers in the ranks, it was retribu- tion—"the men," said a New Yorker, "were inspired with new hope, and they went in with a will."[32]

At the western end of the Union line, William Dwight's division of two brigades spearheaded the attack of the XIX Corps. Dwight, it will be recalled, had been under arrest for his refusal to retract statements in his report on Third Winchester critical of the conduct of Cuvier Grover's division. But, during the afternoon lull, Sheridan returned Dwight to command and, now, the brigadier led his troops toward the left end of Gordon's line.[33]

The Federals, unknowingly, drove straight into the gap between Lowe's Georgians and Pendleton's Louisianans, occupying two timbered crests. A handful of Rebel skirmishers triggered a volley and then fled. Union officers, watching the gray videttes retire, shouted to their troops: "Pour it into them, men! Let them have it. It's our turn now!" The Federals responded with a volley and then surged ahead. Confederate batteries, positioned behind the knolls, opened fire. Suddenly, as the Northerners approached the bases of the hills, a concealed Southern battle line, Lowe's Georgians, blasted the flank of Dwight's right brigade, that of Brigadier General James McMillan. The Federal attack "was brought to a dead halt" by what McMillan termed a "murderous" fire.[34]

Though the Yankees had found the weakness in Gordon's line, they were the ones caught in an enfilading fire. McMillan wheeled his brigade to the right and Colonel Edwin Davis, whose brigade was on McMillan's left, swung two of his regiments in that direction. This movement placed the Federals perpendicular to their original attack path and parallel to Lowe's ranks, which had also wheeled to the right when the Northerners advanced into the gap.[35]

McMillan's regiments, plus Davis's pair, then scrambled up the hillside, covered in cedar trees and thick underbrush. A Yankee described the ground as "a jungle," which aided the defenders and disrupted the Union ranks. The Georgians fought tenaciously, but the Federals took the discharges and kept going. Lowe's line finally collapsed before the swarm, with its shreds spilling down the opposite slope. When the Yankees reached the top, they hollered in triumph, threw their hats into the air and jumped up and down.[36]

Phil Sheridan, riding his gray horse, soon joined the celebrating soldiers on the crest. His presence on this portion of the field indicated a concern with the XIX Corps. Though Dwight's attack had not gone as expected, Sheridan was satisfied with the results for one Confederate brigade had been broken and the division now overlapped the left flank of Gordon's main line. He told McMillan to close with Davis and wait until George Custer's division advanced on their right. When the cavalrymen appeared, the infantry should charge, he stated. The commander instructed "Sandy" Forsyth, who had been with the division from its outset, to oversee the movement. With this done, Sheridan rode toward the center and left of his attacking lines.[37]

Little Phil headed toward a firestorm of combat. From Cuvier Grover's division, aligned east of Dwight, to George Getty's along the Pike, the Federals were engaged in what one called "a square musketry fight."[38] The graycoats of Clement Evans, Joseph Kershaw and Dodson Ramseur, bolstered by well-served cannon, were holding their own behind stone walls. The fighting rivalled some of the morning's worst in its intensity and toll. It was a stand-up struggle, remarkably similar to that at Winchester a month earlier, and, as Sheridan spurred eastward, the Confederates had the best of it.

The division of Cuvier Grover, who also reassumed command during the lull, "advanced with the greatest impetuosity" on the left of Dwight. Grover's four brigades dislodged Rebel skirmishers from a stone wall, approximately 400 yards in advance of the main Southern line, and then came under a killing fire from Pendleton's Louisianans and William Terry's Virginians of Evans and Kershaw's left brigade. The attack stalled. Grover went down with a wound, as did every regimental commander in Colonel David Shunk's brigade. Colonel Henry Birge, mounted on a mule, once more took over the division. Before the musketry and shell bursts, however, Birge could do nothing but maintain his hold on the stone walls.[39]

On Birge's left, Frank Wheaton's VI Corps division was in a similar fix. Opposing mainly Kershaw's veterans, these Yankees, too, wrenched a string of stone walls from the Southerners and then went no farther. They suffered particularly from a battery deployed behind the gray infantry. One piece of shell struck Colonel Ranald Mackenzie on the shoulder, forcing that capable officer to relinquish his brigade. Wheaton brought up his second line, but it was still not enough firepower. This Union division, like Birge's, had been stopped.[40]

The situation was no better, perhaps even worse, in J. Warren Keifer's division, aligned on Wheaton's left. Before the Northerners advanced at four o'clock, Keifer issued strict instructions to his brigade commanders, Colonels William Ball and William Emerson, "to dress to the left in the general advance and close up all intervals." But, when the division moved forward, Emerson angled too rapidly to the left, massing his regiments behind Ball's. This uncovered the right flank, and the Confederates, those on Kershaw's right and Ramseur's left, raked the exposed flank. Keifer's ranks wavered and then broke toward the woods, losing "very heavily." Officers steadied the troops, corrected the alignment and, within five minutes, the Federals recharged. Gray skirmishers, defending some more rock fences, fled before this second surge, falling back to their main line. Keifer's men halted at the walls and volleyed. The musketry roared, but it was, as Emerson said, "a deadlock."[41]

This initial repulse of Keifer's attack, in turn, momentarily disrupted part of George Getty's division as it pressed forward on Keifer's left. Getty's three brigades opposed Ramseur's veterans, whose line centered around the house and brick mill of D. J. Miller. Ramseur had blanketed his front with skirmishers and they, supported by batteries to the rear, scorched the Federals as they emerged from the woods. A Yankee said that the Rebel line "flamed from a wall before them." Each of Getty's brigades fought separate battles for awhile.[42]

On the division's right, next to Keifer, Colonel James Warner's brigade, instead of closing leftward, had to angle westward when Keifer fell back. The 93rd Pennsylvania, on the brigade's right, caused the shift, breaking under a slicing fire on its uncovered flank. Warner, consequently, obliqued his other regiments rightward, and the command drove back the gray videttes from a stone wall. The Pennsylvanians soon rallied; Keifer sealed the gap; and Warner's men duelled with the enemy.[43]

Brigadier General Lewis Grant's Vermont Brigade occupied the center of Getty's division. A low ridge separated Grant's regiments from Warner's, preventing coordination between the commands. The Vermonters went in gamely on an attack path leading directly toward the Miller place. They seized a stone wall and then encountered heavy fire from an indeterminate number of Ramseur's troops, positioned among and in Miller's house, mill and out-buildings. The structures, in the words of a Vermonter, were "swarming with the enemy, our only approach to which was along a narrow road by the side of a little mill-pond formed by a dam across our old annoyance, Meadow Brook." With this obstacle in front and with their left flank unprotected because of the repulse of Getty's third brigade, the Vermonters stayed put.[44]

Covering the ground between Grant's left and the turnpike was the veteran brigade of David Bidwell, under the direction of Lieutenant Colonel Winsor B. French of the 77th New York. Sheridan had hoped that as the Federal divisions charged, the XIX Corps, overlapping the Confederate flank, would initiate a giant left wheel of the entire army which would roll up the Southern line. Consequently, Getty assigned French the dual role of guiding on the Pike and acting as the pivot of the movement. This meant that the brigade had to march slowly across a meadow which sloped downwards into a swale, where Miller's mill was located, and then upwards to a crest edged by another stone wall manned by Bryan Grimes's North Carolinians.[45]

French's three regiments and three battalions thus moved deliberately across the meadow—and into a cauldron of musketry and canister. Tarheel infantrymen, at the mill and on the ridgeline, flailed at the slow-marching Yankees while Southern batteries, behind the North Carolinians and east of the turnpike, shredded French's ranks with sheets of the one-inch slugs. Casualties in the brigade mounted; in succession three color bearers of the 77th New York died after picking up the standard. The line wavered and then cracked, with the men pouring back into the woods.[46]

French rallied his troops in the shelter of the trees and, when he saw Getty, he allegedly exclaimed: "I cannot take my brigade over that field slowly." "Then go quickly," rebutted Getty. It was the order French wanted, and he waved his men forward again. This time the Yankees double-quicked across the meadow, sweeping past the mill and up the hillside. On their right, the Vermonters circled the millpond, rushing among the Miller outbuildings, scattering the Confederates. Both Union brigades then halted and engaged Ramseur's main line a few hundred yards to the south. A Vermonter estimated that for the next thirty minutes each of his comrades expended fifty rounds of ammunition.[47]

From the Valley Pike westward to where Cuvier Grover's troops fought, the Union assault, therefore, had been stalemated. The Northerners had driven back the Confederate skirmishers but no part of the main Southern line had been breached, and it flamed in defiance. The veteran Confederates were holding against the frontal attack, showing the steadfastness they had displayed at Winchester. But, as it had been on that field a month before, it was to be here also—the battle turned with the entry of Union cavalry against the left end of the Confederate line.

George Custer's division—less three regiments pressing Thomas Rosser's troopers at Minebank Ford—entered the action at approximately four-thirty. The cavalrymen came in at a thundering gallop. The three detached companies of the 31st Georgia, spread thinly across the path of the horsemen, fired a round or so and then sprinted toward Cedar Creek. Behind the Georgia skirmishers, their comrades from the brigade were already retreating toward the stream after being routed by Dwight's Yankees. Most of the Georgians eluded Custer's men, who had come under Confederate artillery fire. Many in the saddles were cheering, ignoring the shells bursting over them. "It was a maddening time," claimed a New Yorker.[48]

The appearance of Custer was the signal for Dwight's two brigades to charge perpendicularly down the Confederate line. Dwight advanced promptly, through the swale between the two wooded knolls and up the western face of the hill occupied by Edmund Pendleton's Louisianans. Though Confederate accounts don't describe the initial contact between these forces, it would appear that the Federals, hidden by the woods, surprised the Louisianans. Regardless, Pendleton's line disappeared in a matter of minutes, with the Southerners tumbling down the hillside in flight.[49]

The break by Pendleton's brigade, acting like the first piece in a row of dominoes, toppled the entire front. William Terry's Virginians, on the Louisianans' right, broke next, followed quickly by Joseph Kershaw's division and then Dodson Ramseur's. "Regiment after regiment, brigade after brigade, in rapid succession was crushed," was the way John Gordon painted the collapse, "and, like hard clods of clay under a pelting rain, the superb commands crumbled to pieces."[50]

It was as rapid as it was somewhat unexplainable. Some of the Confederates admitted later that they did not even see the Yankees on their flank when they fled. Jubal Early asserted in his report that the men abandoned their position "not because there was any pressure on them, but from an insane idea of being flanked." Captain D. Augustus Dickert, commanding the 3rd South Carolina in Kershaw's division, stated subsequently that "the stampede of Early was uncalled for, unnecessary, and disgraceful, and I willingly assume my share of the blame and shame. My only title to fame rests upon my leading the Third South Carolina Regiment in the grandest stampede of the Southern Army ... and I hope to be forgiven for saying with pardonable pride that I led them remarkably well to the rear for a boy of eighteen."[51]

It was indeed a "stampede," for panic gripped the Confederates almost from the outset. Memories of Winchester and Fisher's Hill surely impelled many in their flight toward Cedar Creek. A Confederate wrote that they were "running as fast as a herd of wild, stampeded cattle. We just had to get out or be captured, and as we saw it, our officers were losing all controls over us." A trailing Yankee termed it "the wildest race that had ever been witnessed, even in that valley."[52]

Numbers of Confederates, however, formed islands of resistance. Tom Carter's gun crews were usually at the center of these pockets, standing by their pieces with the courage and determination they displayed earlier at Winchester and Fisher's Hill. "Sandy" Forsyth avowed that some of the enemy "fought splendidly—desperately even."[53] But these brave Southerners could not stand long before the numbers in blue. Once the gray line shattered, all of the Union infantry advanced in pursuit, and the Northerners simply engulfed each cluster of butternut.

At one stand, Colonel James P. Simms, whose brigade spearheaded Kershaw's morning attack, was killed almost instantly while imploring his South Carolinians to hold. Not far away, Dodson Ramseur was rallying some of his veterans. Ramseur already had one horse shot from under him and had taken a bullet himself. Few could equal this North Carolinian on a battlefield, and none probably relished being there more. His second mount was shot. Then, before he could remount a third, Ramseur was hit in the right side with another bullet, which penetrated both his lungs. An aide and some soldiers carried the major general to an ambulance.[54]

By now the splinters of the commands of Evans, Kershaw and Ramseur were passing west of Middletown, where the divisions of John Pegram and Gabriel Wharton and the brigade of William Wofford were positioned. These units had stood firm, repulsing attacks from Wesley Merritt's cavalry division, supported by horse artillery. In one of the thrusts, the Federals overran an advanced Confederate battery. Merritt, who seldom allowed humility to intrude upon his reports, stated that "never has the mettle of the division been put to a severer test than at this time, and never did it stand the test better."[55]

The Federals, like the Confederates, lost irreplaceable officers on this day. In the combat between Merritt's horsemen and the gray infantrymen, Colonel Charles R. Lowell, Jr., commander of the Reserve Brigade, was killed by a sharpshooter. A boyish-looking 29-year-old, Lowell was one of the most highly regarded and popular officers in the cavalry corps. One of George G. Meade's staff officers had noted in his diary that "no officer from civil life stood so high in the estimation of the army" than Lowell, a Harvard graduate. "He was the brightest star among the many good officers." Merritt asserted in his report that Lowell's "fall cast a gloom on the entire command. No one in the field appreciated his worth more than his division commander."[56]

During the morning's action, Lowell suffered a painful wound but refused to relinquish his command. He was in acute pain when he led his brigade in the charge on the battery. Ironically, only a few days before, Lowell wrote his bride that "I don't want to be shot til I've had a chance to come home. I have no idea that I shall be hit, but I *want* so much not to now, that it sometimes frightens me." Later this night, Sheridan signed Lowell's posthumous commission as brigadier.[57]

Lowell fell only moments before his opponents abandoned their position outside of Middletown. Jubal Early, who had been near Pegram's division when the Yankees launched their counteroffensive, personally ordered Pegram, Wharton and Wofford back. Pegram, according to one account, told his troops: "Men, you must do this in order—firing as you retreat, for your own and the army's safety demand it." Most of the Virginian's regiments maintained their organization until they reached Cedar Creek. Robert Johnston's brigade, for instance, while crossing at the turnpike bridge, came under "a hot fire" from the pursuing Yankees and the ranks became unglued. Johnston's brigade scattered and disappeared before his eyes.[58]

The commands of Pegram, Wharton and Wofford were the last across the stream. It was probably at or past five-thirty, for the sun had set and twilight dimmed the field. The panic and wild flight had given way to bedlam as the Rebels sought safety. One of them remembered seeing Old Jube, red with rage, trying to rally some of the fugitives, but none heeded him. "Run, run, G-- d-- you, they will get you," the army commander hollered.[59]

Neither imprecation nor example could stem the flood of Rebels coursing toward Fisher's Hill. It was nearly every man for himself; unit organizations almost ceased to exist. Confederates, by the thousands, blanketed the fields between Cedar Creek and Fisher's Hill. Wagons, ambulances and cannon clogged the Valley Pike, bringing movement to a near standstill. One Rebel saw that magnificent warrior, John Gordon, standing in a wagon bed, at the foot of Fisher's Hill, pleading with passersby to return and assist the teamsters. Only three soldiers responded to the Georgian. It was a nightmare of disorder, worsened by the enveloping darkness, and reminiscent of the rout after Fisher's Hill on September 22.[60]

Then, as the night deepened, Union cavalrymen—the 1st Vermont and 5th New York from the west of the jammed highway, the 6th and 19th New York from the east—knived into the retreating column between Strasburg and Cedar Creek. The Northerners, wielding sabers, were among the teams, cutting down the horses. Scores of wagons and ambulances, dozens of cannon and hundreds of prisoners were soon in the possession of the horsemen. In one captured ambulance lay the wounded Dodson Ramseur. At another point along the roadbed a squad of troopers seized a cannon and the Confederates accompanying it. The Yankees, unknowingly, had grabbed Tom Carter, Early's artillery chief, and his staff but, as the prisoners were led away, the Southerners slipped away in the darkness. Many graycoats, in fact, had narrow escapes and were saved primarily because of the blackness.[61]

Some of the troopers entered Strasburg and then turned back. On Fisher's Hill, the Confederate flight was ending, as most of the men hunted their old campsites and slept. Old Jube was there, too, still cursing, still trying to reform the shredded ranks. The only organized body of troops he could find was the 1,300 Union captives and their provost guard. "Nothing saved us," Early groused in his report, "but the inability of the enemy to follow with his infantry and his expectation that we would make a stand there. The state of things was distressing and mortifying beyond measure."[62] Other things, more-over, were "beyond measure" on this night, on the crest of Fisher's Hill.

To the north, across Cedar Creek, the Yankees were back in their old campsites, as Sheridan had promised, jubliantly celebrating the victory. The afternoon's attack and pursuit had exhiliated them because "we were repaying those fellows for our morning's experience."[63] During the chase across the farmlands, the Northerners shouted at the fleeing Southerners:

"Ah! Johnny Reb, we'll learn you to take a joke."

"Say, you, Jeff Davis' pimps, how do you like our style?"

"You are looking after the last ditch, ain't ye?"

"Get out of the way! the mudsills are coming."[64]

This sense of redemption, this settlement of an old score, this excitement of the pursuit now filled the Federals, circling the campfires. Some things here, too, were "beyond measure," but numbers already believed that the day's work had a finality to it. An Iowa veteran said it well in an October 21 letter to his parents. Of the battles he had been in, Cedar Creek "beats them all."[65]

At army headquarters, at the Belle Grove mansion, "the excitement was intense," according to one of those present. In the yard, a bonfire, built by staff officers, lit the night with a crackling blaze. Around it, officers also celebrated, feasting on bacon and hard bread. Many of the army's ranking commanders were there at one time or another. When "Autie" Custer arrived, he hugged Sheridan, lifting the diminutive commander off the ground.[66]

Of the army's three major victories, this final one, more than Winchester or Fisher's Hill, belonged to Sheridan. He had steadied the soldiers, reinstilled their confidence and formulated the plan for a counterattack. Then, as his battle lines swept the Confederates away, he rode among the men, shouting at them to "give them h--l!" to "put a twist on 'em." Though he confided to his old friend, George Crook, as they sat around the campfire, that "I am going to get much more credit for this than I deserve," this was Little Phil's finest moment of the campaign. Like his troops, he justifiably "was feeling very good."[67]

Inside Belle Grove, a different scene, a reminder of the day's cost, was transpiring. On the mansion's main floor, in the front room used as the owner's library, Stephen Dodson Ramseur lay dying. The Confederate major general had been brought here after his capture, and Union surgeons were working in vain to save the 27-year-old North Carolinian. George Custer and Henry DuPont, among others, visited their old academy pal. They comforted him, spoke to him, but nothing could save the splendid fighter from the fatal wound in his lungs.

So much of the Army of Northern Virginia's past lay on that bed with Dodson Ramseur. He had been one of Robert Lee's finest combat officers, earning promotion and reputation at Malvern Hill, Chancellorsville, Gettys-burg and Spotsylvania. No younger graduate of West Point earned his major generalcy in the Confederate service. He did not question the justness of the cause, nor rarely despaired of its ultimate victory. As the war progressed and as he relished combat more, his religious convictions deepened. He had wanted, on this day, nothing more than a furlough home to see his wife and their baby. In his last moments, he requested that a lock of his hair be sent to his wife. Then, among friends and foes, Stephen Dodson Ramseur died on the morning of October 20, 1864. Some things, indeed, were "beyond measure."[68]

Two Union Colonels: Rutherford B. Hayes, later U.S. President, and George M. Love, recipient of the Medal of Honor for service at Cedar Creek. Both are pictured later as Brigadier Generals. *Picerno Collection.*

14

Old Jube and Little Phil: An Evaluation

The Battle of Cedar Creek, Philip Sheridan stated in his report, "practically ended the campaign in the Shenandoah Valley. When it opened we found our enemy boastful and confident, unwilling to acknowledge that the soldiers of the Union were their equal in courage and manliness; when it closed with Cedar Creek this impression had been removed from his mind, and gave place to good sense and a strong desire to quit fighting. The very best troops of the Confederacy had not only been defeated, but had been routed in successive engagements, until their spirit and espirit were destroyed. In obtaining these results, however, our loss in officers and men was severe."[1]

And so it was. This final struggle for the "Daughter of the Stars," spanning three months, ended with members of the Army of the Shenandoah celebrating around fires glowing in a Virginia night. For the Southerners, it had been, from the outset, a gamble against long odds, originating in the June 12 meeting between Robert E. Lee and Jubal Early outside of Cold Harbor. Lee refashioned his grand strategy of two years before and, then, as Ulysses S. Grant responded in kind, with greater numbers and a new field commander, the stakes rose, particularly for the Confederate chieftain. For the Northerners, in turn, the campaign brought redemption, an affirmation that even an invincible symbol of the Confederacy could no longer withstand the massed might of the Union.

The months of maneuver and combat—from the "mimic war" in August, through the stand-up fight in September, to "The Burning" in October—came down to an ultimate resolution on October 19. Cedar Creek, which a Federal participant called "the most remarkable battle of the War," was the last gamble by the Confederates to retrieve what was argumentatively irretrievable. By its nature, by its outcome, by its impact on the reputations of the two leading antagonists, the engagement served as a microcosm of the entire campaign. Perhaps, as a member of the VI Corps argued subsequently, Cedar Creek "was a battle that had to be fought."[2]

Jubal Early said as much years later. "It may be asked," the old warrior wrote, "why with my small force I made the attack. I can only say we had been fighting large odds during the whole war, and I knew there was no chance of lessening them. It was of the utmost consequence that Sheridan should be prevented from sending troops to Grant, and General Lee, in a letter received a day or two before, had expressed an earnest desire that a victory should be gained in the valley if possible, and it could not be gained without fighting for it."[3]

Old Jube, prodded by Lee, risked his outnumbered legions in an offensive that might have salvaged a lost campaign. As he had in August, the southern commander relied upon maneuver to offset his numerical inferiority. Using an audacious plan fashioned primarily by John Gordon and Jed Hotchkiss, Early executed a flank attack at dawn, after a night march, which has no parallel in the Civil War. Union artillery officer Henry DuPont asserted that the Confederate attack scheme "was conceived and executed with very great ability" and "carried out with the utmost precision." Benjamin Crowninshield, a member of Sheridan's staff, thought that "surely never before was battle so carefully and definitely planned," adding that the offensive movement was "as brilliant a feat of arms as the war afforded."[4]

That the Confederates could launch a surprise flank attack, crush two-thirds of the Union infantry, bloody the other third and drive back their opponents a distance of three miles resulted from factors directly attributable to the Federals and their commander. First of all, the Yankees, as noted previously, lulled themselves into the belief that their nemesis had been beaten beyond redemption. A letter of Lieutenant Willie Root of the 75th New York, written shortly after the battle, expressed this complacency well: "We had had the most *awful* day I ever saw—and something I had not the least idea would happen." In addition, the separate reconnaissances by some of George Crook's and George Custer's units on the 18th bolstered the sense of security by reporting that no Confederates were in the army's immediate front.[5]

Cedar Creek, as a defensive position, moreover, was a "poor choice of terrain" by Sheridan. The ground had no particularly strong natural features, except that an attack force had to cross either the creek or the North Fork of the Shenandoah River or both. Neither flank had an anchor, and the series of ridges which ran northward from the convoluted stream, like the fingers of a hand, hampered the movement of one defensive force hurrying to the support of another. In defense of Sheridan, however, he viewed the position as a temporary stopover in the army's retrograde movement.[6]

The Union commander compounded the position's natural weaknesses with a faulty disposition of his units. Joseph Thoburn's division of Crook's command occupied a dangerously isolated position, with a ravine in its rear and a mile from infantry support. When the Southerners wrecked Thoburn's command, the left flank of the XIX Corps and the right flank of the Rutherford Hayes/J. Howard Kitching line were exposed. Additionally, neither Hayes nor Kitching had fieldworks erected, which weakened their position, indicating a probable lack of concern by the Union commanders over the threat to this wing of the army.[7]

The Confederate attack plan was predicated on the exposed position of Thoburn and the weakness of the Hayes/Kitching line, but it still could not have achieved its stunning success without the benefit of surprise. The Second Corps and Joseph Kershaw's division moved to their assault positions because the Union left flank was inadequately guarded by cavalry. This was the chief cause of the disaster which befell the Federals in the morning. Responsibility for the negligence became a matter of subsequent dispute.

When Sheridan returned Wesley Merritt's mounted division to the army on the 16th, he directed Horatio Wright, acting commander, to close William Powell's cavalry division, posted at Front Royal, on the army's left flank. The next day Wright took Colonel Alpheus S. Moore's brigade from Powell, assigning it picket duty at Bowman's and McInturff's Fords on the North Fork. Moore, in turn, placed videttes at the shallows but kept his main body at Buckton's Ford, nearly two miles downstream from Bowman's. When William Payne's Virginians struck the videttes on the 19th, the Federals, who escaped, fled toward their brigade and away from the Union army. Into the vacated gap filed the Second Corps.[8]

George Crook, in an unpublished, postwar account, stated that Wright personally promised him that cavalry pickets would be placed on Crook's unprotected flank. Wright did so with Moore's troopers, but Crook inferred that the cavalrymen were to have come either from Merritt's or George Custer's commands. This was what the senior officer should have done—both of those first-rate divisions did not belong on the same flank. But nothing in Wright's writings on the battle supports Crook's allegation. The acting commander believed, in fact, that, if the Confederates attacked, it would be against the opposite end, where Sheridan had originally placed Merritt and Custer. For Wright to have transferred either of the two divisions, he would have altered Sheridan's dispositions and would have gone against his own predilections. Furthermore, he had complied with Sheridan's instructions by using part of Powell's command on the left flank. Perhaps, Wright and Crook simply misunderstood what the one requested and the other promised. But, as Crook stated in the memoir, "the whole thing hinges on this point" of the inadequacy of the cavalry force on that flank.[9]

Sheridan, in his report, hinted that had he been with the army, he would have corrected the disposition of the two cavalry divisions, because "it had always occurred to me there was little danger of attack" on the right flank. His actions, however, definitely contradict this assertion. Little Phil, like Wright, thought that a Confederate offensive was a remote possibility but, if Jubal Early dared to launch an assault, it would most likely come against the western sector of the Union position where the terrain favored such an operation. His postbattle statement was, most likely, an attempt to lessen his own culpability in the unwise placement of Merritt and Custer. He probably knew, when he penned his report, that if one of those divisions had occupied the ground next to Crook, the surprise could never have happened. And "without the surprise," Crook argued, "the enemy would never have dared to have gotten so near us with their small force."[10]

A combination of factors, therefore, contributed to the initial success of the Confederate offensive: the belief that the campaign had concluded, which fostered a lack of vigilance; the terrain and the faulty arrangement of Union infantry units; and the misplacement of the cavalry which left the army's vulnerable flank improperly guarded. For these errors, Sheridan remains primarily accountable. For, as Henry DuPont correctly noted: "it can hardly be disputed that upon the commander-in-chief rested the responsibility of placing his troops in safe and secure positions."[11]

As a consequence, Old Jube's "invincible but exhausted little army," shielded by the fog, stormed into the weak sector of the Federal position.[12] The divisions of Thoburn, Hayes and Kitching melted before the onslaught, while some units of the XIX Corps, hammered on the front and flank, fought valiantly in an untenable position, erasing partially the stain of their performance at Third Winchester. Within a span of two hours, the Southerners, in what a nineteenth century student of the battle termed "one of the most daring and brilliant attacks recorded in history," had driven two infantry corps, plus Kitching's division, beyond Meadow Brook and were closing on the third.[13] Jubal Early, Gabriel Wharton's reserve division and the army's artillery were coming onto the field. Confederate fortunes neared their zenith.

But, then, as the combat shifted to the western side of Meadow Brook, where the VI Corps stood, the Southern offensive started to unravel for a number of reasons. The fog, which aided the Rebels at the outset, now cursed them. Coordination could not be maintained between the two wings of the army (the Clement Evans/Joseph Kershaw force and the Stephen Ramseur/ John Pegram force) in their attacks on the VI Corps. Evans and Kershaw, for instance, struck the divisions of J. Warren Keifer and Frank Wheaton at approximately 7:30 while the first attack on George Getty by Ramseur and Pegram did not occur until an hour later. The covering mists also prevented the Confederates from seeing that Getty's position could have been turned on either flank by maneuver. Instead, first Pegram, then Ramseur and finally Wharton charged the Union division on the graveyard crest and suffered successive repulses. All the while, the divisions of Evans and Kershaw, under John Gordon's direction, remained stationary, approximately 500 to 600 yards south and west of Getty's right flank.

The inactivity of Evans and Kershaw during this phase of the battle resulted not only from the fog but from disorganization within their own ranks. For over two hours these commands had been engaged in almost ceaseless combat, fighting most of the enemy units. Casualties and those plundering the camps had weakened the ranks, which were in disarray from the continuous movement. Those that had stayed in line were tired and hungry, needing a respite. Kershaw, as related in Chapter Twelve, told Mann Page, Early's aide, precisely this. Though John Gordon pictured the two divisions as poised to strike, the fact remains that from the time they swept back the divisions of Keifer and Wheaton at eight o'clock until nine-thirty, these six Confederate brigades went nowhere. Either Gordon did not act aggressively or the conditions in the brigades necessitated a temporary halt. From the evidence, the latter is the proper conclusion.

Jubal Early entered the action at this stage of the engagement. Sketchily aware of the prevailing tactical conditions and unable to conduct a personal reconnaissance because of the fog, the lieutenant general was drawn into the combat with Getty's Federals. If the Evans/Kershaw wing needed rest, the Ramseur/Pegram wing required direction. The division of Pegram and the stray brigade of William Wofford had been basically wasted for the better part of three hours. When Early reached this wing, he brought guidance, but instead of pushing his only reserve infantry command, Wharton's division, down the Valley Pike, through Middletown, he made a critical mistake by committing it to another attack on Getty. At this point, Early lost the freedom of maneuver, the vital requirement in an offensive operation conducted by a numerically inferior foe against a superior opponent.

The Valley Pike had become the key to the battle, for had the Rebels seized it north of Middletown, they could have outflanked every new defensive position of the retreating Yankees. Surprisingly, unlike the Federals, the Southerners, then or later, did not recognize this. Their discussions of the engagement focused on the delay in pursuing the Northerners after Getty's troops abandoned the area around the cemetery. But, by then, the turning point in the battle had passed—the stalwart defense by Getty's three brigades had bought valuable time for the rest of the broken infantry commands and the cavalry divisions of Merritt and Custer covered the turnpike.[14]

Early's egregious blunder, however, was not sending Wharton against Getty but the detachment of Lunsford Lomax's cavalry division on a mission of minimal value. Payne's understrength brigade could have occupied Powell's attention at Front Royal while Lomax's 1,700 troopers accompanied the Second Corps. Lomax could have readily seized the Pike, preventing the Northern army from regrouping where it did. Early possessed a "peculiar ineptitude for dealing with cavalry" in marked contrast to Sheridan, a former horse officer. Old Jube misused his mounted arm throughout the campaign, but never with more serious consequences than at Cedar Creek.[15]

What, then, of the "fatal delay?" Regardless of the use of Wharton and the absence of Lomax, could the Southerners have swept the Yankees all the way to Winchester, if Early had not halted? John Gordon's version, Early's justifications for the halt and the sequence of events have been fully discussed in Chapter Twelve. Nevertheless, it was the consensus of opinion in the Army of the Valley in the battle's immediate aftermath that their commander's actions doomed the army.

Captain James M. Garnett, an ordnance officer in Ramseur's division, recorded in his diary, one week after the battle: "This is the worst stampede yet, and the harder to bear after our victory of the morning. If 'old Jubal' had only pressed on, I firmly believe, from all I have heard, that we could have driven them beyond Winchester."[16]

The experienced, capable Jed Hotchkiss, moreover, shared the view of an evident majority. Near the end of his journal entry for October 19, the mapmaker wrote: "Thus was one of the most brilliant victories of the war turned into one of the most disgraceful defeats, and all owing to the delay in pressing the enemy after we got to Middletown; as General Early said, 'The Yankees got whipped and we got scared.'"[17]

Four days later, on the 23rd, Hotchkiss entrained for Richmond, carrying a sketch of the battle and Early's report for Robert E. Lee. According to Hotchkiss, before he departed, "General Early told me not to tell General Lee that we ought to have advanced in the morning at Middletown, for, said he, we ought to have done so."[18] Had Old Jube come to believe what other senior officers were stating, had he admitted privately to the staff officer what he never admitted publicly? There is no reason to doubt Hotchkiss's statement.

The Southern commander, perhaps, realized that he should have undertaken a full-scale, vigorous pursuit before one o'clock, when it was neither full-scale nor vigorous. That he did not order such a movement when all his divisions were up, between eleven and eleven-thirty, he deserves censure. Whether an advance at that time would have fared better than the eventual one remains dubious. By the time the Rebels would have closed on the Federal line, all three divisions of the VI Corps were in place and 7,000 cavalrymen covered both flanks. Criticisms of Early, contemporary and subsequent, either ignore or lessen the importance of the timetable and the tactical situation, which by midday favored the Northerners. Early had sound reasons for temporarily suspending the advance but, in the end, he lacked the relentlessness of a Stonewall Jackson, though few others possessed Old Jack's instinct for the jugular.

The physically weary Confederate army thus halted between ten and eleven o'clock, nearly fifteen hours after its initial elements undertook the operation. Its right wing had been stopped by two Union cavalry divisions while its left wing reformed across the fields west of Meadow Brook. The Rebels had achieved a spectacular victory, whose spoils could be readily viewed in captured Yankees, cannon and wagons. For the next two hours the victors rested, until one o'clock when Early ordered Gordon forward with the divisions of Evans, Kershaw and Ramseur to test the concealed Union line. Old Jube expected little from the movement, and little was accomplished. Then, without explanation, in the face of a series of messages from Gordon expressing the subordinate's grave concern over the exposed position of the three divisions, the general commanding maintained, without sound reason, the dangerous alignment. It was Early's most grievous, most inexcusable tactical blunder of the entire campaign, dooming his army to a crushing, irredeemable defeat.

In the Union ranks, meanwhile, the magnetic Philip Sheridan reinvigorated his army. It was the finest moment of the campaign for the aggressive, bantam-sized general, whose battlefield presence overshadowed his tactical and strategic limitations as an army commander. When Little Phil rode onto the battlefield, he entered his element. He belonged along a smoking battleline, inspiring troops, responding to fluid combat conditions with almost instinctive ability. When an opponent gave him an opening, as Early did on this afternoon, he smashed through it. And, as he had at Winchester and Fisher's Hill, he was among his men, from one end of the line to the other, impelling them to victory.

All that had come before in this campaign mattered finally on the late afternoon at Cedar Creek. When the Northerners charged at four o'clock, the graycoats of Evans, Kershaw and Ramseur stood and made the Yankees pay until Evans's flank caved in and word raced down the Southern line that enemy cavalry and infantry again had outflanked them. The Confederate ranks disintegrated as some of the finest fighting men in American military history fled in a panic-stricken rout. What Winchester and Fisher's Hill had given to Sheridan's army, it had taken from Early's.

Not all of the Southerners gave it up without a fight. Small islands of gray infantry resisted until splintered or erased by a floodtide of blue. But none in the Southern army did more in slowing the Union pursuers than the artillerymen. On this field, as on the two before, the conduct of Tom Carter's gunners exceeded those of any other unit in the army. Early praised them highly in his report and recommended promotions for his artillery chief and the battalion commanders. On October 29, Old Jube, in a formal statement, expressed to the gun crews his "high appreciation of their good conduct and gallantry" in the three battles, adding that "I take pleasure in bearing this testimony to their gallantry and devotion to duty in all these actions fought at these places."[19]

The historian of Robert Lee's long arm, however, said it best regarding the Confederate artillery's contribution. He wrote:

> Carter's Artillery formed the very backbone of Early's Army from Winchester to the end of the campaign. Without it, on more than one occasion, withdrawals from before the enemy would have been decisive defeats, and retreats would have become disgraceful routs. It was always at hand . . . in the forefront of the advance, and on every hilltop on the retreat, either to open the battle with encouragement to the infantry, or to deny Sheridan's superb and overwhelming force of cavalry the full fruits of victory.[20]

Not even the valiant rearguard performance of the batteries or of some infantry commands could salvage the wreckage streaming across Cedar Creek toward the haven of Fisher's Hill in the deepening twilight of October 19. The engagement became probably the most bitter defeat for these Southerners. All that had been gained in the morning, and more, had been lost by nightfall. In addition, the casualty totals showed that, once again, the Confederates had inflicted more losses than they had sustained. Union casualties at Cedar Creek were officially reported at 644 killed, 3,430 wounded and 1,591 missing, for a total of 5,665. Though Confederate figures are disputable, one tally placed the losses at possibly 320 killed, 1,540 wounded and 1,050 missing, for 2,910. Added to this list, were 43 cannon, including 20 taken from the Federals in the morning, and at least 300 wagons and ambulances.[21]

The blame for Cedar Creek and the month preceding it would, with and without justifications, fall upon Jubal Early who, even at the end, hunted for men to stand with him. He had executed a masterful offensive against a numerically superior opponent, only to watch it result in ruin. On this day, as on others, against such odds, his army required of him flawless generalship. But conditions beyond his control and a few critical mistakes on his part exacted of him and his army a fatal cost. Cedar Creek epitomized the entire campaign.

Early must have known that the criticism of his generalship, begun after Winchester, would intensify as a result of Cedar Creek. In his report, dated October 21 and carried by Hotchkiss to Lee, the lieutenant general offered to relinquish his command if Lee believed "that the interests of the service would be promoted by a change of commanders." But Old Jube, as was his wont, defended his conduct. "It is mortifying to me, general," he told Lee, "to have to make these explanations of my reverses. They are due to no want of effort on my part, though it may be that I have not the capacity or judgment to prevent them. I have labored faithfully to gain success, and I have not failed to expose my person and to set an example to my men. I know that I shall have to endure censure from those who do not understand my position and difficulties, but I am still willing to make renewed efforts."[22]

But try as he might, then and thereafter, the Valley commander could not explain away that thirty-day drum roll of defeat—Winchester, Fisher's

Hill, "The Burning," Tom's Brook and Cedar Creek. A singular fact mattered above all else—Jubal Anderson Early had suffered full-scale defeat in the Shenandoah Valley, a region associated with Southern invincibility. To the foot cavalry and to the public, the comparison was inevitable and unjust—Old Jube was not Stonewall Jackson, whose legend haunted the hollows, the pastures, and woodlots of the Valley. In the springtime of the Confederacy, Old Jack fired Southern hopes as he rampaged through the Shenandoah but, now, in the winter of a doomed nation, Old Jube stood accused of incompetence, mismanagement, even cowardice and drunkenness, as he so disastrously failed where Jackson so brilliantly succeeded.

Flaws in Early's character and with his generalship surely contributed to the campaign's outcome. His caustic nature, his blindness to his own errors and his penchant for fault-finding affected the relationship between him and his top subordinates. The commander worsened this with his indisposition to accept the advice and suggestions from able officers like John Breckinridge, Richard Anderson, John Gordon and Robert Rodes. Cedar Creek was a notable exception to this latter point. Additionally, once the army tasted defeat at Winchester, the soldiers in the ranks—men who had never before been driven from a field they held—started losing confidence in their commander. Fisher's Hill increased their doubts and, by Cedar Creek, the army, in its morale and in its belief in its prowess, was not the same body of troops as it had been before Winchester. At the head of the Confederate command, therefore, was a general who no longer shared that vital bond of mutual confidence required between a leader and the led.

Early's generalship also suffered from a serious handicap in his utilization of the mounted arm. His cavalry force, in leadership, armament, numbers and horseflesh, definitely paled before the Union mounted command, but Early showed a remarkable misunderstanding of that arm's role. He harbored longstanding prejudices against horse soldiers and, as his units were thrashed time after time by the Federals, his distrust increased while he blamed the cavalry for his woes. Instead, he used infantry as cavalry, which took a physical toll from the foot soldiers. Finally, when he desperately needed his horsemen at Cedar Creek, he had sent most of them away on a mission of little purpose.

John Gordon, one of Early's most ascerbic critics, conceded that the lieutenant general "was an able strategist and one of the coolest and most imperturable of men under fire and in extremity." But Old Jube, the Georgian argued, lacked "the courage of one's convictions." He possessed "blind boldness," not perceiving weak and strong points of an adversary. "He strikes in the dark, madly, wildly, and often impotently," Gordon concluded. To the Georgian, rashness and an underestimation of his opponent led to Early's defeats, beginning and best illustrated by Winchester.[23]

What Gordon and others overlooked or forgot, however, was the campaign, from start to finish, had been predicated upon boldness, a gamble that might stay the inevitable. Burdened with Lee's audacious strategy, confronted by odds of three-to-one, Early could only act with daring, contesting every foot of the Valley. It ultimately brought defeat, but not without accomplishment. He took the war to the doorstep of the enemy capital when Northerners believed such an act an impossibility. As a result, he forced Union authorities—as Lee had hoped—to detach an infantry corps and two-thirds of the cavalry from Petersburg and to reroute another corps destined for that place. In the course of the fighting, his outnumbered band inflicted over 16,500 casualties, the equivalent of another corps and more men than he directed at any time in the campaign, while sustaining losses of less than 10,000. "I think," Private John Worsham of the 21st Virginia concluded, "General Early did everything a commander could do in the Valley with the number of men he had in his command." Jubal Early, burdened with his disadvantages, displayed superior generalship when compared to his Union counterpart.[24]

Two soldiers, a Northerner and a Southerner, left fitting verdicts. "Poor Early!" said the Yankee four days after Cedar Creek. "The fates seem against him." The Confederate, writing many years later, offered this assessment of Early: "He was not a Jackson or a Lee, nor was he, in my judgment, the equal of John B. Gordon, who succeeded him. His queer ways do not lose their freshness with the passage of time, and to those who followed him he will always be 'Old Jube.'"[25]

Philip Sheridan, by contrast, enjoyed instant renown and insured himself a foremost place in American military history because of the Shenandoah Valley. Praise for the general filled Northern newspapers and, within days of Cedar Creek, poet T. Buchanan Read produced "Sheridan's Ride," a widely-read poem which enshrined both rider and mount. Little Phil even changed Rienza's name to Winchester in honor of the deed. William Emory was quite correct when he told an aide on the night after the battle: "This young man, only about thirty years old, has made a great name for himself today."[26]

The acclaim heaped upon Sheridan for the victory on October 19 was well deserved. He had no finer moment during the campaign, a timely opportunity which so fitted the man and the circumstances. Within the army the men came to the universal belief that his presence on the field turned the day. A Vermont veteran, in his regimental history, said it well, asserting that the "secret" of victory "was simply Sheridan's personal magnetism, and all-conquering energy. He felt no doubt, he would submit to no defeat, and he took his army with him as on a whirlwind."[27]

A biographer of Sheridan has argued that the public image of the general—"a daredevil, a hell-for-leather cavalryman whose military assets lay chiefly in his personality rather than his brain"—unfortunately "overwhelmed the truth about the man and his accomplishments." Little Phil, the biographer claimed, was a "truly great and peculiarly American general," who should be placed among the finest commanders in American history.[28]

Sheridan, indeed, stood in the forefront of Civil War army commanders in two particular areas. Few, if any, generals could equal his ability to adapt to fluid conditions on a battlefield. Benjamin Crowninshield, a staff officer, addressed this point, writing: "In one respect Sheridan was especially remarkable: that was in watching the troops in battle, seeing for himself what was done and taking instant advantage of the chances that offered."[29] Winchester, particularly, and Fisher's Hill and Cedar Creek, to a degree, revealed this quality of Sheridan's generalship.

Secondly, Sheridan's use of the mounted arm exceeded that of any army commander, North and South, during the war. He not only enjoyed a decisive superiority with this arm, he exploited it. The cavalry, under his direction, became the equal of the infantry and artillery, the spearhead of the offensive at Winchester and Cedar Creek. He extended the field use of the mounted arm and, in the process, provided a model for armored operations in the Second World War. The contribution of the Union cavalry to the outcome of the campaign was decisive and attributable to Sheridan.[30]

The Union commander forged an army from an amalgam of commands, gave the North and Abraham Lincoln's reelection campaign three timely, major victories, seriously crippled the best fighting corps in the Army of Northern Virginia for the duration of the war, laid waste the granary of the Confederacy and began the descent of the Confederates in Virginia to Appomattox. For these accomplishments, Sheridan received from a grateful government the commission of major general in the Regular Army and, from a grateful people, a place alongside Ulysses Grant and William Sherman in that triumvirate of victors.

Nevertheless, Philip Sheridan, as a tactician and as a strategist, directing an army in the field, had weaknesses as a general. His vast advantage in numbers and armament compensated for his tactical mistakes. If Jubal Early had enjoyed a closer parity in manpower, the outcome of the campaign might have been reversed. Early outgeneraled Sheridan at Winchester but still could not overcome the strength of the Federal host. And, at Cedar Creek, the Southern warrior executed the brilliant offensive of the campaign which still fell short because his lack of muskets could not offset a handful of errors. A Union soldier's description of the final attack at Winchester explained well that, in the end, Confederate bravery and generalship could not stem "those living lines of men like the foaming waves of ocean."[31]

Sheridan, with his decisive numerical edge and with victories at Winchester and Fisher's Hill, finally, missed a splendid opportunity to shorten the war in Virginia. If he had complied with Grant's instructions for a movement on Gordonsville and/or Charlottesville and the Virginia Central Railroad, Richmond might have fallen months before it succumbed. But Sheridan offered a string of excuses and did not comply. L. W. V. Kennon, in his study of the campaign, concluded that "it is remarkable that a campaign so completely victorious in the field should be so barren of decisive results, and this can be accounted for only on the supposition of very faulty strategy."[32] Sheridan, by acting with the daring which guided much of Early's strategy, could have probably delivered the mortal blow to the Confederates in Virginia. Ironically, Robert Lee expected too much of his subordinate, Ulysses Grant too little.

So it had been. The Army of the Shenandoah had conquered what was perceived to be unconquerable. With Cedar Creek, the fate of the Army of the Valley had been sealed. All that remained was a final chapter, a pitiful ending which showed graphically what had been lost, what had been gained in the struggle for the "Daughter of the Stars."

After Cedar Creek, the Confederates retired up the Valley, halting initially at New Market. The Federals undertook a brief pursuit, broke it off and stayed in camp at Cedar Creek. In the weeks that followed, said a Yankee, "Jubal occasionally came up to the front and barked, but there was no more bite in him."[33] Sheridan, in turn, was content with his achievements.

The two armies started disbanding in mid-November as Lee and Grant recalled the units. Joseph Kershaw's division went first, leaving for Petersburg on the 15th. Then, on December 1, the Union VI Corps began its return march to the Army of the Potomac. One of George Crook's divisions followed the corps while his second one was moved to winter quarters at Cumberland, Maryland. Lee countered Grant's moves by ordering the Second Corps, with John Gordon at its head, back to him in mid-December. Early, consequently, with Gabriel Wharton's division and some cavalry and artillery went into winter quarters around Staunton. Sheridan, likewise, established a winter encampment with the XIX Corps and the two cavalry divisions at Winchester.

The opponents then passed the next two months of bitter weather at these locations, with the Rebels suffering grievously from lack of food and supplies. The scarcity of forage forced Early to disband his cavalry and send much of his artillery to the southwestern part of the state. Otherwise, as Early wrote, "the horses of the cavalry and artillery would have perished had they been kept in the Valley."[34]

During the last week of February, Sheridan, with orders from Grant to destroy the Virginia Central Railroad and the James River Canal, and capture Lynchburg, if practicable, headed south from Winchester. His force consisted of the two cavalry divisions, numbering 10,000, under Wesley Merritt's overall command. Departing on February 27, the Yankees met weak resistance from a handful of Rebel cavalry under Thomas Rosser and, sweeping the enemy aside, entered Staunton on the night of March 1.[35]

The next morning, in a chilling rain, George Custer's division rode eastward out of Staunton toward the Blue Ridge. Custer's men crawled through the mud as the rain turned into sleet. Shortly after midday, Custer found Early's remnant of an army in line of battle on a range of low hills west of

Waynesborough. The Confederates belonged to Wharton's division and some artillery units, totalling about 1,500.[36]

Custer, because of the weather and conditions, took three hours to deploy and to prepare an attack plan. At 3:30, the Yankees charged, hitting the Confederate left flank and front almost simultaneously. There was not much left in Wharton's men, who triggered a round or two and then fled precipitately. Nothing could stop the "headlong stampede" of the Southerners, though some officers tried. The Northerners pursued some of them as far as twelve miles into the mountains. Early avoided capture by escaping through a patch of woods, a general riding away from his last battle without a command.[37]

Waynesborough finished the duel between Old Jube and Little Phil. It was not much of a fight, a mockery, in fact, of Winchester, Fisher's Hill and Cedar Creek. But it closed the door. Ahead, for Sheridan, lay further glory at Five Forks and in the West against Indians; ahead, for Early, lay remaining years of bitterness, unreconstruction and defense of a cause he had reluctantly embraced in the beginning and had sacrificed so much for in the end.

Later Union Group Photo: L. to R., Maj. Gen. Philip H. Sheridan, Brig. Gen. James William Forsyth (was Major), Maj. Gen. Wesley Merritt (was Brigadier General), Brig. Gen. Thomas Devin (was Colonel), Maj. Gen. George A. Custer (was Brigadier General). USAMHI.

Four Union Brigadier Generals: Top Left: William Woods Averell; Top Right: David A. Russell (killed at Winchester); Bottom Left: James B. Ricketts; Bottom Right: Cuvier Grover. *Picerno Collection.*

Four Union Brigadier Generals: Top Left: Frank Wheaton; Top Right: Emory Upton (as Colonel); Bottom Left: Lewis Addison Grant; Bottom Right: George Washington Getty. *Picerno Collection.*

Four Union Major Generals: Top Left: George Crook; Top Right: William Hemsley Emory; Bottom Left: Horatio G. Wright; Bottom Right: Alfred T. A. Torbert (was Brigadier General). *Picerno Collection.*

FOOTNOTES
CHAPTER ONE

¹Bruce Catton, *Grant Moves South* (Boston and Toronto: Little, Brown And Company, 1960), p. 389.
²U.S. War Department, *The War Of The Rebellion: A Compilation of the Official Records of the Union and Confederate Armies* (Washington, D.C.: U.S. Government Printing Office, 1880–1901), XXXVI, 2, p. 629; hereafter cited as OR, all references are to Series I.
³Ibid., LII, 2, p. 1003.
⁴Ibid., XXXVII, 1, p. 346.
⁵Robert E. Park, "Diary of Robert E. Park, late Capt. Twelfth Alabama Regt.," *Southern Historical Society Papers*, I, pp. 373–374; hereafter cited as SHSP; Frank E. Vandiver, *Jubal's Raid: General Early's Famous Attack On Washington In 1864* (New York: McGraw-Hill Book Company, 1960; reprint edition, Westport, Connecticut: Greenwood Press, Publishers, 1974), *passim*.
⁶Jeffry D. Wert, "The Snicker's Gap War," *Civil War Times Illustrated*, XVII, 4 (July 1978), pp. 30–40; hereafter cited as *CWTI*; Peter J. Meaney, O.S.B., *The Civil War Engagement at Cool Spring* (Morristown, N.J.: Peter J. Meaney, O.S.B., 1979), *passim*; Jeffry D. Wert, "The Old Killing Ground," *CWTI*, XXIII, 6 (October 1984), pp. 40–47.
⁷Millard Kessler Bushong, *Old Jube: A Biography of General Jubal A. Early* (Boyce, Virginia: Carr Publishing Company, Inc., 1955), p. 222; Liva Baker, "The Burning of Chambersburg," *American Heritage*, XXIV, 5 (August 1973), pp. 38, 39, 97; Sylvester K. Stevens, *Pennsylvania: Birthplace of A Nation* (New York: Random House, 1964), p. 198.
⁸New York *Times*, July 11, 1864.
⁹Everard Hall Smith, "The General and the Valley: Union Leadership During the Threat to Washington in 1864," PhD. Dissertation, University of North Carolina, Chapel Hill, 1977, p. 162.
¹⁰Ibid., p. 162; Ezra J. Warner, *Generals In Blue: Lives of the Union Commanders* (Baton Rouge: Louisiana State University Press, 1964), pp. 195–196.
¹¹Smith, PhD. Diss., UNC, pp. 10, 20; OR, XXXVII, 2, p. 15.
¹²OR, XXXVII, 2, pp. 9, 15; Smith, PhD. Diss., UNC, pp. 20, 162.
¹³OR, XXXVII, 2, pp. 194, 223, 259, 366, 374, 384, 385, 408, 414, 422.
¹⁴Ulysses S. Grant, *Personal Memoirs of U.S. Grant* (New York: Charles L. Webster & Company, 1886) II, p. 317; William C. Davis, *The Battle of New Market* (Garden City, New York: Doubleday & Company, Inc., 1975), pp. 20, 21.
¹⁵OR, XXXVII, 2, pp. 433–434.
¹⁶Ibid., p. 444; John G. Nicolay and John Hay, *Abraham Lincoln: A History* (New York: The Century Co., 1890), IX, p. 179.
¹⁷E. B. Long, with Barbara Long, Foreward by Bruce Catton, *The Civil War Day by Day: An Almanac 1861–1865* (Garden City; New York: Doubleday & Company, Inc., 1971), pp. 545–548; Bruce Catton, *Grant Takes Command* (Boston and Toronto: Little, Brown And Company, 1968), p. 336.
¹⁸Catton, *Grant*, p. 336; OR, XXXVII, 2, pp. 445, 509, 510.
¹⁹Catton, *Grant*, pp. 336, 337; Nicolay and Hay, *Lincoln*, IX, p. 179.
²⁰Catton, *Grant*, pp. 337–340.
²¹Ibid., pp. 342–343; Theodore Lang, *Loyal West Virginia From 1861 to 1865* (Baltimore, Md.: The Deutsch Publishing Co., 1895), pp. 146, 147; L.W.V. Kennon, "The Valley Campaign of 1864: A Military Study," *The Shenandoah Campaigns Of 1862 And 1864 And The Appomattox Campaign 1865: Papers Of The Military Historical Society Of Massachusetts, Vol. VI* (Boston: The Military Historical Society of Massachusetts, 1907), p. 41; hereafter cited as Kennon, *MHSM*, VI.

22 OR, XXXVII, 2, pp. 558, 572.
23 Ibid., pp. 573, 582, 583; Catton, *Grant*, p. 343.
24 Grant, *Memoirs*, II, p. 319; Catton, *Grant*, p. 346.
25 Grant, *Memoirs*, II, p. 319.
26 Ibid., pp. 320, 321; Catton, *Grant*, p. 348.

CHAPTER TWO

1 Aldace F. Walker, *The Vermont Brigade in the Shenandoah Valley, 1864* (Burlington, Vt.: The Free Press Association, 1869), p. 47; Charles R. Perkins to Sister, July 30, 1864, Charles R. Perkins, Letters of, *Civil War Times Illustrated* Collection, Archives, United States Army Military History Institute, Carlisle Barracks, Pa., hereafter cited as USAMHI; OR, XXXVII, 2, pp. 518, 519; James Ellis, Diary of, Roy Bird Cook Collection, West Virginia Collection, West Virginia University.
2 Alanson A. Haines, *History Of The Fifteenth Regiment New Jersey Volunteers* (New York: Jenkins & Thomas, Printers, 1883), p. 238; F. H. Buffum, A *Memorial of The Great Rebellion: Being a History Of The Fourteenth Regiment New-hampshire Volunteers, Covering Its Three Years Of Service With Original Sketches Of Army Life, 1862–1865* (Boston: Franklin Press, Rand, Avery & Company, 1882, p. 189; John V. Young, Diary of, John V. Young Papers, West Virginia Collection, WVU.
3 OR, XLIII, 1, p. 719; Joseph P. Cullen, "Sheridan Wins At Winchester," CWTI, VI, 2 (May 1967), p. 6; William Knowlton to Harriet, August 3, 1864, William Knowlton, Letters and Papers of, Mr. Nick Picerno, Springfield, Vermont.
4 James F. Fitts, "Last Battle of Winchester," *Galaxy*, II (1866), p. 323; Charles C. MacConnell, "Service with Sheridan," *War Papers Read Before the Commandery of the State of Wisconsin, Military Order Loyal Legion of the United States* (Milwaukee: Burdick, Armitage & Allen, 1891), I, p. 285; hereinafter cited as *MOLLUS*; George R. Agassiz, ed., *Meade's Headquarters, 1863–1865: Letters of Colonel Theodore Lyman From The Wilderness To Appomattox* (Boston: The Atlantic Monthly Press, 1922), p. 210.
5 Warner, *Generals In Blue*, pp. 437, 438; Richard O'Connor, *Sheridan the Inevitable* (Indianapolis and New York: The Bobbs-Merrill Company, Inc., 1953), pp. 18, 19.
6 Allan Nevins, ed., A *Diary Of Battle: The Personal Journals Of Colonel Charles S. Wainwright, 1861–1865* (New York: Harcourt, Bruce & World, 1962), p. 517; Orton S. Clark, *The One Hundred And Sixteenth Regiment Of New York State Volunteers* (Buffalo: Printing House of Matthews & Warren, 1868), p. 207; E. R. Hagemann, Editor with an Introduction, *Fighting Rebels And Redskins: Experiences In Army Life Of Colonel George B. Sanford 1861–1892* (Norman: University of Oklahoma Press, 1969), p. 222n; Agassiz, *Meade's Headquarters*, p. 82.
7 A. D. Rockwell, *Rambling Recollections: An Autobiography* (New York: Paul B. Hoeber, 1920), p. 137; O'Connor, *Sheridan*, p. 14; Joseph Warren Keifer, *Slavery And Four Years Of War* (New York and London: G. P. Putnam's Sone, The Knickerbocker Press, 1900), II, p. 104.
8 Frank M. Flinn, *Campaigning With Banks In Louisiana, '63 And '64 And With Sheridan In The Shenandoah Valley, In '64 And '65* (Boston: W. B. Clarke & Co., 1889), p. 227; O'Connor, *Sheridan*, pp. 15, 16; Keifer, *Slavery*, II, pp. 104, 105; Benjamin W. Crowninshield, "Sheridan At Winchester," *Atlantic Monthly*, XLII (1878), p. 690; H. A. DuPont, *The Campaign of 1864 In The Valley Of Virginia and the Expedition To Lynchburg* (New York: National Americana Society, 1925), p. 134.
9 Crowninshield, "Sheridan," *Atlantic Monthly*, XLII, p. 690; Keifer, *Slavery*, II, pp. 104, 105.
10 O'Connor, *Sheridan*, p. 13; Crowninshield, "Sheridan," *Atlantic Monthly*, XLII, p. 690; Keifer, *Slavery*, II, p. 105.

[11] OR, XLIII, 1, pp. 107–108.

[12] Keifer, *Slavery*, II, p. 105; Agassiz, *Meade's Headquarters*, pp. 112, 300.

[13] Walker, *Vermont Brigade*, p. 17; James Madison Murphy, Journal of, J. M. Murphy Papers, William R. Perkins Library, Duke University; Warner, *General In Blue*, p. 404; Agassiz, *Meade's Headquarters*, p. 139.

[14] Warner, *Generals In Blue*, pp. 32, 138, 519, 539, 535.

[15] Walker, *Vermont Brigade*, pp. 23, 24.

[16] DuPont, *Campaign of 1864*, p. 102; OR, XLIII, 1, pp. 108, 109.

[17] Crowninshield, "Sheridan," *Atlantic Monthly*, XLII, p. 684n; Warner, *Generals In Blue*, pp. 142, 143; William H. Emory, Papers of, The Beinecke Rare Book and Manuscript Library, Yale University; Harris H. Beecher, *Record of the 114th Regiment, N.Y.S.V.* (Norwich, N.Y.: J. F. Hubbard, Jr., 1866), p. 395.

[18] Warner, *Generals In Blue*, pp. 33, 134, 135, 193, 194, 305; Homer B. Sprague, *History of the 13th Infantry Regiment of Connecticut Volunteers, During The Great Rebellion* (Hartford, Conn.: Case, Lockwood & Co., 1867), p. 11.

[19] Keifer, *Slavery*, II, p. 106.

[20] DuPont, *Campaign of 1864*, p. 102; Thomas F. Wildes, *Record of the One Hundred And Sixteenth Regiment Ohio Infantry Volunteers in the War Of The Rebellion* (Sandusky, O.: I. F. Mack & Bro., Printers, 1884), p. 220; Warner, *Generals In Blue*, pp. 134, 221; Marshall Moore Brice, *Conquest of A Valley* (Charlottesville: The University Press of Virginia, 1965), p. 65; Isaac H. Duval, "Autobiography," unpublished typed manuscript, *Civil War Times Illustrated* Collection, Archives, USAMHI; Lang, *West Virginia*, p. 351.

[21] OR, XLIII, 1, pp. 108, 109, 110, 271, 413, 414.

[22] Hagemann, *Fighting Rebels*, p. 224; Warner, *Generals In Blue*, p. 508.

[23] Warner, *Generals In Blue*, pp. 80, 108, 109, 123, 124, 321, 566, 567.

[24] OR, XLIII, 1, pp. 111, 112; J. O. Buckeridge, *Lincoln's Choice* (Harrisburg, Pennsylvania: The Stackpole Company, 1956), p. 116; Albert A. Clapp, Diary of, *Civil War Times Illustrated* Collection, Archives, USAMHI.

[25] OR, XLIII, 1, pp. 61, 974.

[26] Robert Stiles, *Four Years Under Marse Robert* (New York & Washington: The Neale Publishing Company, 1903; reprint edition, with Introduction and Index by Robert Krick, Dayton, Ohio: Morningside Bookshop, 1977), p. 109; "Recollections of Jubal Early By One Who Followed Him," *The Century Magazine*, LXX (May–October 1905), p. 311.

[27] Stiles, *Four Years*, pp. 189, 190; J. C. Featherston, "Gen, Jubal Anderson Early," *CV*, XXVI, p. 432.

[28] T. F. Newell, "Gen, Early's Motto: 'Fight 'Em,'" *CV*, V, p. 594; Samuel D. Buck, Papers of, William R. Perkins Library, Duke University.

[29] John B. Gordon, *Reminiscences Of The Civil War* (New York: Charles Scribner's Sons; reprint edition, Gettysburg, Pa.: *Civil War Times Illustrated*, 1974), pp. 317, 318.

[30] John W. Daniel, "General Jubal A. Early," *SHSP*, XXII, p. 328; Gordon, *Reminiscences*, p. 318; Douglas S. Freeman, *Lee's Lieutenants: A Study In Command* (New York: Charles Scribner's Sons, 1942–1944), III, p. xxxiv.

[31] Bushong, *Old Jube*, p. 168; Freeman, *Lee's Lieutenants*, III, p. xxx.

[32] Bradley T. Johnson, "My Ride Around Baltimore In Eighteen Hundred And Sixty-Four," *SHSP*, XXX, pp. 216, 217.

[33] Harry Gilmor, *Four Years In The Saddle* (New York: Harper & Brothers, Publishers, 1866), p. 260; T. T. Munford, "Reminiscences of Cavalry Operations," *SHSP*, XII, pp. 346, 347, 348; Luther W. Hopkins, *From Bull Run To Appomattox: A Boy's View* (Baltimore: Press of Fleet-McGinley Co., 1908), p. 216.

[34] Hopkins, *Bull Run*, p. 216; Munford, "Reminiscences," *SHSP*, XII, p. 346.

35 Nathaniel E. Harris, *Autobiography: The Story Of An Old Man's Life With Reminiscences of Seventy-five Years* (Macon, Ga.: The J. W. Burke Company, Publishers, 1925), pp. 97–98; Vandiver, *Jubal's Raid*, p. 42; Ezra J. Warner, *Generals In Gray: Lives of the Confederate Commanders* (Baton Rouge: Louisiana State University Press, 1959), p. 254.

36 Warner, *Generals In Gray*, p. 79; Stiles, *Four Years*, p. 189; George H. T. Greer, "Riding With Early: An Aide's Diary," *CWTI*, XVII, 8 (December 1978), p. 30.

37 OR, XLIII, 1, p. 1011; Samuel J. C. Moore, "Early's Strength At Winchester," *CV*, XI, p. 396; Smith, "The General and the Valley," PhD. Diss. UNC, pp. 204, 205; John R. Connolly, "Prelude to Victory: Sheridan and the Shenandoah Valley Campaigns of 1864," American History and Literature Honors Paper, Williams College, May 1962, p. 189.

38 Agassiz, *Meade's Headquarters*, p. 100.

39 Ibid., p. 208.

40 Richard Taylor, *Destruction and Reconstruction: Personal Experiences Of The Late War*, Edited by Richard Harwell (New York, London and Toronto: Longmans, Green And Co., 1955), p. 45.

41 John W. Wayland, *Virginia Valley Records: Genealogical and Historical Materials of Rockingham County, Virginia and Related Regions* (Baltimore: Genealogical Publishing Company, 1965), p. 63.

42 Robert G. Tanner, *Stonewall In The Valley: Thomas J. "Stonewall" Jackson's Shenandoah Valley Campaign Spring 1862* (Garden City, New York: Doubleday & Company, Inc., 1976), pp. 18, 20, 21, 22.

43 John William DeForest, *A Volunteers Adventures: A Union Captain's Record of the Civil War* (New Haven: Yale University Press, 1946), p. 85; Crowninshield, "Sheridan," *Atlantic Monthly*, XLII, p. 684.

44 George T. Stevens, *Three Years in the Sixth Corps: A Concise Narrative of Events in the Army of the Potomac, From 1861 To the Close of the Rebellion, April, 1865* (Albany: S. R. Gray, Publisher, 1866), p. 390; Davis, *New Market*, pp. 2, 3.

45 Taylor, *Destruction and Reconstruction*, p. 46; Davis, *New Market*, p. 3.

46 Robert C. Black, III, *The Railroads of the Confederacy* (Chapel Hill: The University of North Carolina Press, 1952), p. 6; Davis, *New Market*, p. 2.

CHAPTER THREE

1 OR, XLIII, 1, pp. 697, 698; Kennon, "Valley Campaign," *MHSM*, VI, p. 40.

2 OR, XLIII, 1, pp. 54, 720, 739.

3 Ibid., pp. 739, 740; U.S. War Department, *Atlas to Accompany The Official Records of the Union And Confederate Armies* (Washington: Government Printing Office, 1891–1895; reprint edition, Gettysburg, Pennsylvania: The National Historical Society, 1978), Plate LXXXIII, 6; hereafter cited as OR *Atlas*.

4 OR *Atlas*, Plate LXXXI, 4.

5 William C. Walker, *History of The Eighteenth Regiment Conn. Volunteers in The War For The Union* (Norwich, Conn.: Published By The Committee, 1885), p. 299; Charles Richard Williams, ed., *Diary And Letters of Rutherford Birchard Hayes* (Columbus: The Ohio State Archaeological and Historical Society, 1922), II, p. 492, hereinafter cited as Williams, *Hayes Diary*; John C. Arnold, Letters of, The Arnold Family Papers, Archives, USAMHI.

6 H. P. Moyer, compiler, *History of the Seventeenth Regiment Pennsylvania Volunteer Cavalry or One Hundred And Sixty-Second In The Line of Pennsylvania Volunteer Regiments, War to Suppress the Rebellion, 1861–1865* (Lebanon, Pa.: Sowers Printing

Company, 1911), p. 94; Penrose G. Mark, *Red: White: and Blue Badge: Pennsylvania Veteran Volunteers, A History of the 93rd Regiment* (Harrisburg, PA.: The Aughinbaugh Press, 1911), p. 287; Haines, *Fifteenth New Jersey*, p. 239; Capt. William W. Old, Diary of, Jubal A. Early Papers, Library of Congress hereafter cited as LC; Archie P. McDonald, ed., *Make Me a Map Of the Valley: The Civil War Journals of Stonewall Jackson's Topographer*, Foreward by T. Harry Williams (Dallas: Southern Methodist University Press, 1973), p. 211; hereafter cited as *Hotchkiss Journal.*

⁷Buffum, *A Memorial*, p. 192; McDonald, *Hotchkiss Journal*, p. 211; Old Diary, LC; OR, XLIII, 1, pp. 42, 760, 761; William Stackhouse, Diary of, The Historical Society of Pennsylvania, Philadelphia; Alonzo Foster, *Reminiscences and Record of the 6th New York V. V. Cavalry* (n.p.: Alonzo Foster, 1892), p. 129; Warner, *Generals In Blue*, pp. 123, 124; J. R. Bowen, *Regimental History of the First New York Dragoons (Originally the 130th N.Y. Vol. Infantry) During Three Years Of Active In The Great Civil War* (n.p.: J. R. Bowen, 1900), p. 247; Hillman A. Hall, compiler, *History of the Sixth New York Cavalry (Second Ira Harris Guard), Second Brigade–First Division–Cavalry Corps, Army Of The Potomac 1861–1865* (Worcester, Mass.: The Blanchard Press, 1908), p. 211; Richard J. DelVecchio, "With The First New York Dragoons: From The Letters of Jared L. Ainsworth," typed unpublished manuscript, Jared L. Ainsworth Papers, Harrisburg Civil War Round Table Collection, Archives, USAMHI; S. L. Gracey, *Annals of the Sixth Pennsylvania Cavalry* (Philadelphia: E. H. Butler & Co., 1868), p. 281.

⁸OR, XLIII, 1, pp. 18–19.

⁹Henry Keiser, Diary of, Harrisburg Civil War Round Table Collection, Archives, USAMHI; William Hewitt, *History of the Twelfth West Virginia Volunteer Infantry: The Part It Took in the War of the Rebellion 1861–1865* (n.p.: Twelfth West Virginia Infantry Association, (1892)), p. 171; McDonald, *Hotchkiss Journal*, p. 222; Jubal Anderson Early, *Autobiographical Sketch And Narrative Of The War Between the States*, With Notes by R. H. Early (Philadelphia & London: J. B. Lippincott Company, 1912), p. 407; OR, XLIII, 1, pp. 42, 63.

¹⁰OR, XLIII, 1, p. 43; D. H. Hanaburgh, *History of the One Hundred And Twenty-eight Regiment, New York Volunteers (U.S. Infantry) In The Late Civil War* (Pokeepsie, N.Y.: Press of Enterprise Publishing Company, 1894), p. 136; William O. Lee, compiler, *Personal And Historical Sketches And Facial History Of And By Members Of The Seventh Regiment Michigan Volunteer Cavalry 1862–1865* (Detroit: 7th Michigan Cavalry Association, (1902)), p. 210; William Fisk, Letters of, *Civil War Times Illustrated* Collection, Archives, USAMHI; George W. Barbour, Diary of, Michigan Historical Collections, Bentley Historical Library, The University of Michigan, Ann Arbor.

¹¹OR, XLIII, 1, p. 43, 423, 801; Haines, *Fifteenth New Jersey*, p. 241; Hewitt, *History*, p. 172.

¹²Buffum, *A Memorial*, p. 194; Hanaburgh, *History*, p. 137, 138.

¹³OR, XLIII, 1, pp. 43, 44, 423; Young, Diary, WVU; Hewitt, *History*, p. 172.

¹⁴OR, XLII, 2, p. 1161.

¹⁵Douglas Southall Freeman, *R. E. Lee: A Biography* (New York: Charles Scribner's Sons, 1932–34), III, p. 479; "Official Diary of First Corps, A.N.V., While Commanded by Lt.-General R. H. Anderson, from June 1st to October 18, 1864," *SHSP*, VII, p. 507.

¹⁶D. Augustus Dickert, *History of Kershaw's Brigade With Complete Roll of Companies, Biographical Sketches, Incidents, Anecdotes, Etc.* (Newberry, S.C.: Elbert H. Aull Co., 1899; reprint edition, with Introduction by Dr. Wm. Stanley Hoole, Dayton, Ohio: Press of Morningside Bookshop, 1973), p. 417; "Official Diary," *SHSP*, VII, p. 507; J. D. Ferguson, "Memoranda of the itinerary and operations of Major General Fitz. Lee's Cavalry Division of the Army of Northern Virginia, from May 4th to October 15th 1864, inclusive by J. D. Ferguson Major & Asst. Adjutant General," typescript

unpublished manuscript, Munford-Ellis Papers, William R. Perkins Library, Duke University; Freeman, *Lee*, III, pp. 480–482; OR, XLII, 2, pp. 1170, 1171, 1177.

[17] Constance Pendleton, ed., *Confederate Memoirs: Early Life And Family History William Frederic Pendleton, Mary Lawson Young Pendleton* (Bryn Athyn, Pennsylvania: Constance Pendleton, 1958), p. 73; "Official Diary," SHSP, VII, p. 507; DeWitt Clinton Gallaher, *A Diary Depicting The Experiences of DeWitt Clinton Gallaher in The War Between The States While Serving In The Confederate Army* (Charleston, W. Va.: DeWitt C. Gallaher, Jr., 1945), p. 10; Ferguson, "Memoranda," Duke.

[18] OR, XLIII, 1, p. 997; Ferguson, "Memoranda," Duke; "Official Diary," SHSP, VII, p. 507; McDonald, *Hotchkiss Journal*, p. 222; OR, XLIII, 1, p. 472.

[19] OR, XLIII, 1, pp. 44, 78, 79, 423, 424; Peter Eltinge, Letters of, Eltinge-Lord Family Papers, William R. Perkins Library, Duke University; pp. 286, 287; Walker, *Vermont Brigade*, p. 58; Louis N. Boudrye, *Historic Records of the Fifth New York Cavalry, First Ira Harris Guard* (Albany, N.Y.: S. R. Gray, 1865), pp. 162–164; W. N. Pickerill, *History of the Third Indiana Cavalry* (Indianapolis, Indiana: Aetna Printing Co., 1906), p. 158.

[20] Early, *Autobiographical Sketch*, pp. 407, 408; McDonald, *Hotchkiss Journal*, p. 222; Ferguson, "Memoranda," Duke; "Official Diary," SHSP, VII, p. 508; Garnett, "Diary," SHSP, XXVII, p. 2; C. L. Shaffner, *Diary of Dr. J. F. Shaffner, Sr.*, (n.p.,n.d.), p. 47.

[21] McDonald, *Hotchkiss Journal*, p. 223; "Official Diary," SHSP, VII, p. 508; Shaffner, *Diary*, p. 48; OR, XLIII, 1, p. 44; Munford, "Reminiscences," SHSP, XII, pp. 348, 349; Irving P. Whitehead, "The Campaigns of Munford and the Second Virginia Cavalry," unpublished typed manuscript, Alderman Library, UVA; "Military Operations in Jefferson County, Virginia (And West VA), 1861–1865," typed copy published by Jefferson County Camp, U.C.V., 1911, reprint 1960, *Civil War Times Illustrated* Collection, Archives, USAMHI, pp. 17, 18; G. G. Benedict, *Vermont In The Civil War: A History of the Part Taken by the Vermont Soldiers And Sailors in the War For The Union, 1861-5* (Burlington, VT: The Free Press Association, 1886–1888), I, p. 504.

[22] DeForest, *Volunteers Adventures*, p. 167; OR, XLIII, 1, p. 45; McDonald, *Hotchkiss Journal*, p. 224; Early, *Autobiographical Sketch*, p. 409; Haines, *Fifteenth New Jersey*, p. 251; Boudrye, *Fifth New York*, p. 166; Bryan Grimes, *Extracts Of Letters of Major-Gen'l Bryan Grimes, To His Wife, Written While In Active Service In The Army of Northern Virginia*, Compiled by Pulaski Cowper (Raleigh: Edwards, Broughton & Co., Steam Printers and Binders, 1883), pp. 62, 63.

[23] DeForest, *Volunteers Adventures*, p. 167; Walker, *Vermont Brigade*, p. 36, 53.

[24] OR, XLIII, 1, pp. 20, 871, 872.

[25] Ibid., p. 893.

[26] Ibid., p. 880; DeForest, *Volunteers Adventures*, p. 166.

[27] Long, *Day-By-Day*, pp. 559, 560–563.

[28] Kennon, "Valley Campaign," MHSM, VI, pp. 39, 41; Grant, *Personal Memoirs*, II, p. 332; OR, XLIII, 1, p. 917.

[29] Philip H. Sheridan, *Personal Memoirs of P. H. Sheridan, General United States Army* (New York: Charles L. Webster & Company, 1888), I, p. 500.

[30] Early, *Autobiographical Sketch*, pp. 414–415.

[31] Ibid., p. 415; Daniel, "Early," SHSP, XXII, p. 318; Gordon, *Reminiscences*, p. 317; Henry Kyd Douglas, *I Rode with Stonewall* (Chapel Hill: The University of North Carolina Press, 1940), p. 307.

[32] Hagemann, *Fighting Rebels*, p. 263; Samuel C. Jones, *Reminiscences of the Twenty-Second Iowa Volunteer Infantry* (Iowa City, Iowa: S.C. Jones, 1907), p. 80; OR, XLIII, 1, pp. 21, 905, 906, 911, 912; McDonald, *Hotchkiss Journal*, p. 225; Kennon, "Valley Campaign," MHSM, VI, p. 39.

[33] OR, XLIII, 1, pp. 45, 426, 461; Early, *Autobiographical Sketch*, pp. 410–412; Mc-

Donald, *Hotchkiss Journal*, p. 226–227; James M. Garnett, "Diary of Captain James M. Garnett, Ordnance Officer Rodes's Division, 2d Corps, Army of Northern Virginia," *SHSP*, XXVII, p. 3.

[34]Mason Whiting Tyler, *Recollections of the Civil War*, Edited by William S. Tyler (New York and London: G. P. Putnam's Sons, The Knickerbocker Press, 1912), p. 273; Jacob Seibert, Letters of, Seibert Family Papers, Harrisburg Civil War Round Table Collection, Archives, USAMHI; Peter B. Boarts, Letters of, The Earl Hess Collection, Archives, USAMHI; Daniel Faust, Papers of, Harrisburg Civil War Round Table Collection, Archives, USAMHI.

[35]Park, "Diary," *SHSP*, I, pp. 434–435; Grimes, *Letters*, p. 66; W. G. Bean, *Stonewall's Man: Sandie Pendleton* (Chapel Hill: The University of North Carolina Press, 1959), p. 208.

[36]OR, XLIII, 1, p. 46.

[37]Sheridan, *Memoirs*, II, pp. 1, 2; Moyer, *Seventeenth Pennsylvania*, p. 222.

[38]OR, XLIII, 2, pp. 49, 57; Kennon, "Valley Campaign," *MHSM*, VI, p. 39.

[39]OR, XLIII, 2, p. 69.

[40]Mary Conner Moffett, *Letters Of General James Conner, C.S.A.* (Columbia, S.C.: Presses of The R. L. Bryan Co., 1950), pp. 157, 158.

[41]"Official Diary," *SHSP*, VII, p. 510; McDonald, *Hotchkiss Journal*, p. 228; Ferguson, "Memoranda," Duke.

[42]Sheridan, *Memoirs*, II, pp. 2, 3; John Worsham, *One of Jackson's Foot Cavalry*, Edited by James I. Robertson, Jr. (Jackson, Tenn.: McCowat-Mercer Press, Inc., 1964), pp. 174, 175.

[43]Sheridan, *Memoirs*, II, pp. 5n, 6n; OR, XLIII, 2, p. 90.

[44]Sheridan, *Memoirs*, II, pp. 4, 5; Letter of Mr. Arthur C. Hodgson to author, September 5, 1979, in author's possession.

[45]Sheridan, *Memoirs*, II, p. 6n.

[46]Ibid., p. 9.

[47]OR, XLIII, 2, pp. 83, 84.

[48]Grant, *Personal Memoirs*, II, p. 327.

[49]Ibid., II, pp. 327, 328, 329; Sheridan, *Memoirs*, II, p. 9; DeForest, *Volunteers Adventures*, p. 172; Jeffry D. Wert, "The Third Battle of Winchester," *American History Illustrated*, XV, 7 (November 1980), p. 8, hereinafter cited as *AHI*.

[50]DeForest, *Volunteers Adventures*, p. 172; Catton, *Grant Takes Command*, p. 363.

[51]OR, XLIII, 2, p. 96.

[52]Sheridan, *Memoirs*, II, p. 9.

[53]Isaac E. Severn, Papers of, Archives, USAMHI; Haines, *Fifteenth New Jersey*, p. 256; Beecher, *Record*, p. 417; Williams, *Hayes Diary*, p. 508.

[54]OR, XLIII, 2, p. 106; Sheridan, *Memoirs*, II, pp. 9, 10.

[55]OR, XLIII, 1, p. 554; Early, *A Memoir*, p. 83; Kennon, "Valley Campaign," *MHSM*, VI, p. 38.

[56]Early, *Autobiographical Sketch*, p. 415; Kennon, "Valley Campaign," *MHSM*, VI, p. 38.

[57]Nichols, *Soldier's Story*, p. 181; OR, XLIII, 1, p. 554; Shaffner, *Diary*, p. 51; I. G. Bradwell, "Early's Valley Campaign, 1864," *CV*, XXVIII, p. 218; Garnett, "Diary," *SHSP*, XXVII, p. 4; McDonald, *Hotchkiss Journal*, p. 229.

[58]OR, XLIII, 1, p. 554; Shaffner, *Diary*, p. 51; Bradwell, "Valley Campaign," *CV*, XXVIII, p. 218.

[59]Shaffner, *Diary*, p. 51; OR, XLIII, 1, pp. 61, 1011; Early, *A Memoir*, p. 81; Connally, "Prelude to Victory," Honors Paper, Williams College; Tenney, *War Diary*, p. 132; Moore, "Early's Strength," *CV*, XI, p. 396.

[60]I. Norval Baker, Diary of, *Civil War Times Illustrated* Collection, Archives, USAMHI.

CHAPTER FOUR

[1] OR, XLIII, 1, pp. 149, 221, 265; Boudrye, *Fifth New York*, p. 171; Henry Norton, editor and compiler, *Deeds Of Daring or History of the Eighth N.Y. Volunteer Cavalry* (Norwich, N.Y.: Chenango Telegraph Printing House, 1889), p. 92; Sheridan, *Memoirs*, II, p. 11; Murphy, Journal, Duke; Charles R. Farr, Diary of, The Charles R. Farr Papers, Archives, USAMHI; Stackhouse, Diary, Hist. Soc. of Pa.

[2] George Crook, *General George Crook: His Autobiography*, Edited and Annotated by Martin F. Schmitt (Norman: University of Oklahoma Press, 1946), p. 124.

[3] OR, XLIII, 1, pp. 517, 518; Norton, *Eighth N.Y.*, p. 92; DuPont, *Campaign Of 1864*, p. 109; Theodore F. Rodenbough, Henry C. Potter and William P. Seal, editors and compilers, *History of the Eighteenth Regiment of Cavalry Pennsylvania Volunteers (163d Regiment of the Line) 1862–1865* (New York: Wynkoop Hallenback Crawford Co., 1909), p. 57; Boudrye, *Fifth New York*, p. 171; T. K. Cartmell, *Shenandoah Valley Pioneers and Their Descendants: A History of Frederick County, Virginia From its Formation in 1738 to 1908* (reprint edition, Berryville, Virginia: Chesapeake Book Company, 1963), p. 483.

[4] Walter Clark, ed., *Histories of the Several Regiments and Battalions From North Carolina, in the Great War 1861–'65* Written by Members of the Respective Commands (Raleigh, N.C.: E. M. Uzzell, Printer, 1901), II, p. 251, 254–256; hereafter cited as Clark, *N.C. Regts*; Clark, *One Hundred And Sixteenth New York*, p. 217; Rodenbough, *Eighteenth Pennsylvania*, p. 57; Norton, *Eighth N.Y.*, p. 92; Boudrye, *Fifth New York*, p. 117.

[5] Clark, *N. C. Regts.*, I, p. 646.

[6] Douglas, *Stonewall*, p. 309.

[7] S. D. Ramseur to David Schenck, October 10, 1864, Stephen D. Ramseur Papers, Southern Historical Collection, University of North Carolina; hereafter cited as SHC/UNC; Worsham, *Foot Cavalry*, p. 177; Early, *Autobiographical Sketch*, p. 442.

[8] Rodenbough, *Eighteenth Pennsylvania*, p. 57; Clark, *One Hundred And Sixteenth New York*, p. 217; Beecher, *Record*, p. 417; McDonald, *Hotchkiss Journal*, p. 229; OR, XLIII, 1, p. 518.

[9] Unsigned Letter to Mrs. Lovina Wilfong, October 3, 1864, John Wilfong Papers, William R. Perkins Library, Duke; S. D. Ramseur to David Schenck, October 10, 1864, Ramseur Papers, SHC/UNC; Clarence R. Hatton, "Gen. Archibald Campbell Godwin," *CV*, XXVIII, p. 136; Clark, *N.C. Regts.*, III, p. 420; Bradley T. Johnson, "Tarheels' Thin Gray Line," *SHSP*, XVII, p. 172.

[10] S. D. Ramseur to David Schenck, October 10, 1864, Ramseur Papers, SHC/UNC; Hatton, "Godwin," *CV*, p. 136.

[11] Tenney, *War Record*, p. 131; Walker, *Vermont Brigade*, p. 91; Sheridan, *Memoirs*, II, pp. 15, 16; OR, XLIII, 1, p. 47.

[12] OR, XLIII, 1, pp. 149, 221, 279; Walker, *Vermont Brigade*, p. 91; Haines, *Fifteenth New Jersey*, pp. 256, 257.

[13] Flinn, *Campaigning*, p. 177; DeForest, *Volunteers Adventures*, p. 173; Flinn, *Campaigning*, p. 177; Haines, *Fifteenth New Jersey*, p. 257; OR, XLIII, 1, pp. 149, 279; Stevens, *Three Years*, pp. 396, 397.

[14] George N. Carpenter, *History of The Eighth Regiment Vermont Volunteers, 1861–1865* (Boston: Press of Deland & Barta, 1886), p. 177; DeForest, *Volunteers Adventures*, p. 173.

[15] Buffum, *A Memorial*, p. 205; Beecher, *Record*, p. 419.

[16] J. H. Kidd, *Personal Recollections of a Cavalryman With Custer's Michigan Cavalry Brigade in the Civil War* (Ionia, Michigan: Sentinel Printing Company, 1908), p. 298; Crook, *Autobiography*, pp. 125, 126.

[17] Sheridan, *Memoirs*, II, p. 30; William R. Cox, *Address on the Life And Character of Maj. Gen. Stephen D. Ramseur* (Raleigh: E. M. Uzzell, Steam Printer And Binder, 1891), p. 39; Kennon, "Valley Campaign," *MHSM*, p. 45.

[18] OR *Atlas*, Plate XCIX, 1.

[19] Sheridan, *Memoirs*, II, p. 31; Kennon, "Valley Campaign," *MHSM*, VI, p. 44; DeForest, *Volunteers Adventures*, p. 173; Crook, *Autobiography*, pp. 125–126.

[20] "Recollections," *The Century Magazine*, LXX, p. 311.

[21] Early, *Autobiographical Sketch*, pp. 414, 415.

[22] Clark, *N. C. Regts.*, I, p. 261.

[23] Ibid., I, pp. 207, 262; Cox, *Address*, p. 39; Cullen, "Sheridan," *CWTI*, VI, 2, pp. 40–41; Jedediah Hotchkiss, Papers of, LC; Marcus D. Herring, "Gen. Robert E. Rodes," *CV*, XXXIV, p. 330; Marcus D. Herring, "General Rodes At Winchester," *CV*, XXVIII, p. 184.

[24] Worsham, *Foot Cavalry*, p. 167.

[25] Ibid., p. 167; Nichols, *Soldier's Story*, pp. 182, 183; Gordon, *Reminiscences*, p. 321; I. G. Bradwell, "With Early In The Valley," *CV*, XXII, p. 504; Wise, *Long Arm*, p. 884; McDonald, *Hotchkiss Journal*, p. 229.

[26] Cartmell, *Shenandoah Valley*, pp. 296, 402; J. E. Norris, ed. *History of the Lower Shenandoah Valley Counties of Frederick, Berkeley, Jefferson and Clarke* (Chicago: A. Warner & Co., Publishers, 1890; reprint edition, Berryville, Virginia: Virginia Book Company, 1972), p. 778; Worsham, *Foot Cavalry*, p. 167.

[27] S. D. Ramseur to David Schenck, October 10, 1864, Ramseur Papers, SHC/UNC; Douglas, *Stonewall*, p. 309.

[28] OR, XLIII, 1, pp. 610, 611; Cullen, "Sheridan," *CWTI*, VI, 2, pp. 8, 40; McDonald, *Hotchkiss Journal*, p. 229; Early, *Autobiographical Sketch*, p. 420; Sheridan, *Memoirs*, II, p. 17; Munford, "Reminiscences," *SHSP*, XII, p. 448; Ferguson, "Memoranda," Duke.

[29] Flinn, *Campaigning*, p. 178; Early, *Autobiographical Sketch*, p. 420; Sheridan, *Memoirs*, II, p. 17; Crook, *Autobiography*, pp. 125, 126; DuPont, *Campaign Of 1864*, pp. 110, 117, 118; John MacGregor Adams and Albert Egerton Adams, eds., *Memorial And Letters of Rev. John R. Adams, D. D.* (Cambridge, Mass.: University Press: John Wilson And Son, 1890), p. 155.

[30] OR, XLIII, 1, pp. 149, 191.

[31] Ibid., pp. 149, 150, 191, 192, 207, 219; Stevens, *Three Years*, p. 398; Walker, *Vermont Brigade*, p. 92.

[32] OR, XLIII, 1, pp. 221, 222, 238.

[33] Ibid., pp. 163, 164; Haines, *Fifteenth New Jersey*, pp. 256, 257.

[34] Philip Van Doren Stern, *Soldier Life in the Union and Confederate Armies* (Bloomington: Indiana University Press, 1961), p. 337; OR, XLIII, 1, pp. 191, 219, 221, 238.

[35] OR, XLIII, 1, pp. 271, 273.

[36] Hatton, "Godwin," *CV*, XXVIII, p. 136.

[37] OR, XLIII, 1, pp. 287, 288, 318, 346; Buffum, *A Memorial*, pp. 206, 207, 208; DeForest, *Volunteers Adventures*, p. 176; Richard B. Irwin, *History of the Nineteenth Army Corps* (New York & London: G. P. Putnam's Sons, 1892), p. 318; John M. Gould, *History of the First-Tenth-Twenty-ninth Maine Regiment* (Portland: Stephen Berry, 1871), p. 490.

[38] OR, XLIII, 1, pp. 287, 288; Gould, *History*, p. 490.

[39] Bayard A. Nettleton, "How The Day Was Saved At The Battle Of Cedar Creek," *Glimpses of the Nation's Struggle*, MOLLUS, Commandery of Minnesota, 1887, I, p. 267.

[40] Buffum, *A Memorial*, pp. 209, 225.

[41] Ibid., p. 210; Munford, "Reminiscences," *SHSP*, XII, p. 448; Nathan G. Dye, Papers of, William R. Perkins Library, Duke University.

[42] Buffum, *A Memorial*, p. 220.

[43] Ibid., p. 211.

[44] Bradwell, "With Early," *CV*, XXII, p. 505.

[45] Buffum, *A Memorial*, pp. 212–214, 219, 226.

46 Peter Eltinge to Father, September 26, 1864, Eltinge Papers, Duke; Buffum, *A Memorial*, p. 212; *OR*, XLIII, 1, pp. 279, 280; Nichols, *Soldier's Story*, p. 183; Bradwell, "With Early," *CV*, XXII, p. 505; Hanaburgh, *History*, pp. 146, 147; Carpenter, *Eighth Vermont*, p. 172; Dye to Dear Friends, October 2, 1864, Dye Papers, Duke.

47 *OR*, XLIII, 1, pp. 325, 555; Buffum, *A Memorial*, p. 218; Hanaburgh, *History*, p. 147; Jennings Cropper Wise, *The Long Arm of Lee: The History of the Artillery of the Army of Northern Virginia* (Lynchburg, Virginia: J. P. Bell Company, Inc., 1915; reprint edition, New York: Oxford University Press, Inc., 1959), p. 885.

48 Allen P. Tankersley, *John B. Gordon: A Study In Gallantry* (Atlanta, Georgia: The Whitehall Press, 1955), pp. 17, 19, 20, 37, 52, 62, 74, 75; Warner, *Generals In Gray*, p. 111; Freeman, *Lee's Lieutenants*, III, p. xxxiv.

49 Tankersley, *Gordon*, p. 2; Stiles, *Four Years*, pp. 188, 212.

50 Worsham, *Foot Cavalry*, pp. 146–147; Tankersley, *Gordon*, pp. 4, 5, 7; Bradwell, "With Early," *CV*, XXII, p. 506.

51 *OR*, XLIII, 1, pp. 318, 319, 344; Flinn, *Campaigning*, pp. 165, 166; Hanaburgh, *History*, p. 147; Carpenter, *Eighth Vermont*, pp. 169, 172; Peter Eltinge to brother, September 28, 1864, Eltinge Papers, Duke; Francis H. Buffum, *Sheridan's Veterans: A Souvenir of their Two Campaigns in the Shenandoah Valley* (Boston, Mass.: W. F. Brown & Company, Printers, 1883), I, p. 89.

52 *OR*, XLIII, 1, pp. 319, 330; William F. Tiemann, compiler, *The 159th Regiment Infantry, New-York State Volunteers, in the War Of The Rebellion, 1862–1865* (Brooklyn, N.Y.: William F. Tiemann, 1891), pp. 98–99.

53 *OR*, LXIII, 1, pp. 330, 331, 337; Sprague, *13th Connecticut*, pp. 226–231; Jones, *Reminiscences*, p. 85.

54 *OR*, XLIII, 1, pp. 346, 349, 350, 355; Dye to Dear Friends, October 5, 1864, Dye Papers, Duke.

55 *OR*, XLIII, 1, pp. 346, 349, 350, 355; Dye to Dear Friends, October 5, 1864, Dye Papers, Duke.

56 DuPont, *Campaign Of 1864*, p. 111.

57 Munford, "Reminiscences," *SHSP*, XII, p. 448; Worsham, *Foot Cavalry*, p. 167; *OR*, XLIII, 1, pp. 356, 357; Francis Dawes, Diary of, *Civil War Times Illustrated* Collection, Archives, USAMHI.

58 Buffum, *A Memorial*, pp. 220, 221, 222; *OR*, XLIII, 1, p. 115; Flinn, *Campaigning*, p. 194.

59 DeForest, *Volunteers Adventures*, p. 179; *OR*, XLIII, 1, pp. 288, 289, 290, 295, 298, 299.

60 Fitts, "Winchester," *Galaxy*, II, pp. 326, 327; Beecher, *Record*, p. 421.

61 Beecher, *Record*, pp. 421, 422; Fitts, "Winchester," *Galaxy*, II, p. 327; Elias P. Pellet, *History of the 114th Regiment, New York State Volunteers* (Norwich, N.Y.: Telegraph & Chronicle Power Press Print., 1866), pp. 253, 254.

62 Clark, *One Hundred And Sixteenth New York*, pp. 220–221; Beecher, *Record*, p. 423; Pellet, *114th New York*, pp. 254, 255.

63 Beecher, *Record*, pp. 423, 424, 425; Pellet, *114th New York*, pp. 254, 255; Clark, *One Hundred And Sixteenth New York*, p. 222; Gould, *History*, p. 490; Fitts, "Winchester," *Galaxy*, II, p. 329.

64 Beecher, *Record*, p. 428; Pellet, *114th New York*, p. 256; *OR*, XLIII, 1, p. 308.

65 DeForest, *Volunteers Adventures*, pp. 175, 181, 182.

66 Ibid., pp. 182, 183; *OR*, XLIII, 1, pp. 315, 316.

67 Carpenter, *Eighth Vermont*, pp. 15, 170, 174, 195, 254, 255; Benedict, *Vermont*, II, p. 80.

68 Benedict, *Vermont*, II, pp. 151, 152.

69 Ibid., II, p. 152.

70 Ibid., II, pp. 148, 152, 153.

71 Jesse C. Osgood to Aunt Fanny, September 22, 1864, Letter of, Americana Collection, The Huntington Library, San Marino, California; DeForest, *Volunteers Adventures*, pp. 183–186; OR, XLIII, 1, p. 316.

72 DeForest, *Volunteers Adventures*, pp. 185, 186; Carpenter, *Eighth Vermont*, pp. 179, 180.

73 Park, "Diary," *SHSP*, II, p. 29; Worsham, *Foot Cavalry*, p. 168.

74 "A Staff Officer's Recollection of The Battle of Opequon, Fought at Winchester, Va. Sept. 19, 1864," Russell Hastings Papers, Library, Rutherford B. Hayes Presidential Center, Fremont, Ohio; hereafter cited as RBHPC.

75 OR, XLIII, 1, pp. 212, 219; Hotchkiss, Papers, LC.

76 OR, XLIII, 1, pp. 196, 197, 204, 205, 212; Hotchkiss, Papers, LC.

77 OR, XLIII, 1, p. 207; Walker, *Vermont Brigade*, pp. 93–96; Hotchkiss, Papers, LC.

78 OR, XLIII, 1, pp. 221, 222, 231, 236, 237, 238; *National Tribune*, October 15, 1891; J. Newton Terrill, *Campaign of the Fourteenth Regiment New Jersey Volunteers*, Second Edition (New Brunswick, N.J.: Daily Home News Press, 1884), p. 87; Lemuel Abijah Abbott, *Personal Recollections and Civil War Diary 1864* (Burlington: Free Press Printing Co., 1908), p. 162; Chaplain E. M. Haynes, *A History of the Tenth Regiment, Vermont Volunteers* (Lewiston, Me.: Journal Steam Press, 1870), p. 111.

79 OR, XLIII, 1, pp. 263, 264; *OR Atlas*, Plate XCIX; Joseph Warren Keifer, Papers, LC.

80 OR, XLIII, 1, pp. 191, 192, 196, 197, 204, 205, 212, 219, 243, 253, 263, 264, 266, 269; Walker, *Vermont Brigade*, p. 96; Wise, *Long Arm*, pp. 738, 878; William H. Runge, ed., *Four Years In The Confederate Artillery: The Diary of Private Henry Robinson Berkeley* (Chapel Hill: The University of North Carolina Press, 1961), pp. 94, 96; Abbott, *Personal Recollections*, p. 156.

81 OR, XLIII, 1, pp. 246, 247; Keifer, Papers, LC.

82 Bradwell, "Valley Campaign," CV, XXVIII, p. 219; Clark, *N.C. Regts.*, I, pp. 207, 208.

83 Garnett, "Diary," *SHSP*, XXVII, p. 5; J. L. Schaub, "Gen. Robert E. Rodes," CV, XVIII, p. 269; Herring, "Rodes At Winchester," CV, XXVIII, p. 184; Herring, "Rodes," CV, XXXIV, p. 330; Wert, "Rodes," *CWTI*, XVI, 8, p. 41–45.

84 Park, "Diary," *SHSP*, II, p. 25; Bradwell, "Valley Campaign," CV, XXVIII, p. 219; OR, XLIII, 1, pp. 192, 197, 205, 221, 222, 231, 232, 243, 247, 260, 264, 266; Walker, *Vermont Brigade*, pp. 96, 97; Garnett, "Diary," *SHSP*, II, pp. 26, 27; Henry R. Morrison to Brother, September 20, 1864, Henry R. Morrison, Letters and Clippings of, *Civil War Times Illustrated* Collection, Archives, USAMHI.

85 Nichols, *Soldier's Story*, p. 185.

86 Ibid., p. 186; OR, XLIII, 1, pp. 260, 261, 263, 264, 344; Bradwell, "Valley Campaign," CV, XXVIII, p. 219; DeForest, *Volunteers Adventures*, p. 177; Alfred Seelye Roe, *The Ninth New York Heavy Artillery* (Worcester, Mass.: Published By The Author, 1899), p. 151.

87 OR, XLIII, 1, p. 150.

88 Nelson V. Hutchinson, *History of the Seventh Massachusetts Volunteer Infantry in the War of the Rebellion of the Southern States Against Constitutional Authority, 1861–1865* (Taunton, Mass.: Published by Authority of the Regimental Association, 1890), p. 288.

89 OR, XLIII, 1, pp. 164, 168, 184, 185, 259, 277, 278, 279; James L. Bowen, *History of the Thirty-seventh Regiment Mass. Volunteers, In The Civil War of 1861–1865* (Holyoke, Mass., and New York City: Clark W. Bryan & Company, Publishers, 1884), pp. 376, 377; Edmund Halsey, Papers of, Archives, USAMHI; James M. Gaspar, Diary of, Civil War Miscellaneous Collection, Archives, USAMHI.

90 OR, XLIII, 1, p. 605; W. A. Smith, *The Anson Guards: Company C, Fourteenth Regiment North Carolina Volunteers, 1861-1865* (Charlotte, N.C.: Stone Publishing Co., 1914; reprint edition, Wendell, N.C.: Broadfoot's Bookmark, 1978), p. 279; Clark, N.C. *Regts.*, I, p. 728; Halsey, Papers, USAMHI.

91 Tyler, *Recollections*, p. 279; Gaspar, Diary, USAMHI.

92 OR, XLIII, 1, p. 151; Sheridan, *Memoirs*, II, pp. 23-24; Paul, Diary, USAMHI.

93 DeForest, *Volunteers Adventures*, p. 190; OR, XLIII, 1, pp. 164, 168, 169, 187, 188; Haines, *Fifteenth New Jersey*, p. 259; Park, "Diary," SHSP, II, pp. 26, 27; Halsey, Papers, USAMHI.

94 Peter S. Michie, *The Life And Letters Of Emory Upton* (New York: D. Appleton, 1885), pp. 3, 5, 6, 6, 4; Isaac D. Best, *History of the 121st New York State Infantry* (Chicago, Ill.: Lieut. Jas. H. Smith, 1921), pp. 30, 31; Warner, *Generals In Blue*, pp. 519, 520; Bruce Catton, *A Stillness at Appomattox* (Garden City, New York: Doubleday & Company, Inc., 1953), p. 111; Keiser, Diary, USAMHI.

95 Michie, *Upton*, pp. xxvii, 68; Best, *121st New York*, p. 31.

96 Jeffry D. Wert, "Spotsylvania", CWTI, XXII, 2, pp. 12-15, 19-21; Best, *121st New York*, p. 135; Catton, *Stillness*, p. 112.

97 Henry A. DuPont to James A. Wilson, February 11, 1889, Letter of, Crook-Kennon Papers, Archives, USAMHI; Theodore F. Vaill, *History of the Second Connecticut Volunteer Heavy Artillery, Originally The Nineteenth Connecticut Vols.* (Winsted, Conn.: Winsted Printing Company, 1868), pp. 94, 95; DuPont, *Campaign Of 1864*, pp. 114, 115; Best, *121st New York*, pp. 34, 180, 181.

98 Flinn, *Campaigning*, p. 185; OR, XLIII, 1, pp. 173, 180, 182; DuPont, *Campaign Of 1864*, p. 115; Best, *121st New York*, pp. 181, 182; Bradwell, "Valley Campaign," CV, XXVIII, p. 219; Smith, *Anson Guards*, pp. 279, 280.

99 OR, XLIII, 1, p. 150; Paul Singer Thompson, "The Summer Campaign In The Lower Valley 1864," PhD. Dissertation, University of Virginia, 1966, p. 383.

CHAPTER FIVE

1 OR, XLIII, 2, pp. 104, 105.

2 Hagemann, *Fighting Rebels*, p. 22; Warner, *Generals In Blue*, p. 321; Kidd, *Personal Recollections*, pp. 237, 238.

3 OR, XLIII, 1, pp. 443, 454, 481; Lee, *Seventh Michigan*, p. 168; Hall, *Sixth New York*, p. 223; Barbour, Diary, UMICH; Hagemann, *Fighting Rebels*, p. 225.

4 "An Incident of the Battle of Winchester, or Opequon," SHSP, XXXVII, p. 232; OR, XLIII, 1, pp. 1003, 1004; John H. Bobbitt, "That Moorefield Surprise," CV, X, p. 70; Harris, *Autobiography*, p. 74; Ferguson, "Memoranda," Duke.

5 George A. Forsyth, *Thrilling Days In Army Life* (New York and London: Harper & Brothers, 1900), p. 148; "Incident," SHSP, XXXVII, 1, p. 232; OR, XLIII, 1, p. 443.

6 OR, XLIII, 1, p. 443; Hagemann, *Fighting Rebels*, p. 267.

7 Hagemann, *Fighting Rebels*, p. 276; Catherine S. Crary, ed., *Dear Belle: Letters from a Cadet & Officer to his Sweetheart, 1858-1865* (Middletown, Connecticut: Wesleyan University Press, 1965), pp. 214, 215; Kidd, *Personal Recollections*, pp. 130, 131; Warner, *Generals In Blue*, pp. 108, 109; Marguerite Merington, ed., *The Custer Story: The Life and Intimate Letters of General George A. Custer and His Wife Elizabeth* (New York: The Devin-Adair Company, 1950), pp. 97, 110, 111.

8 Kidd, *Personal Recollections*, p. 130; Agassiz, *Meade's Headquarters*, p. 130.

9 Hagemann, *Fighting Rebels*, pp. 225-226.

10 OR, XLIII, 1, pp. 454, 462; Kidd, *Personal Recollections*, pp. 385, 386.

11 OR, XLIII, 1, pp. 454, 455; Kidd, *Personal Recollections*, p. 387; Isham, *Seventh Michigan*, p. 69.

[12] OR, XLIII, 1, pp. 443, 454, 455, 462; Kidd, *Personal Recollections*, pp. 387–389; Asa B. Isham, *An Historical Sketch of the Seventh Regiment Michigan Volunteer Cavalry: From Its Organization, In 1862, To Its Muster Out, In 1865* (New York: Town Topics Publishing Company, (1893)), p. 69.

[13] OR, XLIII, 1, p. 455; Hagemann, *Fighting Rebels*, p. 267; OR *Atlas*, Plate, LXXXV, 12.

[14] OR, XLIII, 1, p. 555; Milton Humphrey, Diary of, Alderman Library, University of Virginia; OR *Atlas*, Plate XCIX, 1.

[15] OR, XLIII, 1, pp. 455, 1003; Hagemann, *Fighting Rebels*, p. 267; Humphrey, Diary, UVA; OR *Atlas*, Plate 12.

[16] OR, XLIII, 1, pp. 427, 443, 455, 482, 490; Moyer, *Seventeenth Pennsylvania*, p. 347; OR *Atlas*, Plate LXXXV, 12.

[17] OR, XLIII, 1, pp. 425, 427, 443, 482, 490; pt. 2, p. 113; Hall, *Sixth New York*, p. 223.

[18] Humphrey, Diary, UVA; OR *Atlas*, Plate LXXXV, 12, 13; Hagemann, *Fighting Rebels*, p. 267.

[19] OR, XLIII, 1, pp. 443, 455; Humphrey, Diary, UVA; Morton L. Hawkins, "Sketch of the Battle of Winchester, September 19, 1864," *Sketches of War History, 1861–1865*, MOLLUS, Ohio Commandery (Cincinnati: Robert Clarke & Co., 1888), I, p. 152.

[20] OR, XLIII, 2, p. 876.

[21] Ibid., 1, p. 498; pt. 2, p. 106; Charles T. O'Ferrall, *Forty Years Of Active Service* (New York And Washington: The Neale Publishing Company, 1904), p. 114.

[22] O'Ferrall, *Forty Years*, pp. 114, 115.

[23] Ibid., p. 115; OR, XLIII, 1, p. 498; William Davis Slease, *The Fourteenth Pennsylvania in the Civil War* (Pittsburgh, Pa.: Art Engraving & Printing Co., (1915?), p. 183; Humphrey, Diary, UVA; Baker, Diary, USAMHI.

[24] OR, XLIII, 1, pp. 456, 555; Garnett, "Diary," SHSP, XXVII, p. 5; Ferguson, "Memoranda," Duke; Wise, *Long Arm*, p. 886; O'Ferrall, *Forty Years*, p. 115.

[25] Garnett, "Diary," SHSP, XXVII, p. 5.

[26] OR, XLIII, 1, pp. 444, 482; Moyer, *Seventeenth Pennsylvania*, pp. 98, 99; O'Ferrall, *Forty Years*, p. 115.

[27] Moyer, *Seventeenth Pennsylvania*, pp. 99, 347; OR, XLIII, 1, pp. 444, 482; O'Ferrall, *Forty Years*, p. 115; Harris, *Autobiography*, p. 74.

[28] OR, XLIII, 1, pp. 444, 482; Bowen, *Dragoons*, pp. 229, 230; O'Ferrall, *Forty Years*, p. 115.

[29] Ferguson, "Memoranda," Duke; OR, XLIII, 1, p. 456; Isham, *Seventh Michigan*, p. 70.

[30] OR, XLIII, 1, pp. 427, 444, 456, 498; Kidd, *Personal Recollections*, pp. 390, 391; Wiley Sword, "Cavalry on Trial at Kelly's Ford," CWTI, XIII, 1, (April 1974), p. 33.

[31] OR, XLIII, 1, pp. 444, 456; Kidd, *Personal Recollections*, p. 391; O'Ferrall, *Forty Years*, p. 115; Ferguson, "Memoranda," Duke.

[32] OR, XLIII, 1, pp. 456, 555; Kidd, *Personal Recollections*, p. 392; Wise, *Long Arm*, p. 886; Isham, *Seventh Michigan*, p. 70; Humphrey, Diary, UVA; Garnett, "Diary," SHSP, XXVII, p. 6.

[33] OR, XLIII, 1, pp. 456, 457, 498; Humphrey, Diary, UVA; Kidd, *Personal Recollections*, p. 392; Garnett, "Diary," SHSP, XXVII, p. 6.

[34] OR, XLIII, 1, p. 444.

[35] OR *Atlas*, Plate XCIX, 1.

[36] OR, XLIII, 1, p. 47; Sheridan, *Memoirs*, II, p. 24.

[37] OR, XLIII, 2, p. 103; DuPont, *Campaign Of 1864*, p. 108.

[38] OR, XLIII, 1, p. 47; Sheridan, *Memoirs*, II, p. 24.

[39] OR, XLIII, 1, p. 361; Crook, *Autobiography*, p. 127; DuPont, *Campaign Of 1864*, pp. 119, 120–121; "Staff Officer's Recollection," RBHPC.

40 DuPont, *Campaign Of 1864*, p. 127; DuPont to James Wilson, February 11, 1889, Letter, Crook-Kennon Papers, USAMHI; Kennon, "Valley Campaign," *MHSM*, VI, p. 43.

41 DuPont, *Campaign Of 1864*, pp. 109, 110; OR, XLIII, 1, p. 361; Crook, *Autobiography*, p. 126; Stern, *Soldier Life*, p. 338.

42 Hewitt, *History*, p. 177; OR, XLIII, 1, pp. 361, 368; Crook, *Autobiography*, p. 125; Charles H. Lynch, *The Civil War Diary 1862–1865 of Charles H. Lynch, 18th Conn. Vol's.* (Hartford, Conn.: The Case, Lockwood & Brainard Co., 1915), p. 114.

43 William S. Lincoln, *Life With the Thirty-Fourth Mass. Infantry In The War Of The Rebellion* (Worcester: Press of Noyes, Snow & Company, 1879), p. 354; Crook, *Autobiography*, p. 126; OR, XLIII, 1, p. 401.

44 Ibid., pp. 361, 368; DuPont, *Campaign Of 1864*, p. 119; DuPont to James Wilson, February 11, 1889, Letter, Crook-Kennon Papers, USAMHI.

45 OR, XLIII, 1, pp. 361, 401; DuPont, *Campaign Of 1864*, p. 120; OR *Atlas*, Plate, XCIX, 1.

46 DuPont, *Campaign Of 1864*, pp. 121, 122; OR, XLIII, 1, pp. 361, 362, 401; OR *Atlas*, Plate, XCIX, 1.

47 OR *Atlas*, Plate, XCIX, 1; Early, *A Memoir*, p. 88; OR, XLIII, 1, p. 555; Garnett, "Diary," *SHSP*, XII, p. 6; Cullen, "Sheridan," *CWTI*, VI, 2, p. 42.

48 Williams, *Hayes Diary*, p. 510; Hawkins, "Sketch," *MOLLUS*, Ohio, I, p. 158; OR, XLIII, 1, p. 412; Jonathan Harlan to R. B. Hayes, July 8, 1887, Jonathan Harlan, Letter of, Library, RBHPC.

49 Comly, Diary, RBHPC; OR, XLIII, 1, p. 401; Williams, *Hayes Diary*, pp. 509, 511.

50 William S. Wilson to R. B. Hayes, April 9, 1887, William S. Wilson, Letter of, Library, RBHPC; Comly, Diary, RBHPC; James W. DeLay to R. B. Hayes, December 22, 1886, James W. DeLay, Letters of, Library, RBHPC; John T. Booth to R. B. Hayes, May 26, 1887, John T. Booth, Letter of, Library, RBHPC; B. F. Stearns to R. B. Hayes, July 18, 1887, B. F. Stearns, Letter of, Library, RBHPC; J. Reasoner to R. B. Hayes, September 18, 1887, J. Reasoner, Letter of, Library, RBHPC; Williams, *Hayes Diary*, p. 509.

51 Williams, *Hayes Diary*, p. 510; OR, XLIII, 1, p. 362; Benedict, *Vermont*, II, p. 149; Hastings, "Memoirs," RBHPC; Comly, Diary, RBHPC; OR, XLIII, 1, pp. 362, 402.

52 OR, XLIII, 1, pp. 368, 375, 376, 387, 388; Wildes, *Record*, p. 170.

53 OR, XLIII, 1, pp. 368, 369, 376; Wildes, *Record*, p. 171; OR *Atlas*, Plate XCIX, 1.

54 OR, XLIII, 1, pp. 369, 389, 402; OR *Atlas*, Plate XCIX, 1.

55 OR, XLIII, 1, pp. 362, 369, 376; OR *Atlas*, Plate XCIX, 1.

56 OR, XLIII, 1, p. 376; John P. Suter, Papers of, Harrisburg Civil War Round Table Collection, Archives, USAMHI; Lincoln, *Thirty-Fourth Mass.*, p. 356.

57 Lincoln, *Thirty-Fourth Mass.*, pp. 362–363.

58 Ibid., p. 356.

59 Wildes, *Record*, pp. 171–172.

60 Bradwell, "With Early," CV, XXII, p. 505.

61 Crook, *Autobiography*, p. 128; Wilson to R. B. Hayes, April 9, 1887, Wilson, Letter, RBHPC.

62 Comly, Diary, RBHPC.

63 Ibid.; "Journal of the 23rd Regiment," RBHPC.

64 DuPont, *Campaign Of 1864*, pp. 122, 124; Crook, *Autobiography*, p. 128.

65 Carpenter, *Eighth Vermont*, pp. 181, 182; Benedict, *Vermont*, II, p. 149; Buffum, *A Memorial*, pp. 222, 223; OR, XLIII, 1, pp. 314, 315.

66 Carpenter, *Eighth Vermont*, pp. 182, 190; OR, XLIII, 1, p. 314.

67 Carpenter, *Eighth Vermont*, p. 196; OR, XLIII, 1, p. 314; Benedict, *Vermont*, II, pp. 154, 155.

[68] Benedict, *Vermont*, II, p. 150; Carpenter, *Eighth Vermont*, p. 182.

[69] DuPont, *Campaign Of 1864*, p. 124; Crook, *Autobiography*, pp. 128, 129; OR, XLIII, 1, pp. 281, 291, 314; Irwin, *History*, p. 390.

[70] OR, XLIII, 1, pp. 150, 162, 179, 182; OR *Atlas*, Plate XCIX, 1.

[71] John C. Arnold to wife, September 23, 1864, John C. Arnold, Letters of, The Arnold Family Papers, Archives, USAMHI; OR, XLIII, 1, pp. 162, 177, 179; OR *Atlas*, Plate XCIX, 1.

[72] Buffum, *A Memorial*, p. 227; OR, XLIII, 1, p. 271.

[73] OR, XLIII, 1, pp. 162, 163, 177, 179, 182.

[74] Vaill, *Second Connecticut*, p. 96; OR, XLIII, 1, pp. 163, 164, 182; OR *Atlas*, XCIX, 1; Best, *121st New York*, p. 184.

[75] OR, XLIII, 1, pp. 163, 164; Vaill, *Second Connecticut*, pp. 96, 97; Adams, *Memorial*, p. 156; Michie, *Upton*, p. xxiii.

[76] Boudrye, *Fifth New York*, p. 172; OR, XLIII, 1, pp. 222, 232; Haynes, *Tenth Vermont*, p. 114; OR *Atlas*, Plate XCIX, 1.

[77] Hotchkiss, Papers, LC; OR *Atlas*, Plate XCIX, 1; OR, XLIII, 1, pp. 192, 197, 212; Murphy, Papers, Duke.

[78] OR, XLIII, 1, pp. 192, 198, 208; Walker, *Vermont Brigade*, p. 102.

[79] Hotchkiss, Papers, LC; Humphrey, Diary, UVA; OR *Atlas*, Plate XCIX, 1.

[80] OR *Atlas*, Plate XCIX, 1; Walker, *Vermont Brigade*, p. 103; Morrison to Brother, September 20, 1864, Morrison, Letters, USAMHI.

[81] Williams, *Hayes Diary*, p. 510; OR, XLIII, 1, pp. 198, 208.

[82] Bell I. Wiley, "The Common Soldier of the Civil War," *CWTI*, XII, 4, (July 1973), p. 5.

[83] Humphrey, Diary, UVA; Clark, *N.C. Regts.*, II, p. 141; Morrison to Brother, September 20, 1864, Morrison, Letters, USAMHI; Garnett, "Diary," *SHSP*, XXVII, p. 5.

[84] Sheridan, *Memoirs*, II, p. 25; O'Connor, *Sheridan*, pp. 14, 15; Flinn, *Campaigning*, p. 227; Carpenter, *Eighth Vermont*, p. 183.

[85] Hagemann, *Fighting Rebels*, pp. 222–224.

[86] Paul, Diary, USAMHI; Arnold to wife, September 23, 1864, Arnold, Letters, USAMHI; Flinn, *Campaigning*, p. 188; OR, XLIII, 1, p. 189; Mark, *93rd Pennsylvania*, p. 289; Stevens, *Three Years*, p. 401.

[87] O'Connor, *Sheridan*, p. 17.

[88] OR, XLIII, 1, pp. 444, 445; Samuel Clarke Farrar, *The Twenty-Second Pennsylvania Cavalry and the Ringgold Battalion 1861–1865* (Pittsburgh: The New Werner Company, 1911), p. 371n.

[89] Wilson to R. B. Hayes, April 9, 1887, Wilson, Letter, RBHPC; Benedict, *Vermont*, II, p. 150; Carpenter, *Eighth Vermont*, p. 183; Lee, *Seventh Michigan*, p. 168; Bowen, *Dragoons*, p. 232.

[90] Bowen, *Dragoons*, p. 232; OR, XLIII, 1, pp. 444, 445, 457, 458; Newel Cheney, *History of the Ninth Regiment, New York Volunteer Cavalry, War of 1861 to 1865* (Poland Center, N.Y.: Martin Merz & Son, 1901), p. 221.

[91] Arnold to wife, September 23, 1864, Arnold, Letters, USAMHI; Bowen, *Dragoons*, p. 232; S. D. Ramseur to David Schenck, October 10, 1864, Ramseur, Papers, SHC/UNC; Worsham, *Foot Cavalry*, p. 169; Munford, "Reminiscences," *SHSP*, XII, p. 449; Wise, *Long Arm*, p. 887; Humphrey, Diary, UVA.

[92] Humphrey, Diary, UVA; Wise, *Long Arm*, p. 887; OR, XLIII, 1, p. 445.

[93] OR, XLIII, 1, pp. 550, 551; Cheney, *Ninth New York*, p. 291; Bowen, *Dragoons*, p. 234.

[94] Gordon, *Reminiscences*, p. 322.

[95] Grimes, *Letters*, pp. 69–70.

[96] Ibid., pp. 67, 70; Clark, *N. C. Regts.*, I, p. 174; S. D. Ramseur to David Schenck, October 10, 1864, Ramseur, Papers, SHC/UNC.

[97] S. D. Ramseur to David Schenck, October 10, 1864, Ramseur, Papers, SHC/ UNC; Clark, *N. C. Regts.*, II, p. 123; III, pp. 256, 257, Cox, *Address*, p. 42.

[98] S. D. Ramseur to David Schenck, October 10, 1864, Ramseur, Papers, SHC/ UNC; Clark, *N. C. Regt.*, III, p. 421; Hatton, "Godwin," CV, XXVIII, pp. 133, 136.

[99] Unsigned letter to Mrs. Lovina Wilfong, October 3, 1864, Wilfong, Papers, Duke.

[100] I. G. Bradwell, "The Fight At Winchester, VA.-Jim Graham," CV, XV, p. 411; I. G. Bradwell, "The Battle Of Fisher's Hill," CV, XXVIII, p. 338; Bradwell, "Valley Campaign," CV, XXVIII, p. 218; Worsham, *Foot Cavalry*, p. 169; S. D. Ramseur to David Schenck, October 10, 1864, Ramseur, Papers, SHC/UNC.

[101] Farrar, *Twenty-Second Pennsylvania*, p. 377; Slease, *Fourteenth Pennsylvania*, p. 239; Whitehead, "Campaigns of Munford," UVA; B. F. Whittle, "Notebook, September 12, 1864–February 18, 1865," Adlerman Library, UVA; Munford, "Reminiscences," SHSP, XII, p. 450; P. S. White, "Recollections of Battle At Winchester," CV, XV, p. 566; Wise, *Long Arm*, p. 887.

[102] Slease, *Fourteenth Pennsylvania*, pp. 185, 186, 239, 240; Farrar, *Twenty-Second Pennsylvania*, p. 377; Munford, "Reminiscences," SHSP, XII, p. 450; Rufus H. Peck, *Reminiscences Of A Confederate Soldier Of Co. C, 2nd Va. Cavalry* (Reprint edition, Ann Arbor, Michigan: University Microfilms, 1971), p. 53.

[103] Hawkins, "Sketch," *MOLLUS*, Ohio, I, p. 149; Pickerill, *Third Indiana*, p. 162; OR, XLIII, 1, p. 518; Benedict, *Vermont*, II, p. 658; OR *Atlas*, Plate XCIX, 1.

[104] OR, XLIII, 1, pp. 47, 518; Boudrye, *Fifth New York*, pp. 172, 173; OR *Atlas*, Plate XCIX, 1; Munford, "Reminiscences," SHSP, XII, p. 450.

[105] J. S. Lloyd to Sister, October 21, 1864, J. S. Lloyd, Letter of, Americana Collection, The Huntington Library, San Marino, California; Ruth Woods Dayton, ed., *The Diary of A Confederate Soldier James E. Hall* (Philippi, W.Va.: Elizabeth Teter Phillips, 1961), p. 120; Garnett, "Diary," SHSP, XXVII, p. 7.

[106] Buffum, *A Memorial*, pp. 228, 229; Haines, *Fifteenth New Jersey*, p. 263; Shelby Foote, *The Civil War—A Narrative: Red River to Appomattox* (New York: Random House, 1974), p. 554.

[107] Sheridan, *Memoirs*, II, pp. 28, 29; Hagemann, *Fighting Rebels*, p. 268; Hanaburgh, *History*, p. 152.

[108] Washington *Daily National Intelligence*, September 29, 1864; Robert W. Hatton, ed., "Just a Little Bit of the Civil War, As Seen by W. J. Smith, Company M, 2nd O. V. Cavalry—Part I," *Ohio History*, LXXXIV, 3 (Summer 1975), p. 121; Tyler, *Recollections*, p. 279; Garland R. Quarles, *Occupied Winchester 1861–1865* (Winchester, Virginia: Farmers & Merchants National Bank, 1976), pp. 44, 94, 102, 117; Shaffner, *Diary*, p. 51; Bradwell, "Fight At Winchester," CV, XV, p. 411.

CHAPTER SIX

[1] George F. Skoch, ed., "With a Special in the Shenandoah," CWTI, XXI, 2, (April 1982), pp. 36, 37.

[2] Ibid., pp. 37, 38.

[3] Ibid., p. 38.

[4] Ibid., pp. 38, 39.

[5] J. D. Lloyd to Sister, September 21, 1864, Lloyd Papers, HL; Flinn, *Campaigning*, p. 189; Adams, *Memorial*, p. 156.

[6] Best, *121st New York*, p. 184.

[7] Stackhouse, Diary, Hist. Soc. of PA; OR, XLIII, 1, pp. 139, 140, 141; Haines, *Fifteenth New Jersey*, pp. 262, 263; Quarles, *Occupied Winchester*, pp. 44, 94, 117; John H. Brinton, *Personal Memoirs of John H. Brinton* (New York: The Neale Publishing Company, 1914), p. 293.

[8] Early reported 226 killed and 1,567 wounded to Lee, or a difference of 27 killed and 59 wounded, OR, XLIII, 1, pp. 555, 557; Grady McWhiney and Perry D. Jamieson, *Attack and Die: Civil War Military Tactics and the Southern Heritage* (University, Alabama: The University of Alabama Press, 1982), pp. 19-21.

[9] OR, XLIII, 1, p. 557; Robert K. Krick, *Lee's Colonels: A Biographical Register of the Field Officers of the Army of Northern Virginia* (Dayton, Ohio: Press of Morningside Bookshop, 1979), *passim*; regiments which lost commanders were Alabama: 12th; Georgia: 12th, 21st, 44th; Louisiana: 1st, 5th; North Carolina: 4th, 5th, 13th, 23rd Battalion, 26th, 45th, 48th, 60th.

[10] OR, XLIII, 1, p. 118; McWhiney and Jamieson, *Attack And Die*, Chapter 1.

[11] OR, XLIII, 1, pp. 114-118; Otis F. R. Waite, *New Hampshire in the Great Rebellion* (Claremont, N.H.: Tracy, Chase & Company, 1870), p. 511.

[12] OR, XLIII, 1, pp. 113-115, 116, 118.

[13] Runge, *Four Years*, p. 96; White, "Recollections," CV, XV, p. 566; Lyman S. Walker, Diary of—1864, Civil War Miscellaneous Collection, Archives, USAMHI; Lee, *Seventh Michigan*, p. 167; Norton, *Eighth N.Y.*, p. 92.

[14] J. S. Lloyd to Sister, September 21, 1864, Lloyd Papers, HL; Gould, *History*, p. 507; Beecher, *Record*, p. 432; Hewitt, *History*, p. 180; Nettleton, "Cedar Creek," *MOLLUS*, Minn., I, p. 269.

[15] Munford, "Reminiscences," *SHSP*, XII, p. 344; Worsham, *Foot Cavalry*, p. 173.

[16] Boudrye, *Fifth New York*, p. 172; White, "Recollections," CV, XV, p. 566; Thompson, PhD. Diss., UVA, p. 384.

[17] DeForest, *Volunteers Adventures*, p. 190; Nettleton, "Cedar Creek," *MOLLUS*, Minn., I, pp. 268, 26.

[18] Kidd, *Personal Recollections*, p. 394; Nettleton, "Cedar Creek," *MOLLUS*, Minn., I, pp. 263-264.

[19] OR, XLIII, 1, pp. 458, 555; O'Ferrall, *Forty Years*, p. 116; Ferguson, "Memoranda," Duke; Garnett, "Diary," *SHSP*, XXVII, p. 7; Slease, *Fourteenth Pennsylvania*, p. 186.

[20] Thompson, PhD. Diss, UVA, pp. 382, 383; Ferguson, "Memoranda," Duke.

[21] Thompson, PhD. Diss., UVA, pp. 383, 386.

[22] Ibid., pp. 384, 386; OR, XLIII, 1, p. 555; Farr, Diary, USAMHI.

[23] John D. Casler, *Four Years in the Stonewall Brigade* (reprint edition, edited by James I. Robertson, Jr., Dayton, Ohio: Morningside Bookshop, 1971), p. 234.

[24] OR, XLIII, 1, pp. 47, 152, 428, 498; Haines, *Fifteenth New Jersey*, p. 264; DuPont, *Campaign Of 1864*, p. 133; Barbour, Diary, UMICH.

[25] Tyler, *Recollections*, p. 288; Haines, *Fifteenth New Jersey*, p. 264.

[26] OR, XLIII, 1, pp. 48, 152, 203, 213, 232, 428, 499; Wayland, *Virginia Valley Records*, pp. 193, 235; Sheridan, *Personal Memoirs*, II, p. 34.

[27] Beecher, *Record*, p. 433; Keiser, Diary, USAMHI; Wayland, *Virginia Valley Records*, pp. 124, 125, 129, 130, 293.

[28] Gordon, *Reminiscences*, p. 324.

[29] Ibid., pp. 322-323; O'Ferrall, *Forty Years*, p. 116; Bradwell, "Fisher's Hill," CV, XXVIII, p. 338; Grimes, *Letters*, p. 70.

[30] Gordon, *Reminiscences*, p. 325; McDonald, *Hotchkiss Journal*, p. 230.

[31] Grimes, *Letters*, pp. 70, 71; Gordon, *Reminiscences*, p. 324.

[32] OR, XLIII, 1, pp. 555, 556; Early, *Autobiographical Sketch*, p. 429.

[33] Haynes, *Tenth Vermont*, p. 116.

[34] Adams, *Memorial*, pp. 156, 157; Bennett, *First Massachusetts*, p. 178; Walker, *Vermont Brigade*, pp. 110, 111; Haines, *Fifteenth New Jersey*, p. 239; Irwin, *History*, p. 396.

[35] Jeffry D. Wert, "First Fair Chance," CWTI, XVIII, 5 (August 1979), pp. 8, 9; DeForest, *Volunteers Adventures*, p. 192.

[36] Wert, "First Fair Chance," CWTI, XVIII, 5, p. 9; McDonald, *Hotchkiss Journal*, p. 230; Early, *Autobiographical Sketch*, p. 429; Bean, *Stonewall's Man*, p. 209; Wayland, *Virginia Valley Records*, pp. 185, 186; Humphrey, Diary, UVA.

[37] McDonald, *Hotchkiss Journal*, p. 230; Early, *Autobiographical Sketch*, p. 429; Garnett, "Diary," *SHSP*, XXVII, p. 7; OR, XLIII, 2, p. 877; Bradwell, "Fight," *CV*, XV, p. 411; Grimes, *Letters*, p. 68; Worsham, *Foot Cavalry*, p. 168; Alexander D. Betts, *Experience Of A Confederate Chaplain 1861–1864* (Reprint Edition, Ann Arbor, Michigan: University Microfilms, 1973), p. 65.

[38] McDonald, *Hotchkiss Journal*, p. 230; Early, *Autobiographical Sketch*, p. 429; Hatton, "Valley Campaign," *CV*, XXVII, p. 170; OR *Atlas*, Plates LXXXII, 11; XCIX, 2; OR, XLIII, 2, p. 883.

[39] McDonald, *Hotchkiss Journal*, p. 230; Early, *Autobiographical Sketch*, p. 429; Hatton, "Valley Campaign," *CV*, XXVII, p. 170; Bean, *Stonewall's Man*, p. 209; OR *Atlas*, Plate LXXXII, 11.

[40] Adams, *Memorial*, p. 156; DeForest, *Volunteers Adventures*, pp. 191, 192; Walker, *Vermont Brigade*, p. 113.

[41] Sheridan, *Personal Memoirs*, II, p. 34.

[42] OR, XLIII, 2, p. 136; Stevens, *Three Years*, p. 388; Crook, *Autobiography*, p. 129; George Crook, "Gen George Crook's Statement on Shenandoah Valley Campaign, 1864 dictated to L. W. V. Kennon Sept. 28, 1888," Crook-Kennon Papers, Archives, USAMHI.

[43] Kennon, "Valley Campaign," *MHSM*, VI, p. 46; Crook, *Autobiography*, p. 129; Henry A. DuPont to James A. Wilson, February 11, 1889, Crook-Kennon Papers, USAMHI; Crook, "Statement," Crook-Kennon Papers, USAMHI; Lang, *Loyal West Virginia*, p. 334n; Williams, *Hayes Diary*, pp. 511, 514; Walker, *Vermont Brigade*, p. 117; Clark, *One Hundred And Sixteenth*, p. 204.

[44] OR, XLIII, 1, pp. 136, 137; Wert, "First Fair Chance," *CWTI*, XVIII, 5, p. 9; DuPont, *Campaign Of 1864*, p. 135.

[45] OR, XLIII, 1, p. 48; Sheridan, *Personal Memoirs*, II, p. 35; Williams, *Hayes Diary*, pp. 511, 514, 517; DuPont, *Campaign Of 1864*, p. 134; O'Connor, *Sheridan*, p. 208; J. W. Howard, "Interviews with Rutherford B. Hayes," Transcript, Library of RBHPC; Henry A. DuPont to James A. Wilson, February 11, 1889, Crook-Kennon Papers, USAMHI; Crook, "Statement," Crook-Kennon Papers, USAMHI.

[46] OR, XLIII, 2, pp. 120, 136; Wert, "First Fair Chance," *CWTI*, XVIII, 5, p. 9; Barbour, Diary, UMICH.

[47] OR, XLIII, 1, pp. 518, 519; pt. 2, p. 113; Warner, *Generals In Blue*, pp. 566, 567; Tenney, *War Diary*, p. 132; Early, *Memoir*, p. 81; Ferguson, "Memoranda," Duke.

[48] Ibid., 1, pp. 428, 519; Farr, Diary, USAMHI; Ferguson, "Memoranda," Duke; Whittle, Notebook, UVA.

[49] OR, XLIII, 1, p. 428, 519; Ferguson, "Memoranda," Duke; Whittle, Notebook, UVA; Farr, Diary, USAMHI; Barbour, Diary, UMICH; OR *Atlas*, Plate LXXXII, 8.

[50] Sheridan, *Personal Memoirs*, II, p. 36; Haines, *Fifteenth New Jersey*, p. 265; OR, XLIII, 1, pp. 152, 282; McDonald, *Hotchkiss Journal*, p. 230; Williams, *Hayes Diary*, p. 508.

[51] Comly, Diary, RBHPC; OR, XLIII, 1, p. 61; pt. 2, pp. 117, 118.

[52] OR, XLIII, 1, pp. 152, 162, 192, 208, 223; Sheridan, *Personal Memoirs*, II, p. 36; Haines, *Fifteenth New Jersey*, p. 265; McDonald, *Hotchkiss Journal*, p. 230; OR *Atlas*, Plate XCIX, 2.

[53] OR, XLIII, 1, pp. 152, 162, 169; pt. 2, p. 134; Warner, *Generals In Blue*, p. 553.

[54] OR, XLIII, 1, pp. 205, 208, 213, 254, 274; Walker, *Vermont Brigade*, pp. 114, 115.

[55] Sheridan, *Personal Memoirs*, II, p. 36; OR, XLIII, 1, p. 152.

[56] OR, XLIII, 1, pp. 205, 206, 248, 264.

[57] Ibid., pp. 223, 253.

[58] Ibid., pp. 192, 199, 203; Mark, *Red: White: And Blue*, p. 293.

[59] OR, XLIII, 1, pp. 208, 209, 282; Wert, "First Fair Chance," *CWTI*, XVIII, 5, p. 40.

[60] Clark, *One Hundred And Sixteenth*, p. 226.

CHAPTER SEVEN

[1] OR, XLIII, 1, pp. 152, 169, 178, 199; Walker, *Vermont Brigade*, p. 115; Haines, *Fifteenth New Jersey*, p. 266; Skoch, "With a Special," *CWTI*, XXI, 1, p. 41; OR *Atlas*, Plate XCIX, 2.

[2] OR, XLIII, 1, pp. 282, 297, 312, 331; pt. 2, pp. 135, 136; Irwin, *History*, p. 398.

[3] Sheridan, *Personal Memoirs*, II, p. 36; DuPont, *Campaign Of 1864*, p. 135; Young, Diary, WVAU; OR *Atlas*, Plate XCIX, 2.

[4] Clark, *One Hundred And Sixteenth*, p. 228; McDonald, *Hotchkiss Journal*, p. 230; Wert, "First Fair Chance," *CWTI*, XVIII, 5, p. 41.

[5] McDonald, *Hotchkiss Journal*, p. 230; OR, XLIII, 1, pp. 183, 223, 254, 316, 319; DeForest, *Volunteers Adventures*, p. 194; Beecher, *Record*, p. 434; Pellet, *History*, p. 263.

[6] OR, XLIII, 2, p. 137; Walker, *Vermont Brigade*, p. 116.

[7] OR, XLIII, 1, pp. 283, 293, 312, 319, 320, 357; Irwin, *History*, p. 398; Hanaburgh, *History*, p. 153; Clark, *One Hundred And Sixteenth*, p. 229.

[8] OR, XLIII, 1, pp. 223, 237, 242, 258, 266, 272, 274; Hayes, *Tenth Vermont*, p. 117; Runge, *Four Years*, p. 100; Garnett, "Diary," *SHSP*, XXVII, p. 8; McDonald, *Hotchkiss Journal*, p. 230; OR *Atlas*, Plate XCIX, 2.

[9] OR, XLIII, 1, p. 556; Early, *Autobiographical Sketch*, p. 430.

[10] OR, XLIII, 2, pp. 864–873; McDonald, *Hotchkiss Journal*, p. 230; Early, *Autobiographical Sketch*, p. 429.

[11] Wert, "First Fair Chance," *CWTI*, XVIII, 5, p. 42.

[12] Crook, *Autobiography*, p. 130; OR, XLIII, 1, p. 363; Keifer, *Four Years*, II, p. 122; OR *Atlas*, Plate XCIX, 2.

[13] Crook, *Autobiography*, p. 130; OR, XLIII, 1, pp. 363, 499; pt. 2, p. 137; OR *Atlas*, Plate XCIX, 2.

[14] OR, XLIII, 1, p. 363; Crook, *Autobiography*, p. 130; Wildes, *Record*, p. 181.

[15] DuPont, *Campaign Of 1864*, p. 136; OR, XLIII, 1, pp. 363, 390; Crook, *Autobiography*, p. 130.

[16] Grimes, *Letters*, p. 71.

[17] Runge, *Four Years*, pp. 99–100.

[18] Crook, *Autobiography*, p. 131; OR, XLIII, 1, pp. 363, 370, 390, 403; Williams, *Hayes Diary*, p. 512; Howard, "Interviews," RBHPC.

[19] Wildes, *Record*, p. 182; Williams, *Hayes Diary*, p. 517; Crook, *Autobiography*, p. 131; OR, XLIII, 1, pp. 364, 370, 378; Howard, "Interviews," RBHPC.

[20] OR, XLIII, 1, p. 378.

[21] Williams, *Hayes Diary*, p. 517; M. S. Watts, "General Battle And The Stolen Colt," *CV*, XXX, p. 169; O'Ferrall, *Forty Years*, pp. 118, 119; W. W. Goldsborough, *The Maryland Line in the Confederate Army, 1861–1865* (reprint edition, Port Washington, N.Y. and London: Kennikat Press, 1972), pp. 212, 213; Williams, *Hayes Diary*, p. 517; OR, XLIII, 1, pp. 364, 370; Wert, "First Fair Chance," *CWTI*, XVIII, 5, p. 43.

[22] Early, *Autobiographical Sketch*, p. 430; McDonald, *Hotchkiss Journal*, p. 230; P. J. Rast, "Fisher's Hill," *CV*, XXIII, p. 123; Watts, "Battle," *CV*, XXX, p. 169; Runge, *Four Years*, p. 100; Crook, *Autobiography*, p. 131; OR, XLIII, 1, pp. 364, 370, 378, 390; Wildes, *Record*, p. 182.

[23] Watts, "Battle," *CV*, XXX, p. 169; Rast, "Fisher's Hill," *CV*, XXIII, p. 123; Garnett, "Diary," *SHSP*, XXVII, p. 8; Wise, *Long Arm*, p. 888; Crook, *Autobiography*, p. 131.

[24] OR, XLIII, 1, p. 364; Rast, "Fisher's Hill," *CV*, XXIII, p. 123; Runge, *Four Years*, p. 100; Watts, "Battle," *CV*, XXX, p. 169.

[25] Cox, *Address*, p. 43; Warner, *Generals In Gray*, pp. 64–65; Ledford, *Reminiscences*, p. 77.

[26] Cox, *Address*, p. 43; T. B. Beall, "That Stampede At Fisher's Hill," *CV*, V, p. 26; McDonald, *Hotchkiss Journal*, p. 230.

[27] OR, XLIII, 1, pp. 364, 370, 378; Williams, *Hayes Diary*, p. 517; Early, *Autobiographical Sketch*, p. 430; McDonald, *Hotchkiss Journal*, p. 230; Wise, *Long Arm*, pp. 888, 889.

[28] Grimes, *Letters*, p. 72; OR, XLIII, 1, pp. 370, 378, 605.

[29] OR, XLIII, 1, pp. 153, 223, 264.

[30] Ibid., pp. 223, 232, 242, 266, 272, 275; OR *Atlas*, Plate LXXXII, 11.

[31] Crook, *Autobiography*, pp. 131–132; OR, XLIII, 1, pp. 223, 232, 364, 370, 378; Wise, *Long Arm*, p. 888.

[32] OR *Atlas*, Plate LXXXII, 11; Grimes, *Letters*, p. 72; Buck, Papers, Duke.

[33] Grimes, *Letters*, p. 72; OR, XLIII, 1, p. 605; Buck, Papers, Duke; Bushong, *Old Jube*, p. 241.

[34] Grimes, *Letters*, pp. 72–73; Clark, *N.C. Regts.*, I, p. 174.

[35] McDonald, *Hotchkiss Journal*, p. 231; Bushong, *Old Jube*, p. 241; Buck, Papers, Duke.

[36] OR, XLIII, 1, pp. 192, 199, 200, 203, 209, 213; Walker, *Vermont Brigade*, pp. 118, 119, 120; Murphy, Journal, Duke.

[37] OR, XLIII, 1, pp. 192, 203, 213; Mark, *Red: White: And Blue*, p. 293; Vaill, *History*, p. 106; Wayland, *Virginia Valley Records*, p. 345; Walker, *Vermont Brigade*, p. 120; Murphy, Journal, Duke.

[38] Walker, *Vermont Brigade*, p. 120; Mark, *Red: White: And Blue*, pp. 293, 294; OR, XLIII, 1, pp. 192, 200, 203, 204, 213, 214, 217, 218, 221; Early, *Autobiographical Sketch*, p. 430; Wise, *Long Arm*, p. 888; Humphrey, Diary, UVA.

[39] OR, XLIII, 1, pp. 170, 181, 183; Haines, *Fifteenth New Jersey*, pp. 266, 267; Best, *121st New York*, p. 186.

[40] Lewis, *One Hundred And Thirty-Eighth Pennsylvania*, p. 127; McDonald, *Hotchkiss Journal*, p. 231; OR, XLIII, 1, pp. 283, 320, 340, 345, 356; Buffum, *A Memorial*, p. 250; Benedict, *Vermont*, II, p. 159; Hanaburgh, *History*, p. 153; Ewer, *Third Massachusetts*, p. 210.

[41] Halsey, Papers, USAMHI; Haines, *Fifteenth New Jersey*, p. 267.

[42] Nichols, *Soldier's Story*, p. 189; Clark, *One Hundred and Sixteenth*, p. 230.

[43] Bradwell, "Troops," CV, XXV, p. 109; Bradwell, "Fisher's Hill," CV, XXVIII, p. 339; Wildes, *Record*, pp. 183, 184.

[44] Clark, *N.C. Regts.*, pp. 257–258.

[45] McDonald, *Hotchkiss Journal*, p. 231; Garnett, "Diary," SHSP, XXVII, p. 9; Clark, *N.C. Regts.*, I, p. 208; III, p. 55; Buck, Papers, Duke.

[46] Bean, *Stonewall's Man*, pp. 111, 182, 207, 210, 211, 216; Moore, "Early's Strength," CV, XI, p. 396; Early, *Autobiographical Sketch*, p. 431; Hotchkiss, Papers, LC; Marcellus Moorman, "Recollections of Cedar Creek and Fisher's Hill, October 19th, 1864," Unpublished letter, February 19, 1903, The Huntington Library, San Marino, CA.

[47] Nichols, *Soldier's Story*, p. 190; Early, *Autobiographical Sketch*, p. 430; McDonald, *Hotchkiss Journal*, p. 231.

[48] OR, XLIII, 2, p. 878.

[49] Ibid., 1, p. 558; Gordon, *Reminiscences*, p. 326.

[50] OR, XLIII, 1, pp. 556, 557; J. A. Early to Thomas Henry Carter, December 13, 1866, Lee Family Papers, Virginia Historical Society, Richmond; Runge, *Four Years*, p. 101.

[51] Adams, *Memorial*, p. 160; Williams, *Hayes Diary*, p. 518; OR, XLIII, 1, pp. 59, 153.

[52] Hagemann, *Fighting Rebels*, p. 269; Crowninshield, "Sheridan," *Atlantic Monthly*, XLII, p. 685, 686; Walker, *Vermont Brigade*, p. 120.

[53] OR, XLIII, 1, pp. 26–27.

[54] Ibid., pp. 193, 283, 320, 332, 370, 390.

[55] Hewitt, *History*, pp. 180–181; OR, XLIII, 1, pp. 283, 294, 320, 326, 332, 340; DeForest, *Volunteers Adventures*, p. 196; Hanaburgh, *History*, p. 155; Irwin, *History*, pp. 400,

401; Powers, *Thirty Eighth Massachusetts*, p. 169; Joseph Ward to Father and Mother, October 26, 1864, Ward Letters, CHS.

56 OR, XLIII, 1, pp. 283, 320, 326, 333; Walker, *Vermont Brigade*, p. 124; Haines, *Fifteenth New Jersey*, p. 268; Vaill, *Second Connecticut*, p. 107.

57 OR, XLIII, 2, p. 137; Barbour, Diary, UMICH; Boudrye, *Fifth New York*, p. 173.

58 Ferguson, "Memoranda," Duke; Munford, "Reminiscences," SHSP, XII, p. 455; Pickerill, *History*, p. 163; OR, XLIII, 1, p. 428; Hagemann, *Fighting Rebels*, p. 273; Barbour, Diary, UMICH; OR *Atlas*, Plate LXXXIV, 1.

59 Munford, "Reminiscences," SHSP, XII, pp. 454, 455; Ferguson, "Memoranda," Duke; OR, XLIII, 1, p. 428; Barbour, Diary, UMICH.

60 OR, XLIII, 1, p. 428; Munford, "Reminiscences," SHSP, XII, p. 455; Ferguson, "Memoranda," Duke; Whittle, Notebook, UVA; Barbour, Diary, UMICH; Boudrye, *Fifth New York*, pp. 173, 174.

61 OR, XLIII, 1, pp. 428, 429, 441; Boudrye, *Fifth New York*, p. 174; Ferguson, "Memoranda," Duke.

62 OR, XLIII, 1, p. 48; Sheridan, *Personal Memoirs*, II, pp. 40–42.

63 Sheridan, *Personal Memoirs*, II, pp. 42–43; OR, XLIII, 1, p. 499.

64 Sheridan, *Personal Memoirs*, II, p. 44; OR, XLIII, 1, p. 499; Walker, *Vermont Brigade*, p. 124; Haines, *Fifteenth New Jersey*, p. 268; Vaill, *Second Connecticut*, p. 107; McDonald, *Hotchkiss Journal*, pp. 231, 232.

65 Sheridan, *Personal Memoirs*, II, p. 44; OR, XLIII, 1, pp. 48, 499; Slease, *Fourteenth Pennsylvania*, pp. 193, 194.

66 Keiser, Diary, USAMHI; Runge, *Four Years*, p. 101; McDonald, *Hotchkiss Journal*, pp. 231, 232; OR *Atlas*, Plate LXXXV, 22.

67 OR, XLIII, 1, p. 49; Sheridan, *Personal Memoirs*, II, pp. 45, 46; Dye, Papers, Duke; Haines, *Fifteenth New Jersey*, pp. 268, 269; Walker, *Vermont Brigade*, pp. 124, 125.

68 Runge, *Four Years*, p. 101; McDonald, *Hotchkiss Journal*, p. 232.

69 Haines, *Fifteenth New Jersey*, p. 269.

70 Ibid., p. 268; OR, XLIII, 1, p. 49; Sheridan, *Personal Memoirs*, II, pp. 46, 47; Walker, *Vermont Brigade*, p. 125; Dye, Papers, Duke; Keiser, Diary, USAMHI.

71 OR, XLIII, 1, pp. 429, 491; Barbour, Diary, UMICH; Ferguson, "Memoranda," Duke.

72 McDonald, *Hotchkiss Journal*, p. 232; Runge, *Four Years*, p. 101; Ferguson, "Memoranda," Duke.

73 Keiser, Diary, USAMHI; OR, XLIII, 1, p. 49; Dye, Papers, Duke; Barbour, Diary, UMICH.

CHAPTER EIGHT

1 The figures are a composite taken from OR, XLIII, 2, pp. 882, 883, 903; Connally, "Prelude to Victory," Honors paper, Williams College; Hatton, "Valley Campaign," CV, XXVII, p. 170.

2 OR, XLIII, 2, pp. 600–601.

3 Ibid., pp. 595–598.

4 Ibid., 1, p. 558; Clark, N.C. Regts., II, p. 142; Bradwell, "Fisher's Hill," CV, XXVIII, p. 338; John Gill, *Reminiscences of Four Years As A Private Soldier In The Confederate Army 1861-1865* (Baltimore: Sun Printing Office, 1904), pp. 112–113.

5 Gill, *Reminiscences*, p. 113.

6 OR, XLIII, 2, p. 894.

7 Ibid., p. 894.

8 Ibid., pp. 893–896.

9 Ibid., pp. 897–898.

10 Richmond *Enquirer*, September 27, 1864; Freeman, *Lee's Lieutenants*, III, pp. 586, 587.

[11] Sommers, *Richmond Redeemed,* p. 421.

[12] OR, XLIII, 1, pp. 558, 559.

[13] Ibid., 2, pp. 873, 874, 877, 878; Sommers, *Richmond Redeemed,* p. 421.

[14] Dickert, *Kershaw's Brigade,* p. 436; McDonald, *Hotchkiss Journal,* p. 232; Shaffner, *Diary,* p. 52.

[15] OR, XLIII, 1, pp. 557, 558; pt. 2, pp. 879, 881, 882, 885.

[16] Ibid., 1, p. 558.

[17] Ibid., pp. 558–559.

[18] Ibid., p. 62.

[19] Bruce Catton, *The Centennial History of the Civil War, Volume Three: Never Call Retreat* (Garden City, New York: Doubleday & Company, Inc., 1965), p. 338; Vaill, *Second Connecticut,* p. 108; Foote, *Civil War,* pp. 558, 559; Allan Nevins, *The War for the Union, Volume IV: the Organized War To Victory, 1864–1865* (New York: Charles Scribner's Sons, 1971), pp. 104, 105; Washington *Daily National Intelligencer,* September 26, 1864.

[20] John A. Rawlins to Colonel Ely Parker, September 25, 1864, Letter of, Civil War Miscellaneous Collection, Archives, USAMHI.

[21] OR, XLIII, 1, pp. 28, 29, 30; David Siebert to Parents and All, October 17, 1864, Seibert Family Papers, Harrisburg Civil War Round Table Papers, Archives, USAMHI; Young, Diary, WVAU.

[22] OR, XLIII, 2, pp. 152, 177, 187; Foote, *Civil War,* p. 563; Hotchkiss, Papers, LC.

[23] OR, XLIII, 2, pp. 152, 177, 187.

[24] Sommers, *Richmond Redeemed,* p. 420; Sommers's book is a monumentally detailed study of the Fifth Offensive, noting fully its relationship to events beyond the Blue Ridge.

[25] OR, XLIII, 1, p. 28; Wayland, *Virginia Valley Records,* pp. 197, 198.

[26] OR, XLIII, 2, p. 210.

[27] Ibid., 1, p. 50; pt. 2, p. 249.

[28] Ibid., 2, pp. 249, 258.

[29] Ibid., pp. 210, 249.

[30] Ibid., 1, p. 29; DeForest, *Volunteers Adventures,* p. 197.

[31] Murphy, Journal, Duke; OR, XLIII, 1, pp. 29, 49, 429, 491, 519; Boudrye, *Fifth New York,* p. 175; Brice, *Conquest,* pp. 131, 132; Hanaburgh, *History,* p. 158; Vaill, *Second Connecticut,* p. 108; McDonald, *Hotchkiss Journal,* p. 232; Haines, *Fifteenth New Jersey,* p. 270; Williams, *Hayes Diary,* p. 513; Farr, Diary, USAMHI.

[32] OR, XLIII, 1, pp. 441, 442, 459, 463, 467, 477, 507, 611; Kidd, *Personal Recollections,* pp. 396, 397; Slease, *Fourteenth Pennsylvania,* p. 254; Barbour, Diary, UMICH; McDonald, *Hotchkiss Journal,* p. 232, 233; Ferguson, "Memoranda," Duke; Whittle, Notebook, UVA.

[33] Benedict, *Vermont,* II, p. 661; Norton, *Deeds,* p. 93; OR, XLIII, 1, p. 508; pt. 2, p. 170; Gause, *Four Years,* p. 321; Rodenbough, *Eighteenth Pennsylvania,* p. 59.

[34] Boudrye, *Fifth New York,* p. 176; The disputed evidence is found in Sheridan, *Personal Memoirs,* II, pp. 50–51; OR, XLIII, 1, p. 30; pt. 2, p. 314; Alexander Neil to Parents, October 5, 1864, Neil Letters, UVA; John E. Armstrong, Memoirs, *Civil War Times Illustrated* Collection, Archives, USAMHI; *National Tribune,* February 16, 1911; Hotchkiss, Papers, LC; O'Ferrall, *Forty Years,* pp. 128, 129; John W. Wayland, *A History of Rockingham County Virginia* (Dayton, Virginia: Ruebush-Elkins Company, 1912), pp. 434, 435.

[35] Sheridan, *Personal Memoirs,* II, pp. 51, 52; OR, XLIII, 1, p. 30; pt. 2, 318; Hagemann, *Fighting Rebels,* p. 303.

[36] Horst, *Mennonites,* pp. 101, 102; Wayland, *Virginia Valley Records,* pp. 149, 189, 194; Brice, *Conquest,* p. 132; Wildes, *Record,* pp. 189–192; Sheridan, *Personal Memoirs,* II, p. 52; Boudrye, *Fifth New York,* pp. 176, 177.

CHAPTER NINE

[1] Williams, *Hayes Diary*, pp. 501–502.

[2] James F. Fitts, "Mosby And His Men," *Galaxy*, II, p. 644; Hagemann, *Fighting Rebels*, p. 261.

[3] John W. Munson, *Reminiscences Of A Mosby Guerrilla* (New York: Moffat, Yard And Company, 1906), pp. 4, 6; Virgil Carrington Jones, *Ranger Mosby* (Chapel Hill: The University of North Carolina Press, 1944), Chapter 8.

[4] Munson, *Reminiscences*, pp. 21, 22, 243, 244, 245; John H. Alexander, *Mosby's Men* (New York and Washington: The Neale Publishing Company, 1907), pp. 27–31; Jones, *Mosby*, p. 175.

[5] John Stewart Bryan, *Joseph Bryan: His Times, His Family, His Friends*, A Memoir (Richmond, Virginia: Whittet & Shepperson, 1935), p. 123; Munson, *Reminiscences*, pp. 7, 15, 16, 17, 30, 31, 36; W. W. Badger, "My Capture And Escape From Mosby," *United States Service Magazine*, June 1865, p. 551.

[6] Alexander, *Mosby's Men*, pp. 15, 17, 24, 25, 27; Jones, *Mosby*, p. 15; Channing M. Smith, "Survivors of Mosby's Command," *CV*, XXXI, p. 356.

[7] Bryan, *Joseph Bryan*, p. 126n; John S. Mosby, *The Memoirs Of Colonel John S. Mosby*, Edited by Charles Wells Russell, Preface by Virgil Carrington Jones (Bloomington: Indiana University Press, 1959), pp. 284, 285; Munson, *Reminiscences*, pp. 22, 23, 24; Alexander, *Mosby's Men*, p. 21; Jones, *Mosby*, p. 11.

[8] Alexander, *Mosby's Men*, pp. 16–19; Munson, *Reminiscences*, pp. 35, 36; J. Marshall Crawford, *Mosby And His Men: A Record Of The Adventures Of That Renowned Partisan Ranger, John S. Mosby* (New York: G. W. Carleton & Co., Publishers, 1867), p. 238.

[9] Mosby, *Memoirs*, pp. 283, 284, 286, 290; John Scott, *Partisan Life With Col. John S. Mosby* (New York: Harper & Brothers, Publishers, 1867), p. 279.

[10] Munson, *Reminiscences*, p. 102; Scott, *Partisan Life*, pp. 271, 272; Crawford, *Mosby*, p. 260; James J. Williamson, *Mosby's Rangers: A Record Of The Operations of the Forty-third Battalion Virginia Cavalry* (New York: Ralph B. Kenyon, Publisher, 1896), p. 207; George Perkins, *A Summer In Maryland and Virginia, Or Campaigning with the 149th Ohio Volunteer Infantry* (Chillicothe, Ohio: The School Printing Company, n.d.), pp. 34, 35; *National Tribune*, October 28, 1909.

[11] OR, XLIII, 1, pp. 811, 822, 842, 843.

[12] OR, XLIII, 1, p. 860; Munson, *Reminiscences*, pp. 115, 116; Scott, *Partisan Life*, p. 364.

[13] Munson, *Reminiscences*, p. 116; Williamson, *Mosby's Rangers*, p. 300; Scott, *Partisan Life*, pp. 364, 365; Jones, *Mosby*, p. 200.

[14] Scott, *Partisan Life*, p. 365; Jones, *Mosby*, p. 200.

[15] Williamson, *Mosby's Rangers*, pp. 301–305; Scott, *Partisan Life*, pp. 365–368; Munson, *Reminiscences*, pp. 120–121; OR, XLIII, 2, p. 654.

[16] OR, XLIII, 1, p. 909.

[17] Mosby, *Memoirs*, p. 290; OR, XLIII, 1, pp. 616, 617, 942; pt. 2, p. 273; Jones, *Mosby*, p. 203.

[18] Scott, *Partisan Life*, pp. 317, 318; John S. Mosby, "Retaliation: The Execution Of Seven Prisoners By Col. John S. Mosby—A Self-Protective Necessity," *SHSP*, XXVII, p. 314; Jones, *Mosby*, p. 207; Jones, *Mosby*, p. 207; "Hanging of Mosby's Men In 1864," *SHSP*, XXIV, p. 24; Laura Virginia Hale, *Four Valiant Years: In The Lower Shenandoah Valley 1861–1865* (Strasburg: Shenandoah Publishing House, Inc., 1968), p. 429.

[19] Thomas A. Ashby, *The Valley Campaigns, Being the Reminiscences of a Non-Combatant while Between the Lines in the Shenandoah Valley During the War of the States* (New York: The Neale Publishing Company, 1914), p. 291; Hale, *Valiant Years*, p. 431; Williamson, *Mosby's Rangers*, p. 240; Moyer, *Seventeenth Pennsylvania*, p. 217;

"Hanging," *SHSP*, XXIV, p. 109; Mosby, "Retaliation," *SHSP*, XXVII, pp. 315, 316; Jones, *Mosby*, p. 208; Scott, *Partisan Life*, p. 319; Francis B. Heitman, *Historical Register and Dictionary of the United States Army* (Washington: Government Printing Office, 1903), p. 677; Charles H. Veil, "An Old Boy's Personal Recollections and Reminiscences of the Civil War," Civil War Miscellaneous Collection, Archives, USAMHI.

20 Barbour, Diary, UMICH; Emerson, *Lowell*, p. 353; "Hanging," *SHSP*, XXIV, p. 109; Scott, *Partisan Life*, p. 320; Jones, *Mosby*, p. 208; "The Monument To Mosby's Men," *SHSP*, XXVII, pp. 254, 282.

21 Ashby, *Valley Campaigns*, p. 293; Jones, *Mosby*, p. 209; Hale, *Valiant Years*, p. 431; "Hanging," *SHSP*, XXIV, p. 109; Scott, *Partisan Life*, p. 320; Williamson, *Mosby's Rangers*, p. 240.

22 Hale, *Valiant Years*, p. 433; Barbour, Diary, UMICH; Ashby, *Valley Campaigns*, p. 293; "Hanging," *SHSP*, XXIV, p. 109; Mosby, *Memoirs*, p. 301; Moyer, *Seventeenth Pennsylvania*, p. 217; Scott, *Partisan Life*, p. 320; Jones, *Mosby*, p. 210.

23 Jones, *Mosby*, pp. 210, 211; Lee, *Seventh Michigan*, p. 258; Badger, "My Capture," *United States Service Magazine*, June 1865, p. 552; Moyer, *Seventeenth Pennsylvania*, p. 218; Williamson, *Mosby's Rangers*, p. 242; "Hanging," *SHSP*, XXIV, p. 109; Scott, *Partisan Life*, p. 320; Hale, *Valiant Years*, p. 433; Cartmell, *Shenandoah Valley Pioneers*, p. 234.

24 Scott, *Partisan Life*, p. 320; Ashby, *Valley Campaigns*, p. 294; Jones, *Mosby*, p. 209; Hale, *Valiant Years*, p. 432; Mosby, "Retaliation," *SHSP*, XXVII, p. 314; "Monument," *SHSP*, XXVII, pp. 250–253.

25 Mosby, "Retaliation," *SHSP*, XXVII, p. 316; OR, XLIII, 2, p. 910.

26 Crawford, *Mosby*, pp. 268, 269; Haines, *Fifteenth New Jersey*, p. 273; Stevens, *Three Years*, p. 410; George Haven Putnam, *Memories of My Youth, 1844–1865* (New York and London: G. P. Putnam's Sons, The Knickerbocker Press, 1914), pp. 350, 351; Alexander Neil to Friends, October 13, 1864, Neil Letters, UVA; Walker, *Vermont Brigade*, p. 165.

27 Mosby, "Retaliation," *SHSP*, XXVII, pp. 316, 319; Scott, *Partisan Life*, pp. 356, 357; Alexander, *Mosby's Men*, pp. 143, 144, 145; OR, XLIII, 2, p. 566.

28 Alexander, *Mosby's Men*, p. 145; Scott, *Partisan Life*, pp. 357, 358; Williamson, *Mosby's Rangers*, p. 290; Mosby, "Retaliation," *SHSP*, XXVII, p. 319.

29 Mosby, "Retaliation," *SHSP*, XXVII, p. 319; Alexander, *Mosby's Men*, p. 147; Scott, *Partisan Life*, p. 358.

30 Munson, *Reminiscences*, pp. 140, 141, 150; Bryan, *Joseph Bryan*, p. 125n; Alexander, *Mosby's Men*, p. 147; Lee, *Seventh Michigan*, p. 93; Scott, *Partisan Life*, p. 358.

31 OR, XLIII, 2, p. 566; Munson, *Reminiscences*, p. 151; Scott, *Partisan Life*, p. 358; Williamson, *Mosby's Rangers*, pp. 293, 294; Alexander, *Mosby's Men*, p. 147.

32 OR, XLIII, 2, p. 920.

33 Ibid., 2, pp. 671–673, 679; Jones, *Mosby*, Chapter 20.

34 Hagemann, *Fighting Rebels*, p. 261; J. S. Lloyd to Sister, September 21, 1864, Lloyd Letter, HL; OR, XLIII, 1, p. 55; pt. 2, p. 64; Hewitt, *History*, p. 192; N. M. Burkholder, "The Barn-Burners: A Chapter of Sheridan's Raid up the Valley," *SHSP*, XXVIII, p. 98; William Thompson to Eliza, September 25, 1864, Baldridge Papers, PSU.

CHAPTER TEN

1 Catton, *Grant Takes Command*, pp. 389–390.

2 OR, XLIII, 1, p. 698.

3 Ibid., 2, pp. 288–289.

4 Adams, *Memorial*, p. 159.

[5] Kidd, *Personal Recollections*, p. 400; Walker, *Vermont Brigade*, p. 128; Moyer, *Seventeenth Pennsylvania*, p. 216; Keiser, Diary, USAMHI.

[6] Frank M. Myers, *The Comanches: A History of White's Battalion, Virginia Cavalry, Laurel Brig., Hampton Div., A.N.V., C.S.A.* (Baltimore: Kelly, Piet & Co., Publishers, 1871; reprint edition, Marietta, Georgia: Continental Book Company, 1956), pp. 335–336; Gilmor, *Four Years*, pp. 264, 265; Whittle, Notebook, UVA.

[7] Wayland, *Rockingham*, p. 151.

[8] OR, XLIII, 1, p. 443.

[9] Ibid., pp. 30, 31.

[10] Wayland, *Rockingham*, pp. 150, 151.

[11] Andrew Stairwalt, Sr., Diary, 1861–1864, Russell Hastings Papers, Library, RBHPC; Wildes, *Record*, p. 188; OR, XLIII, 1, p. 30; McDonald, *Hotchkiss Journal*, p. 235; Horst, *Mennonites*, pp. 15, 16; Stevens, *Three Years*, p. 411.

[12] OR, XLIII, 2, p. 88; McDonald, *Hotchkiss Journal*, p. 234; Myers, *Comanches*, pp. 333, 334.

[13] OR, XXXIII, p. 1166; Freeman, *Lee's Lieutenants*, III, pp. xi, 328, 596; Warner, *Generals In Gray*, pp. 264, 265; McDonald, *Hotchkiss Journal*, p. 234.

[14] Thomas T. Munford to L. W. V. Kennon, April 1, 1889, Letter of, Crook-Kennon Papers, Archives, USAMHI; Warner, *Generals In Gray*, p. 336; Freeman, *Lee's Lieutenants*, III, p. 596.

[15] Myers, *Comanches*, pp. 333–335, 340, 341; Munford, *Reminiscences*, SHSP, XIII, p. 135; Freeman, *Lee's Lieutenants*, III, p. 596.

[16] OR, XLIII, 1, pp. 442, 460, 477, 491, 612; pt. 2, pp. 296, 297, 302, 313; OR *Atlas*, Plate LXXXIV, 2; McDonald, *Hotchkiss Journal*, p. 235; Myers, *Comanches*, pp. 335, 336; Boudrye, *Fifth New York*, p. 177; Ferguson, "Memoranda," Duke; Whittle, Notebook, UVA; Barbour, Diary, UMICH; Farr, Diary, USAMHI; Dye, Papers, Duke.

[17] OR, XLIII, 1, p. 698; pt. 2, p. 329; Sheridan, *Personal Memoirs*, II, pp. 56–58; Hagemann, *Fighting Rebels*, pp. 282, 283.

[18] OR, XLIII, 1, pp. 447, 483, 491, 612, 613; Kidd, *Personal Recollections*, p. 402; Gilmor, *Four Years*, p. 268; Farr, Diary, USAMHI.

[19] OR, XLIII, 1, pp. 520, 549; Munford, "Reminiscences," SHSP, XIII, p. 136.

[20] Munford, "Reminiscences," SHSP, XIII, pp. 136–137; OR *Atlas*, Plate LXXXV, 34; OR, XLIII, 1, p. 520.

[21] OR, XLIII, 1, pp. 520, 521, 539, 541, 549, 550.

[22] Ibid., pp. 521, 541, 543, 544.

[23] Boudrye, *Fifth New York*, p. 180; Farr, Diary, USAMHI; OR, XLIII, 1, pp. 521, 541, 542, 544, 545; Myers, *Comanches*, p. 338; OR *Atlas*, Plate LXXXV, 34; Ferguson, "Memoranda," Duke; Whittle, Notebook, UVA; Munford, "Reminiscences," SHSP, XIII, pp. 136, 137.

[24] OR, XLIII, 1, pp. 538, 541; Boudrye, *Fifth New York*, pp. 296, 297; Ferguson, "Memoranda," Duke; Munford, "Reminiscences," SHSP, XII, p. 343; Pickerill, *History*, p. 167.

[25] Munford, "Reminiscences," SHSP, XIII, p. 138; OR, XLIII, 1, p. 521, 612; Ferguson, "Memoranda," Duke.

[26] OR, XLIII, 1, pp. 447, 460, 461, 483, 491, 559, 612, 613.

[27] OR, XLIII, 1, pp. 447, 483, 491, 612; Goldsborough, *Maryland Line*, pp. 291, 292.

[28] OR, XLIII, 1, pp. 447, 612; Humphrey, Diary, UVA.

[29] OR, XLIII, 1, pp. 448, 550; Barbour, Diary, UMICH.

[30] OR, XLIII, 2, p. 339, 431, 448; John Suter to wife, October 13, 1864, Suter Papers, USAMHI.

[31] Ferguson, "Memoranda," Duke; Whitehead, "Campaigns," UVA.

[32] Munford, "Reminiscences," SHSP, XIII, p. 135; XII, p. 453.

[33] Willard Glazier, *Three Years in the Federal Cavalry* (New York: R. H. Ferguson & Company, Publishers, 1874), p. 144.

[34] Peter Eltinge to Father, October 9, 1864, Eltinge Papers, Duke.

[35] Nettleton, "Cedar Creek," *MOLLUS*, Minn., I, p. 259; John Ollivett to Sister, October 12, 1864, Ollivett Letters, Duke.

[36] OR, XLIII, 1, pp. 51, 461, 477, 492, 508; Murphy, Journal, Duke; Dye, Papers, Duke; Haines, *Fifteenth New Jersey*, p. 272; Walker, *Vermont Brigade*, p. 128.

[37] OR, XLIII, 2, p. 327.

[38] Ibid., p. 340.

[39] Ibid., p. 340.

[40] Ibid., 1, pp. 51, 461, 477, 492; Haines, *Fifteenth New Jersey*, p. 273; Boudrye, *Fifth New York*, p. 178; Barbour, Diary, UMICH; Murphy, Journal, Duke; Wildes, *Record*, pp. 196, 197; Garnett, "Diary," *SHSP*, XXVII, p. 12; Sheridan, *Personal Memoirs*, II, p. 59.

[41] OR, XLIII, 1, pp. 508, 509; OR *Atlas*, Plate LXXXV, 1.

[42] OR, XLIII, 1, p. 51; pt. 2, pp. 345, 346; Sheridan, *Personal Memoirs*, p. 59.

[43] McDonald, *Hotchkiss Journal*, pp. 235–236; Runge, *Four Years*, p. 105; S. D. Ramseur to David Schenck, October 10, 1864, Ramseur Papers, SHC/UNC.

[44] OR, XLIII, 1, pp. 559–560.

[45] McDonald, *Hotchkiss Journal*, pp. 236–237; Runge, *Four Years*, p. 105; Shaffner, *Diary*, p. 54; Ferguson, "Memoranda," Duke.

[46] McDonald, *Hotchkiss Journal*, p. 236; DeForest, *Volunteers Adventures*, p. 200; Lincoln, *Thirty-Fourth Mass.*, p. 371.

[47] OR, XLIII, 1, p. 371; Lincoln, *Thirty-Fourth Mass.*, p. 372; Wildes, *Record*, pp. 197, 198; Garnett, "Diary," *SHSP*, XXVII, p. 12; Dickert, *Kershaw Brigade*, p. 438; McDonald, *Hotchkiss Journal*, p. 236; Cartmell, *Shenandoah Valley Pioneers*, p. 488.

[48] McDonald, *Hotchkiss Journal*, pp. 236–237; Ferguson, "Memoranda," Duke; Runge, *Four Years*, p. 105; OR, XLIII, 1, p. 372.

[49] OR, XLIII, 1, p. 51; Sheridan, *Personal Memoirs*, II, pp. 61–62; Murphy, Journal, Duke; Haines, *Fifteenth New Jersey*, p. 273; Walker, *Vermont Brigade*, pp. 128, 129.

[50] OR, XLIII, 2, p. 345.

[51] Ibid., 1, p. 51.

[52] Ibid., 1, p. 51; pt. 2, 355; Sheridan, *Personal Memoirs*, II, p. 62.

[53] DeForest, *Volunteers Adventures*, p. 202; OR, XLIII, 1, p. 432; Boudrye, *Fifth New York*, p. 179; Shaffner, *Diary*, p. 55; McDonald, *Hotchkiss Journal*, p. 237; Ferguson, "Memoranda," Duke.

[54] Cartmell, *Shenandoah Valley Pioneers*, pp. 235, 236; OR *Atlas*, Plate XCIX, 2.

[55] DuPont, *Campaign Of 1864*, p. 141; Crowninshield, "Cedar Creek," *MHSM*, VI, p. 161; Walker, *Vermont Brigade*, p. 131; OR *Atlas*, Plate XCIX, 2.

[56] Raoul S. Naroll, "Sheridan And Cedar Creek—A Reappraisal," *Military Analysis Of The Civil War: An Anthology by the Editors of Military Affairs*, Introduction by T. Harvey Williams (Millwood, N.Y.: KTO Press, 1977), pp. 370, 371, hereinafter cited as Naroll, "Sheridan," MA; DeForest, *Volunteers Adventures*, p. 204.

[57] DeForest, *Volunteers Adventures*, p. 204; DuPont, *Campaign Of 1864*, p. 142; Irwin, *History*, p. 414; Crowninshield, "Cedar Creek," *MHSM*, VI, pp. 161, 162.

[58] Irwin, *History*, p. 414; Putnam, *Memories*, pp. 362, 363; Crowninshield, "Cedar Creek," *MHSM*, VI, p. 162.

[59] Theodore Irving, *"More than Conqueror," or Memorials of Col. J. Howard Kitching* (New York: Published by Hurd and Houghton, 1873), pp. 4, 190–193.

[60] Buffum, *A Memorial*, p. 275; DuPont, *Campaign Of 1864*, p. 142; Crook, *Autobiography*, p. 132; DeForest, *Volunteers Adventures*, pp. 204, 205; Crowninshield, "Cedar Creek," *MHSM*, VI, p. 163; OR *Atlas*, Plate LXXXII, 9; XCIX, 2.

61 Crowninshield, "Cedar Creek," *MHSM*, VI, p. 162; Bradwell, "Cedar Creek," *CV*, XXVII, p. 411; DuPont, *Campaign Of 1864*, p. 142; Crook, *Autobiography*, p. 132; DeForest, *Volunteers Adventures*, p. 205; Buffum, A *Memorial*, p. 275.

62 James K. Ewer, *The Third Massachusetts Cavalry in the War For The Union* (Maplewood, Mass.: Historical Committee of The Regimental Association, 1903), p. 216; Naroll, "Sheridan," *MA*, p. 371; Crook, *Autobiography*, p. 132; DeForest, *Volunteers Adventures*, p. 205; Walker, *Vermont Brigade*, pp. 132, 134.

63 OR, XLIII, 1, p. 51; Sheridan, *Personal Memoirs*, II, p. 62; Forsyth, *Thrilling Days*, pp. 130, 131; Hall, *Sixth New York*, p. 233.

64 OR, XLIII, 1, pp. 51–52, 466; Sheridan, *Personal Memoirs*, II, p. 62.

65 OR, XLIII, 1, p. 52; Sheridan, *Personal Memoirs*, II, pp. 62, 63; Foote, *Civil War*, p. 565.

66 Sheridan, *Personal Memoirs*, II, pp. 65, 66, 67; Forsyth, *Thrilling Days*, pp. 133, 134; Nettleton, "Cedar Creek," *MOLLUS*, Minn., I, p. 263.

67 Early, *Autobiographical Sketch*, p. 438.

68 OR, XLIII, 2, pp. 891–892.

69 Ibid., pp. 891–892; Freeman, *Lee's Lieutenants*, III, pp. 595, 611.

70 McDonald, *Hotchkiss Journal*, p. 237; Gordon, *Reminiscences*, p. 333.

71 McDonald, *Hotchkiss Journal*, pp. 237–238; Gordon, *Reminiscences*, pp. 333–335.

72 Nettleton, "Cedar Creek," *MOLLUS*, Minn., I, p. 265; Crowninshield, "Cedar Creek," *MHSM*, VI, p. 164; Dye, Papers, Duke; Peter Eltinge to Father, October 18, 1864, Eltinge Papers, Duke; Murphy, Journal, Duke; Vaill, *Second Connecticut*, pp. 119, 120; Best, *121st New York*, pp. 190, 191; DeForest, *Volunteers Adventures*, p. 203; OR, XLIII, 1, p. 158.

73 McDonald, *Hotchkiss Journal*, p. 238.

74 Ibid., p. 238; Gordon, *Reminiscences*, pp. 335–336.

75 McDonald, *Hotchkiss Journal*, p. 238; Gordon, *Reminiscences*, p. 336; Daniel, "Early," *SHSP*, XXII, p. 307; Wayland, *Virginia Valley Records*, pp. 449, 451; OR *Atlas*, Plate LXXXII, 9.

76 McDonald, *Hotchkiss Journal*, p. 238; Nichols, *Soldier's Story*, p. 193; Betts, *Experience*, p. 68; Hatton, "Valley Campaign," *CV*, XXVII, p. 170; Bradwell, "Cedar Creek," *CV*, XXII, p. 315.

77 Shaffner, *Diary*, p. 55; Gordon, *Reminiscences*, p. 336; Samuel Buck, "Battle of Cedar Creek, VA.," Oct. 19th, 1864," *SHSP*, XXX, p. 105; Bradwell, "Cedar Creek," *CV*, XXII, p. 411; Hatton, "Valley Campaign," *CV*, XXVII, p. 170; McDonald, *Hotchkiss Journal*, p. 238; OR *Atlas*, Plate LXXXII, 9; XCIX, 2.

78 Gordon, *Reminiscences*, p. 337; Buck, "Cedar Creek," *SHSP*, XXX, p. 105; W. A. L. Jett, "Corrected Account of Battle of Cedar Creek," *CV*, XIII, p. 251; Nichols, *Soldier's Story*, p. 194; *National Tribune*, August 29, 1901; OR *Atlas*, Plate LXXXII, 9; XCIX, 2.

79 E. Ruffin Harris, "Battle Near Cedar Creek, VA.," *CV*, IX, p. 390; Bradwell, "Cedar Creek," *CV*, XXII, p. 315; Hatton, "Valley Campaign, *CV*, pp. 170, 171; *National Tribune*, August 29, 1901; Moses M. Granger, "The Battle of Cedar Creek," *Sketches of War History 1861-1865* , Vol. III, Ohio Commandery, MOLLUS (Cincinnati: Robert Clarke & Co., 1890), p. 102; DuPont, *Campaign Of 1864*, pp. 153, 156; OR *Atlas*, Plate LXXXII, 9; XCIX, 2.

CHAPTER ELEVEN

1 Hanaburgh, *History*, p. 164; *National Tribune*, September 13, 1883.

2 Hanaburgh, *History*, p. 164; *National Tribune*, September 13, 1883; OR, XLIII, 1, pp. 158, 184.

[3] OR, XLIII, 1, p. 382; Wildes, *Record*, p. 214n; Crook, *Autobiography*, p. 133.

[4] Wildes, *Record*, p. 214n; OR, XLIII, 1, pp. 379, 380, 382, 383, 384, 591.

[5] OR, XLIII, 1, p. 591; Warner, *Generals In Gray*, p. 171; Freeman, *Lee's Lieutenants*, III, p. xlvi.

[6] OR, XLIII, 1, pp. 591, 593; Dickert, *Kershaw Brigade*, p. 438; McDonald, *Hotchkiss Journal*, p. 239; OR *Atlas*, Plate LXXXII, 9.

[7] OR, XLIII, 1, pp. 160, 382, 383, 591; Joseph Ward to Father and Mother, October 26, 1864, Ward Letters, CHS; G. B. Gerald, "Notes on the Battle of Cedar Creek," *SHSP*, XVI, p. 392; H. H. Stevens, "Battle Of Cedar Creek, VA.," *CV*, XXVII, p. 390.

[8] *National Tribune*, August 29, 1901.

[9] OR, XLIII, 1, pp. 372, 391, 398, 591; Dye, Papers, Duke.

[10] DeForest, *Volunteers Adventures*, p. 209.

[11] OR, XLIII, 1, pp. 391, 398, 591.

[12] Ibid., pp. 372–374, 392–394, 398, 591; Lang, *Loyal West Virginia*, pp. 277, 299; Dickert, *Kershaw's Brigade*, p. 448.

[13] Joseph Ward to Father and Mother, October 26, 1864, Ward Letters, CHS; OR, XLIII, 1, p. 381; Lincoln, *Thirty-Fourth Mass.*, p. 381; Wildes, *Record*, p. 381.

[14] Lincoln, *Thirty-Fourth Mass.*, p. 381.

[15] Wildes, *Record*, pp. 203, 204; OR, XLIII, 1, pp. 380, 383, 384, 385, 591; Stevens, "Cedar Creek," *CV*, XXVII, p. 390; OR *Atlas*, Plate LXXXII, 9.

[16] OR, XLIII, 1, p. 414; DuPont, *Campaign Of 1864*, p. 158.

[17] OR, XLIII, 1, pp. 365, 413, 414, 418; DuPont, *Campaign Of 1864*, pp. 152–154.

[18] OR, XLIII, 1, pp. 418, 419, 591; DuPont, *Campaign Of 1864*, p. 156.

[19] DuPont, *Campaign Of 1864*, p. 175; OR, XLIII, 1, pp. 414, 415, 419, 591.

[20] DuPont, *Campaign Of 1864*, pp. 152, 156; OR, XLIII, 1, p. 414.

[21] DuPont, *Campaign Of 1864*, pp. 156, 157; OR, XLIII, 1, p. 414.

[22] OR, XLIII, 1, pp. 414, 417; DuPont, *Campaign Of 1864*, pp. 158–159; OR *Atlas*, Plate LXXXII, 9.

[23] OR, XLIII, 1, pp. 415, 416; DuPont, *Campaign Of 1864*, pp. 159, 160, 161, 162, 175.

[24] DuPont, *Campaign Of 1864*, pp. 159, 160; OR, XLIII, 1, pp. 414, 415, 417.

[25] DuPont, *Campaign Of 1864*, pp. 175, 176, 177.

[26] OR, XLIII, 1, p. 591; Dickert, *Kershaw's Brigade*, pp. 438, 448, 452.

[27] Dickert, *Kershaw's Brigade*, pp. 448, 449; Stevens, "Cedar Creek," *CV*, XXVII, p. 390.

[28] OR, XLIII, 1, pp. 591, 593; Dickert, *Kershaw's Brigade*, p. 448; OR *Atlas*, Plate LXXXII, 9; XCIX, 2.

[29] OR, XLIII, 1, p. 598; Gordon, *Reminiscences*, p. 339; OR *Atlas*, Plate LXXXII, 9.

[30] Gordon, *Reminiscences*, p. 64; Charles M. Steadman, "Gen. Stephen Dodson Ramseur," *CV*, XXVIII, p. 456.

[31] OR, XLIII, 1, pp. 403, 561, 591, 593; Dickert, *Kershaw's Brigade*, p. 447; Humphrey, Diary, UVA; *National Tribune*, August 29, 1901; McDonald, *Hotchkiss Journal*, pp. 238–239; Jubal A. Early, "Winchester, Fisher's Hill, And Cedar Creek," *B & L*, IV, p. 526.

[32] OR, XLIII, 1, p. 365; "Fisher's Hill and 'Sheridan's Ride,'" *CV*, X, p. 165.

[33] Catton, *Glory Road*, pp. 45, 46; Nichols, *Soldier's Story*, p. 194; Bradwell, "Cedar Creek," *CV*, XXVII, p. 412.

[34] OR, XLIII, 1, pp. 403, 404, 406, 408, 410; Nichols, *Soldier's Story*, pp. 194, 195; OR *Atlas*, Plate LXXXII, 9.

[35] OR, XLIII, 1, pp. 404, 406; OR *Atlas*, Plate LXXXII, 9; Krick, *Lee's Colonels*, p. 277.

[36] Nichols, *Soldier's Story*, p. 195; Bradwell, "Cedar Creek," *CV*, XXVII, p. 411; Krick, *Lee's Colonels*, p. 224; OR, XLIII, 1, pp. 404, 410, 411; OR *Atlas*, Plate LXXXII, 9.

[37] Rutherford B. Hayes, "Incidents at the Battle of Cedar Creek," *Sketches of War*

History 1861–1865 , Vol. IV, *Ohio Commandery, MOLLUS* (Cincinnati: Robert Clarke & Co., 1896), p. 239; Hayes, Diary, RBHPC; Howard, "Interviews," RBHPC.

[38] OR, XLIII, 1, p. 598.

[39] Ibid., pp. 366, 598, 606; Harris, "Cedar Creek," *CV,* IX, p. 390; Irving, *Kitching,* p. 199; OR *Atlas,* Plate LXXXII, 9.

[40] OR, XLIII, 1, pp. 366, 415, 417, 598; DuPont, *Campaign Of 1864,* p. 163; Warner, *Generals In Gray,* p. 20.

[41] Best, *121st New York,* p. 194; Walker, *Vermont Brigade,* pp. 136–137.

[42] DeForest, *Volunteers Adventures,* pp. 210–211.

[43] OR, XLIII, 1, pp. 380, 384, 404, 406; Wildes, *Record,* pp. 206, 207; Crowninshield, "Cedar Creek," *MHSM,* VI, pp. 164, 165.

[44] OR, XLIII, 1, p. 413; William Sanders to Sister, October 23, 1864, William Sanders, Letters of, *Civil War Times Illustrated* Collection, Archives, USAMHI; *National Tribune,* August 29, 1901; Benedict, *Vermont,* I, p. 549; James F. Fitts, "In The Enemy's Lines," *Galaxy,* IV, p. 700.

[45] Wildes, *Record,* p. 207; OR, XLIII, 1, pp. 380, 404, 406, 598; OR *Atlas,* Plate LXXXII, 9.

[46] OR, XLIII, 1, pp. 366, 404, 406, 598, 599; Hewitt, *History,* p. 188; Slease, *Fourteenth Pennsylvania,* pp. 212, 213; Brice, *Conquest,* p. 65; *National Tribune,* September 13, 1883; Goudy, Diary, WVAU; Alexander Neil to Friends, October 21, 1864, Neil Letters, UVA; OR *Atlas,* Plate, LXXXII, 9.

[47] OR, XLIII, 1, pp. 380, 404, 406, 598, 599; Wildes, *Record,* p. 207; OR *Atlas,* Plate LXXXII, 9.

[48] DeForest, *Volunteers Adventures,* p. 208; Buffum, *A Memorial,* pp. 278, 279; OR, XLIII, 1, p. 284; Dye, Papers, Duke.

[49] DeForest, *Volunteers Adventures,* pp. 208, 209; OR, XLIII, 1, p. 284.

[50] OR, XLIII, 1, pp. 284, 306.

[51] The documents pertinent to the dispute can be found in Ibid., pp. 287–295, 300–307, 322; originals are in Emory Papers, Yale.

[52] OR, XLIII, 1, pp. 284, 308; Irwin, *History,* pp. 418, 419.

[53] Benedict, *Vermont,* II, pp. 162, 163; DeForest, *Volunteers Adventures,* p. 211; Carpenter, *Eighth Vermont,* p. 215.

[54] Benedict, *Vermont,* II, p. 163; Wharton J. Green, *Recollections And Reflections: An Auto of Half A Century And More* (n.p.: Presses of Edwards And Boughton Printing Company, 1906), p. 177; OR, XLIII, 1, p. 308; Carpenter, *Eighth Vermont,* p. 215; Dickert, *Kershaw's Brigade,* p. 448; OR *Atlas,* Plate LXXXII, 9.

[55] Benedict, *Vermont,* II, pp. 163, 164, 167; *National Tribune,* January 26, 1911.

[56] Benedict, *Vermont,* II, pp. 166, 167, 168; Carpenter, *Eighth Vermont,* pp. 209, 210, 216; *National Tribune,* January 26, 1911; OR, XLIII, 1, p. 133.

[57] DeForest, *Volunteers Adventures,* p. 212; Carpenter, *Eighth Vermont,* p. 218; *National Tribune,* January 26, 1911; OR, XLIII, 1, pp. 133, 308.

[58] Agassiz, *Meade's Headquarters,* p. 300; OR, XLIII, 1, p. 158, 184; Wildes, *Record,* p. 205; Hagemann, *Fighting Rebels,* p. 290.

[59] OR, XLIII, 1, p. 284.

[60] Ibid., pp. 284, 308, 322, 338, 342; Flinn, *Campaigning,* pp. 213, 214; Hanaburgh, *History,* p. 163; Powers, *Thirty Eighth Massachusetts,* p. 172; Irwin, *History,* pp. 418, 419.

[61] John Suter to Wife, November 10, 1864, Suter Papers, USAMHI; OR, XLIII, 1, p. 358; Irwin, *History,* pp. 418, 420; Humphrey, Diary, UVA; Wise, *Long Arm,* p. 891; OR *Atlas,* Plate LXXXII, 9; Granger, "Cedar Creek," *MOLLUS,* Ohio, III, p. 113.

[62] OR, XLIII, 1, pp. 591, 593; Dickert, *Kershaw's Brigade,* p. 448; OR *Atlas,* Plate LXXXII, 9.

[63] Stevens "Cedar Creek," *CV,* XXVII, p. 390; OR, XLIII, 1, pp. 323, 342, 358; Putnam, *Memories,* pp. 368, 369; Sumner, *First Rhode Island,* p. 144.

[64] Peter Eltinge to Father, October 20, 1864, Eltinge Papers, Duke; OR, XLIII, 1, pp. 323, 342, 358; Flinn, *Campaigning*, pp. 216, 217; Powers, *Thirty Eighth Massachusetts*, p. 172; Putnam, *Memories*, pp. 369, 371.

[65] OR, XLIII, 1, pp. 134, 342; Powers, *Thirty Eighth Massachusetts*, pp. 172, 175; Flinn, *Campaigning*, p. 218.

[66] Sumner, *First Rhode Island*, p. 145; Irwin, *History*, p. 421; Putnam, *Memories*, pp. 372, 373; OR, XLIII, 1, pp. 347, 348, 352, 353; OR *Atlas*, Plate LXXXII, 9.

[67] OR, XLIII, 1, pp. 322, 358; Irwin, *History*, p. 421.

[68] OR, XLIII, 1, pp. 323, 327, 338, 339; Jones, *Reminiscences*, p. 88; Peter Boarts to Parents, October 21, 1864, Boarts Letters, USAMHI.

[69] Buffum, *A Memorial*, pp. 293–294; OR, XLIII, 1, pp. 133, 327, 328; Jones, *Reminiscences*, p. 88; Willie Root, Letters and Diary, September–October 1864, Civil War Times Illustrated Collection, Archives, USAMHI; Waite, *New Hampshire*, p. 513.

[70] OR, XLIII, 1, pp. 323, 333, 334, 336, 339; Sprague, *History*, p. 236.

[71] Fitts, "Cedar Creek," *Galaxy*, I, p. 537; OR, XLIII, 1, pp. 308, 309, 323; Beecher, *Record*, p. 445; Pellet, *History*, p. 268.

[72] Beecher, *History*, p. 446; Fitts, "Cedar Creek," *Galaxy*, I, p. 538; OR, XLIII, 1, p. 309.

[73] OR, XLIII, 1, pp. 309, 323; Beecher, *History*, p. 447; Orton S. Clark, "Sheridan's Shenandoah Valley Campaign," *Glimpses of the Nation's Struggle*, MOLLUS, Minn. Commandery, Sixth Series (Minneapolis, Minn.: Aug. Davis, Publisher, 1909), p. 46; Irwin, *History*, p. 421.

[74] Irwin, *History*, pp. 422, 423; Fitts, "Cedar Creek," *Galaxy*, I, p. 538; OR, XLIII, 1, p. 285; DeForest, *Volunteers Adventures*, p. 214; Buffum, *A Memorial*, p. 294.

[75] DeForest, *Volunteers Adventures*, p. 213; Ezra Farnsworth, Jr., "Reminiscences of the Shenandoah Valley in 1864," *Glimpses of the Nation's Struggle*, MOLLUS, Minn. Commandery, Fifth Series (St. Paul, Minn.: Review Publishing Co., 1903), p. 183.

[76] OR, XLIII, 1, p. 285; Irwin, *History*, pp. 422, 423; OR *Atlas*, Plate XCIX, 2.

[77] Haynes, *History*, p. 125; Irwin, *History*, p. 421; Carpenter, *Eighth Vermont*, p. 213; Dickert, *Kershaw's Brigade*, p. 448; Humphrey, Diary, UVA.

CHAPTER TWELVE

[1] Early, "Winchester," *B & L*, IV, p. 527; Freeman, *Lee's Lieutenants*, III, p. 601.

[2] Early, "Winchester," *B & L*, IV, p. 527; Freeman, *Lee's Lieutenants*, III, p. 601.

[3] Early, "Winchester," *B & L*, IV, p. 527; Freeman, *Lee's Lieutenants*, III, pp. 601, 602; Humphrey, Diary, UVA; McDonald, *Hotchkiss Journal*, p. 239; OR *Atlas*, Plate LXXXII, 9.

[4] David Faust to Mother, October 21, 1864, Faust Papers, USAMHI; Haines, *Fifteenth New Jersey*, p. 275; OR, XLIII, 1, p. 193; pt. 2, p. 501; Best, *121st New York*, p. 193; Walker, *Vermont Brigade*, p. 139.

[5] Walker, *Vermont Brigade*, p. 139; OR, XLIII, 1, pp. 226, 261; OR *Atlas*, Plate, XCIX, 2; Crowninshield, "Cedar Creek," *MHSM*, VI, p. 167.

[6] OR, XLIII, 1, pp. 167, 174, 193, 209, 225, 261; Walker, *Vermont Brigade*, p. 140; OR *Atlas*, Plate XCIX, 2.

[7] OR, XLIII, 1, pp. 158, 159, 167, 193, 209, 225, 261; Gilson, *History*, p. 102.

[8] OR, XLIII, 1, pp. 226, 233, 251, 259, 261; Granger, "Cedar Creek," *MOLLUS*, Ohio, III, pp. 118, 119.

[9] OR, XLIII, 1, pp. 226, 233, 251, 255, 278; Granger, "Cedar Creek," *MOLLUS*, Ohio, III, p. 119.

[10] OR, XLIII, 1, pp. 226, 233, 251, 256, 276, 278, 323, 333, 336, 342; OR *Atlas*, Plate XCIX, 2; Buffum, *A Memorial*, p. 285.

[11] OR, XLIII, 1, pp. 174, 176; Best, *121st New York*, pp. 193, 195; Vaill, *Second Connecticut*, p. 121.

[12] OR, XLIII, 1, pp. 167, 168; Haines, *Fifteenth New Jersey*, pp. 276, 282; *National Tribune*, September 13, 1883; OR *Atlas*, Plate XCIX, 2.

[13] OR, XLIII, 1, pp. 226, 233, 251, 334; OR *Atlas*, Plate LXXXII, 9; XCIX, 2; Dickert, *Kershaw's Brigade*, p. 449.

[14] OR, XLIII, 1, p. 226.

[15] Keifer, *Four Years*, II, p. 115; OR, XLIII, 1, pp. 226, 233, 251, 276, 278.

[16] OR, XLIII, 1, pp. 226, 233; Prowell, *History*, p. 214; Haines, *Tenth Vermont*, p. 128.

[17] Haines, *Tenth Vermont*, p. 128; OR, XLIII, 1, pp. 121, 226, 233, 244, 255, 278.

[18] Roe, *Ninth New York*, p. 182; OR, XLIII, 1, pp. 251, 256.

[19] OR, XLIII, 1, pp. 251, 256.

[20] Roe, *Ninth New York*, p. 181; OR, XLIII, 1, pp. 256, 257.

[21] OR, XLIII, 1, pp. 251, 256, 257; Roe, *Ninth New York*, p. 181.

[22] *National Tribune*, September 13, 1883; OR, XLIII, 1, p. 167; Haines, *Fifteenth New Jersey*, p. 276.

[23] OR, XLIII, 1, p. 167; Haines, *Fifteenth New Jersey*, pp. 276, 277; *National Tribune*, September 13, 1883.

[24] OR, XLIII, 1, p. 167; Haines, *Fifteenth New Jersey*, p. 277; *National Tribune*, September 13, 1883; Halsey, Papers, USAMHI.

[25] OR, XLIII, 1, pp. 174, 176; Best, *121st New York*, p. 195; OR *Atlas*, Plate LXXXII, 9; XCIX, 2.

[26] John Knight Bucklyn, "Battle of Cedar Creek, October 19, 1864," *Personal Narratives of Events in the War of the Rebellion, Being Papers Read Before The Rhode Island Soldiers And Sailors Historical Society*, Second Series, No. 19 (Providence: N. Bangs Williams & Company, 1882), p. 14.

[27] The primary map of the battle prepared by Hotchkiss is Plate LXXXII, 9, while the most extensive one prepared by the Federals is XCIX, 2, OR *Atlas*.

[28] Gordon, *Reminiscences*, p. 354.

[29] Official Confederate reports are in OR, XLIII, 1, pp. 561–613.

[30] Ibid., pp. 174, 193; Best, *121st New York*, pp. 194, 195, 196; Vaill, *Second Connecticut*, p. 123; OR *Atlas*, LXXXII, 9; XCIX, 2.

[31] Hatton, "Valley Campaign," CV, XXVII, p. 171; Buck, "Cedar Creek," SHSP, XXX, p. 106; Buck, Papers, Duke; OR *Atlas*, Plate XCIX, 2.

[32] OR, XLIII, 1, p. 174; Best, *121st New York*, p. 195; Vaill, *Second Connecticut*, pp. 122, 123; OR *Atlas*, Plate LXXXII, 9; XCIX, 2.

[33] OR, XLIII, 1, pp. 174, 175, 206; Best, *121st New York*, pp. 195, 196; Vaill, *Second Connecticut*, pp. 105, 123; Bucklyn, "Cedar Creek," *Personal Narratives*, p. 14.

[34] OR, XLIII, 1, pp. 175, 176; Best, *121st New York*, p. 196; Vaill, *Second Connecticut*, pp. 123, 124.

[35] OR, XLIII, 1, pp. 193, 226, 323, 334, 342; OR *Atlas*, Plate XCIX, 2.

[36] DuPont, *Campaign Of 1864*, p. 165; OR, XLIII, 1, pp. 193, 209, 215; Stevens, *Three Years*, p. 419; Walker, *Vermont Brigade*, p. 141; Warner, *Generals In Blue*, p. 170; OR *Atlas*, Plate XCIX, 2.

[37] OR, XLIII, 1, pp. 193, 194, 201, 209, 214, 215; Keiser, Diary, USAMHI; Bidwell, *History*, p. 74; Walker, *Vermont Brigade*, p. 141; OR *Atlas*, Plate XCIX, 2; Ewer, *Third Massachusetts*, p. 224.

[38] OR, XLIII, 1, pp. 193, 194, 201; DuPont, *Campaign of 1864*, p. 166; OR *Atlas*, Plate XCIX, 2.

[39] OR, XLIII, 1, pp. 598, 599, 606, 607, 608.

[40] Ibid., pp. 598, 599.

[41] Crowninshield, "Sheridan," *Atlantic Monthly*, XLII, p. 690; DuPont, *Campaign*

Of 1864, p. 167.

42 Hatton, "Valley Campaign," *CV*, XXVII, p. 171; Lewis A. Grant, "The Second Division of the Sixth Corps at Cedar Creek," *Glimpses of the Nation's Struggle, MOLLUS*, Minn. Commandery, Sixth Series (Minneapolis, Minn.: Aug. Davis, Publisher, 1909), p. 18; OR, XLIII, 1, p. 599; OR *Atlas*, Plate LXXXII, 9.

43 Hatton, "Valley Campaign," *CV*, XXVII, p. 171; Buck, "Cedar Creek," *SHSP*, XXX, p. 106; OR, XLIII, 1, pp. 194, 201, 209; pt. 2, p. 882; DuPont, *Campaign Of 1864*, p. 166.

44 Hatton, "Valley Campaign," *CV*, XXVII, p. 171; OR, XLIII, 1, pp. 194, 201, 209; Walker, *Vermont Brigade*, p. 142; Buck, Papers, Duke.

45 OR, XLIII, 1, pp. 194, 201, 209, 599; Bidwell, *History*, p. 75; Walker, *Vermont Brigade*, p. 142; DuPont, *Campaign Of 1864*, p. 166.

46 Walker, *Vermont Brigade*, p. 142; OR, XLIII, 1, pp. 194, 209.

47 Walker, *Vermont Brigade*, pp. 18, 19; Warner, *Generals In Blue*, pp. 182–183.

48 OR, XLIII, 1, pp. 599, 606, 607; Steadman, "Ramseur," *CV*, XXVIII, p. 456; Ledford, *Reminiscences*, p. 78.

49 Walker, *Vermont Brigade*, pp. 142, 143; Bidwell, *History*, pp. 98, 99; OR, XLIII, 1, pp. 209, 215, 606, 607; Warner, *Generals In Blue*, p. 32.

50 OR, XLIII, 1, pp. 209, 210, 215, 599, 606, 607; Walker, *Vermont Brigade*, p. 143.

51 Douglas, *Stonewall*, p. 317; Early, "Winchester," *B & L*, IV, p. 527; Freeman, *Lee's Lieutenants*, III, p. 602.

52 Early, "Winchester," *B & L*, IV, p. 527.

53 McDonald, *Hotchkiss Journal*, p. 238.

54 Crowninshield, "Sheridan," *Atlantic Monthly*, XLII, p. 690; DuPont, *Campaign Of 1864*, pp. 167–168.

55 Freeman, *Lee's Lieutenants*, III, pp. 604–608.

56 OR, XLIII, 1, pp. 210, 215; Walker, *Vermont Brigade*, p. 144; Early, "Winchester," *B & L*, IV, p. 527; Humphrey, Diary, UVA.

57 Early, "Winchester," *B & L*, IV, p. 527; OR, XLIII, 1, p. 562; Humphrey, Diary, UVA; Daniel, "Early," *SHSP*, XXII, p. 308; OR *Atlas*, Plate LXXXII, 9; XCIX, 2.

58 Early, "Winchester," *B & L*, IV, p. 527; OR *Atlas*, Plate LXXXII, 9.

59 DelVecchio, "First New York," Ainsworth Papers, USAMHI; Early, "Winchester," *B & L*, IV, p. 527; OR, XLIII, 1, pp. 193, 201, 210, 215; Walker, *Vermont Brigade*, p. 144.

60 Crowninshield, "Cedar Creek," *MHSM*, VI, p. 168; Grant, "Second Division," *MOLLUS*, Minn., VI, pp. 20, 21; Walker, *Vermont Brigade*, pp. 144, 145.

61 OR, XLIII, 1, p. 562; Early, "Winchester," *B & L*, IV, p. 527.

62 Gordon, *Reminiscences*, p. 359; Early, "Winchester," *B & L*, IV, p. 527; Freeman, *Lee's Lieutenants*, III, p. 603.

63 OR, XLIII, 1, pp. 415, 417, 562; Early, "Winchester," *B & L*, IV, pp. 527, 528; DuPont, *Campaign Of 1864*, pp. 164, 165; Humphrey, Diary, UVA; OR *Atlas*, Plate LXXXII, 9; XCIX, 2.

64 OR, XLIII, 1, pp. 433, 438; Lee, *Seventh Michigan*, p. 59; Isham, *Historical Sketch*, p. 73; OR *Atlas*, Plate XCIX, 2.

65 OR, XLIII, 1, pp. 448, 522, 561; Lee, *Seventh Michigan*, p. 59; Isham, *Historical Sketch*, p. 73; Kidd, *Personal Recollections*, p. 410; OR *Atlas*, Plate XCIX, 2; Gallaher, *Diary*, p. 13.

66 OR, XLIII, 1, pp. 448, 522; Kidd, *Personal Recollections*, p. 411; Gallaher, *Diary*, p. 13.

67 Hagemann, *Fighting Rebels*, p. 287; Crowninshield, "Sheridan," *Atlantic Monthly*, XLII, p. 686, OR, XLIII, 1, p. 433.

68 OR, XLIII, 1, pp. 433, 449, 478.

69 Hall, *Sixth New York*, p. 235; OR, XLIII, 1, p. 478; Bowen, *History*, p. 252.

70 OR, XLIII, 1, pp. 478, 562; Granger, "Cedar Creek," *MOLLUS*, Ohio, III, pp. 105, 111; OR *Atlas*, Plate XCIX, 2.

71 OR, XLIII, 1, pp. 433, 522.

72 Wesley Merritt, "Sheridan In The Shenandoah Valley," *B & L*, IV, p. 518; Kidd, *Personal Recollections*, p. 416.

73 OR, XLIII, 1, pp. 433, 449, 478, 523; *National Tribune*, September 13, 1883; OR *Atlas*, Plate XCIX, 2; Naroll, "Sheridan," *MA*, p. 368.

74 OR, XLIII, 1, pp. 433, 449, 478, 562; Merritt, "Sheridan," *B & L*, IV, p. 518; Humphrey, *Diary*, UVA; OR *Atlas*, Plate XCIX, 2.

75 OR, XLIII, 1, p. 562; Early, "Winchester," *B & L*, IV, p. 528; Freeman, *Lee's Lieutenants*, III, p. 605.

76 OR, XLIII, 1, pp. 562, 613; Early, "Winchester," *B & L*, IV, p. 528; Freeman, *Lee's Lieutenants*, III, p. 609.

77 Early, "Winchester," *B & L*, IV, p. 528; OR, XLIII, 1, pp. 562, 613; Daniel, "Early," *SHSP*, XXII, pp. 308, 309.

78 Freeman, *Lee's Lieutenants*, III, p. 604n.

79 Gordon, *Reminiscences*, pp. 341–342.

80 Freeman, *Lee's Lieutenants*, III, p. 609.

81 Mark, *Red: White: And Blue*, p. 301; Cartmell, *Shenandoah Valley Pioneers*, p. 409.

82 Gordon, *Reminiscences*, p. 341.

83 Ibid., pp. 365–368; OR, XLIII, 1, p. 562; Early, "Winchester," *B & L*, IV, p. 528.

84 Shaffner, *Diary*, p. 56; Stevens, "Cedar Creek," *CV*, XXVII, p. 390; Dickert, *Kershaw's Brigade*, p. 449.

85 William A. Wilson, *A Borderland Confederate*, Edited by Festus P. Summers (Pittsburgh: University of Pittsburgh Press, 1962), p. 83; Nettleton, "Cedar Creek," *MOLLUS*, Minn., I, pp. 268, 275; Haines, *Fifteenth New Jersey*, p. 279; Vaill, *Second Connecticut*, p. 130; DuPont, *Campaign Of 1864*, pp. 168, 169.

86 Clark, *N. C. Regts.*, I, p. 327; Smith, *Anson Guards*, p. 285.

87 Worsham, *Foot Cavalry*, p. 177.

88 Freeman, *Lee's Lieutenants*, III, p. 605; Bushong, *Old Jube*, p. 260; Harris, "Cedar Creek," *CV*, IX, p. 390.

89 Bushong, *Old Jube*, p. 260.

CHAPTER THIRTEEN

1 Quarles, *Occupied Winchester*, pp. 83–84; Sheridan, *Personal Memoirs*, II, pp. 67–70.

2 Crowninshield, "Sheridan," *Atlantic Monthly*, XLII, p. 690; Benedict, *Vermont*, I, p. 556n; MacConnell, "Sheridan," *War Papers*, MOLLUS, Wis., I, pp. 285, 286.

3 Sheridan, *Personal Memoirs*, II, pp. 71–75; Forsyth, *Thrilling Days*, p. 136; Moyer, *Seventeenth Pennsylvania*, p. 115.

4 Forsyth, *Thrilling Days*, p. 136; Rawling, *History*, p. 212; Sheridan, *Personal Memoirs*, II, p. 75; Hewitt, *History*, pp. 184, 185; Moyer, *Seventeenth Pennsylvania*, p. 116.

5 Sheridan, *Personal Memoirs*, II, p. 76; Forsyth, *Thrilling Days*, p. 136; Moyer, *Seventeenth Pennsylvania*, p. 116.

6 Sheridan, *Personal Memoirs*, II, pp. 79, 80; Hewitt, *History*, p. 186; Forsyth, *Thrilling Days*, p. 136; Moyer, *Seventeenth Pennsylvania*, p. 116; Stackhouse, *Diary*, Hist. Soc. of PA.; Irwin, *History*, p. 430n.

7 Moyer, *Seventeenth Pennsylvania*, p. 116; Albert Stearns, *Reminiscences of the Late War* (Green Point, Brooklyn, N.Y.: Albert Stearns, 1881), p. 30; Forsyth, *Thrilling Days*, p. 142.

[8] Hayes, "Incidents," *Sketches, MOLLUS*, Ohio, IV, p. 240; Sheridan, *Personal Memoirs*, II, pp. 81–82; Forsyth, *Thrilling Days*, pp. 144, 145; Moyer, *Seventeenth Pennsylvania*, pp. 116, 117.

[9] Sheridan, *Personal Memoirs*, II, pp. 82, 83; Forsyth, *Thrilling Days*, pp. 145, 146; DuPont, *Campaign Of 1864*, p. 170.

[10] Hagemann, *Fighting Rebels*, p. 291.

[11] OR, XLIII, 1, p. 53; Sheridan, *Personal Memoirs*, II, pp. 83, 84.

[12] *National Tribune*, September 13, 1883, December 1, 1910; Sheridan, *Personal Memoirs*, II, pp. 85, 86.

[13] Root, Letters and Diary, USAMHI; Buffum, *A Memorial*, p. 291; Nettleton, "Cedar Creek," *Glimpses, MOLLUS*, Minn., I, p. 270; Adams, *Memorial*, p. 165; Hewitt, *History*, p. 187; Walker, *Vermont Brigade*, p. 148; Flinn, *Campaigning*, p. 226; O'Connor, *Sheridan*, p. 16.

[14] McDonald, *Hotchkiss Journal*, p. 239; OR Atlas, Plate LXXXII, 9.

[15] McDonald, *Hotchkiss Journal*, p. 239; Irwin, *History*, p. 427; Crowninshield, "Cedar Creek," *MHSM*, VI, p. 173; Buck, "Cedar Creek," *SHSP*, XXX, p. 107; OR *Atlas*, Plate LXXXII, 9; Humphrey, *Diary*, UVA.

[16] OR, XLIII, 1, p. 562.

[17] Freeman, *Lee's Lieutenants*, III, pp. 605, 606.

[18] Early, "Winchester," *B & L*, IV, p. 528.

[19] OR, XLIII, 1, p. 194; Sheridan, *Personal Memoirs*, p. 86; Walker, *Vermont Brigade*, p. 149.

[20] Forsyth, *Thrilling Days*, p. 152; *National Tribune*, December 1, 1910; OR, XLIII, 1, p. 194; Early, "Winchester," *B & L*, IV, p. 528.

[21] Farnsworth, "Reminiscences," *Glimpses, MOLLUS*, Minn., V, p. 193; Benedict, *Vermont*, I, p. 558; OR *Atlas*, Plate LXXXII, 9; XCIX, 2.

[22] Forsyth, *Thrilling Days*, p. 155; Walker, *Vermont Brigade*, p. 149; Sheridan, *Personal Memoirs*, II, p. 87.

[23] Early, "Winchester," *B & L*, IV, p. 528.

[24] Gordon, *Reminiscences*, pp. 346–347.

[25] Ibid., p. 346; OR, XLIII, 1, p. 523; *National Tribune*, September 13, 1883.

[26] Gordon, *Reminiscences*, p. 347; Bradwell, "Cedar Creek," *CV*, XXII, p. 315; OR *Atlas*, Plate LXXXII, 9; XCIX, 2.

[27] Gordon, *Reminiscences*, p. 347.

[28] Sheridan, *Personal Memoirs*, II, p. 86.

[29] OR, XLIII, 1, p. 53.

[30] Ibid., pp. 449, 450; Sheridan, *Personal Memoirs*, II, pp. 87–88; DeForest, *Volunteers Adventures*, p. 222.

[31] Flinn, *Campaigning*, p. 201; DeForest, *Volunteers Adventures*, p. 225; Forsyth, *Thrilling Days*, pp. 157–158.

[32] Adams, *Memorial*, p. 165; Nettleton, "Cedar Creek," *Glimpses, MOLLUS*, Minn., I, p. 271; Slease, *Fourteenth Pennsylvania*, p. 209; DeForest, *Volunteers Adventures*, p. 223; OR, XLIII, 1, p. 159.

[33] OR, XLIII, 1, p. 310; Pellet, *History*, p. 270.

[34] Forsyth, *Thrilling Days*, p. 162; OR, XLIII, 1, p. 310; Beecher, *Record*, p. 451; Irwin, *History*, p. 433.

[35] OR, XLIII, 1, p. 310; Irwin, *History*, p. 433; Forsyth, *Thrilling Days*, p. 163.

[36] OR, XLIII, 1, p. 310; Carpenter, *Eighth Vermont*, pp. 221–223; Irwin, *History*, p. 433; Forsyth, *Thrilling Days*, p. 164.

[37] Sheridan, *Personal Memoirs*, II, p. 89; Forsyth, *Thrilling Days*, p. 164; OR, XLIII, 1, p. 310; Irwin, *History*, p. 433.

[38] Vaill, *Second Connecticut*, p. 126.

[39] OR, XLIII, 1, pp. 323, 324, 334, 335.

40 Ibid., pp. 167, 168, 175; Vaill, *Second Connecticut*, pp. 125, 126; Best, *121st New York*, p. 197; Haines, *Fifteenth New Jersey*, p. 280.

41 OR, XLIII, 1, pp. 227, 228, 234.

42 Walker, *Vermont Brigade*, p. 150; OR, XLIII, 1, pp. 194, 195, 201, 210, 216; Mark, *Red: White: and Blue*, p. 301.

43 OR, XLIII, 1, pp. 194, 201; Walker, *Vermont Brigade*, p. 150.

44 Walker, *Vermont Brigade*, p. 150; OR, XLIII, 1, pp. 195, 210.

45 OR, XLIII, 1, pp. 195, 216, 220; *National Tribune*, December 1, 1910; Stevens, *Three Years*, p. 424; OR *Atlas*, Plate LXXXII, 9.

46 OR, XLIII, 1, pp. 216, 220; *National Tribune*, December 1, 1910; Stevens, *Three Years*, pp. 424, 425.

47 *National Tribune*, December 1, 1910; OR, XLIII, 1, pp. 195, 210, 216, 220; Walker, *Vermont Brigade*, pp. 150, 151; Stevens, *Three Years*, p. 425.

48 Boudrye, *Fifth New York*, p. 181; Kidd, *Personal Recollections*, pp. 422, 423; OR, XLIII, 1, pp. 523–524.

49 OR, XLIII, 1, p. 310; Forsyth, *Thrilling Days*, p. 165; Irwin, *History*, p. 434.

50 Gordon, *Reminiscences*, p. 348.

51 OR, XLIII, 1, p. 562; Dickert, *Kershaw's Brigade*, p. 470.

52 Nichols, *Soldier's Story*, p. 197; Mark, *Red: White: and Blue*, p. 302.

53 Forsyth, *Thrilling Days*, p. 165.

54 Gerald, "Cedar Creek," *SHSP*, XVI, p. 391; Freeman, *Lee's Lieutenants*, III, p. 607; Garnett, "Diary," *SHSP*, XXVII, p. 14; Clark, *N. C. Regts.*, II, p. 143; Stevens, "Cedar Creek," *CV*, XXVII, p. 396.

55 OR, XLIII, 1, p. 450; Kidd, *Personal Recollections*, pp. 422–423.

56 Nevins, *Diary*, p. 475; OR, XLIII, 1, p. 450.

57 Emerson, *Lowell*, pp. 357–358, 475n; Kidd, *Personal Recollections*, pp. 412, 417; Warner, *Generals In Blue*, p. 284.

58 Clark, *N.C. Regts.*, II, pp. 143, 260; S. D. Buck, "Gen. Early in the Valley," *CV*, XII, p. 23; OR, XLIII, 1, p. 562; Humphrey, Diary, UVA.

59 Moorman, "Recollections," HL.

60 Bradwell, "Cedar Creek," *CV*, XXVII, p. 412; Bradwell, "Cedar Creek," *CV*, XXII, p. 315; Buck, "Cedar Creek," *SHSP*, XXX, p. 107.

61 OR, XLIII, 1, pp. 53, 451, 480; Bradwell, "Cedar Creek," *CV*, XXII, p. 315; *National Tribune*, January 26, 1911; Benedict, *Vermont*, II, p. 667; McDonald, *Hotchkiss Journal*, p. 240; Paul, Diary, USAMIII; Merington, *Custer Story*, pp. 126, 127; George Percy Hawes, "The Battle of Cedar Creek," *CV*, XXXI, pp. 169–170.

62 OR, XLIII, 1, p. 563.

63 Clark, "Sheridan's," *Glimpses*, MOLLUS, Minn., VI, p. 50.

64 Beecher, *Record*, p. 453.

65 Peter B. Boarts to Parents, October 21, 1864, Boarts Letters, USAMHI.

66 Hagemann, *Fighting Rebels*, p. 296; Forsyth, *Thrilling Days*, p. 167; *National Tribune*, September 13, 1883.

67 Crook, *Autobiography*, p. 134; Lee, *Seventh Michigan*, p. 217.

68 Garnett, "Diary," *SHSP*, XXVII, p. 14; Hagemann, *Fighting Rebels*, p. 296; DuPont, *Campaign Of 1864*, pp. 172, 173, 174.

CHAPTER FOURTEEN

1 OR, XLIII, 1, p. 54.

2 Vaill, *Second Connecticut*, p. 111; Mark, *Red: White: and Blue*, p. 297.

3 Early, "Winchester," *B & L*, IV, p. 530.

4 DuPont, *Campaign Of 1864*, p. 152; Crowninshield, "Cedar Creek," *MHSM*, VI, pp. 163, 176.

5 Root, Letters, USAMHI; DeForest, *Volunteers Adventures*, p. 203; OR, XLIII, 1, pp. 158, 160.

6 Naroll, "Sheridan," *MA*, pp. 379, 380; DuPont, *Campaign Of 1864*, p. 147.

7 Naroll, "Sheridan," *MA*, p. 380; Kennon, "Valley Campaign," *MHSM*, VI, p. 51.

8 OR, XLIII, 1, p. 52; DuPont, *Campaign Of 1864*, p. 144; OR *Atlas*, Plate XCIX, 2.

9 Crook, "Campaign," USAMHI; OR, XLIII, 1, pp. 158–161; Crook, *Autobiography*, p. 134.

10 OR, XLIII, 1, p. 52; Crook, *Autobiography*, p. 134; Naroll, "Sheridan," *MA*, p. 380; Kennon, "Valley Campaign," *MHSM*, VI, p. 51.

11 DuPont, *Campaign Of 1864*, p. 147.

12 Joseph T. Durkin, (ed.), *Confederate Chaplain: A War Journal of Rev. James B. Sheeran, c. ss. r. 14th Louisiana, C.S.A.*, With a Preface by Bruce Catton (Milwaukee: The Bruce Publishing Company, 1960), p. 107.

13 Kennon, "Valley Campaign," *MHSM*, VI, p. 48.

14 Ibid., pp. 50–51; Naroll, "Sheridan," *MA*, p. 379; Crowninshield, "Cedar Creek," *MHSM*, VI, p. 379.

15 Freeman, *Lee's Lieutenants*, III, p. 609.

16 Garnett, "Diary," *SHSP*, XXVII, p. 13.

17 McDonald, *Hotchkiss Journal*, p. 240.

18 Ibid., p. 241.

19 OR, LI, 2, p. 1048.

20 Wise, *Long Arm*, p. 894.

21 OR, XLIII, 1, pp. 33, 137, 564; Long, *Day By Day*, p. 585; Garnett, "Diary," *SHSP*, XXVII, p. 13; J. A. Early to Thomas Henry Carter, December 13, 1866, Early, Va. Hist. Soc.

22 OR, XLIII, 1, p. 563.

23 Gordon, *Reminiscences*, pp. 317–318.

24 Foote, *Civil War*, p. 572; Worsham, *Foot Cavalry*, p. 179.

25 Wilson, *Borderland*, p. 176; "Recollections," *Century Magazine*, LXX, p. 313.

26 DeForest, *Volunteers Adventures*, p. 228; Foote, *Civil War*, p. 574.

27 Walker, *Vermont Brigade*, p. 155.

28 O'Connor, *Sheridan*, p. 13.

29 Crowninshield, "Sheridan," *Atlantic Monthly*, XLII, p. 686.

30 Samuel B. M. Young, Papers of, USAMHI.

31 Boudrye, *Fifth New York*, p. 172.

32 Kennon, "Valley Campaign," *MHSM*, VI, pp. 52–53, 57.

33 Vaill, *Second Connecticut*, p. 131.

34 Early, *Autobiographical Sketch*, p. 459; McDonald, *Hotchkiss Journal*, pp. 244, 246; OR, XLIII, 1, pp. 63–105.

35 OR, XLVI, 1, pp. 475, 485, 501, 502.

36 Ibid., pp. 476, 502; McDonald, *Hotchkiss Journal*, pp. 258, 259.

37 OR, XLVI, 1, pp. 502, 505; McDonald, *Hotchkiss Journal*, p. 260; Runge, *Four Years*, p. 122.

Bibliography

MANUSCRIPTS

Chicago Historical Society, Chicago, Illinois: Joseph F. Ward Letters.

Duke University, William R. Perkins Library, Durham, North Carolina:
Samuel D. Buck Papers
Mary E. Cloud Papers, Letter August 8, 1864, from a Smith to "Miss Mary"
Henry I. Cowan, Letter of September 15, 1864, Helen L. and Mary Virginia Shell Papers
Nathan G. Dye Diary
Peter Eltinge Letters, Eltinge-Lord Family Papers
J. D. Ferguson, "Memoranda of the itinerary and operations of Major General Fitz. Lee's Cavalry Division of the Army of Northern Virginia, from May 4th to October 15th 1864, inclusive by J. D. Ferguson Major & Asst. Adjutant General." Typescript manuscript, Munford-Ellis Papers
James Madison Murphy Journal, J. M. Murphy Papers
John M. Ollivett Letters
Green W. Penn Papers
John Wilfong Papers, Unsigned letter to Mrs. Lovina Wilfong, October 3, 1864

Emory University, Robert W. Woodruff Library for Advanced Studies, Atlanta, Georgia:
Thomas Bomar Letter of September 17, 1864 to "My Dear Sister," Bomar Family Papers

The Historical Society of Pennsylvania, Philadelphia, Pennsylvania:
James A. Congdon Letters, Clement H. Congdon Papers
William Stackhouse Diary

The Huntington Library, San Marino, California:
Americana Collection:
Samuel Buck, "Battle of Cedar Creek, VA., October 19, 1864," Samuel Buck Papers
J. S. Lloyd Letter to Sister, September 21, 1864
Jesse C. Osgood Letter to Aunt Fanny, September 22, 1864
Philip H. Sheridan Papers
Jubal A. Early Papers
Maj. Marcellus Moorman, "Recollections of Cedar Creek and Fisher's Hill, October 19th, 1864," Unpublished letter February 19, 1903

Library of Congress, Washington, D.C.:
Jedediah Hotchkiss Papers
Joseph Warren Keifer Papers
Capt. William W. Old Diary, Jubal A. Early Papers

The Pennsylvania State University, Pattee Library, University Park, Pennsylvania:
William Thompson Letters, The Baldridge Collection of Civil War Letters

Mr. Nick Picerno, Springfield, Vermont:
William Knowlton Letters and Papers
Levi Winslow, "The Memoirs of Rev. Levi Winslow, 12th Maine Volunteers, Co. A," unpublished, typescript manuscript

Rutherford B. Hayes Presidential Center, Library, Fremont, Ohio:

John T. Booth Letter to R. B. Hayes, May 26, 1887
James M. Comly Diary
James W. DeLay Letters to R. B. Hayes, December 22, 1886 and January 7, 1886
Jonathan Harlan Letter to R. B. Hayes, July 8, 1887
Rutherford B. Hayes Diary, Rutherford B. Hayes Papers, Civil War Records, Series 7
J. Q. Howard, "Interviews with Rutherford B. Hayes," Transcript
J. Reasoner Letter to J. T. Booth, September 18, 1887
B. F. Stearns Letter to R. B. Hayes, July 18, 1887
William S. Wilson Letter to R. B. Hayes, April 9, 1887

Russell Hastings Papers:
  Russell Hastings, "Memoirs"
  "Journal of the 23rd Regiment, O.V.I."
  "Memoirs of General Russell Hastings"
  "Records 23rd Ohio Regiment, Veteran Volunteer Infantry, Colonel Rutherford B. Hayes, Dedication of Monument"
  "A Staff Officer's Recollection of The Battle of Opequon, Fought at Winchester Va. Sept. 19, 1864"
  Andrew Stairwalt, Sr. Diary, 1861–1864

United States Army Military History Institute, Archives, Carlisle Barracks, Pennsylvania:
  Civil War Times Illustrated Collection:
  James Abraham, "Reminiscences and Letters," typed copy
  John E. Armstrong Memoirs, typed copy
  I. Norval Baker Diary, typed copy
  Albert A. Clapp Diary
  Francis Dawes Diary
  Isaac H. Duval, "Autobiography"
  William Fisk Letters
  David B. Lang, "The Life of Lt. Col. David B. Lang of the 62nd Virginia Regiment"
  William A. McIlhenny Memoirs, typed copy
  "Military Operations in Jefferson County, Virginia (And West VA), 1861–1865," typed copy published by Jefferson County Camp, U.C.V., 1911, reprint 1960
  Hance Morgan Diary
  Henry R. Morrison Letters and Clippings
  Charles R. Perkins Letters
  David Powell, "Memoirs of a Union Officer During Civil War 1861–1865"
  Willie Root Letters and Diary, September–October 1864
  William Sanders Letters
  James L. Sharp Letter, July 31, 1864
  Perry Smith Letters
  Civil War Miscellaneous Collection:
  "Charles," 10th New Jersey Volunteer Infantry Letter, July 15, 1864
  Dayton E. Flint Letters
  James M. Gaspar Diary, June 5–October 19, 1864
  Lewis Josselyn Memoirs
  John A. Rawlins Letter to Colonel Ely Parker, September 25, 1864
  Benjamin F. Ridenour Memoir
  Samuel Burks Rucker, Sr., "Recollections of My War Record During The Confederacy," typescript

Shenandoah, Army of the, Letter from an unidentified Union soldier at Halltown, West Virginia, August 25, 1864
Charles H. Veil, "An Old Boy's Personal Recollections and Reminiscences of the Civil War," typed copy
Lyman S. Walker Diary—1864
Harrisburg Civil War Round Table Collection:
Richard J. Del Vecchio, "With The First New York Dragoons: From the Letters of Jared L. Ainsworth," Jared L. Ainsworth Papers
Daniel Faust Papers
Henry Keiser Diary
David Seibert Letters, Seibert Family Papers
Jacob Seibert Letters, Seibert Family Papers
John P. Suter Papers
The Earl W. Hess Collection:
John W. Barnard, Deposition made before Regimental Quartermaster, September 1, 1864
Peter B. Boarts Letters
John C. Arnold Letters, The Arnold Family Papers, typed copy
George Bain Papers, Ronald D. Boyer Collection
Allen Baker, Jr. Diary
Richard Castle Letter, July 12, 1864, The William Prince Collection
George Crook, "Gen. George Crook's Statement on Shenandoah Valley Campaign, dictated to L. W. V. Kennon September 28, 1888," Crook-Kennon Papers
Henry A. DuPont Letter to James A. Wilson, February 11, 1889, Crook-Kennon Papers
Charles R. Farr Diary, The Charles R. Farr Papers
Edmund Halsey Papers
Thomas T. Munford Letter to L. W. V. Kennon, April 1, 1889, Crook-Kennon Papers
Charles R. Paul Diary, Murray J. Smith Collection, typed copy
Isaac E. Severn Papers
Philip H. Sheridan, copy of telegram to U. S. Grant, 11:30 a.m., October 20, 1864, Autograph Collection, Vol. 2, #233, Massachusetts Commandery, Military Order Loyal Legion of the United States
Albert A. Wright Diary, George J. Fluhr Collection, typed copy
Samuel B. M. Young Papers
United States Military Academy, Library, West Point, New York:
George A. Custer Letter, dated September 16, 1864, addressed to "My dear Friend"
The University of Michigan, Bentley Historical Library, Ann Arbor, Michigan:
George W. Barbour Diary, Michigan Historical Collections
University of North Carolina, Library, Chapel Hill, North Carolina:
Stephen Dodson Ramseur Papers, Southern Historical Collection
University of Virginia, Alderman Library, Charlottesville, Virginia:
Edwin Bouldin, "Reminiscences"
Milton W. Humphrey Diary
Alexander Neil Letters
I. P. Whitehead, "The Campaigns of Munford and the Second Virginia Cavalry," unpublished typed manuscript
B. F. Whittle Notebook, September 12, 1864–February 18, 1865

Virginia Historical Society, Richmond, Virginia:
J. A. Early Letter to Thomas Henry Carter, December 13, 1866, Lee Family Papers
William Barksdale Myers Letters to his father, Adolphus Gustavus Myers, Papers of Adolphus Gustavus Myers

Virginia Military Institute, Preston Library, Lexington, Virginia:
William G. Watson Reminiscences

Virginia State Library, Richmond, Virginia:
Joseph McMurran Diary

Washington and Lee University, Library, Lexington, Virginia:
Alexander Barclay Letters

Jeffry D. Wert, Centre Hall, Pennsylvania:
Arthur C. Hodgson Letter to author, September 5, 1979

West Virginia University, Library, Morgantown, West Virginia:
West Virginia Collection:
James Ellis Diary, Roy Bird Cook Collection
William M. Goudy Diary
John V. Young Diary, John V. Young Civil War Papers

Yale University, The Beinecke Rare Book and Manuscript Library, New Haven, Connecticut:
William H. Emory Papers

PUBLISHED SOURCES

GOVERNMENT RECORDS

Heitman, Francis B. *Historical Register and Dictionary of the United States Army.* Washington: Government Printing Office, 1903.

U.S. War Department. *Atlas To Accompany The Official Records of the Union And Confederate Armies.* Washington: Government Printing Office, 1891–1895; reprint edition, Gettysburg, Pennsylvania: The National Historical Society, 1978.

U.S. War Department. *The War Of The Rebellion: A Compilation of the Official Records of the Union and Confederate Armies.* 128 Vols. Washington, D.C.: U.S. Government Printing Office, 1880–1901.

MEMOIRS, REMINISCENCES, DIARIES, LETTERS

Abbott, Lemuel Alijah. *Personal Recollections and Civil War Diary 1864.* Burlington: Free Press Printing Co., 1908.

Adams, John MacGregor and Albert Egerton Adams, (editors). *Memorial And Letters of Rev. John R. Adams, D. D.* Cambridge, Mass.: University Press: John Wilson and Son, 1890.

Agassiz, George R., (editor). *Meade's Headquarters, 1863–1865: Letters of Colonel Theodore Lyman From The Wilderness To Appomattox.* Boston: The Atlantic Monthly Press, 1922.

Alexander, E. P. *Military Memoirs Of A Confederate,* with a new introduction and notes by T. Harry Williams. Bloomington: Indiana University Press, 1962.

Ashby, Thomas A. *The Valley Campaigns, Being the Reminiscences of a Non-Combatant While Between the Lines in the Shenandoah Valley During the War of the States.* New York: The Neale Publishing Company, 1914.

Badger, W. W. "My Capture And Escape From Mosby," *United States Service Magazine,* June 1865.

"The Battle of Cedar Creek," *Confederate Veteran*, XIV (1906).
Beall, T. B. "That Stampede At Fisher's Hill," *Confederate Veteran*, V (1897).
Berkeley, F. Carter. "Imboden's Dash Into Charlestown." *Confederate Veteran*, XXV (1917).
Betts, Alexander D. *Experiences Of A Confederate Chaplain 1861–1864* , Edited by W. A. Betts. Reprint edition; Ann Arbor, Michigan: University Microfilms, 1973.
Blackford, Charles M. "The Campaign and Battle of Lynchburg, Va., June, 1864," *Southern Historical Society Papers*, XXX (1902).
Bobbitt, John H. "That Moorefield Surprise," *Confederate Veteran*, X (1902).
Bourne, R. G. "Capture Of The Fort At New Creek," *Confederate Veteran*, XXIV (1916).
Bradwell, I. G. "The Battle Of Cedar Creek, VA." *Confederate Veteran*, XXII (1914).
————. "Battle Of Cedar Creek, VA." *Confederate Veteran*, XXVII (1919).
————. "The Battle Of Fisher's Hill," *Confederate Veteran*, XXVIII (1920).
————. "Early's Demonstration Against Washington In 1864," *Confederate Veteran*, XXII (1914).
————. "Early's Valley Campaign, 1864," *Confederate Veteran*, XXVIII (1920).
————. "The Fight At Winchester, VA.—Jim Graham," *Confederate Veteran*, XV (1907).
————. "First Of Valley Campaign By General Early," *Confederate Veteran*, XIX (1911).
————. "Scouting In The Valley," *Confederate Veteran*, XXVII (1919).
————. "Troops Demoralized At Fisher's Hill," *Confederate Veteran*, XXV (1917).
————. "When General Mulligan Was Killed," *Confederate Veteran*, XXXV (1927).
————. "With Early In The Valley," *Confederate Veteran*, XXII (1914).
Brinton, John H. *Personal Memoirs of John H. Brinton*. New York: The Neale Publishing Company, 1914.
Bryan, John Stewart. *Joseph Bryan: His Times, His Family, His Friends, A Memoir*. Richmond, Virginia: Whittet & Shepperson, 1935.
Buck, Lucy Rebecca. *Sad Earth, Sweet Heaven: The Diary of Lucy Rebecca Buck, During the War Between the States, Front Royal, Virginia, December 25, 1861–April 15, 1865*, Edited by William P. Buck. Birmingham, Alabama: The Cornerstone, Publisher, 1973.
Bucklyn, John Knight. "Battle of Cedar Creek, October 19, 1864," *Personal Narratives of Events in the War of The Rebellion, Being Papers Read Before The Rhode Island Soldiers And Sailors Historical Society*, Second Series, No. 19. Providence: N. Bangs Williams & Company, 1882.
Buck, Samuel D. "Battle Of Cedar Creek—Tribute To Early," *Confederate Veteran*, II (1894).
————. "Battle of Cedar Creek, VA., Oct. 19th, 1864," *Southern Historical Society Papers*, XXX (1902).
————. "Battle of Fisher's Hill," *Confederate Veteran*, II (1894).
————. "Gen. Early in the Valley," *Confederate Veteran*, XII (1904).
Burkholder, N. M. "The Barn-Burners: A Chapter of Sheridan's Raid up the Valley," *Southern Historical Society Papers*, XXVIII (1900).
"Capt. Frank Bennett," *Confederate Veteran*, VIII (1900).
Casler, John O. *Four Years in the Stonewall Brigade*. Reprint edition, edited by James I. Robertson, Jr., Dayton, Ohio: Morningside Bookshop, 1971.
Chamberlayne, C. G. (editor). *Ham Chamberlayne—Virginian: Letters And Papers Of An Artillery Officer in the War for Southern Independence 1861–1865* . Richmond, VA.: Press of The Dietz Printing Co., Publishers, 1932.
Chamberlin, George E. *Letters of George E. Chamberlin, Who Fell in the Service of his Country near Charlestown, Va., August 21st, 1864*. Springfield, Ill.: H. W. Rokker's Publishing House, 1883.

Clark, Orton S. "Sheridan's Shenandoah Valley Campaign," *Glimpses of the Nation's Struggle, Minnesota Commandery, Military Order Loyal Legion of the United States*, Sixth Series. Minneapolis, Minn.: Aug. Davis, Publisher, 1909.

Clay, James B. "Jubal A. Early And His Campaigns," *Confederate Veteran*, I (1893).

Crary, Catherine S., (editor). *Dear Belle: Letters from a Cadet & Officer to his Sweetheart, 1858–1865.* Middletown, Connecticut: Wesleyan University Press, 1965.

Crook, George. *General George Crook: His Autobiography*, Edited and Annotated by Martin F. Schmitt. Norman: University of Oklahoma Press, 1946.

Crowninshield, Benjamin W. "Cedar Creek," *Papers Of The Military Historical Society Of Massachusetts: The Shenandoah Campaigns Of 1862 And 1864 And The Appomattox Campaign 1865*, Vol. VI. Boston: The Military Historical Society of Massachusetts, 1907.

————. "Sheridan At Winchester," *Atlantic Monthly*, XLII (1878).

Dalzell, James M. *Private Dalzell: His Autobiography, Poems And Comic War Papers.* Cincinnati: Robert Clarke & Co., 1888.

Daniel, John W. "General Jubal A. Early," *Southern Historical Society Papers*, XXII (1894).

Dayton, Ruth Woods, (editor). *The Diary of A Confederate Soldier James E. Hall.* Philippi, W. Va.: Elizabeth Teter Phillips, 1961.

DeForest, John William. *A Volunteers Adventures: A Union Captain's Record of the Civil War*, Edited, with Notes, by James H. Croushore, With an Introduction by Stanley T. Williams. New Haven: Yale University Press, 1946; reprint edition, Hamden, Conn.: Archon Books, 1970.

Douglas, Henry Kyd. *I Rode With Stonewall.* Chapel Hill: The University of North Carolina Press, 1940.

DuPont, Henry A. *The Campaign Of 1864 In The Valley Of Virginia and the Expedition To Lynchburg.* New York: National Americana Society, 1925.

Durkin, Joseph T., (editor). *Confederate Chaplain: A War Journal of Rev. James B. Sheeran, c. ss.r. 14th Louisiana, C.S.A.*, With a Preface by Bruce Catton. Milwaukee: The Bruce Publishing Company, 1960.

Early, Jubal Anderson. *Autobiographical Sketch And Narrative Of The War Between The States*, With Notes By R. H. Early. Philadelphia & London: J. B. Lippincott Company, 1912.

————. *A Memoir of The Last Year of the War For Independence in the Confederate States Of America.* Lynchburg: Charles W. Button, 1867.

————. "Early's March To Washington In 1864," Clarence Clough Buel and Robert Underwood Johnson, (editors). *Battles and Leaders of the Civil War*, IV. Reprint edition, New York: Thomas Yoseloff, Inc., 1956.

————. "Winchester, Fisher's Hill, And Creek Creek," Clarence Clough Buel and Robert Underwood Johnson, (editors). *Battles and Leaders of the Civil War*, IV. Reprint edition, New York: Thomas Yoseloff, Inc., 1956.

Ely, Cecil D. Jr. (editor). *A Virginia Yankee in the Civil War: The Diaries of David Hunter Strother.* Chapel Hill: The University of North Carolina Press, 1961.

Emerson, Edward W. *Life And Letters of Charles Russell Lowell.* Reprint edition, Port Washington, N.Y.: Kennikat Press, 1971.

Farnsworth, Ezra. "The Battle of Cedar Creek," *Glimpses of the Nation's Struggle, Minnesota Commandery, Military Order Loyal Legion of the United States*, Sixth Series. Minneapolis, Minn.: Aug. Davis, Publisher, 1909.

————. "Reminiscences of the Shenandoah Valley in 1864," *Glimpses of the Nation's Struggle, Minnesota Commandery, Military Order Loyal Legion of the United States*, Fifth Series. St. Paul, Minn.: Review Publishing Co., 1903.

Featherston, J. C. "Gen. Jubal Anderson Early," *Confederate Veteran*, XXVI (1918).

"Fisher's Hill And 'Sheridan's Ride,'" *Confederate Veteran*, X (1902).

Fitts, James F. "In The Enemy's Lines," *Galaxy*, IV (1867).
————. "In The Ranks At Cedar Creek," *Galaxy*, I (1866).
————. "Last Battle of Winchester," *Galaxy*, II (1866).
————. "Mosby And His Men," *Galaxy*, II (1866).
Flinn, Frank M. *Campaigning With Banks In Louisiana, '63 And '64 And With Sheridan In The Shenandoah Valley, In '64 And '65*, Second Edition. Boston: W. B. Clarke & Co., 1889.
Forsyth, George A. "Sheridan's Ride," *Harper's New Monthly Magazine*, Vol. XCV, No. DLXVI (July, 1897).
————. *Thrilling Days In Army Life*. New York and London: Harper & Brothers, 1900.
Gallaher, De Witt Clinton. *A Diary Depicting The Experiences of De Witt Clinton Gallaher In The War Between The States While Serving In The Confederate Army*. Charleston, W. Va.: De Witt C. Gallaher, Jr., 1945.
Gallaher, D. C. "The Myth of Sheridan's Ride," *Confederate Veteran*, XXXI (1923).
Garnett, James M. "Diary of Captain James M. Garnett, Ordnance Officer Rodes's Division, 2d Corps, Army of Northern Virginia," *Southern Historical Society Papers*, XXVII (1899).
Gause, Isaac. *Four Years With Five Armies*. New York And Washington: The Neale Publishing Company, 1908.
Gerald, G. B. "Notes on the Battle of Cedar Creek," *Southern Historical Society Papers*, XVI (1888).
Gill, John. *Reminiscences Of Four Years As A Private Soldier In The Confederate Army 1861-1865*. Baltimore: Sun Printing Office, 1904.
Gilmor, Harry. *Four Years In The Saddle*. New York: Harper & Brothers, Publishers, 1866.
Glazier, Willard. *Three Years in the Federal Cavalry*. New York: R. H. Ferguson & Company, Publishers, 1874.
Gordon, John B. *Reminiscences Of The Civil War*. New York: Charles Scribner's Sons, 1904; reprint edition, Gettysburg, Pa.: *Civil War Times Illustrated*, 1974.
Granger, Moses M. "The Battle of Cedar Creek," *Sketches of War History 1861-1865*, Vol. III, *Ohio Commandery, Military Order Loyal Legion of the United States*. Cincinnati: Robert Clarke & Co., 1890.
Grant, Lewis A. "The Second Division of the Sixth Corps at Cedar Creek," *Glimpses Of the Nation's Struggle, Minnesota Commandery, Military Order Loyal Legion of the United States*, Sixth Series. Minneapolis, Minn.: Aug. Davis, Publisher, 1909.
Grant, Ulysses S. *Personal Memoirs of U.S. Grant, In Two Volumes*. New York: Charles L. Webster & Company, 1886.
Green, Wharton J. *Recollections and Reflections: An Auto of Half A Century And More*. n.p.: Presses of Edwards And Broughton Printing Company, 1906.
Greer, George H. T. "Riding with Early: An Aide's Diary," *Civil War Times Illustrated*, Volume XVII, Number 8 (December 1978).
Grimes, Bryan. *Extracts Of Letters Of Major-Gen'l Bryan Grimes, To His Wife, Written While In Active Service In The Army of Northern Virginia*, Compiled by Pulaski Cowper. Raleigh: Edwards, Broughton & Co., Steam Printers and Binders, 1883.
Hagemann, E. R., Editor with an Introduction. *Fighting Rebels And Redskins: Experiences In Army Life Of Colonel George B. Sanford 1861-1892*. Norman: University of Oklahoma Press, 1969.
"Hanging Of Mosby's Men In 1864," *Southern Historical Society Papers*, XXIV (1896).
Harrar, William. *With Drum And Gun In '61: A Narrative of the Adventures of William Harrar of the Fourteenth New York State Volunteers, in the War for the Union from 1861 to 1863*. Greenville, PA: The Beaver Printing Company, 1908.
Harris, E. Ruffin. "Battle Near Cedar Creek, VA." *Confederate Veteran*, IX (1901).

Harris, Nathaniel E. *Autobiography: The Story Of An Old Man's Life With Reminiscences Of Seventy-five Years*. Macon, Ga.: The J. W. Burke Company, Publishers, 1925.

Harris, Samuel. *Personal Reminiscences of Samuel Harris*. Chicago: The Rogerson Press, 1897.

Hatton, Clarence R. "Gen. Archibald Campbell Godwin," *Confederate Veteran*, XXVIII (1920).

————. "The Valley Campaign Of 1864," *Confederate Veteran*, XXVII (1919).

Hatton, Robert W., (editor), "Just a Little Bit of the Civil War, As Seen by W. J. Smith, Company M, 2nd O. V. Cavalry—Part I." *Ohio History*, Volume 84, Number 3 (Summer 1975).

Harves, George Percy. "The Battle of Cedar Creek," *Confederate Veteran*, XXXI (1923).

Hawkins, Morton L. "Sketch of the Battle of Winchester, September 19, 1864," *Sketches of War History 1861-1865* , Vol. I, Ohio Commandery, Military Order Loyal Legion of the United States. Cincinnati: Robert Clarke & Co., 1888.

Hayes, Rutherford B. "Incidents at the Battle of Cedar Creek," *Sketches of War History 1861-1865* , Vol. IV, Ohio Commandery, Military Order Loyal Legion of the United States. Cincinnati: Robert Clarke & Co., 1896.

Herring, Marcus D. "General Rodes At Winchester," *Confederate Veteran*, XXVIII (1910).

————. "Gen. Robert E. Rodes," *Confederate Veteran*, XXIV (1926).

Hopkins, Luther W. *From Bull Run To Appomattox: A Boy's View*. Baltimore: Press of Fleet-McGinley Co., 1908.

Hunter, Alexander. *Johnny Reb And Billy Yank*. New York and Washington: The Neale Publishing Company, 1905.

"An Incident of the Battle of Winchester, or Opequon," *Southern Historical Society Papers*, XXXVII (1909).

Irving, Theodore. "*More Than Conqueror*," or Memorials of Col. J. Howard Kitching. New York: Published By Hurd And Houghton, 1873.

Jett, W. A. L. "Corrected Account of Battle of Cedar Creek," *Confederate Veteran*, XIII (1905).

Johnson, Bradley T. "My Ride Around Baltimore In Eighteen Hundred And Sixty-Four," *Southern Historical Society Papers*, XXX (1902).

————. "Tarheels' Thin Gray Line," *Southern Historical Society Papers*, XXVII (1889).

Kahle, M. S. "Gen. Jubal A. Early," *Confederate Veteran*, II (1894).

Keifer, Joseph Warren. *Slavery And Four Years Of War*. New York and London: G. P. Putnam's Sons, the Knickerbocker Press, 1900.

Kidd, James H. *Personal Recollections of a Cavalryman With Custer's Michigan Cavalry Brigade in the Civil War*. Ionia, Michigan: Sentinel Printing Company, 1908.

Ledford, Preston L. *Reminiscences of The Civil War 1861-1865* . Thomasville, N.C.: News Printing House, 1909.

Leon, L. *Diary of A Tar Heel Confederate Soldier*. Charlotte, N.C.: Stone Publishing Company, 1913.

Lynch, Charles H. *The Civil War Diary 1862-1865 of Charles H. Lynch, 18th Conn. Vol's*. Hartford, Conn.: The Case, Lockwood & Brainard Co., 1915.

MacConnell, Charles C. "Service with Sheridan," *War Papers Read Before the Commandery of the State of Wisconsin, Military Order Loyal Legion of the United States, Vol. I*. Milwaukee: Burdick, Armitage & Allen, 1891.

M' Chesney, James Z. "Scouting On Hunter's Raid to Lynchburg, Va.," *Confederate Veteran*, XXVIII (1920).

McCollum, J. L. "Sketch Of The Raccoon Roughs," *Confederate Veteran*, VI (1898).

Merritt, Wesley. "Sheridan In The Shenandoah Valley," Clarence Clough Buel and Robert Underwood Johnson, (editors). *Battles and Leaders of the Civil War, IV.* Reprint edition, New York: Thomas Yoseloff, Inc., 1956.

Meyer, Henry C. *Civil War Experiences Under Bayard, Gregg, Kilpatrick, Custer, Raulston, And Newberry, 1862, 1863, 1864.* New York: The Knickerbocker Press, 1911.

"Military Career Of Gen. Bryan Grimes," *Confederate Veteran*, VII (1899).

Moffett, Mary Conner, (editor). *Letters Of General James Conner C. S. A.* Columbia, S.C.: Presses of The R. L. Bryon Co., 1950.

Moore, J. Scott. "Unwritten History: A Southern Account of the Burning of Chambersburg," *Southern Historical Society Papers*, XXVI (1898).

Moore, Robert A. *A Life For The Confederacy*, Edited by James W. Silver; Foreword by Bell Irvin Wiley. Jackson, Tenn.: McCowat-Mercer Press, Inc., 1959.

Moore, Samuel J. C. "Early's Strength At Winchester," *Confederate Veteran*, XI (1903).

Mosby, John S. *The Memoirs Of Colonel John S. Mosby*, Edited by Charles Wells Russell; Preface By Virgil Carrington Jones. Bloomington: Indiana University Press, 1959.

————. "Retaliation: The Execution Of Seven Prisoners By Col. John S. Mosby—A Self-Protective Necessity," *Southern Historical Society Papers*, XXVII (1899).

Munford, T. T. "Reminiscences of Cavalry Operations," *Southern Historical Society Papers*, XII (1884) and XIII (1885).

Munson, John W. *Reminiscences Of A Mosby Guerrilla.* New York: Moffat, Yard And Company, 1906.

Nettleton, A. Bayard. "How the Day was Saved at the Battle of Cedar Creek," *Glimpses of the Nation's Struggle, Minnesota Commandery, Military Order Loyal Legion of the United States*, First Series. St. Paul, Minn.: St. Paul Book And Stationery Company, 1887.

Nevins, Allan, (editor). *A Diary Of Battle: The Personal Journals of Colonel Charles S. Wainwright, 1861–1865.* New York: Harcourt, Brace & World, 1962.

Newell, T. F. "Gen. Early's Motto: 'Fight 'Em,'" *Confederate Veteran*, V (1897).

Nichols, G. W. *A Soldier's Story Of His Regiment (61st Georgia) And Incidentally of the Lawton-Gordon-Evans Brigade Army Northern Virginia.* Kennesaw, Georgia: Continental Book Company, 1961.

Nielson, T. H. "Thrilling Experiences Of Lieut. Col. Lang," *Confederate Veteran*, XIII (1905).

O'Ferrall, Charles T. *Forty Years Of Active Service.* New York And Washington: The Neale Publishing Company, 1904.

"Official Diary of First Corps, A.N.V., While Commanded by Lt.-General R. H. Anderson, from June 1st to October 18, 1864," *Southern Historical Society Papers*, VII (1879).

Park, Robert E. "Diary of Robert E. Park, late Capt. Twelfth Alabama Reg't.," *Southern Historical Society Papers*, I (1875) and II (1876).

Patterson, W. W. "Swift Retribution for House-Burning," *Confederate Veteran*, XII (1904).

Peck, Rufus H. *Reminiscences Of A Confederate Soldier Of Co. C., 2nd Va. Cavalry.* Reprint edition, Ann Arbor, Michigan: University Microfilms, 1971.

Pendleton, Constance, (editor). *Confederate Memoirs: Early Life And Family History William Frederic Pendleton, Mary Lawson Young Pendleton.* Bryn Athyn, Pennsylvania: Constance Pendleton, 1958.

Potts, J. N. "Hard-Fighting Virginians—Lieut. Col. Lang," *Confederate Veteran*, XIII (1905).

Putnam, George Haven. *Memories of My Youth, 1844–1865.* New York and London: G. P. Putnam's Sons, The Knickbocker Press, 1914.

Rast, P. J. "Fisher's Hill," *Confederate Veteran*, XXIII (1915).

"Recollections Of Jubal Early By One Who Followed Him," *The Century Magazine*, LXX (May–October 1905).

Reed, Thomas Benton. *A Private in Gray*. Camden, Ark.: T. B. Reed, 1905.

Rockwell, A. D. *Rambling Recollections: An Autobiography*. New York: Paul B. Hoeber, 1920.

Runge, William H., (editor). *Four Years In The Confederate Artillery: The Diary of Private Henry Robinson Berkeley*. Chapel Hill: The University of North Carolina Press, 1961.

Shaffner, C. L. (editor). *Diary of Dr. J. F. Shaffner, Sr.* n.p., n.d.

Scott, John. *Partisan Life With Col. John S. Mosby*. New York: Harper & Brothers, Publishers, 1867.

Sheridan, Philip H. *Personal Memoirs of P. H. Sheridan, General United States Army*. New York: Charles L. Webster & Company, 1888.

Sorrel, G. Mosley. *Recollections of a Confederate Staff Officer*, Edited by Bell Irvin Wiley. Jackson, Tennessee: McCowat-Mercer Press, Inc., 1958.

Stearns, Albert. *Reminiscences of the Late War*. Green Point, Brooklyn, N.Y.: Albert Stearns, 1881.

Stevens, H. H. "Battle Of Cedar Creek, VA.," *Confederate Veteran*, XXVII (1919).

Stiles, Robert. *Four Years Under Marse Robert*. New York & Washington: The Neale Publishing Company, 1903; reprint edition, with introduction and Index by Robert Krick, Dayton, Ohio: Morningside Bookshop, 1977.

Taylor, Richard. *Destruction and Reconstruction: Personal Experiences Of The Late War*, Edited by Richard Harwell. New York, London and Toronto: Longman, Green And Co., 1955.

Tenney, Luman Harris. *War Diary of Luman Harris Tenney 1861–1865*. Cleveland, Ohio: Evangelical Publishing House, 1914.

Traylor, John H. "Battle of Cedar Creek," *Confederate Veteran*, X (1902).

A Troopers Adventures in the War For The Union, By A Cavalryman. New York: Hurst And Company, Publishers, n.d.

Tyler, Mason Whiting. *Recollections of the Civil War*, Edited by William S. Tyler. New York and London: G. P. Putnam's Sons, The Knickerbocker Press, 1912.

Van Alstyne, Lawrence. *Diary of An Enlisted Man*. New Haven, Conn.: The Tuttle, Morehouse & Taylor Company, 1910.

Watts, M. S. "General Battle And The Stolen Colt," *Confederate Veteran*, XXX (1922).

White, P. J. "Recollections of Battle At Winchester," *Confederate Veteran*, XV (1907).

Williams, Charles Richard, (editor). *Diary And Letters of Rutherford Birchard Hayes*, Vol. II. Columbus: The Ohio State Archaeological and Historical Society, 1922.

Wilson, William A. *A Borderland Confederate*, Edited by Festus P. Summers. Pittsburgh: University of Pittsburgh Press, 1962.

Worsham, John H. *One Of Jackson's Foot Cavalry*, Edited by James I. Robertson, Jr., Jackson, Tenn.: McCowat-Mercer Press, Inc., 1964.

Zell, Robert R. "The Raid Into Pennsylvania – The First Armored Train," *Confederate Veteran*, XXVIII (1920).

UNIT HISTORIES

Alexander, John H. *Mosby's Men*. New York and Washington: The Neale Publishing Company, 1907.

Beecher, Harris H. *Record of the 114th Regiment, N.Y.S.V.* Norwich, N.Y.: J. F. Hubbard, Jr., 1866.

Benedict, G. G. *Vermont In The Civil War: A History of the Part Taken by the Vermont Soldiers And Sailors in the War For The Union, 1861–5, Two Volumes.* Burlington, VT.: The Free Press Association, 1886–1888.

Bennett, A. J. *The Story of the First Massachusetts Light Battery, Attached to the Sixth Corps.* Boston: Press of Deland and Barta, 1886.

Best, Isaac O. *History of the 121st New York State Infantry.* Chicago, Ill.: Lieut. J. H. Smith, 1921.

Bidwell, Frederick David, (compiler). *History of the Forty-Ninth New York Volunteers.* Albany: J. B. Lyon Company, Printers, 1916.

Boudrye (Beaudry), Louis N. *Historic Records of the Fifth New York Cavalry, First Ira Harris Guard . . .* Albany, N.Y.: S. R. Gray, 1865.

Bowen, James L. *History of the Thirty-seventh Regiment Mass. Volunteers, In the Civil War of 1861–1865 .* Holyoke, Mass., and New York City: Clark W. Bryan & Company, Publishers, 1884.

Bowen, J. R. *Regimental History of the First New York Dragoons (Originally the 130th N.Y. Vol. Infantry) During Three Years Of Active Service In The Great Civil War.* n.p.: J. R. Bowen, 1900.

Buffum, F. H. *A Memorial of The Great Rebellion: Being A History Of The Fourteenth Regiment New-Hampshire Volunteers, Covering Its Three Years Of Service, With Original Sketches Of Army Life, 1861–1865 .* Boston: Franklin Press: Rand, Avery, & Company, 1882.

Carpenter, George N. *History of The Eighth Regiment Vermont Volunteers, 1861–1865.* Boston: Press Of Deland & Barta, 1886.

Cheney, Newel. *History of the Ninth Regiment, New York Volunteer Cavalry, War Of 1861 To 1865.* Poland Center, N.Y.: Martin Merz & Son, 1901.

Clark, Orton S. *The One Hundred And Sixteenth Regiment Of New York State Volunteers.* Buffalo: Printing House of Matthews & Warren, 1868.

Clark, Walter, (editor). *Histories of the Several Regiments and Battalions From North Carolina, in the Great War 1861–'65.* Written by Members of the Respective Commands, 5 Vols. Pub. by the State. Raleigh, N.C.: E. M. Uzzell, Printer, 1901.

Crawford, J. Marshall. *Mosby And His Men: A Record Of The Adventures Of That Renowned Partisan Ranger, John S. Mosby.* New York: G. W. Carleton & Co., Publishers, 1867.

Denison, Frederic. *Sabres And Spurs: The First Regiment Rhode Island Cavalry in the Civil War, 1861–1865 .* Central Parks, R.I.: Press of E. L. Freeman & Co., 1876.

Dickert, D. Augustus. *History of Kershaw's Brigade With Complete Roll of Companies, Biographical Sketches, Incidents, Anecdotes, Etc.* Newberry, S.C.: Elbert H. Aull Co., 1899; reprint edition, with Introduction by Dr. Wm. Stanley Hoole, Dayton, Ohio: Press of Morningside Bookshop, 1973.

Ewer, James K. *The Third Massachusetts Cavalry in the War For The Union.* Maplewood, Mass.: Historical Committee of The Regimental Association, 1903.

Ewing, E. E. *Bugles And Bells; Or, Stories Told Again, Including The Story of the Ninety-first Ohio Volunteer Infantry.* Cincinnati: Press of Curtis & Jennings, 1899.

Farrar, Samuel Clarke. *The Twenty-Second Pennsylvania Cavalry and the Ringgold Battalion 1861–1865 .* Pittsburgh: The New Werner Company, 1911.

Foster, Alonzo. *Reminiscences and Record of the 6th New York V. V. Cavalry.* n.p.: Alonzo Foster, 1892.

Gilson, J. H., (compiler). *Concise History of the One Hundred and Twenty-sixth Regiment, Ohio Volunteer Infantry, From the Date of Organization to the End of the Rebellion; with a Complete Roster Of Each Company.* Salem, Ohio: Walton, Steam Job And Label Printer, 1883.

Goldsborough, W. W. *The Maryland Line in the Confederate Army, 1861–1865 .* Reprint edition, Port Washington, N. Y. and London: Kennikat Press, 1972.

Gould, John M. *History of the First-Tenth-Twenty-ninth Maine Regiment.* Portland: Stephen Berry, 1871.

Gracey, S. L. *Annals of the Sixth Pennsylvania Cavalry.* Philadelphia: E. H. Butler & Co., 1868.

Haines, Alanson A. *History Of The Fifteenth Regiment New Jersey Volunteers.* New York: Jenkins & Thomas, Printers, 1883.

Hall, Hillman A., *et al*, (compilers). *History of the Sixth New York Cavalry (Second Ira Harris Guard), Second Brigade — First Division — Cavalry Corps, Army Of The Potomac 1861–1865.* Worcester, Mass.: The Blanchard Press, 1908.

Hanaburgh, D. H. *History of the One Hundred And Twenty-eight Regiment, New York Volunteers (U.S. Infantry) In The Late Civil War.* Pokeepsie, N.Y.: Press of Enterprise Publishing Company, 1894.

Haynes, E. M. *A History of the Tenth Regiment, Vermont Volunteers . . .* Lewiston, Me.: Journal Steam Press, 1870.

Hewitt, William. *History of the Twelfth West Virginia Volunteer Infantry: The Part It Took in the War of the Rebellion 1861–1865.* n.p.: Published by the Twelfth West Virginia Infantry Association, (1892).

Howell, Helena Adelaide (compiler). *Chronicles of the One hundred fifty-first Regiment New York State Volunteer Infantry 1862–1865, Contributed By Its Surviving Members.* Albion, N.Y.: A. M. Eddy, Printer, 1911.

Hutchinson, Nelson V. *History of the Seventh Massachusetts Volunteer Infantry in the War of the Rebellion of the Southern States Against Constitutional Authority, 1861–1865.* Taunton, Mass.: Published by Authority of the Regimental Association, 1890.

Irwin, Richard B. *History of the Nineteenth Army Corps.* New York & London: G. P. Putnam's Sons, The Knickbocker Press, 1892.

Isham, Asa B. *An Historical Sketch of the Seventh Regiment Michigan Volunteer Cavalry: From Its Organization, In 1862, To Its Muster Out, In 1865.* New York: Town Topics Publishing Company, (1893).

Jones, Samuel C. *Reminiscences of the Twenty-Second Iowa Volunteer Infantry.* Iowa City, Iowa: S. C. Jones, 1907.

Keyes, Charles M., (editor). *The Military History of the 123d Regiment of Ohio Volunteer Infantry.* Sandusky: Register Press, 1874.

Lee, William O., (compiler). *Personal and Historical Sketches And Facial History Of And By Members Of The Seventh Regiment Michigan Volunteer Cavalry 1862–1865.* Detroit: 7th Michigan Cavalry Association, (1902).

Lewis, Osceola. *One Hundred and Thirty-Eighth Regiment, Pennsylvania Volunteer Infantry.* Norristown, Pa.: Wills, Iredell & Jenkins, 1866.

Lincoln, William S. *Life With The Thirty-Fourth Mass. Infantry In The War Of The Rebellion.* Worcester: Press Of Noyes, Snow & Company, 1879.

Lufkin, Edwin B. *History of the Thirteenth Maine Regiment From Its Organization In 1861 To Its Muster-out In 1865.* Bridgton, Me.: H. A. Shorey & Son, Publishers, 1898.

Mark, Penrose G. *Red: White: and Blue Badge: Pennsylvania Veteran Volunteers, A History of the 93rd Regiment. . .* Harrisburg, PA.: The Aughinbaugh Press, 1911.

McDonald, William N. *A History Of The Laurel Brigade, Originally The Ashby Cavalry of the Army of Northern Virginia And Chew's Battery,* Edited by Bushrod C. Washington. Baltimore: Kate S. McDonald, 1907; Reprint edition, Arlington, Virginia: R. W. Beatty, Ltd., 1969.

Moyer, H. P., (compiler). *History of the Seventeenth Regiment Pennsylvania Volunteer Cavalry or One Hundred And Sixty-second In The Line of Pennsylvania Volunteer Regiments, War to Suppress the Rebellion, 1861–1865.* Lebanon, Pa.: Sowers Printing Company, 1911.

Murray, Thomas Hamilton. *History of the Ninth Regiment, Connecticut Volunteer Infantry, "The Irish Regiment," In The War Of The Rebellion, 1861-65.* New Haven, Conn.: The Price, Lee & Adkins Co., 1903.

Myers, Frank M. *The Comanches: A History of White's Battalion, Virginia Cavalry, Laurel Brig., Hampton Div.,* A.N.V., C.S.A. Baltimore: Kelly, Piet & Co., Publishers, 1871; Reprint edition, Marietta, Georgia: Continental Book Company, 1956.

Newcomer, C. Armour. *Cole's Cavalry; or Three Years In The Saddle in the Shenandoah Valley.* Baltimore: Cushing & Company, 1895.

Norton, Henry, (editor and compiler). *Deeds Of Daring or History of the Eighth N.Y. Volunteer Cavalry.* Norwich, N.Y.: Chenango Telegraph Printing House, 1889.

Pellet, Elias P. *History of the 114th Regiment, New York State Volunteers.* Norwich, N.Y.: Telegraph & Chronicle Power Press Print., 1866.

Perkins, George. *A Summer In Maryland and Virginia, Or Campaigning with the 149th Ohio Volunteer Infantry.* Chillicothe, Ohio: The Scholl Printing Company, n.d.

Pickerill, W. N. *History of the Third Indiana Cavalry.* Indianapolis, Indiana: Aetna Printing Co., 1906.

Powers, George W. *The Story of the Thirty Eighth Regiment of Massachusetts Volunteers.* Boston: Dakin and Metcalf, 1866.

Prowell, George R. *History of the Eighty-Seventh Regiment, Pennsylvania Volunteers.* York, Pa.: Press of the York Daily, 1903.

Rawling, Charles J. *History of the First Regiment Virginia Infantry.* Philadelphia: J. B. Lippincott Company, 1887.

Reader, Frank S. *History of the Fifth West Virginia Cavalry, Formerly The Second Virginia Infantry, and of Battery G, First West Va. Light Artillery.* New Brighton, PA.: Daily News, Frank S. Reader, Editor and Prop'r, 1890.

Rodenbough, Theodore F., Henry C. Potter and William P. Seal, (compilers and editors). *History of the Eighteenth Regiment of Cavalry Pennsylvania Volunteers (163d Regiment of the Line) 1862-1865.* New York: Wynkoop Hallenbeck Crawford Co., 1909.

Roe, Alfred Seelye. *The Ninth New York Heavy Artillery.* Worcester, Mass.: Published By The Author, 1899.

Slease, William Davis. *The Fourteenth Pennsylvania in the Civil War.* Pittsburgh, Pa.: Art Engraving & Printing Co., n.d.

Smith, W. A. *The Anson Guards: Company C, Fourteenth Regiment North Carolina Volunteers 1861-1865.* Charlotte, N.C.: Stone Publishing Co., 1914; reprint edition, Wendell, N.C.: Broadfoot's Bookmark, 1978.

Sprague, Homer B. *History of the 13th Infantry Regiment of Connecticut Volunteers, During The Great Rebellion.* Hartford, Conn.: Case, Lockwood & Co., 1867.

Stevens, George T. *Three Years in the Sixth Corps. A Concise Narrative of Events in the Army of the Potomac, From 1861 To the Close of the Rebellion, April, 1865.* Albany: S. R. Gray, Publisher, 1866.

Sumner, George C. *Battery D, First Rhode Island Light Artillery, In The Civil War, 1861-1865.* Providence: Rhode Island Printing Company, 1897.

Sutton, Joseph J. *History of the Second Regiment West Virginia Cavalry Volunteers During The War Of The Rebellion.* Portsmouth, Ohio: Joseph J. Sutton, 1892.

Terrill, J. Newton. *Campaign of the Fourteenth Regiment New Jersey Volunteers,* Second Edition. New Brunswick, N.J.: Daily Home News Press, 1884.

Thomas, Henry W. *History of the Doles-Cook Brigade Army of Northern Virginia,* C.S.A. Atlanta, Ga.: The Franklin Printing and Publishing Company, 1903; reprint edition, Dayton, Ohio: Press of Morningside Bookshop, 1981.

Tiemann, William F., (compiler). *The 159th Regiment Infantry, New-York State Volun-*

teers, in the War Of The Rebellion, 1862–1865. Brooklyn, N.Y.: William F. Tiemann, 1891.

Vaill, Theodore F. *History of the Second Connecticut Volunteer Heavy Artillery. Originally The Nineteenth Connecticut Vols.* Winsted, Conn.: Winsted Printing Company, 1868.

Waite, Otis F. R. *New Hampshire in the Great Rebellion.* Claremont, N.H.: Tracy, Chase & Company, 1870.

Walker, Aldace F. *The Vermont Brigade in the Shenandoah Valley, 1864.* Burlington, VT.: The Free Press Association, 1869.

Walker, William C. *History of The Eighteenth Regiment Conn. Volunteers in The War For The Union.* Norwich, Conn.: Published By The Committee, 1885.

Westbrook, Robert S. *History of the 49th Pennsylvania Volunteers.* Altoona, Pa.: Altoona Times Print, 1898.

Wildes, Thos. F. *Record of the One Hundred And Sixteenth Regiment Ohio Infantry Volunteers in the War Of The Rebellion.* Sandusky, Ohio: I. F. Mack & Bro., Printers, 1884.

Williamson, James J. *Mosby's Rangers: A Record Of The Operations of the Forty-third Battalion Virginia Cavalry.* New York: Ralph B. Kenyon, Publisher, 1896.

Wise, Jennings Cropper. *The Long Arm of Lee: The History of the Artillery of the Army of Northern Virginia.* Lynchburg, Virginia: J. P. Bell Company, Inc., 1915; reprint edition, New York: Oxford University Press, Inc., 1959.

NEWSPAPERS

National Tribune.
New York *Herald.*
New York *Times.*
Richmond *Enquirer.*
Washington *Daily National Intelligencer.*

SECONDARY SOURCES

Baker, Liva. "The Burning of Chambersburg," *American Heritage,* Volume XXIV, Number 5 (August 1973).

Bean, W. G. *Stonewall's Man: Sandie Pendleton.* Chapel Hill: The University of North Carolina Press, 1959.

Black, Robert C. III. *The Railroads of the Confederacy.* Chapel Hill: The University of North Carolina Press, 1952.

Brice, Marshall Moore. *Conquest Of A Valley.* Charlottesville: The University Press of Virginia, 1965.

Buckeridge, J. O. *Lincoln's Choice.* Harrisburg, Pennsylvania: The Stackpole Company, 1956.

Buffum, Francis H. *Sheridan's Veterans: A Souvenir of their Two Campaigns in the Shenandoah Valley, Volume I.* Boston, Mass.: W. F. Brown & Company, Printers, 1883.

Bushong, Millard Kessler, PhD. *Old Jube: A Biography of General Jubal A. Early.* Boyce, Virginia: Carr Publishing Company, Inc., 1955.

Cartmell, T. K. *Shenandoah Valley Pioneers and Their Descendants: A History of Frederick County, Virginia From its Formation in 1738 to 1908.* Reprint edition, Berryville, Virginia: Chesapeake Book Company, 1963.

Catton, Bruce. *The Army Of The Potomac: Glory Road.* Garden City, New York: Doubleday & Company, Inc., 1952.

———. *The Centennial History of the Civil War, Volume Three: Never Call Retreat.* Garden City, New York: Doubleday & Company, Inc., 1965.

————. *Grant Moves South.* Boston and Toronto: Little, Brown And Company, 1960.
————. *Grant Takes Command.* Boston and Toronto: Little, Brown And Company, 1968.
————. *A Stillness at Appomattox.* Garden City, New York: Doubleday & Company, Inc., 1953.
Connolly, John R. "Prelude to Victory: Sheridan and the Shenandoah Valley Campaign of 1864." American History and Literature Honors paper, Williams College, May 1962.
Coulter, E. Merton. *The Confederate States of America 1861–1865,* A History Of The South, Volume VII, Edited by Wendell Holmes Stephenson and E. Merton Coulter. Baton Rouge: Louisiana State University Press, 1950.
Cox, William R. *Address on the Life And Character of Maj. Gen. Stephen D. Ramseur.* Raleigh: E. M. Uzzell, Steam Printer And Binder, 1891.
Cullen, Joseph P. "Cedar Creek," *Civil War Times Illustrated,* Vol VIII, No. 8 (December 1969).
————. "Sheridan Wins at Winchester," *Civil War Times Illustrated,* Vol. VI, No. 2 (May 1967).
Davis, William C. *The Battle of New Market.* Garden City, New York: Doubleday & Company, Inc., 1975.
Foote, Shelby. *The Civil War—A Narrative: Red River to Appomattox.* New York: Random House, 1974.
Freeman, Douglas S. *Lee's Lieutenants: A Study In Command.* New York: Charles Scribner's Sons, 1942–44.
————. *R. E. Lee: A Biography.* New York: Charles Scribner's Sons, 1932–34.
Hale, Laura Virginia. *Four Valiant Years: In The Lower Shenandoah Valley 1861–1865.* Strasburg: Shenandoah Publishing House, Inc., 1968.
Horst, Samuel. *Mennonites In The Confederacy: A Study in Civil War Pacifism.* Scottdale, Pennsylvania: Herald Press, 1967.
Jones, Virgil Carrington. *Ranger Mosby.* Chapel Hill: The University of North Carolina Press, 1944.
Kellogg, Sanford C. *The Shenandoah Valley and Virginia, 1861 to 1865: A War Study.* New York & Washington: The Neale Publishing Company, 1903.
Kennon, L. W. V. "The Valley Campaign Of 1864: A Military Study," *The Shenandoah Campaigns Of 1862 And 1864 And The Appomattox Campaign 1865: Papers Of The Military Historical Society Of Massachusetts,* Vol. VI. Boston: The Military Historical Society of Massachusetts, 1907.
Krick, Robert K. *Lee's Colonels: A Biographical Register of the Field Officers of the Army of Northern Virginia.* Dayton, Ohio: Press of Morningside Bookshop, 1979.
Lang, Theodore F. *Loyal West Virginia From 1861 To 1865.* Baltimore, MD.: The Deutsch Publishing Co., 1895.
Long, E. B., with Barbara Long, *The Civil War Day by Day: An Almanac 1861–1865,* Foreword by Bruce Catton. Garden City, New York: Doubleday & Company, Inc., 1971.
Matheny, H. E. *Major General Thomas Maley Harris.* Parsons, West Virginia: McClain Printing Company, 1963.
McDonald, Archie P., (editor). *Make Me A Map Of The Valley: The Civil War Journal Of Stonewall Jackson's Topographer,* Foreword by T. Harry Williams. Dallas: Southern Methodist University Press, 1973.
McWhiney, Grady and Perry D. Jamieson. *Attack and Die: Civil War Military Tactics and the Southern Heritage.* University, Alabama: The University of Alabama Press, 1982.
Meaney, Peter J., O.S.B. *The Civil War Engagement at Cool Spring July 18, 1864.* Morristown, N.J.: Peter J. Meaney, O.S.B., 1979.

Merington, Marguerite, (editor). *The Custer Story: The Life and Intimate Letters of General George A. Custer and His Wife Elizabeth.* New York: The Devin-Adair Company, 1950.

Michie, Peter S. *The Life And Letters of Emory Upton.* New York: D. Appleton, 1885; Reprint edition, New York: Arn Press, 1979.

"The Monument To Mosby's Men," *Southern Historical Society Papers,* XXVII (1899).

Naroll, Raoul S. "Sheridan And Cedar Creek—A Reappraisal," *Military Analysis Of The Civil War: An Anthology by the Editors of Military Affairs,* Introduction by T. Harry Williams. Millwood, N.Y.: KTO Press, 1977.

Nevins, Allan. *The War for the Union, Volume IV: The Organized War To Victory, 1864–1865.* New York: Charles Scribner's Sons, 1971.

Nicolay, John G. and John Hay. *Abraham Lincoln: A History.* New York: The Century Co., 1890.

Norris, J. E., (editor). *History of the Lower Shenandoah Valley Counties of Frederick, Berkeley, Jefferson, And Clarke.* Chicago: A. Warner & Co., Publishers, 1890; reprint edition, Berryville, Virginia: Virginia Book Company, 1972.

Nye, Wilbur Sturtevant. *Here Come The Rebels!* Baton Rouge: Louisiana State University Press, 1965.

O'Connor, Richard. *Sheridan the Inevitable.* Indianapolis and New York: The Bobbs-Merrill Company, Inc., 1953.

Pond, George E. *The Shenandoah Valley In 1864.* New York: Charles Scribner's Sons, 1883.

Porter, Charles H. "Operations Of Generals Sigel And Hunter In The Shenandoah Valley, May And June, 1864," *The Shenandoah Campaigns Of 1862 And 1864 And The Appomattox Campaign 1865, Papers Of The Military Historical Society Of Massachusetts, Vol. VI.* Boston: The Military Historical Society Of Massachusetts, 1907.

Quarles, Garland R. *Occupied Winchester 1861–1865.* Winchester, Virginia: Farmers & Merchants National Bank, 1976.

Randall, J. G. and Current, Richard N. *Lincoln, The President: Last Full Measure.* New York: Dodd, Mead & Company, 1955.

Robertson, James I., Jr. *The Stonewall Brigade.* Baton Rouge: Louisiana State University Press, 1963.

Schaub, J. L. "Gen. Robert E. Rodes," *Confederate Veteran,* XVIII (1908).

Skoch, George F., (editor). "With a Special in the Shenandoah," *Civil War Times Illustrated,* Vol. XXI, No. 2 (April 1982).

Smith, Channing M. "Survivors Of Mosby's Command," *Confederate Veteran,* XXXI (1923).

Smith, Everard Hall. "The General and the Valley: Union Leadership During the Threat to Washington in 1864," Ph.D. Dissertation, University of North Carolina, 1977.

Sommers, Richard J. *Richmond Redeemed: The Siege at Petersburg.* Garden City, New York: Doubleday & Company, Inc., 1981.

Stackpole, Edward J. *Sheridan In The Shenandoah: Jubal Early's Nemesis.* Harrisburg, Pa.: Stackpole Co., 1961.

Steadman, Charles M. "Gen. Stephen Dodson Ramseur," *Confederate Veteran,* XXVIII (1920).

Stern, Philip Van Doren. *Soldier Life in the Union and Confederate Armies.* Bloomington: Indiana University Press, 1961.

Stevens, Sylvester K. *Pennsylvania: Birthplace Of A Nation.* New York: Random House, 1964.

Sword, Wiley. "Cavalry on Trial at Kelly's Ford," *Civil War Times Illustrated,* Vol. XIII, No. 1 (April 1974).

Tankersley, Allen P. *John B. Gordon: A Study In Gallantry.* Atlanta, Georgia: The Whitehall Press, 1955.

Tanner, Robert G. *Stonewall In The Valley: Thomas J. "Stonewall" Jackson's Shenandoah Valley Campaign Spring 1862.* Garden City, New York: Doubleday & Company, Inc., 1976.

Thompson, Paul Singer. "The Summer Campaign In The Lower Valley 1864," Ph.D. Dissertation, University of Virginia, 1966.

Vandiver, Frank E. *Jubal's Raid: General Early's Famous Attack On Washington In 1864.* New York: McGraw-Hill Book Company, 1960; reprint edition, Westport, Connecticut: Greenwood Press, Publishers, 1974.

Warner, Ezra J. *Generals In Blue: Lives of the Union Commanders.* Baton Rouge: Louisiana State University Press, 1964.

————. *Generals In Gray: Lives of the Confederate Commanders.* Baton Rouge: Louisiana State University Press, 1959.

Wayland, John W. *A History of Rockingham County, Virginia.* Dayton, Virginia: Ruebush-Elkins Company, 1912.

————. *A History of Shenandoah County, Virginia.* Strasburg: Shenandoah Publishing House, 1927.

————. *Virginia Valley Records: Genealogical and Historical Materials of Rockingham County, Virginia and Related Regions.* Reprint edition, Baltimore: Genealogical Publishing Company, 1965.

Wellman, Manly Wade. *Rebel Boast: First At Bethel—Last At Appomattox.* New York: Henry Holt And Company, 1956.

Wert, Jeffry D. "Attacking The Invincible," *Civil War Times Illustrated,* Vol. XX, No. 10 (February 1982).

————. "The Confederate Belle," *Civil War Times Illustrated,* Vol. XV, No. 5 (August 1976).

————. "'First Fair Chance,'" *Civil War Times Illustrated,* Vol. XVIII, No. 5 (August 1979).

————. "George Crook: Sheridan's Second Fiddle," *Civil War Times Illustrated,* Vol. XXII, No. 8 (December 1983).

————. "In One Deadly Encounter," *Civil War Times Illustrated,* Vol. XIX, No. 7 (November 1980).

————. "'Old John,'" *Civil War Times Illustrated,* Vol. XX, No. 2 (May 1981).

————. "Old Jubilee's Last Battle," *Civil War Times Illustrated,* Vol. XVI, No. 5 (August 1977).

————. "Robert E. Rodes," *Civil War Times Illustrated,* Vol. XVI, No. 8 (December 1977).

————. "The Snicker's Gap War," *Civil War Times Illustrated,* Vol. XVII, No. 4 (July 1978).

————. "Spotsylvania: Charge On The Mule Shoe," *Civil War Times Illustrated,* Vol. XXII, No. 2 (April 1983).

————. "Stephen D. Ramseur," *Civil War Times Illustrated,* Vol. XII, No. 2 (May 1973).

————. "The Third Battle of Winchester," *American History Illustrated,* Vol. XV, No. 7 (November 1980).

————. "Woodstock Races," *Civil War Times Illustrated,* Vol. XIX, No. 2 (May 1980).

Wharton, J. U. H. "Major Gen. Gabriel C. Wharton," *Confederate Veteran,* XIII (1900).

White, P. J. "Gen. Robert E. Rodes," *Confederate Veteran,* XXXV (1927).

Wiley, Bell I. "The Common Soldier of the Civil War," *Civil War Times Illustrated,* Vol. XII, No. 4 (July 1973).

————. *The Life of Billy Yank: The Common Soldier of the Union.* Indianapolis and New York: The Bobbs-Merrill Company, Publishers, 1951.

Williams, T. Harry. *Lincoln And His Generals.* New York: Vintage Books, 1967.

Table of Organizations

Army of the Shenandoah
Maj. Gen. Philip H. Sheridan
Maj. Gen. Horatio G. Wright

Headquarters Escort
6th U.S. Cavalry
17th Pennsylvania Cavalry (detachment)

Sixth Army Corps
Maj. Gen. Horatio G. Wright
Brig. Gen. James B. Ricketts
Brig. Gen. George W. Getty

First Division:
Brig. Gen. David A. Russell
Brig. Gen. Emory Upton
Col. Oliver Edwards
Brig. Gen. Frank Wheaton

First Brigade:
Lt. Col. Edward L. Campbell

4th New Jersey	15th New Jersey
10th New Jersey	

Second Brigade:
Brig. Gen. Emory Upton
Col. Joseph E. Hamblin
Col. Ranald S. MacKenzie
Lt. Col. Egbert Olcott

2nd Connecticut Heavy Artillery	95th Pennsylvania
65th New York	96th Pennsylvania
121st New York	

Third Brigade:
Col. Oliver Edwards
Col. Isaac C. Bassett

37th Massachusetts	119th Pennsylvania
49th Pennsylvania	2nd Rhode Island (battalion)
82nd Pennsylvania	5th Wisconsin (battalion)

Second Division:
Brig. Gen. George W. Getty
Brig. Gen. Lewis A. Grant

First Brigade:
Brig. Gen. Frank Wheaton
Col. James M. Warner

62nd New York	102nd Pennsylvania
93rd Pennsylvania	139th Pennsylvania
98th Pennsylvania	

Second Brigade:
Col. James M. Warner
Brig. Gen. Lewis A. Grant
Lt. Col. Amasa S. Tracy

2nd Vermont	5th Vermont
3rd Vermont	6th Vermont
4th Vermont	11th Vermont

Third Brigade:
Brig. Gen. Daniel D. Bidwell
Lt. Col. Winsor B. French

7th Maine	77th New York
43rd New York	122nd New York
49th New York (battalion)	61st Pennsylvania (battalion)

Third Division:
Brig. Gen. James B. Ricketts
Col. J. Warren Keifer

First Brigade:
Col. William Emerson

14th New Jersey	184th New York (battalion)
106th New York	87th Pennsylvania
151st New York	10th Vermont

Second Brigade:
Col. J. Warren Keifer
Col. William H. Ball

6th Maryland	126th Ohio
9th New York	67th Pennsylvania
110th Ohio	138th Pennsylvania
122nd Ohio	

Artillery Brigade:
Col. Charles H. Tompkins

Maine Light, 5th Battery (E)	1st Rhode Island Light, Battery C
Massachusetts Light, 1st Battery (A)	1st Rhode Island Light, Battery G
New York Light, 1st Battery	5th United States, Battery M

Nineteenth Corps
Bvt. Maj. Gen. William H. Emory

First Division:
Brig. Gen. William Dwight
Brig. Gen. James W. McMillan

First Brigade:
Col. George L. Beal
Col. Edwin P. Davis

29th Maine	114th New York
30th Massachusetts	116th New York
90th New York	153rd New York

Second Brigade:
Brig. Gen. James W. McMillan
Col. Stephen Thomas

12th Connecticut
160th New York

47th Pennsylvania
8th Vermont

Third Brigade:
Col. Leonard D. H. Currie

30th Maine
133rd New York
162nd New York

165th New York (six companies)
173rd New York

Artillery:
New York Light, 5th Battery

Second Division:
Brig. Gen. Cuvier Grover
Brig. Gen. Henry W. Birge

First Brigade:
Brig. Gen. Henry W. Birge
Col. Thomas W. Porter

9th Connecticut
12th Maine
14th Maine

26th Massachusetts
14th New Hampshire
75th New York

Second Brigade:
Col. Edward L. Molineux

13th Connecticut
11th Indiana
22nd Iowa

3rd Massachusetts Cavalry
(dismounted)
131st New York
159th New York

Third Brigade:
Col. Jacob Sharpe
Lt. Col. Alfred Neafie
Col. Daniel Macauley

38th Massachusetts
128th New York
156th New York

175th New York (battalion)
176th New York

Fourth Brigade:
Col. David Shunk

8th Indiana
18th Indiana

24th Iowa
28th Iowa

Artillery:
Maine Light, 1st Battery

Reserve Artillery:
Capt. Elijah Taft
Maj. Albert W. Bradbury

Indiana Light, 17th Battery

1st Rhode Island Light,
Battery D

Army of West Virginia
Bvt. Maj. Gen. George Crook

First Division:
Col. Joseph Thoburn
Col. Thomas M. Harris

First Brigade:
Col. George D. Wells
Lt. Col. Thomas F. Wildes

34th Massachusetts	116th Ohio
5th New York Heavy Artillery, 2nd Battalion	123rd Ohio

Second Brigade:
Lt. Col. Robert S. Northcott
Col. William B. Curtis

1st West Virginia	12th West Virginia
4th West Virginia	

Third Brigade:
Col. Thomas M. Harris
Col. Milton Wells

23rd Illinois (battalion)	11th West Virginia
54th Pennsylvania	15th West Virginia
10th West Virginia	

Second Division:
Col. Isaac H. Duval
Col. Rutherford B. Hayes

First Brigade:
Col. Rutherford B. Hayes
Col. Hiram F. Devol

23rd Ohio	5th West Virginia (battalion)
36th Ohio	13th West Virginia

Second Brigade:
Col. Daniel D. Johnson
Lt. Col. Benjamin F. Coates

34th Ohio (battalion)	9th West Virginia
91st Ohio	14th West Virginia

Artillery Brigade:
Capt. Henry A. DuPont

1st Ohio Light, Battery L	5th United States, Battery B
1st Pennsylvania Light, Battery D	

Cavalry
Bvt. Maj. Gen. Alfred T. A. Torbert

Escort
1st Rhode Island

First Division:
Brig. Gen Wesley Merritt

First Brigade:
Brig. Gen. George A. Custer
Col. James H. Kidd

1st Michigan   7th Michigan
5th Michigan   25th New York
6th Michigan

Second Brigade:
Bvt. Brig. Gen. Thomas C. Devin
4th New York   19th New York (1st Dragoons)
6th New York   17th Pennsylvania
9th New York

Reserve Brigade:
Col. Charles R. Lowell, Jr.
Lt. Col. Casper Crowninshield
2nd Massachusetts   2nd United States
6th Pennsylvania   5th United States
1st United States

Artillery:
New York Light Artillery, 6th Battery   1st U.S. Artillery, Batteries
                                              K and L

Second Division:
Bvt. Maj. Gen. William W. Averell
Brig. Gen. George A. Custer
Col. William H. Powell

First Brigade:
Col. James M. Schoonmaker
Col. Alpheus S. Moore
8th Ohio (detachment)   22nd Pennsylvania
14th Pennsylvania

Second Brigade:
Col. Henry Capehart
1st New York   2nd West Virginia
1st West Virginia   3rd West Virginia

Artillery:
5th United States, Battery L

Third Division:
Brig. Gen. James H. Wilson
Brig. Gen. George A. Custer

First Brigade:
Brig. Gen. John B. McIntosh
Lt. Col. George A. Purington
Col. Alexander C. M. Pennington
1st Connecticut   5th New York
3rd New Jersey   2nd Ohio
2nd New York   18th Pennsylvania

Second Brigade:
Brig. Gen. George H. Chapman
Col. William Wells
3rd Indiana (two companies)   22nd New York
1st New Hampshire (battalion)   1st Vermont
8th New York

Horse Artillery:
2nd United States, Batteries B and L   3rd United States, Batteries C,
F and K

Provisional Division:
J. Howard Kitching*

*Engaged only at Cedar Creek.

Army of the Valley
Lt. Gen. Jubal A. Early

Breckinridge's Corps
Maj. Gen. John C. Breckinridge
Unofficial command consisted of the divisions of John B. Gordon and
Gabriel C. Wharton from June 27 to September 21 and directed by Breck-
inridge.

Second Corps
Maj. Gen. John B. Gordon

Rodes's Division:
Maj. Gen. Robert E. Rodes
Maj. Gen. Stephen D. Ramseur

Battle's Brigade:
Brig. Gen. Cullen A. Battle
Lt. Col. Edwin L. Hobson
3rd Alabama   12th Alabama
5th Alabama   61st Alabama
6th Alabama

Grimes's Brigade:
Brig. Gen. Bryan Grimes
32nd North Carolina   43rd North Carolina
53rd North Carolina   45th North Carolina
2nd North Carolina Battalion

Cook's Brigade:
Brig. Gen. Philip Cook
4th Georgia   21st Georgia
12th Georgia   44th Georgia

Cox's Brigade:
Brig. Gen. William R. Cox
1st North Carolina   4th North Carolina
2nd North Carolina   14th North Carolina
3rd North Carolina   30th North Carolina

Ramseur's Division:
Maj. Gen. Stephen D. Ramseur
Brig. Gen. John Pegram

Pegram's Brigade:
Brig. Gen. John Pegram
Col. John S. Hoffman

13th Virginia
31st Virginia
49th Virginia

52nd Virginia
58th Virginia

Johnston's Brigade:
Brig. Gen. Robert D. Johnston

5th North Carolina
12th North Carolina
20th North Carolina

23rd North Carolina
1st North Carolina Battalion
Sharpshooters

Godwin's Brigade:
Brig. Gen. Archibald C. Godwin
Lt. Col. William S. Davis

6th North Carolina
21st North Carolina

54th North Carolina
57th North Carolina

Gordon's Division:
Maj. Gen. John B. Gordon
Brig. Gen. Clement A. Evans

Evans's Brigade:
Brig. Gen. Clement A. Evans
Col. Edmund N. Atkinson
Col. John H. Lowe

13th Georgia
26th Georgia
31st Georgia
38th Georgia

60th Georgia
61st Georgia
12th Georgia Battalion

Terry's Brigade:
Brig. Gen. William Terry*

2nd Virginia
4th Virginia
5th Virginia
27th Virginia
33rd Virginia
21st Virginia
25th Virginia

42nd Virginia
44th Virginia
48th Virginia
50th Virginia
10th Virginia
23rd Virginia
37th Virginia

York's Brigade:
Brig. Gen. Zebulon York**
Col. Edmund Pendleton

5th Louisiana
6th Louisiana
7th Louisiana
8th Louisiana
9th Louisiana

1st Louisiana
14th Louisiana
2nd Louisiana
10th Louisiana
15th Louisiana

* This command consisted of the fragments of fourteen regiments which had formed the Stonewall Division.
** Remnants of two Louisiana brigades merged into one command.

Wharton's Division
Brig. Gen. Gabriel C. Wharton

Wharton's Brigade:
Col. Augustus Forsberg
Capt. Robert H. Logan

45th Virginia	51st Virginia
50th Virginia	30th Virginia Battalion
	Sharpshooters

Patton's Brigade:
Col. George S. Patton
Capt. Edmund S. Read
Lt. Col. John C. McDonald

22nd Virginia	26th Virginia Battalion
23rd Virginia Battalion	

Smith's Brigade:
Col. Thomas Smith

36th Virginia	45th Virginia Battalion
60th Virginia	Thomas Legion

Kershaw's Division
Maj. Gen. Joseph B. Kershaw

Kershaw's Brigade:
Col. John W. Henagan
Brig. Gen. James Conner
Maj. James M. Goggin

2nd South Carolina	15th South Carolina
3rd South Carolina	20th South Carolina
7th South Carolina	3rd South Carolina Battalion
8th South Carolina	

Humphreys's Brigade:
Brig. Gen. Benjamin G. Humphreys

13th Mississippi	18th Mississippi
17th Mississippi	21st Mississippi

Wofford's Brigade:
Brig. Gen. William T. Wofford

16th Georgia	3rd Georgia Battalion
18th Georgia	Cobb's (Georgia) Legion
24th Georgia	Phillips (Georgia) Legion

Bryan's Brigade:
Brig. Gen. Goode Bryan
Col. James P. Simms

10th Georgia	51st Georgia
50th Georgia	53rd Georgia

Cavalry
Maj. Gen. Fitzhugh Lee

Lomax's Division:
Maj. Gen. Lunsford L. Lomax

Imboden's Brigade:
Brig. Gen. John Imboden
Col. George Smith

18th Virginia
23rd Virginia

62nd Virginia Mounted
Infantry

Johnson's Brigade:
Brig. Gen. Bradley T. Johnson

8th Virginia
21st Virginia
22nd Virginia

34th Virginia Battalion
36th Virginia Battalion

McCausland's Brigade:
Brig. Gen. John McCausland

14th Virginia
16th Virginia
17th Virginia

25th Virginia
37th Virginia Battalion

Jackson's Brigade:
Brig. Gen. William L. Jackson
Brig. Gen. Henry B. Davidson

2nd Maryland
19th Virginia
20th Virginia

46th Virginia Battalion
47th Virginia Battalion

Lee's Division:
Maj. Gen. Fitzhugh Lee
Brig. Gen. Williams C. Wickham
Brig. Gen. Thomas L. Rosser

Wickham's Brigade:
Brig. Gen. Williams C. Wickham
Col. Thomas T. Munford

1st Virginia
2nd Virginia

3rd Virginia
4th Virginia

Rosser's Brigade:
Brig. Gen. Thomas L. Rosser
Lt. Col. Richard H. Dulany
Col. Oliver R. Funsten, Jr.

7th Virginia
11th Virginia

12th Virginia
35th Virginia Battalion

Payne's Brigade:
Col. William H. Payne

5th Virginia
6th Virginia

15th Virginia

Artillery
Brig. Gen. Armistead L. Long
Col. Thomas H. Carter

Baxton's Battalion:
Lt. Col. Carter M. Braxton

Alleghany Battery (Va.),
   Capt. John C. Carpenter
Stafford Battery (Va.),
   Capt. R. L. Cooper

Lee Battery (Va.), Capt.
William W. Hardwicke

Nelson's Battalion:
Lt. Col. William Nelson

Amherst Battery (Va.),
Capt. Thomas J. Kirkpatrick
Georgia Regular Battery,
Capt. John Milledge, Jr.

Fluvanna Battery (Va.),
Capt. John L. Massie

King's Battalion:
Lt. Col. J. Floyd King
Maj. William McLaughlin

Lewisburg Battery (Va.),
Capt. Thomas A. Bryan
Monroe Battery (Va.),
Capt. George B. Chapman

Wise Legion Battery (Va.),
Capt. William M. Lowry

Cutshaw's Battalion:
Maj. Wilfred E. Cutshaw

Charlottesville Battery (Va.),
Capt. James McD. Carrington
Staunton Battery (Va.),
Capt. Asher W. Garber

Richmond Courtney Battery
(Va.), Capt. William A.
Tanner

Breathed's Battalion Horse Artillery:
Maj. James Breathed

2nd Maryland Battery,
Capt. William H. Griffin
Charlottesville Battery (Va.),
Capt. Thomas E. Jackson
Roanoke Battery (Va.),
Capt. Warren S. Lurty
Staunton Battery (Va.),
Capt. John H. McClannahan

1st Stuart H. A. Battery (Va.),
Capt. Philipp P. Johnston
Lynchburg Battery (Va.),
Capt. John J. Shoemaker
Ashby Battery (Va.),
Capt. James W. Thomson

Index

Garrett, John W., president of the Baltimore & Ohio Railroad, 11, 12

Getty, Brig. Gen. George Washington, 19, 49, 50, 54, 64, 66, 90, 91, 92, 94, 104, 114, 115, 117, 118, 125, 126, 198, 204, 205, 206, 207, 208, 210, 214, 217, 224, 225, 227, 231, 232, 233, 242, 243.

Godwin, Brig. Gen. Archibald C., 51, 64, 97, 103, 110.

Gordon, Maj. Gen. John B., 23, 24, 26, 38, 44, 45, 52, 53, 54, 58, 59, 61, 65, 66, 70, 74, 75, 79, 84, 85, 86, 88, 91, 92, 95, 96, 97, 103, 104, 106, 108, 109, 110, 126, 127, 128, 133, 135, 136, 168, 174, 175, 176, 182, 184, 185, 189, 197, 203, 204, 206, 207, 211, 212, 215, 216, 217, 218, 219, 226, 227, 228, 229, 230, 231, 234, 236, 240, 243, 244, 245, 247, 248, 250.

Grant, Brig. Gen. Lewis Addison, 198, 205, 206, 207, 208, 211, 216, 223, 224, 225, 232.

Grant, Lieut. Gen. Ulysses S., 3, 4, 5, 6, 7, 8, 9, 10, 11, 12, 13, 15, 20, 28, 29, 32, 33, 37, 40, 42, 43, 45, 99, 113, 138, 140, 141, 142, 143, 144, 150, 151, 157, 167, 169, 172, 239, 249, 250.

Grimes, Brig. Gen. Bryan, 26, 35, 39, 52, 66, 68, 84, 86, 89, 90, 91, 92, 96, 97, 109, 120, 121, 122, 123, 124–125, 135, 186, 203, 206, 208, 209, 233.

Grover, Brig. Gen. Cuvier, 20, 50, 55, 56, 57, 58, 59, 60, 61, 63, 65, 66, 83, 103, 115, 117, 118, 126, 129, 130, 177, 189, 195, 221, 230, 231, 233.

Hackwood farm, 53, 59, 83, 84, 85, 88.

Halleck, Maj. Gen. Henry Wager, 9, 10, 12, 13, 18, 31, 32, 42, 43, 141, 142, 143, 151, 166, 169, 172, 173.

Harpers Ferry, 12, 13, 15, 26, 29, 30, 43, 44, 55, 149.

Hayes, Col. Rutherford B., 21, 30, 44, 83, 84, 85, 92, 104, 111, 112, 119, 120, 121, 123, 129, 147, 171, 182, 184, 185, 186, 187, 189, 191, 211, 241, 242.

Hobson, Lieut. Col. Edwin L., 186, 206, 207, 208.

Hotchkiss, Jedediah, 118, 124, 126, 127, 174, 175, 203, 225, 240, 244, 246.

Hunter, Maj. Gen. David, 7, 12, 13.

Jackson, Lieut. Gen. Thomas J. "Stonewall," 6, 23, 24, 61, 127, 135, 138, 176, 244, 247, 248.

Keifer, Col. J. Warren, 18, 19, 54, 65, 66,

91, 92, 114, 123, 198, 199, 200, 202, 204, 205, 207, 208, 217, 224, 232, 242, 243.

Kershaw, Maj. Gen. Joseph B., 33, 40, 41, 42, 45, 106, 128, 134, 139, 142, 168, 175, 176, 178, 179, 180, 181, 182, 183, 184, 185, 186, 189, 192, 193, 194, 197, 199, 200, 202, 203, 204, 205, 207, 211, 212, 217, 218, 225, 226, 227, 230, 231, 232, 234, 235, 241, 242, 243, 245, 250.

Kitching, Col. J. Howard, 171, 182, 184, 186, 187, 189, 191, 206, 211, 214, 241, 242.

Laws, Tom, 41, 42.

Lee, Maj. Gen. Fitzhugh, 33, 54, 77, 78, 79, 111, 119.

Lee, Gen. Robert E., 5, 6, 7, 13, 24, 33, 36, 106, 119, 137, 138, 139, 140, 141, 142, 143, 148, 153, 168, 173, 174, 178, 239, 240, 245, 248, 250.

Lincoln, President Abraham, 3, 4, 9, 10, 11, 12, 18, 36, 39, 113, 140, 141, 249.

Little North Mountain, 28, 109, 110, 111, 112, 118, 119, 121.

Lomax, Brig. Gen. Lunsford, 53, 98, 111, 119, 120, 121, 122, 123, 128, 133, 135, 140, 161, 162, 163, 164, 168, 215, 229, 243, 244.

Longstreet, Lieut. Gen. James, 31, 33, 137, 172, 212, 229, 230.

Lowell, Col. Charles R., Jr., 72, 73, 75, 76, 77, 78, 94, 95, 112, 131, 151, 152, 161, 162, 163, 215, 230, 235.

McCausland, Brig. Gen. John, 8, 11, 25, 72, 76, 77, 78, 79, 111, 167.

McClellan, Maj. Gen. George B., 6, 11, 36, 39, 104, 138, 224.

McMaster, Lieut. Charles, 152, 153, 155.

McMillan, Brig. Gen. James W., 20, 56, 60, 62, 89, 90, 91, 189, 190, 194, 195, 231.

Massanutten Mountains, 27, 34, 109, 112, 126, 134, 159, 172, 174, 175, 177, 228.

Meade, Maj. Gen. George G., 5, 7, 10, 11, 12, 105, 142.

Meadow Brook, 170, 171, 186, 187, 188, 189, 192, 193, 194, 195, 197, 198, 199, 200, 202, 203, 204, 205, 206, 207, 208, 209, 225, 233, 242, 245.

Meigs, Lieut. John R., 145.

Merritt, Brig. Gen. Wesley, 22, 33, 34, 47, 71, 72, 75, 76, 77, 78, 79, 80, 94, 95, 97, 107, 108, 112, 113, 130, 131, 134, 152, 155, 159, 161, 162, 163, 164, 166, 167, 173, 212,

Two Confederate Leaders: Brig. Gen. Lunsford Lindsay Lomax and Maj. Gen. John Cabell Breckinridge. USAMHI.

Four Union Officers Killed at Cedar Creek: Top Left: Col. Joseph Thoburn, 1st West Va. Inf.; Top Right: Col. John Q. Wilds, 24th Iowa Inf.; Bottom Left: Brig. Gen. Daniel D. Bidwell, VI Corps 2nd & 3rd Brig.; Bottom Right: Col. George Wells, 34th Mass. Inf. *Picerno Collection.*